PERSONALITY CHARACTERISTICS OF THE PERSONALITY DISORDERED

PERSONALITY CHARACTERISTICS OF THE PERSONALITY DISORDERED

Edited by

Charles G. Costello

A Wiley-Interscience Publication

John Wiley & Sons, Inc.

New York • Chichester • Brisbane • Toronto • Singapore

Library of Congress Cataloging-in-Publication Data:
Personality characteristics of the personality disordered / edited by
    Charles G. Costello.
        p.   cm.
    Includes index.
    ISBN 0-471-01529-6 (alk. paper)
    1. Personality disorders—Diagnosis.   2. Personality.
    3. Temperament.   I. Costello, Charles G., 1929–
    RC554.P455   1995
    616.85′8—dc20   95-7510

Printed in the United States of America

10 9 8 7 6 5 4 3 2 1

Contributors

Ernest S. Barratt, PhD
Professor of Psychology
Department of Psychiatry and
    Behavioral Sciences
The University of Texas
    Medical Branch
Galveston, Texas

Howard Berenbaum, PhD
Professor of Psychology
Department of Psychology
University of Illinois
Urbana-Champaign, Illinois

John Birtchnell, PhD
Honorary Senior Lecturer
Institute of Psychiatry
University of London
London, England

Robert F. Bornstein, PhD
Professor of Psychology
Department of Psychology
Gettysburg College
Gettysburg, Pennsylvania

Emil F. Coccaro, MD
Associate Professor of Psychiatry
Eastern Pennsylvania Psychiatric
    Institute
Medical College of Pennsylvania
Philadelphia, Pennsylvania

Charles G. Costello, PhD
Professor Emeritus of Psychology
Department of Psychology
University of Calgary
Calgary, Alberta, Canada

Allan Fenigstein, PhD
Professor of Psychology
Department of Psychology
Kenyon College
Gambier, Ohio

Richard J. Kavoussi, MD
Assistant Professor of Psychiatry
Eastern Pennsylvania Psychiatric
    Institute
Medical College of Pennsylvania
Philadelphia, Pennsylvania

Jennifer D. Lish, PhD
Assistant Professor of Psychiatry
Eastern Pennsylvania Psychiatric
    Institute
Medical College of Pennsylvania
Philadelphia, Pennsylvania

Bruce Pfohl, MD
Professor of Psychiatry
Department of Psychiatry
University of Iowa
Iowa City, Iowa

Michele R. Spoont, PhD
Psychology Service
Veterans Administration
  Medical Center
Minneapolis, Minnesota

Matthew S. Stanford, PhD
Assistant Professor of Psychology
Department of Psychology
University of New Orleans
New Orleans, Louisiana

Paul Wink, PhD
Professor of Psychology
Department of Psychology
Wellesley College
Wellesley, Massachusetts

Marvin Zuckerman, PhD
Professor of Psychology
Department of Psychology
University of Delaware
Newark, Delaware

Preface

This book is a companion to *Symptoms of Depression* (John Wiley & Sons, 1993) and *Symptoms of Schizophrenia* (John Wiley & Sons, 1993). My purpose in editing the first two books was to encourage research on *symptoms* of psychopathology as an alternative to the predominant research strategy that focuses on *syndromes*. Similarly, I hope the present book will encourage research on the personality characteristics that appear to be associated with personality disorders as an alternative to research on questionable diagnostic categories, such as Borderline Personality Disorder.

The fourth edition of the *Diagnostic and Statistical Manual of Mental Disorders* (DSM-IV), the most commonly used diagnostic system, was published in 1994. The writers of this new edition of DSM made an effort to thoroughly review research findings so that the empirical bases supporting DSM-IV diagnoses would be firmer than the bases of diagnoses in the earlier editions of the manual. Unfortunately, the entry point for review of the research was the diagnostic categories of previous editions of the DSM or similar diagnostic systems thus casting doubt on the strength of the empirical bases that were constructed.

I believe that we are in a *reculer pour mieux sauter* situation. We should not try to develop diagnoses by reviewing the questionable data of research using diagnostic systems that were previously constructed in a similar manner. In the case of personality disorders, we should research specific personality characteristics, such as impulsiveness, that appear in those whose personalities are disordered. When we have gained thorough knowledge of the nature of these personality characteristics, we should then begin to investigate their interrelationships. In this way, we are likely to arrive at more valid diagnoses and at some understanding of the process underlying the conditions diagnosed.

I am very grateful to Herb Reich, Senior Editor at John Wiley & Sons, for encouraging the editing of this book and its companion volumes,

Symptoms of Depression and *Symptoms of Schizophrenia.* I am also grateful to him and his staff for the amiable and efficient manner in which they have produced the book.

CHARLES G. COSTELLO

Calgary, Alberta
October 1995

Contents

PERSONALITY CHARACTERISTICS OF THE PERSONALITY DISORDERED

CHAPTER 1

The Advantages of Focusing on the Personality Characteristics of the Personality Disordered

CHARLES G. COSTELLO

Not surprisingly, a disordered personality can turn a person's life into chaos. It increases the likelihood of substance abuse, suicidal attempts, and mental illness; it decreases the response to therapy for mental illnesses; and it increases the probability of relapse if recovery from such an illness does occur. Consequently, there is an urgent need to understand the nature of personality disorders. Unfortunately, the assessments of such disorders are also in a state of chaos.

Clinical lore, as reflected for instance in the third revised edition of the *Diagnostic and Statistical Manual of Mental Disorders* (DSM-III-R; American Psychiatric Association [APA], 1987),* leads us to believe that there are a fair number of different kinds of personality disorder. DSM-III-R lists 11 kinds: paranoid, schizoid, schizotypal, antisocial, borderline, histrionic, narcissistic, avoidant, dependent, obsessive-compulsive, and passive-aggressive. But research has failed to put these diagnoses on a firm footing. Furthermore, the use in research of such complex polythetic categories of personality disorder made up of heterogeneous sets of experiences and behaviors makes it very difficult to interpret research findings. The heterogeneity of the components of some of the diagnostic categories is enormous. Widiger (1993a) noted that there are 93 different ways to meet the DSM-III-R criteria for borderline personality disorder and

---

* The fourth edition (DSM-IV; American Psychiatric Association, 1994) has now been published, but research findings from studies that have used this new edition have yet to be published. Therefore, the research findings covered in this chapter are from studies using earlier published editions of the DSM. However, the approach to personality disorders taken in DSM-IV has not changed from that taken in earlier editions in any way that would essentially alter the critique in the present chapter.

1

149,495,616 different ways to meet the DSM-III-R criteria for antisocial personality disorder! It is not as though the heterogeneity is held together by sound theory. Turning again to Widiger, he has described the basis of the DSM taxonomy as "a sort of theoretical stew, with psychoanalytic theory represented by the narcissistic, social learning by the avoidant, and biogenetic by the schizotypal" (1993b, p. 35).

There is a need to focus research on the nature of the specific personality characteristics of people whose personalities are disordered and that is the raison d'être of this book. In this introductory chapter I shall (a) present some of the evidence for the chaos produced in the lives of those with a personality disorder, (b) review research data that reflect the chaotic state of current taxonomies, (c) discuss dimensional approaches to personality disorder, and (d) present concluding arguments for a focus on the specific personality characteristics of the personality disordered.

THE EFFECTS OF PERSONALITY DISORDER

One unfortunate effect of personality disorders is depression. The rates of clinical depression in people with personality disorders range from 24% to 87% (Barash, Frances, Hurt, Clarkin, & Cohen, 1985; Docherty, Fiester, & Shea, 1986; Fyer, Frances, Sullivan, Hurt, & Clarkin, 1988; Jonas & Pope, 1992; Zanarini, Gunderson, & Frankenburg, 1989; Zimmerman & Coryell, 1989). It also seems that the symptoms of psychopathological conditions, such as depression and anxiety, are more severe if a personality disorder is present (Flick, Roy-Byrne, Cowley, Shores, & Dunner, 1993; Mavissakalian & Hamann, 1986; Tyrer et al., 1990).

Although there are two studies (Mellman et al., 1992; Tyrer et al., 1990) that did not find any evidence that the presence of a personality disorder (Axis II disorder) reduced the effects of therapy for Axis I disorders, most studies do find such evidence. The rates of recovery from depression with antidepressant treatment in four studies ranged from 50% to 76% ($M = 59\%$) in patients without a concomitant personality disorder and from 9% to 36% ($M = 22\%$) in those with such a disorder (Black, Bell, Hulbert, & Nasrallah, 1988; Charney, Nelson, & Quinlan, 1981; Pfohl, Stangl, & Zimmerman, 1984; Tyrer, Casey, & Gall, 1983). Pfohl, Coryell, Zimmerman, and Stangl (1987) found no difference in 6-month outcome for 31 patients with major depression alone and 34 patients with major depression and at least one personality disorder, but their data indicated that the patients with more than the median number of personality disorder criteria were less likely to show improvement at follow-up than those with less than the median number of criteria. For instance, 11 (58%) of the 19 patients with less than a median number of personality disorder criteria in the Structured Interview for DSM-III Personality Disorder (SIDP; Stangl, Pfohl, Zimmerman, Bowers, & Corenthal, 1985) had 8 consecutive weeks without symptoms compared with 4 (21%) of the 19 patients above the median.

Rate of recovery from depression with electroconvulsive therapy (ECT) was found by Black et al. (1988) to be 66% in those without a personality disorder and 40% in those with such a disorder. The comparable figures in the study by Zimmerman, Coryell, Pfohl, Corenthal, and Stangl (1986) were 53% and 20%.

In a study of the effects on depression of one or other of cognitive therapy, interpersonal therapy, imipramine plus clinical management and pill-placebo plus clinical management, Shea et al. (1990) found that 51% of 61 depressed patients with no personality disorder showed residual symptoms of depression compared with 70% of 178 depressed patients with a personality disorder. Even after 3 to 4 years, patients with major depression who also had a personality disorder, if they were over 25 years of age when the personality disorder diagnosis was made, showed a worse course and outcome.

The presence of personality disorders also seems to worsen and reduce response to treatment for other Axis I disorders. Tyrer and Seivewright (1988) found that in patients with a variety of Axis I disorders those who also had a personality disorder had more psychiatric admissions and spent longer in hospital than those without such a disorder. Pfohl, Black, Noyes, Coryell, and Barrash (1990) found that 11 obsessive-compulsive disorder (OCD) patients who responded to clomipramine had fewer criteria for Axis II personality disorders than the 11 nonresponders. Jenike, Baer, Minichiello, Schwartz, and Carey (1986) found that, whereas 90% of 26 OCD patients without schizotypal personality disorder responded to medication, only 7% of 14 OCD patients with such a disorder responded. Similar poor prognosis for treatment of anxiety disorders in the presence of personality disorders has been reported by Mavissakalian and Hamann (1987), Reich (1988), and Turner (1987). Eighteen of 19 patients with co-occurring Axis I and Axis II disorders in the study by Andreoli, Gressot, Aapro, Tricot, and Cognalons (1989) were in treatment once again for their Axis I disorders 2 years after discharge from the treatment on entry into the study compared with 8 of 14 patients with Axis I disorders but no Axis II disorder.

When considering data such as the preceding, which concern the mutual influence of Axis I and Axis II disorders, clinicians must keep in mind that the presence of an Axis I disorder is likely to influence the Axis II experiences and behaviors that individuals will attribute to themselves and vice versa. But this may be a problem only if self-report questionnaires are used. Loranger et al. (1991) found no effects of level of anxiety or depression on the assessment of personality disorder when a structured interview, the Personality Disorder Examination (PDE: Loranger, Susman, Oldham, & Russakoff, 1987), was used.

Personality disorder also increases the rates of suicide attempts. Pfohl et al. (1984) found that 16 (39%) of 41 patients with major depression and a personality disorder made nonserious suicide attempts compared with 14 (11%) of 37 patients with major depression alone. Friedman, Aronoff, Clarkin, Corn, and Hurt (1983) found that 92% of patients with depression and borderline personality disorder made suicide attempts compared with 59% of depressed patients without a personality disorder. Black, Warrack, and Winokur (1985), examining data on unnatural deaths (principally suicide), found the standardized mortality ratio (SMR: the ratio of observed to expected deaths) in personality-disordered men to be 4.6 and in personality-disordered women 17.8. The comparable figures for men and women with affective disorders were 3.1 and 13.0. Martin, Cloninger, Guze, and Clayton (1985) found the SMR for patients with personality disorder to be 8.75 compared with .84 for unipolar disorder and .62 for bipolar affective disorder. Finally, Andreoli et al. (1989) reported that in a group of patients with Axis I disorders, followed up 2 years after discharge from treatment, 6 of 23 patients with a personality disorder had died—2 through suicide—and none of 14 patients free of such disorder had died.

Personality disorder also appears to increase the risk of substance abuse. Reich and Troughton (1988) found that those with a personality disorder were more likely to have a lifetime history of substance abuse than those without.

The evidence is overwhelming then that personality disorders put individuals at risk for a number of serious consequences. The need for their reliable and valid assessment is pressing. The most common approach is the attempt to assign people to diagnostic categories of personality disorder. But, as we shall see in the next section, the approach has not been successful.

THE INADEQUACIES OF CURRENT TAXONOMIES

There is poor agreement between different methods of determining the presence of personality disorders not only when one wishes to identify a specific disorder but also when one simply wants to determine if *any* personality disorder exists. In the following three studies, the investigators examined the agreement between different methods of assessment in detecting the presence of any personality disorder. Pfohl et al. (1987) used the SIDP and the Personality Diagnostic Questionnaire (PDQ; Hyler, Rieder, Spitzer, & Williams, 1983) and found kappa (Cohen, 1960) to be .31. Reich, Noyes, and Troughton (1987) found a kappa of .19 when comparing the SIDP and the Millon Clinical Multiaxial Inventory (MCMI; Millon, 1987) and .29 when comparing the SIDP and PDQ. Piersma (1987) compared the MCMI and discharge diagnoses made by psychiatrists and found a kappa of .11. Rennenberg, Chambless, Dowdall, Fauerbach, and Gracely (1992) compared the Structured Clinical Interview for DSM-III-R, Axis II (SCID-II; Spitzer, Williams, & Gibbon, 1987) and the MCMI-II (Millon, 1987) and found kappas of .20, .28, or .21 depending on the method of scoring the MCMI-II.

Perry (1992) reviewed the findings of nine other studies that compared two or more instruments for the diagnosis of personality disorder. The studies were those of Hyler et al. (1989); Hyler, Skodol, Kellman, Oldham, and Rosnick (1990); Hogg, Jackson, Rudd, and Edwards (1990); Jackson, Gazis, Rudd, and Edwards (1991); O'Boyle and Self (1990); Perry, Lavori, Cooper, Hoke, and O'Connell (1987); Pilkonis, Heape, Ruddy, and Serrao (1991); Skodol, Oldham, Rosnick, Kellman, and Hyler (1991); and Zimmerman and Coryell (1990). Perry found that the range of kappa values was .08 to .54 with a median of .25. He commented that a concordance of .25 between instruments "suggests that 75% of the variance in personality disorder diagnoses in the average study represent variance not attributable to the patients. This puts considerable constraint on comparing the findings from any one study with those from another" (p. 1650). One might add that such poor concurrent validity of personality disorder diagnoses casts serious doubt on their construct validity.

As would be expected, the poor agreement between different methods of assessment in the detection of the presence of any personality disorder is also apparent in studies examining the detection of specific disorders. For instance, Swartz et al. (1989) reported a kappa of .67 between their diagnostic index to identify borderline personality disorder based on the NIMH Diagnostic Interview Schedule (DIS; Robins, Helzer, Croughan, & Ratcliff, 1981) and the Diagnostic Interview for Borderline Patients (DIB; Kolb & Gunderson, 1980), which some may consider acceptable. But it should be noted that there was only a 62% agreement on the presence of the disorder. The kappa statistic is the best available measure of overall agreement because it corrects for chance agreement. However, the same kappa may result from different patterns of relationships between the data obtained by two measures. The measures may be in agreement primarily on the absence of the phenomenon being measured or on the presence of the phenomenon. Table 1.1 provides the kappas for the presence or absence of specific disorders using the SCID-II and the MCMI-II as presented in Table 2 of Rennenberg, Chambless, Dowdall, Fauerbach, and Gracely (1992). Also included in Table 1.1 are the percentages of agreement on the presence of each disorder calculated from the raw cross-tabulation data kindly made available to me by Dianne L. Chambless.

The large extent to which the DSM-III-R diagnoses of personality disorder co-occur casts serious doubt on their discriminant validity. Widiger et al. (1991) normalized through arcsin transformations and then averaged the co-occurrence rates across four studies (Dahl, 1986; Morey, 1988; Pfohl, Coryell, Zimmerman, & Stangl, 1986; Zanarini, Frankenburg, Chauncey, & Gunderson, 1987). They found that only compulsive personality disorder occurred by itself more than 25% of the time and then only 31% of the time. Of borderline personality disorder cases, 96% had a comorbid personality disorder. Pfohl et al. (1984) found that 41 of 78 patients with major depression met criteria for at least one DSM-III personality disorder and 22 (54%) of these 41 patients met criteria for more than one such disorder. Alnaes and Torgersen (1988) reported that 81% of their outpatients had at least one personality disorder with half of the patients having more than one. In a study of 352 outpatients

TABLE 1.1   Kappa Coefficients for Agreement and Percentage of Agreement of MCMI-II and SCID-II Personality Disorder Diagnoses of 54 Agoraphobic Outpatients Using Two Different Methods of Scoring the MCMI[a]

| | BR > 74[b] | | BR > 84[c] | |
Diagnoses	Kappa	% Agreement on Presence	Kappa	% Agreement on Presence
Avoidant	.51	52	.16	19
Dependent	.28	24	.35	27
Obsessive-compulsive	.38	31	.06	9
Passive-aggressive	.30	25	.47	36
Paranoid	.21	14	.21	14
Histrionic	.14	18	−.06	0
Narcissistic	.16	13	—	—
Borderline	.25	20	—	—
Self-defeating	.20	14	.41	29

Note: Kappa coefficients were only computed for diagnoses with an occurrence rate higher than 10% on at least one of the measures.
[a] Modification of Rennenberg et al.'s (1992) Table 2.
[b] BR > 74 is Millon's (1983) original criterion of a base rate score > 74 on the MCMI to indicate presence of a disorder.
[c] BR > 84 is Millon's (1983) criterion of a base rate score > 84 on the MCMI to indicate the predominant disorder.

attending a center for anxiety and depression Flick, Roy-Byrne, Cowley, Shores, and Dunner (1993) found that of 201 patients with personality disorder 123 had one to six other such disorders. Other studies reporting similar levels of comorbidity are Pfohl et al. (1986) and Nurnberg et al. (1991).

Noting the findings by Fyer, Frances, Sullivan, Hurt, and Clarkin (1988) that pure borderline personality disorder was only present in 8% of patients, whereas 46% had one additional diagnosis and 46% two or more additional diagnoses, Tyrer, Casey, and Ferguson (1991) justifiably commented, "Diagnosis ceases to become an economical exercise with such profligacy of pathology" (p. 467).

Although data that indicate high rates of comorbidity serve a useful function in raising the question of the validity of the diagnoses, they cannot be used to further an understanding of personality disorders. This is because investigations of comorbidity are vulnerable to a host of methodological problems that have been thoroughly reviewed by Widiger et al. (1991). Among the problems they noted are the changes in rates of comorbidity with changes in the criteria of DSM-III (APA, 1980). For instance, Morey (1988) found that for the same 291 patients 36% had at least one comorbid pair of diagnoses using DSM-III criteria whereas the rate was 52% using DSM-III-R criteria.

Widiger and Shea (1991) succinctly stated how a focus on specific features of disorder rather than on diagnoses may produce comorbidity data that are less confusing: "It may be easier to interpret the comorbidity of mood disorder with fears of abandonment or identity disturbances than with borderline personality disorder, which includes affective instability in the diagnosis. Likewise, the covariation of theft (from substance abuse) with failure to conform to social norms (from antisocial personality disorder) may be tautological, but the covariation of theft with the failure to function as a responsible parent is not" (p. 403).

Another observation casting doubt on the validity of personality disorder diagnoses is their temporal instability given that such disorders are supposed to be persistent. Loranger et al. (1991) found that the kappas measuring 6-month stability of diagnoses were low: .57 for each of borderline, avoidant, and dependent disorders and .26 for compulsive disorder. Barash et al. (1985) interpreted their findings as indicating stability for the diagnosis of borderline personality disorder. But not everyone would agree with such an interpretation because only 6 of 10 DSM-III borderline patients received the same diagnosis 3 years later and only 7 of 13 borderlines diagnosed according to the Diagnostic Interview for Borderlines (DIB; Gunderson, Kolb, & Austin, 1981) met DIB criteria for the same diagnosis 3 years later. McGlashan (1983) found that only 44% of patients with a diagnosis of borderline personality disorder received the same diagnosis after an average of 15 years; 24% were given the diagnosis of schizophrenia. The comparable figure for stability of borderline personality disorder after a similar period of time was even lower (25%) in the study by Paris, Brown, and Nowlis (1987). Although, as Perry, Lavori, and Hoke (1987) have noted, such follow-up data are complicated by the treatment that may have been received by some of the patients, they still give one pause.

A finding that makes one wonder about the construct validity of borderline personality disorder, one of the most frequently diagnosed personality disorders, is the lack of differential response to pharmacotherapy of patients with a diagnosis of pure borderline personality disorder and those with a diagnosis of mixed borderline/schizotypy disorder (Soloff, George, Cornelius, Nathan, & Schulz, 1991). With respect to personality disorders in general, Coccaro (1993) concluded from his review of the clinical psychopharmacological literature that no one treatment is efficacious in treating any particular DSM-III-R personality disorder. However, he did find evidence in his review that some medications are specifically efficacious in alleviating specific symptoms such as aggressiveness.

As might be expected from the findings already reviewed in this section, the data on the validity of specific DSM-III criteria in predicting particular personality disorder diagnoses are not impressive. Pfohl et al. (1986) using the SIDP found that the median positive predictive value for all the criteria was only 33%.

It may be argued that the validity of the criteria in predicting diagnoses and the predictive validity of the diagnoses themselves will improve with improvements in the DSM criteria. Unfortunately, changing the criteria in the DSM makes it impossible to compare the findings of studies over even short periods. Morey (1988) pointed out that the revisions made to the DSM-III to produce DSM-III-R resulted in an 800% increase in the rate of schizoid personality disorder and a 350% increase in narcissistic personality disorder!

Many psychopathologists now believe that a dimensional rather than a categorical approach is more promising, and I shall now discuss their arguments and data.

DIMENSIONAL APPROACHES

Frances (1993) wrote, "Although the categorical method has all sorts of problems and limitations, especially in the research setting, it does have a long historical tradition precisely because it conforms to the way clinicians work" (p. 110). But that is not sufficient reason to continue working with the categorical approach; other approaches must be tried. The most popular alternative approach is the dimensional one.

One reason many psychopathologists are advocating a dimensional approach is that there is so much overlap in the personality characteristics of the different personality disorders. This was demonstrated, for instance, by Hyler, Lyons, et al. (1990), who conducted a factor analysis of the entire item set of the DSM-III criteria set to determine the extent to which the factors that emerged corresponded to the 11 personality disorders listed in DSM. They found that a broad number of criteria used to diagnose different personality disorders are, to a great extent, assessing the same thing. They also found that in many cases a single factor was composed of criteria from a number of different personality disorders.

Livesley, Schroeder, Jackson, and Jang (1994), on the basis of their review of research data, presented the following reasons a dimensional rather than a categorical approach to personality disorders would be of more value:

1. There is an absence of bimodality in the distribution of scores on the personality characteristics thought to be associated with different personality disorders. Personality disorders appear to merge with each other and with normality.
2. Measurements of social dysfunctions associated with personality disorder are also continuously distributed.
3. Similar patterns of correlations among traits delineating abnormal personality are found in personality-disordered and nonpersonality-disordered individuals.
4. Individuals who meet a subthreshold number of DSM-III-R criteria for personality disorder are more like individuals with such disorder than those who meet none of the criteria.
5. Measures of normal personality are predictive of measures of personality disorder supporting the assumption that disorders of personality are maladaptive variants of normal traits.
6. Similar heritability estimates have been reported for normal personality traits and for traits of personality disorder.

Siever and Davis (1991) also make a good general case for a dimensional rather than a categorical approach to personality disorders.

Reliability and validity data are also in favor of a dimensional approach. Widiger (1992) found that only 1 of 16 studies in which data on personality disorders were analyzed in terms of DSM diagnoses and dimensionality found the reliability and validity data better for the diagnostic analyses.

Findings reported by Lee Anna Clark (1993b) also support the dimensional approach. Clark compared the interrater reliabilities when raters, using the Structured Interview for DSM-III-R Personality (SIDP-R: Pfohl, Blum, Zimmerman, & Stangl, 1989) and examining 82 patients were given a dimensional task (rating patients' manifestations of the various characteristics of the personality disordered) and when given a categorical task (diagnosing the patients). Her results were as follows, with the first figure in parentheses being the Pearson r for dimensional ratings and the second figure Cohen's kappa for categories: antisocial disorder (.95; .86); borderline (.84; .42); dependent (.89; .37); avoidant (.83; .28).

Data presented by Clark, Vorhies, and McEwen (1994) suggest that a dimensional approach may be particularly useful for Axis II disorders. They asked judges to rate patients on clusters of symptoms using a 1-to-3 scale. For symptoms of personality disorder, all three ratings levels were used frequently; 46% of the patients were rated as showing symptoms of a given cluster either fully (21%) or at a subclinical level (25%), an indication that the clusters were seen as having varying degrees of expression and were not simply present or absent. The data contrasted sharply with the data for Axis I symptoms, which were rated on average as subclinically present only 11% of the time with an average of 18% of patients per cluster clearly showing the symptoms and 71% of patients per cluster rated as symptom-free.

There also seems to be a greater stability of personality disorders when they are measured dimensionally than when a categorical approach is taken. Trull (1993) found 3-month temporal stability for self-report personality disorder scores from the Personality Diagnostic Questionnaire-Revised (PDQ-R; Hyler & Rieder, 1987) and the MMPI-Personality Disorder Scales (MMPI-PD; Morey, Waugh, & Blashfield, 1985).

Unfortunately, using dimensions as the entry point for research on personality disorders still tends to leave the researcher enmeshed in heterogeneous sets of experiences and behaviors even though statistical procedures indicate homogeneity as with the scales in Clark's (1993b) Schedule for Nonadaptive and Adaptive Personality (SNAP), where the median alpha reliabilities ranged from .76 to .85 in three student and three patient samples. For instance, the SNAP Negative Temperament Scale correlates significantly with the following symptom clusters: Demoralization, Suicide Proneness, Self-Derogation, and Hypersensitivity (Clark, McEwen, Collard, & Hickok, 1993). Other indications that the dimensional approach does not enable us to escape the problems of heterogeneity can be found in an examination of Widiger's (1993a) Table 2, showing the relationship between the Five-Factor Model of personality disorders and DSM-III-R diagnoses. Livesley, Jackson, and Schroeder's (1992) factor analyses of the personality characteristics that clinicians believe to be associated with personality disorders identified 15 factors. Such investigations are valuable first steps in indicating the behaviors and experiences that are linked together some way or another. For instance the factor of Rejection indicates that feelings of entitlement, rigid cognitive style, and hypervigilance are linked in some way or another. But now there is a need for research focusing on the way they may be linked. Simply searching for the correlates of the factor of Rejection is likely to leave us very much in the dark. This is more of a problem for some factors than for others. For instance, the factor of Narcissism seems to be a homogeneous factor with items such as need for adulation, grandiosity, attention-seeking, and need for approval.

One of the problems stemming, in part, from the heterogeneity of the experiences and behaviors of the dimensions obtained by researchers is that there is often disagreement between the researchers concerning what it is that the dimensions measure. Widiger et al. (1991) noted that the third dimension obtained in the study by Kass, Skodol, Charles, Spitzer, and Williams (1985) correlated highly ($r = .79$) with the second dimension in Widiger, Trull, Hurt, Clarkin, & Frances (1987); the first dimension in Blashfield, Sprock, Pinkston, and Hodgin (1985)—$r = .67$; the first factor in Morey et al. (1985)—$r = .84$; and the third factor in Millon (1987)—$r = .77$. But, despite this consistency, the four sets of researchers gave quite different interpretations to the dimension. Kass interpreted it as representing the dramatic/emotional cluster of personality disorders, Morey as representing the anxious/fearful cluster, Widiger as representing assertion/dominance, and Blashfield as representing interpersonal involvement.

When researchers study the association of specific criteria with specific personality disorders, they find considerable inconsistency. McGlashan and Fenton (1991) noted that, for borderline personality disorder (BPD), whereas unstable relations had the lowest positive predictive power in two samples they investigated, it had the highest positive predictive power in three studies (Clarkin, Widiger, Frances, Hurt, & Gilmore, 1983; Nurnberg, Hurt, Feldman, & Suh, 1987; Pfohl et al., 1986). On the other hand, affective instability had high positive predictive values for BPD in the McGlashan and Fenton samples but the lowest value in the Widiger, Frances, Warner, & Bluhm (1986) study. More generally, McGlashan and Fenton (1991) commented:

> Positive predictive power absolute values also varied widely. Symptoms with the best positive predictive power in each study had values ranging between 0.63 and 0.89, whereas symptoms with the lowest positive predictive power had values ranging between 0.31 and 0.74. Therefore, a symptom with the lowest positive predictive power in one sample could have a higher value than a symptom with the highest positive predictive power in another sample. Also, the best two-symptom combinations were

not consistent, although as a general rule, positive predictive power increased and sensitivity decreased as more symptoms were combined. Finally, the symptoms that discriminated best between BPD and SPD [schizotypal personality disorder] also changed from study to study. In fact, each of the five investigations studying this dimension came up with a different BPD symptom that was the most discriminating. (p. 141)

The need to focus investigations on more specific behaviors and experiences becomes apparent when one considers the problem of distinguishing between *disorders* of personality and what Livesley et al. (1994) call "extreme personality variation." Following the component of Wakefield's (1992a, 1992b) definition of mental disorder in general, which states that a condition is a mental disorder only if "the condition results from the inability of some mental mechanism to perform its natural function" (Wakefield, 1992b, p. 385), Livesley et al. (1994) wrote that we need to define the natural functions of personality and proposed that the functions are those designed to enable people to attain the universal tasks of identity, attachment, intimacy, or affiliation. But to identify specific dysfunctional mechanisms at a biological or psychological level, it would seem that we must focus on something more specific than these tasks.

The dimensional approach becomes more problematic the more broad the dimensions. Blashfield (1991) suggested that a single-factor model accounts well for the co-occurrence of personality disorders. However, as Clark (1992) commented, this solution is not satisfactory, lumping, for instance, aggressive, self-aggrandizing patients with passive, dependent individuals. In his arguments for the Five-Factor Model, Widiger (1993a) commented "Conceptualizing borderline personality disorder as extreme neuroticism is helpful in explaining the excessive prevalence and comorbidity of this popular but controversial diagnosis" (p. 83). That is true but as Clark, Vorhies, and McEwen (1994) noted, in their extensive factor analytic studies, Neuroticism was found to be defined by Mistrust/Cynicism, Aggression, Schizotypal Thought, Suicide Potential, Negative Temperament; and Detachment. Manipulativeness also loaded on this factor in the college sample. Similar complexity is evident with the other broad factors studied by Clark and her colleagues: Extroversion was defined by Exhibitionism and Entitlement on the high end, with Detachment and Dependency loading on the low end; the broad factor Disinhibition versus Conscientiousness was associated with Impulsivity and Manipulativeness on the high end and Propriety and Workaholism on the low end. Aggression was also loaded on the latter broad factor in the patients' sample. Clark and her colleagues also made an important observation when they noted that there were more significant correlations between the self-report primary scales of the SNAP and the rated symptom cluster of the personality disorders than between the higher order factors emerging from the data on the SNAP scales and the symptom clusters. At the same time, it is also important to remember that Clark and her colleagues found that "seven of the SNAP scales have substantial loadings on more than one factor, which indicates . . . that certain (lower order) traits in the domain of personality disorder are factorially complex" (Clark et al., 1994).

Harkness (1992) has generated 39 narrower trait dimensions yet the instrument he and his colleagues have developed (Harkness, McNulty, & Ben-Porath, 1993) is designed to measure five broad factors that are similar to the five factors measured by Costa and McCrae (1992). It would seem to be better at this stage to work at least at the narrower level of the 39 trait dimensions though, even at that level, it would probably be better to focus research efforts on only 2 or 3 of the narrow traits and their relationships rather than investigating all 39 dimensions at the same time.

THE ADVANTAGES OF FOCUSING ON PERSONALITY CHARACTERISTICS

I noted at the beginning of this chapter that because the current diagnostic categories of personality disorder are heterogeneous in nature and because of the existence of comorbidity, research using such categories produces data that are difficult to interpret. Other writers have made the same point. For instance, Kavoussi and Siever (1991) reviewed research data indicating that patients with a diagnosis of borderline personality disorder show nonsuppression of cortisol in response to dexamethasone, a blunted thyrotropin-stimulating hormone response to thyrotropin-releasing hormone and decreased rapid eye movement latency. "However," they commented, "It is unclear whether these tests are assessing affective dysregulation . . . , a coexisting Axis I affective disorder, or some other variable" (p. 77). Noting Reich's (1989) report of heritability for the dependent personality disorder, Widiger (1993a) commented that the finding should raise questions concerning the validity, or at least assessment, of dependent personality disorder, and suggest that a more heritable mood or anxiety pathology was being assessed rather than a personality disorder.

I also noted that a more molecular approach is needed. The need for such an approach is also indicated by evidence for the complexity of specific personality characteristics themselves. For instance, Livesley, Schroeder, and Jackson (1990) found two separate dimensions underlying dependent personality disorder: attachment-related behaviors (a need for and proximity to a secure base) and dependency as a need for instrumental help.

Pfohl et al. (1990), noting that in their study obsessive-compulsive disorder (OCD) patients had the highest rate of passive-aggressive personality disorder, commented:

This may represent an expression of OCD symptoms rather than an independent diagnosis. It may be difficult to sort out of the difference between procrastination, dawdling, and stubbornness due to preoccupation with OCD symptoms, from resistance to demands expressed indirectly through procrastination and dawdling, as required by the criterion [for passive-aggressive personality disorder]. (p. 152)

Widiger (1991) in his account of the complexities and confusions of the DSM approach to the taxonomy of personality disorders noted the problems involved in any attempt to reduce the heterogeneity and co-morbidity of diagnostic categories by requiring just one or more features for a diagnosis leaving the rest as optional:

A limitation of requiring a core feature, however, is determining which feature to require. The central or fundamental feature can be defined in a variety of ways, such as the item with the highest prototypicality rating, the feature that is most often seen in typical or prototypical cases, the item that is most specific to the disorder, the item that has the highest positive predictive power, or the feature that is theoretically central to the disorder's pathology. (p. 7)

Widiger and Shea (1991) add:

In addition, to be effective in differential diagnosis, a core feature must be pathognomonic (i.e., maximally sensitive and specific), and there are few mental disorders that have a pathognomonic criterion (e.g., social isolation differentiates the avoidant from the dependent but not the avoidant from the schizoid). (p. 403)

Perhaps the attempt to further our knowledge of personality disorders and to help those suffering from them by clustering experiences and behaviors whether using a categorical or a dimensional model is a fundamentally wrong approach, at least at this stage of our knowledge. Researchers should perhaps concentrate on gaining further knowledge of a specific experience or behavior believed to be important in disorders of personality. A clinician should perhaps start with an experience or behavior that seems to lie at the heart of the patient's problem and with the patient's help investigate how it is related to other aspects of the patient's problem.

One reason we need to more closely examine the behaviors and experiences associated with personality disorders is that, despite their similarity as they appear in different disorders, the motivations and reasons for them may differ. Shea (1992) gave the following example. For the person with an avoidant personality disorder, not having close friends is the result of an intense fear of rejection; whereas for the person with a schizoid personality disorder, it is the result of a lack of desire for closeness to others. Shea commented, "Assessment at the behavioral level, without attention to precipitants or context, will miss this important aspect and is likely to result in artificial overlap of disorders and a decrease in validity of assessment" (p. 379). Schact (1993) has expressed similar concerns.

Livesley and Jackson (1992) in their excellent presentation of guidelines for the developing, evaluating, and revising the classification of personality disorders recommended "establishing an iterative process in which empirical evaluation of criteria sets is used to modify the theoretical definitions of diagnoses from which they were originally derived. It is this interplay between theory and empirical evaluation, which is fundamental to scientific progress, that will lead to the progressive evolution of a valid classification" (p. 610). I agree that there is a need for theory in our investigations of personality disorders. However, I believe that the testing of the theories should be done by investigating the relationship between specific behaviors and experiences rather than by investigating the correlates of trait constructs derived from the multivariate statistical analysis of the covariation between such specific behaviors and experiences.

Researchers should not focus on specific experiences and behaviors simply to produce more reliable data. As many psychopathologists point out, one must not make a fetish of reliability as the designers of DSM seem to have done. Frances and Widiger (1986) commented:

> As the description of personality disorders become increasingly atomistic and narrowly behavioral, the underlying more inferential and abstract construct may be lost or obscured. . . . This already appears to have occurred in the DSM-III definition of the antisocial personality disorder. . . . This criteria set consists of simply behavioral descriptors that are wonderfully reliable, but define a narrow disorder of questionable validity, perhaps because methodological rigor was a higher priority than adherence to a useful but more inferential and hard to operationalize construct. (p. 248)

But some attention has to be paid to reliability. Clark et al. (1993) presented interrater reliabilities for 22 personality disorder symptom clusters in 52 patients. For the most part, they were reassuringly high but the intraclass coefficient was .00 for Rigidity/Conventionality and was less than .60 for Self-Centered Exploitation, Passive-Aggression, High Energy, and Grandiose Egocentrism.

Gunderson, Links, and Reich (1991) raised the possibility that the DSM-III-R personality disorder criteria are poorly articulated, secondary features of more basic pathological processes. Harkness, McNulty, and Ben-Porath (1993) noted that two of their Psy-5 scales, one measuring aggressiveness and the other constraint, were intercorrelated ($r = -.42$), and they suggest that the organismic systems creating stable dispositions in both domains are both subsumed by serotonergic systems. Further work on personality disorders must be guided by theories of this sort, but the work must also involve detailed analyses of the disordered behaviors and experiences as well as tests of the interrelationships between them that are postulated by the theories.

REFERENCES

Alnaes, R., & Torgersen, S. (1988). DSM-III symptom disorders (Axis I) and personality disorders (Axis II) in an outpatient population. *Acta Psychiatrica Scandinavica, 78,* 348–355.

American Psychiatric Association. (1980). *Diagnostic and statistical manual of mental disorders* (3rd. ed.). Washington, DC: Author.

American Psychiatric Association. (1987). *Diagnostic and statistical manual of mental disorders* (3rd ed. rev.; DSM-III-R). Washington, DC: Author.

American Psychiatric Association. (1994). *Diagnostic and statistical manual of mental disorders* (4th ed.). Washington, DC: Author.

Andreoli, A., Gressot, G., Aapro, N., Tricot, L., & Cognalons, M. Y. (1989). Personality disorders as a predictor of outcome. *Journal of Personality Disorders, 3,* 307–320.

Barash, A., Frances, A., Hurt, S., Clarkin, J., & Cohen, S. (1985). Stability and distinctness of borderline personality disorder. *American Journal of Psychiatry, 142,* 1484–1486.

Black, D. W., Bell, S., Hulbert, J., & Nasrallah, A. (1988). The importance of Axis II in patients with major depression: A controlled study. *Journal of Affective Disorders, 14,* 115–122.

Black, D. W., Warrack, G., & Winokur, G. (1985). The Iowa record linkage study: I. Suicide and accidental deaths among psychiatric patients. *Archives of General Psychiatry, 42,* 71–75.

Blashfield, R. K. (1991). LISREL analyses of diagnoses of personality-disorder using the SIDP-R. Unpublished raw data.

Blashfield, R., Sprock, J., Pinkston, K., & Hodgin, J. (1985). Exemplar prototypes of personality disorder diagnoses. *Comprehensive Psychiatry, 26,* 11–21.

Charney, D. S., Nelson, J. C., & Quinlan, D. M. (1981). Personality traits and disorders in depression. *American Journal of Psychiatry, 138,* 1601–1604.

Clark, L. A. (1992). Resolving taxonomic issues in personality disorders: The value of large-scale analyses of symptom data. *Journal of Personality Disorders, 6,* 360–376.

Clark, L. A. (1993a). *Manual for the schedule for nonadaptive and adaptive personality (SWAP).* Minneapolis: University of Minnesota Press.

Clark, L. A. (1993b, September). *The relevance of trait theory to the assessment of personality disorder.* Paper presented at ISSPD Third International Congress, Boston, MA.

Clark, L. A., McEwen, J. L., Collard, L. M., & Hickok, L. G. (1993). Symptoms and traits of personality disorder: Two new methods for their assessment. *Psychological Assessment, 5,* 81–91.

Clark, L. A., Vorhies, L., & McEwen, J. L. (1994). Personality disorder symptomatology from the five-factor perspective. In P. T. Costa, Jr. & T. A. Widiger, *Personality disorders and the five-factor model of personality* (pp. 95–116). Washington, DC: American Psychological Association.

Clarkin, J. F., Widiger, T. A., Frances, A., Hurt, S. W., & Gilmore, M. (1983). Prototypic typology and the borderline personality disorder. *Journal of Abnormal Psychology, 92,* 263–275.

Coccaro, E. F. (1993). Psychopharmacologic studies in patients with personality disorders: Review and perspective. *Journal of Personality Disorders,* Supplement, 181–192.

Cohen, J. (1960). A coefficient of agreement for nominal scales. *Educational and Psychological Measurement, 20,* 37–46.

Costa, P. T., Jr., & McCrae, R. R. (1992). *NEO-PI-R professional manual.* Odessa, FL: Psychological Assessment Resources.

Dahl, A. (1986). Some aspects of the DSM-III personality disorders illustrated by a consecutive sample of hospitalized patients. *Acta Psychiatrica Scandinavica, 73,* 62–66.

Docherty, J. P., Fiester, S. J., & Shea, T. (1986). Syndrome diagnosis and personality disorder. *American Psychiatric Association Annual Review, 5,* 315–355.

Flick, S. N., Roy-Byrne, P. P., Cowley, D. S., Shores, M. M., & Dunner, D. L. (1993). DSM-III-R personality disorders in a mood and anxiety disorders clinic: Prevalence, comorbidity, and clinical correlates. *Journal of Affective Disorders, 27,* 71–79.

Frances, A. (1993). Dimensional diagnosis of personality—not whether but when and which. *Psychological Inquiry, 4,* 110–111.

Frances, A. J., & Widiger, T. (1986). The classification of personality disorders: An overview of problems and solutions. In A. J. Frances & R. E. Hales (Eds.), *American Psychiatric Association annual review: Vol. 5* (pp. 240–278). Washington, DC: American Psychiatric Press.

Friedman, R. C., Aronoff, M. S., Clarkin, J. F., Corn, R., & Hurt, S. W. (1983). History of suicidal behavior in depressed borderline patients. *American Journal of Psychiatry, 140,* 1023–1026.

Fyer, M. R., Frances, A. J., Sullivan, T., Hurt, S. W., & Clarkin, J. (1988). Comorbidity of borderline personality disorder. *Archives of General Psychiatry, 45,* 348–352.

Gunderson, J. G., Kolb, J. E., & Austin, V. (1981). The diagnostic interview for borderline patients. *American Journal of Psychiatry, 138,* 896–903.

Gunderson, J. G., Links, P. S., & Reich, J. H. (1991). Competing models of personality disorders. *Journal of Personality Disorders, 5,* 60–68.

Harkness, A. R. (1992). Fundamental topics in the personality disorders: Candidate trait dimensions from the lower regions of the hierarchy. *Psychological Assessment, 4,* 251–259.

Harkness, A. R., McNulty, J. L., & Ben-Porath, Y. S. (1993, August). *The Personality Psychopathology Five (PSY-5): Constructs and preliminary MMPI-2 scales.* Paper presented at the American Psychological Association, Toronto, Ontario.

Hogg, B., Jackson, H. J., Rudd, R. P., & Edwards, J. (1990). Diagnosing personality disorders in recent-onset schizophrenia. *Journal of Nervous and Mental Diseases, 178,* 194–199.

Hyler, S. E., Lyons, M., Rieder, R. O., Young, L., Williams, J. B. W., & Spitzer, R. L. (1990). The factor structure of self report DSM-III Axis II symptoms and their relationship to clinicians' ratings. *American Journal of Psychiatry, 147,* 751–757.

Hyler, S., & Rieder, R. (1987). *PDQ-R personality questionnaire.* New York: New York State Psychiatric Institute.

Hyler, S. E., Rieder, R. O., Spitzer, R. L., & Williams, J. B. W. (1983). *Personality Diagnostic Questionnaire (PDQ).* New York: New York State Psychiatric Institute.

Hyler, S. E., Rieder, R. O., Williams, J. B. W., Spitzer, R. L., Lyons, M., & Hendler, J. (1989). A comparison of clinical and self-report diagnoses of DSM-III personality disorders in 552 patients. *Comprehensive Psychiatry, 30,* 170–178.

Hyler, S. E., Skodol, A. E., Kellman, H. D., Oldham, J. M., & Rosnick, L. (1990). Validity of the Personality Diagnostic Questionnaire—Revised: Comparison with two structured interviews. *American Journal of Psychiatry, 147,* 1043–1048.

Jackson, H. J., Gazis, J., Rudd, R. P., & Edwards, J. (1991). Concordance between two personality disorder instruments with psychiatric inpatients. *Comprehensive Psychiatry, 32,* 252–260.

Jenike, M. A., Baer, L., Minichiello, W. E., Schwartz, C. E., & Carey, R. J., Jr. (1986). Concomitant obsessive-compulsive disorder and schizotypal personality disorder. *American Journal of Psychiatry, 143,* 530–532.

Jonas, J. M., & Pope, H. G. (1992). Axis I comorbidity of borderline personality disorder: Clinical implications. In J. F. Clarkin, E. Morziali, & H. Monroe-Blum (Eds.), *Borderline personality disorder: Clinical and empirical perspectives* (pp. 149–160). New York: Guilford.

Kass, F., Skodol, A. E., Charles, E., Spitzer, R. L., & Williams, J. B. W. (1985). Scaled ratings of DSM-III personality disorders. *American Journal of Psychiatry, 142,* 627–630.

Kavoussi, R. J., & Siever, L. J. (1991). Biologic validators of personality disorders. In J. M. Oldham (Ed.), *Personality disorders: New perspectives on diagnostic validity* (pp. 73–87). Washington, DC: American Psychiatric Press.

Kolb, J. E., & Gunderson, J. G. (1980). Diagnosing borderline patients with a semistructured interview. *Archives of General Psychiatry, 37,* 37–41.

Livesley, W. J., & Jackson, D. N. (1992). Guidelines for developing, evaluating, and revising the classification of personality disorders. *Journal of Nervous and Mental Disease, 180,* 609–618.

Livesley, W. J., Jackson, D. N., & Schroeder, M. L. (1992). Factorial structure of traits delineating personality disorders in clinical and general population samples. *Journal of Abnormal Psychology, 101,* 432–440.

Livesley, W. J., Schroeder, M. L., & Jackson, D. N. (1990). Dependent personality disorder and attachment problems. *Journal of Personality Disorders, 4,* 131–140.

Livesley, W. J., Schroeder, M. L., Jackson, D. N., & Jang, K. L. (1994). Categorical distinctions in the study of personality disorder: Implications for classification. *Journal of Abnormal Psychology, 103,* 6–17.

Loranger, A. W., Lenzenweger, M. F., Gartner, A. F., Susman, V. L., Herzig, J., Zammit, G. K., Gartner, J. D., Abrams, R. C., & Young, B. C. (1991). Trait-state artifacts and the diagnosis of personality disorders. *Archives of General Psychiatry, 48,* 720–728.

Loranger, A., Susman, V., Oldham, J., & Russakoff, L. (1987). The personality disorders examination: A preliminary report. *Journal of Personality Disorders, 1,* 1–13.

Martin, R. L., Cloninger, C. R., Guze, S. V., & Clayton, P. J. (1985). Mortality in a follow-up of 500 psychiatric outpatients. I. Total mortality. *Archives of General Psychiatry, 42,* 47–54.

Mavissakalian, M., & Hamann, M. S. (1986). DSM-III personality disorders in agoraphobia. *Comprehensive Psychiatry, 27,* 471–479.

Mavissakalian, M., & Hamann, M. S. (1987). DSM-III personality disorder in agoraphobia. II. Changes with treatment. *Comprehensive Psychiatry, 28,* 356–361.

McGlashan, T. H. (1983). The borderline syndrome, II: Is it a variation of schizophrenia or affective disorder? *Archives of General Psychiatry, 40,* 1319–1323.

McGlashan, T. H., & Fenton, W. S. (1991). Diagnostic efficiency of DSM-III borderline personality disorder and schizotypal disorder. In J. M. Oldham

(Ed.), *Personality disorders: New perspectives on diagnostic validity* (pp. 123–143). Washington, DC: American Psychiatric Press.

Mellman, T. A., Leverich, G. S., Hauser, P., Kramlinger, K., Post, R. M., & Uhde, T. W. (1992). Axis II pathology in panic and affective disorders: Relationship to diagnosis, course of illness, and treatment response. *Journal of Personality Disorders, 6,* 53–63.

Millon, T. (1983). *Millon Clinical Multiaxial Inventory* (3rd ed.). Minneapolis: National Computer Systems.

Millon, T. (1987). *Manual for the MCMI-II* (2nd ed.). Minneapolis: National Computer Systems.

Morey, L. (1988). Personality disorders under DSM-III and DSM-III-R: An examination of convergence, coverage and actual consistency. *American Journal of Psychiatry, 145,* 573–577.

Morey, L., Waugh, M., & Blashfield, R. (1985). MMPI scales for DSM-III personality disorders: Their derivation and correlates. *Journal of Personality Assessment, 49,* 245–251.

Nurnberg, H. G., Hurt, S. W., Feldman, A., & Suh, R. (1987). Efficient diagnosis of borderline personality disorder. *Journal of Personality Disorders, 1,* 307–315.

Nurnberg, H. G., Raskin, M., Levine, P. E., Pollack, S., Siegel, O., & Prince, R. (1991). Hierarchy of DSM-III criteria efficiency for the diagnosis of borderline personality disorder. *Journal of Personality Disorders, 5,* 211–224.

O'Boyle, M., & Self, D. (1990). A comparison of two interviews for DSM-III-R personality disorders. *Psychiatric Research, 32,* 85–92.

Paris, J., Brown, R., & Nowlis, D. (1987). Long-term follow-up of borderline patients in a general hospital. *Comprehensive Psychiatry, 28,* 530–535.

Perry, J. C. (1992). Problems and considerations in the valid assessment of personality disorders. *American Journal of Psychiatry, 149,* 1645–1653.

Perry, J. C., Lavori, P. W., Cooper, S. H., Hoke, L., & O'Connell, M. E. (1987). The Diagnostic Interview Schedule and DSM-III antisocial personality disorder. *Journal of Personality Disorders, 1,* 121–131.

Perry, J. C., Lavori, P. W., & Hoke, L. (1987). A Markov model for predicting levels of psychiatric service use in borderline and antisocial personality disorders and bipolar type II affective disorder. *Journal of Psychiatric Research, 21,* 214–232.

Pfohl, B., Black, D., Noyes, R., Coryell, W. H., & Barrash, J. (1990). Axis I/Axis II comorbidity findings. In J. M. Oldham (Ed.), *Personality disorders: New perspectives on validity* (pp. 145–161). Washington DC: American Psychiatric Association Press.

Pfohl, B., Blum, H., Zimmerman, M., & Stangl, D. (1989). *Structured Interview for DSM-III-R. Personality. SIDP-R.* Iowa City, IA: Department of Psychiatry, University of Iowa.

Pfohl, B., Coryell, W., Zimmerman, M., & Stangl, D. (1986). DSM-III personality disorders: Diagnostic overlap and internal consistency of individual DSM-III criteria. *Comprehensive Psychiatry, 27,* 21–34.

Pfohl, B., Coryell, W., Zimmerman, M., & Stangl, D. (1987). Prognostic validity of self-report and interview measures of personality disorder in depressed inpatients. *Journal of Clinical Psychiatry, 48,* 468–472.

Pfohl, B., Stangl, D., & Zimmerman, M. (1984). The implications of DSM-III personality disorders for patients with major depression. *Journal of Affective Disorders, 7,* 309–318.

Piersma, H. L. (1987). The MCMI as a measure of DSM-III Axis II diagnoses: An empirical comparison. *Journal of Clinical Psychology, 43,* 479–483.

Pilkonis, P. A., Heape, C. L., Ruddy, J., & Serrao, P. (1991). Validity in the diagnosis of personality disorders: The use of the LEAD standard. *Psychological Assessment, 3,* 1–9.

Reich, J. H. (1988). DSM-III personality disorders and the outcome of treated panic disorder. *American Journal of Psychiatry, 145,* 1149–1152.

Reich, J. H. (1989). Familiality of DSM-III dramatic and anxious personality clusters. *Journal of Nervous and Mental Disease, 147,* 96–100.

Reich, J. H., Noyes, R., & Troughton, E. (1987). Comparison of three DSM-III personality disorder instruments. In Conference on the Millon Clinical Inventories (MCMI, MBHI, MAPI). Minneapolis, MN: National Computer Systems.

Reich, J., & Troughton, E. (1988). Frequency of DSM-III personality disorders in patients with panic disorder: Comparison with psychiatric and normal control subjects. *Psychiatric Research, 26,* 89–100.

Rennenberg, B., Chambless, D. L., Dowdall, D. J., Fauerbach, J. A., & Gracely, E. J. (1992). The structured clinical interview for DSM-III-R, Axis II and the Millon Clinical Multiaxial Inventory: A concurrent validity study of personality disorders among anxious outpatients. *Journal of Personality Disorders, 6,* 117–124.

Robins, L. N., Helzer, J. E., Croughan, J., & Ratcliff, K. S. (1981). National Institute of Mental Health Diagnostic Interview Schedule: Its history, characteristics and validity. *Archives of General Psychiatry, 38,* 381–389.

Schact, T. E. (1993). How do I diagnose thee? Let me count the dimensions. *Psychological Inquiry, 4,* 115–118.

Shea, M. T. (1992). Some characteristics of the Axis II criteria sets and their implications for assessment of personality disorders. *Journal of Personality Disorders, 6,* 377–381.

Shea, M. T., Pilkonis, P. A., Beckham, E., Colins, J. F., Elkin, I., Sotsky, S. M., & Docherty, J. P. (1990). Personality disorders and treatment outcome in the NIMH treatment of depression collaborative research program. *American Journal of Psychiatry, 147,* 711–718.

Siever, L. J., & Davis, K. L. (1991). A psychobiological perspective on the personality disorders. *American Journal of Psychiatry, 148,* 1647–1658.

Skodol, A., Oldham, J., Rosnick, L., Kellman, H. D., & Hyler, S. (1991). Diagnosis of DSM-III-R personality disorders: A comparison of two structured interviews. *International Journal of Methods in Psychiatric Research, 1,* 13–26.

Soloff, P. H., George, A., Cornelius, J., Nathan, S., & Schulz, P. (1991). Pharmacotherapy and borderline subtypes. In J. M. Oldham (Ed.), *Personality disorders: New perspectives on diagnostic validity* (pp. 91–103). Washington, DC: American Psychiatric Press.

Spitzer, R. L., Williams, J. B., & Gibbon, M. (1987). *Structured Clinical Interview for DSM-III-R—Outpatient version, personality disorders.* New York: Biometrics Research Department, New York State Psychiatric Institute.

Stangl, D., Pfohl, B., Zimmerman, M., Bowers, W., & Corenthal, C. (1985). A structured interview for the DSM-III personality disorders. *Archives of General Psychiatry, 42,* 591–596.

Swartz, M. S., Blazer, D. G., George, L. K., Winfield, I., Zakris, J., & Dye, E. (1989). Identification of borderline personality disorder with the NIMH Diagnostic Interview Schedule. *American Journal of Psychiatry, 146,* 200–205.

Trull, T. J. (1993). Temporal stability and validity of two personality disorder inventories. *Psychological Assessment, 5,* 11–18.

Turner, R. M. (1987). The effects of personality disorder diagnosis on the outcome of social anxiety reduction. *Journal of Personality Disorders, 1,* 136–143.

Tyrer, P., Casey, P., & Ferguson, B. (1991). Personality disorder in perspective. *British Journal of Psychiatry, 159,* 463–471.

Tyrer, P., Casey, P., & Gall, J. (1983). Relationship between neurosis and personality disorder. *British Journal of Psychiatry, 142,* 404–408.

Tyrer, P., & Seivewright, H. (1988). Studies of outcome. In P. Tyrer (Ed.), *Personality disorders: Diagnosis, treatment and course* (pp. 119–136). London: Wright.

Tyrer, P., Seivewright, N., Ferguson, B., Murphy, S., Darling, C., Brothwell, J., Kingdon, D., & Johnson, A. L. (1990). The Nottingham study of neurotic disorder: Relationship between personality status and symptoms. *Psychological Medicine, 20,* 423–431.

Wakefield, J. C. (1992a). The concept of mental disorder: On the boundary between biological facts and social values. *American Psychologist, 47,* 373–388.

Wakefield, J. C. (1992b). Disorder as harmful dysfunction: A conceptual critique of DSM-III-R's definition of mental disorder. *Psychological Review, 99,* 232–247.

Widiger, T. A. (1991). Critical issues in the design of DSM-IV, Axis II. In R. Michels (Ed.), *Psychiatry* (pp. 1–10). Philadelphia: Lippincott.

Widiger, T. A. (1992). Categorical versus dimensional classification: Implications from and for research. *Journal of Personality Disorders, 6,* 287–300.

Widiger, T. A. (1993a). The DSM-III-R categorical personality disorder diagnoses: A critique and an alternative. *Psychological Inquiry, 4,* 75–90.

Widiger, T. A. (1993b). Validation strategies for the personality disorders. *Journal of Personality Disorders,* Supplement, 34–43.

Widiger, T. A., Frances, A. J., Harris, M., Jacobsberg, L. B., Fyer, M., & Manning, D. (1991). Comorbidity among Axis II disorders. In J. M. Oldham (Ed.), *Personality disorders: New perspectives on diagnostic validity* (pp. 165–194). Washington, DC: American Psychiatric Press.

Widiger, T. A., Frances, A., Warner, L., & Bluhm, C. (1986). Diagnostic criteria for the borderline and schizotypal personality disorders. *Journal of Abnormal Psychology, 95,* 43–51.

Widiger, T. A., & Shea, T. (1991). Differentiation of Axis I and Axis II disorders. *Journal of Abnormal Psychology, 100,* 399–406.

Widiger, T., Trull, T., Hurt, S. W., Clarkin, J., & Frances, A. (1987). A multidimensional scaling of the DSM-III personality disorders. *Archives of General Psychiatry, 44,* 557–563.

Zanarini, M. C., Frankenburg, F. R., Chauncey, D. L., & Gunderson, J. G. (1987). The Diagnostic Interview for Personality Disorders: Interrater and test-retest reliability. *Comprehensive Psychiatry, 28,* 467–480.

Zanarini, M. C., Gunderson, J. G., & Frankenburg, F. R. (1989). Axis I phenomenology of borderline personality disorder. *Comprehensive Psychiatry, 30,* 149–156.

Zimmerman, M., & Coryell, W. (1989). The reliability of personality disorder diagnoses in a nonpatient sample. *Journal of Personality Disorders, 3,* 53–57.

Zimmerman, M., & Coryell, W. H. (1990). Diagnosing personality disorders in the community: A comparison of self report and interview measures. *Archives of General Psychiatry, 47,* 527–531.

Zimmerman, M., Coryell, W., Pfohl, B., Corenthal, C., & Stangl, D. (1986). ECT response in depressed patients with and without a DSM-III personality disorder. *American Journal of Psychiatry, 143,* 1030–1032.

CHAPTER 2

Aggressiveness

JENNIFER D. LISH, RICHARD J. KAVOUSSI, and EMIL F. COCCARO

This chapter will review heightened aggressiveness as a characteristic of persons with personality disorders. We will review the DSM-IV diagnosis, epidemiology, situational stability, temporal stability, familial aggregation, genetics, psychobiology, etiology, measurement, and treatment of heightened aggressiveness. Finally, we suggest the wider use of an existing diagnosis, and the adoption of a new diagnosis for aggressiveness that we believe would facilitate future research and clinical endeavors. We will begin by defining aggressiveness.

DEFINITION OF AGGRESSIVENESS

Aggression is behavior intended to inflict discomfort, hurt, harm, injure, or destroy. Aggression can be physical or verbal, and can be directed at other human beings, at the self, at animals, or at inanimate objects. Aggressiveness is the disposition to engage in aggressive behavior. Anger is the emotional state that usually precedes an aggressive act. Trait anger is the disposition to experience the state of anger. The disposition toward anger and aggression can also be referred to as irritability. All human beings have this disposition to some degree and will therefore experience anger, and behave in an aggressive manner, given certain circumstances or provocation. Individuals who have certain psychiatric disorders are hypothesized to have a greater disposition toward anger and aggression than normal persons.

DSM-IV DIAGNOSTIC CRITERIA FOR AGGRESSIVENESS

The psychiatric taxonomy of pathologically heightened aggressiveness is complex. The *Diagnostic and Statistical Manual of Mental Disorders* of the American Psychiatric Association (DSM-IV; APA, 1994) contains seven diagnoses that explicitly include aggressive behavior as part of their diagnostic criteria: Antisocial Personality Disorder (ASPD), Borderline Personality Disorder (BPD), Intermittent Explosive Disorder (IED), Conduct Disorder, Oppositional-Defiant Disorder, Adjustment Disorder with disturbance of conduct, and Adjustment Disorder with mixed disturbance of emotions and conduct.

The diagnosis of Oppositional-Defiant Disorder is made primarily in persons under age 18. The DSM-IV criteria for Oppositional-Defiant Disorder refer to several kinds of angry, aggressive behavior; "often loses temper; often argues with adults; often deliberately annoys people; often . . . easily annoyed by others; often angry and resentful" (pp. 93–94).

Conduct Disorder is also primarily diagnosed in persons under age 18. The DSM-IV criteria for Conduct Disorder include the following forms of aggressive behavior; "often bullies, threatens, or intimidates others; often initiates physical fights; has used a weapon that can cause serious physical harm to others; has been physically cruel to people; has been physically cruel to animals; has forced someone into sexual activity" (p. 90). The DSM-IV criteria for Conduct Disorder also include violence that is directed at property rather than another person; "has deliberately engaged in fire setting with the intention of causing serious damage; has deliberately destroyed others' property" (p. 90).

Oppositional-Defiant Disorder is not diagnosed if the person meets criteria for Conduct Disorder. Adjustment disorders must be reactions to specific stressors, last less than 6 months after the termination of the stressor, and not meet criteria for another Axis I disorder. Thus, the DSM-IV diagnoses that are most frequently potentially applicable to adults with an increased disposition to anger and aggressiveness are Antisocial Personality Disorder, Borderline Personality Disorder, and Intermittent Explosive Disorder.

The DSM-IV criteria for Antisocial Personality Disorder (ASPD) include "irritability and aggressiveness, as indicated by repeated physical fights or assaults" (p. 650). Furthermore, a diagnosis of Antisocial Personality Disorder can only be made if the person has met the criteria for Conduct Disorder before age 15, which might have included some of the forms of aggressive behavior listed earlier.

The DSM-IV criteria for Borderline Personality Disorder (BPD) also refer to an increased disposition toward anger and aggressiveness; "inappropriate, intense anger or difficulty controlling anger (e.g., frequent displays of temper, constant anger, recurrent physical fights)"; "intense episodic . . . irritability" (p. 654). The DSM-IV criteria for BPD also include aggression directed toward the self; "recurrent suicidal behavior, gestures, or threats, or self-mutilating behavior" (p. 654).

The DSM-IV criteria for Intermittent Explosive Disorder (IED) require "several discrete episodes of failure to resist aggressive impulses that result in serious assaultive acts or destruction of property," that "the degree of aggressiveness is grossly out of proportion to any precipitating psychosocial stressors" (p. 612), and that "the aggressive episodes are not better accounted for by another mental disorder (e.g., Antisocial Personality Disorder, Borderline Personality Disorder, a Psychotic Disorder, a Manic Episode, Conduct Disorder, or Attention-Deficit/Hyperactivity Disorder) and are not due to the direct physiological effects of a substance (e.g., a drug of abuse, a medication) or a general medical condition (e.g., head trauma, Alzheimer's disease)" (p. 612). "Episodic behavioral dyscontrol" is a non-DSM-IV diagnostic term that has sometimes been used for patients with these symptoms.

Persons who have problems with aggression but do not meet the criteria for Borderline or Antisocial Personality Disorder may be given diagnoses of Personality Disorder Not Otherwise Specified, and persons who do not meet criteria for Intermittent Explosive Disorder may be given the diagnosis of Impulse-Control Disorder Not Otherwise Specified.

The preceding DSM-IV criteria suggest that patients who meet criteria for Borderline and Antisocial Personality Disorders can be expected to exhibit increased levels of aggressive behavior, as can patients who meet criteria for Personality Disorder Not Otherwise Specified by virtue of having borderline and/or antisocial traits.

MEASUREMENT OF AGGRESSIVENESS AND OF ASPD, BPD, AND IED

There is some evidence for the convergent validity of the many measures of anger and aggressiveness used in this area of research. Moreno, Fuhriman, and Selby (1993) found good convergent validity between the Buss-Durkee Hostility Inventory (Buss & Durkee, 1957), the State-Trait Anger Scale (Spielberger, Jacobs, Russell, & Crane, 1983), and Fould's Hostility and Direction of Hostility Inventory. Spielberger et al. (1983) found that his State-Trait Anger Scale correlated moderately (.43–.59) with the Cook-Medley Hostility Inventory (Cook & Medley, 1954). Romanov et al. (1994) developed a new three-item hostility scale composed of the sum of Likert ratings of the stems "seldom prone to get into arguments," "do not get angry easily," and "do not get irritated easily." This scale correlated well with the Spielberger anger scale ($r = .71$ for males, .62 for females). Schill and Wang (1990) demonstrated that the MMPI-2 anger content scales are correlated with Spielberger's anger expression scale (Spielberger et al., 1985), with Zelin, Adler, and Myerson's (1972) anger self-report scale, and with the Cook-Medley Hostility scale. Schill, Ramanaiah, and Conn (1990) developed overt and covert hostility subscales of the Buss-Durkee, each of which had good internal consistency, and demonstrated predicted relationships between these scales and several existing measures of anger expression. Muntaner et al. (1990) found moderate correlations between self-report and interview measures of aggression and antisocial personality. Buss and Perry (1992) recently introduced a new aggressiveness questionnaire with four scales; Anger, Hostility, Verbal Aggression, and Physical Aggression. Buss and Perry's questionnaire has good internal consistency.

There is also evidence of temporal stability for some measures of aggressiveness. Moreno et al. (1993) found that Buss-Durkee's Hostility Inventory (Buss & Durkee, 1957, the State-Trait Anger Scale (Spielberger et al., 1983), and Fould's Hostility and Direction of Hostility Inventory had good temporal stability. Romanov et al. (1994) had good long-term stability; the Pearson correlation between two administrations separated by 9 years was .57. Buss and Perry's new questionnaire (1992) has also demonstrated good temporal stability.

There is also evidence that some self-report measures of aggressiveness have external validity. Smith, Sanders, and Alexander (1990) have demonstrated in the context of marital interaction between normal individuals that Cook-Medley hostility scores predict actual anger and hostile behavior. Pope, Smith, and Rhodewalt (1990) found similar relationships between Cook-Medley hostility ratings and anger and aggressive behavior in interaction between strangers. Buss and Perry's scale (1992) predicted peer nominations for aggressiveness.

EPIDEMIOLOGY OF AGGRESSIVENESS

Anger and aggressiveness in personality-disordered individuals can best be understood in the context of information on the prevalence of violence in the general population. A survey of high school students found that 28% of boys and 7% of girls had been in a physical fight in the previous month (Kaplan, Sadock, & Greb, 1994). Data on over 10,000 U.S. community residents from the Epidemiological Catchment Area study (Swanson, Holzer, Ganju, & Jono, 1990), shows that 3.7% of Americans, 5.3% of men and 2.2% of women, have committed one or more acts of violence in the past year (abused a child, repeatedly hit a spouse, gotten into physical fights, used a weapon in a fight). Male gender, youth, low socioeconomic status, or an Axis I psychiatric disorder (especially substance abuse comorbid with another disorder) increase the odds that one has recently committed a violent act (Swanson et al., 1990). Bland and Orn (1986) found that 24% of the population had exhibited one or more violent behaviors; 19.7% of adults (14% of men, 22% of women) had hit or thrown things at their spouse; 2% (1.1% of men, 2.5% of women) had physically abused a child; 10.4% (21.1% of men, 3.1% of women) had been in physical fights with a nonspouse adult; and 2.3% (3.7% of men, 1.4% of women) had used a weapon in a fight. Unfortunately, the survey instrument used by Bland and Orn did not allow them to differentiate between a single incident of mild marital violence (e.g., throwing a piece of paper) and more serious violence (e.g., repeated assault and battery). However, interpersonal aggression is clearly common in the general population; one quarter of North Americans have committed an act of interpersonal violence, and one fifth have committed an act of marital violence, during the past year. Any increased prevalence of aggressive behavior among persons with personality disorders must be understood in the context of this information about the high prevalence of violence in the population in general.

Empirical Data Associating Anger and Aggressiveness with Selected DSM-IV Disorders

There is empirical data demonstrating that persons with antisocial personality disorder do indeed display increased anger and aggressiveness. The body of research regarding anger and aggressiveness in borderline personality disorder is smaller, and the literature on intermittent explosive disorder is smaller yet.

Anger and Aggression in Antisocial Personality Disorder

Bland and Orn (1986) examined the association of antisocial personality disorder (ASPD) with violence in their community epidemiological study. Bland and Orn found that community residents who have ASPD are 4.7 times more likely than others to have committed one or more acts of violence. Men who hit or throw things at their spouses are eight times, and women 24 times, more likely than others to have ASPD. Men who have physical fights are 9.3 times, and women 35 times, more likely than others to have ASPD. Men who use weapons are 18 times, and women 61 times, more likely than others, to have ASPD. Men who have abused children are 6 times, and women 11 times, more likely than others to have ASPD. Bland and Orn thus provided evidence that a range of intrafamilial and extrafamilial violent acts are associated with ASPD. Interestingly, the occurrence of these acts is more restricted to those with personality disorders among women than men: A woman who engages in interpersonal violence appears to be more deviant from her gender, and to be more likely to have engaged in other socially unacceptable acts, than a man.

Other studies have also demonstrated an association between ASPD and violence. Among male relatives of alcoholics, those who have battered their wives have a higher prevalence of antisocial personality disorder than non-batterers, even when spouse battery is not counted as a symptom of ASPD (Dinwiddie, 1992). Hart, Dutton, and Newlove (1993) found that 29% of male wife assaulters had ASPD according to the Personality Disorder Examination (PDE). Self-identified child batterers have an increased prevalence of ASPD compared with nonbatterers (Dinwiddie & Bucholz, 1993). Famularo, Kinscherff, and Fenton (1992) found an increased prevalence of personality disorder on the SCID-II in mothers who had abused their children, although the types of personality disorders were not reported. Yarvis (1990), in clinical evaluations of a referred sample of murderers, found a 38% prevalence of ASPD. Men who batter women have elevated scores on the antisocial personality scales derived from the MMPI (Else, Wonderlich, Beatty, Christie, & Staton, 1993). In prison populations, the prevalence of antisocial personality disorder may be as high as 75% (Kaplan et al., 1994).

In addition to showing an association of actual violent behavior with ASPD, several studies have shown an association between ASPD and various indexes of anger and the disposition toward aggression. Else and colleagues (1993) found that male spouse batterers had elevated scores, compared with controls, on the acting-out hostility scale of the Hostility and Direction of Hostility Questionnaire. Haertzen, Hickey, Rose, and Jaffe (1990) found that individuals with ASPD score high on the Buss-Durkee Hostility Inventory items reflecting overt aggression. Angst and Clayton (1986) have shown that persons with ASPD score high on measures of aggression. Davis et al. (1993) showed that prison inmates' scores on measures of hostility and anger were directly correlated with the degree of violence in their criminal offense histories and in prison.

Anger and Aggression in Borderline Personality Disorder

The research demonstrating the association of borderline personality disorder (BPD) with anger and aggressiveness is sparser than that for ASPD. Yarvis (1990) found that 18% of a referred sample of murderers had BPD. Hart et al. (1993) found that 24% of male wife assaulters had BPD according to the Personality Disorder Examination (PDE). Men who batter women have elevated scores on the Borderline Personality scale derived from the MMPI (Else et al., 1993).

As with ASPD, in addition to studies showing an association between BPD and actual violent acts, there have been studies that show an increased disposition to anger and aggressiveness in persons with BPD. Gardner, Liebenluft, O'Leary, and Cowdry (1991) found that these patients had significantly higher total scores than normal volunteers on the Buss-Durkee Hostility Inventory, as well as higher scores on five subscales: Irritability, Negativism, Resentment, Suspicion, and Guilt, but not on other subscales: Assault, Indirect Hostility, or Verbal Hostility. Gardner et al. (1991) found that the Buss-Durkee Hostility scores of patients with borderline personality disorder were not related to the presence or absence of major depression, or to a history of depression, implying that proneness to anger and hostility is an enduring characteristic of borderline personality disorder. Raine (1993) found a linear relationship between the degree of violence in crimes committed by imprisoned murderers, violent offenders (assault, wounding, rape), and nonviolent offenders (drugs, blackmail, burglary, robbery) and their scores on a continuous measure of borderline personality derived from the Diagnostic Interview for Borderlines (Kolb & Gunderson, 1980).

Several studies showing an association between personality disorder and violence have not reported the nature of the personality disorder. Lindqvist (1991) found a high prevalence of personality disorder among alcohol and drug abusers who had committed a homicide. Rix (1994) found that the prevalence of personality disorder among arsonists was 50%. Convit, Isay, Otis, and Volavka (1990) found that female residents of a state mental hospital who had committed repeated assaults had a higher prevalence of personality disorders than women who had committed one, or no, assaults.

Anger and Aggression in Intermittent Explosive Disorder

There has been little research on anger and aggressiveness in patients with the DSM-IV diagnosis of Intermittent Explosive Disorder, or on the relationship of this Axis I condition to BPD and ASPD. Indeed, DSM-IV states that the disorder itself is rare (APA, 1994). Mattes (1990) studied 51 IED patients; 86% were male, 22% had BPD, and 16% had ASPD. Felthous, Bryant, Wingerter, and Barratt (1991) studied 443 men from the community who sought help for violent episodes characterized by loss of control followed by regret. Felthous and colleagues (1991) found that, because of various exclusion criteria, the IED diagnosis could only be applied to 1.5% of the men who complained of problems with violence. They therefore remarked upon the inadequacy of the DSM-III Intermittent Explosive Disorder diagnosis in classifying individuals who complain of problems controlling violent impulses. Felthous et al. also questioned whether IED is actually rare, or just rarely included in differential diagnoses. One of the exclusion criteria referred to by Felthous—that the person not be impulsive between episodes of extreme violence—has been removed from the criteria in DSM-IV. However, for the other reasons outlined by Felthous and colleagues, the diagnosis of IED is still not adequately able to cover patients who have problems with violence that become a focus of clinical attention.

There have, however, been a number of reports on a condition that appears to resemble IED. Fava and colleagues (Fava, Anderson, & Rosenbaum, 1990, 1993; Fava, Rosenbaum, et al., 1993) have described a syndrome that they call "anger attacks," in which patients have spontaneous or provoked sudden, intense spells of anger that are out of proportion to the circumstances and that may be associated with a surge of autonomic arousal. The criteria for this condition included, over the past 6 months, irritability, overreaction to minor annoyances, and recurrent anger attacks, at least one of which included anger or rage plus four or more of the following symptoms; tachycardia or palpitations, hot flashes, chest tightness or discomfort, parasthesias, dizziness or light-headedness, dyspnea, sweating, trembling, panic or anxiety, feeling out of control or about to explode, feeling like physically attacking or yelling at others, actually attacking others physically or verbally, or throwing or destroying objects. In fact, the most common symptoms during anger attacks in patients studied by Fava's group were feeling like attacking others, feeling out of control, tachycardia, and hot flashes. Among Fava's patients, 63% reported actually attacking others physically or verbally, and 30% reported throwing or destroying objects. Fava, Anderson, and Rosenbaum (1993) found this syndrome in 44% of their outpatients with major depressive disorder (56% of the men and 38% of the women), as well as in 21% of "normal controls" (Fava, Grandi, et al., 1993). Fava and colleagues did not report what proportion of anger attacks actually came "out of the blue" rather than being provoked in interpersonal situations, as are most angry outbursts in patients that our group has studied. The symptoms reported as most common in these anger attacks seem to be the most common symptoms of an experience of extreme anger or rage in normal, nondepressed persons as well. Thus, it appears that the abnormality in patients studied by this research group is not in the nature of the subjective experience but rather is in the frequency of their experiences of extreme anger, the degree of provocation required to elicit anger, and the occurrence of overt aggressive behavior in circumstances in which it would not normally be expected. It seems especially likely that anger attacks are not as deviant an experience as recurrent panic attacks because fully one fifth of community adults reported having "anger attacks." It is intriguing that this is approximately the proportion of community adults who reported commiting at least one act of interpersonal or marital violence in the past year in the Bland and Orn (1986) study.

According to the Personality Disorder Questionnaire Revised (PDQ-R; Hyler & Rieder, 1987), depressed patients with anger attacks were more likely than depressed patients without them to have histrionic, narcissistic, borderline, antisocial, schizotypal, or passive-aggressive personality traits. Indeed, in Fava's study, the rate of borderline personality disorder according to the PDQ-R was 75% among the patients with anger attacks, compared with 47% among depressed patients who did not have anger attacks. These extremely high rates of prevalence are a function of the use of the PDQ-R, which is a self-report questionnaire that renders much higher rates of personality disorder prevalence than structured interviews (Zimmerman, 1994). Fava and colleagues (Fava, Anderson, & Rosenbaum, 1993; Fava, Rosenbaum et al., 1993) state that they also found higher rates of Cluster B personality disorders (histrionic, narcissistic, borderline, antisocial) on the SCID-II, in patients with anger attacks, but they do not report the SCID-II data. Patients with anger attacks scored higher on the Hostility scale of Kellner's Symptom Questionnaire (1987) and on the Cook-Medley Hostility scale than patients without anger attacks (Fava, Anderson, & Rosenbaum, 1993; Fava, Rosenbaum et al., 1993).

According to DSM-III-R (APA, 1987) criteria, these patients would not have met criteria for Intermittent Explosive Disorder, because they were required by the diagnostic criteria used by Fava's group to be irritable between the outbursts. This was an exclusion criterion for IED that was included in DSM-III-R, but was dropped in DSM-IV; namely, "There are no signs of generalized impulsiveness or aggressiveness between the episodes" (p. 322). Thus, it would appear that many of Fava's patients with anger attacks would meet criteria for Intermittent Explosive Disorder according to DSM-IV criteria. The prevalence of IED in the community and in psychiatric populations, and its relationship to BPD and ASPD have not been adequately explored.

Epidemiology of Aggressive Personality Disorders

Weissman (1993), on the basis of all epidemiologic studies conducted prior to 1990, found that the prevalence rate of borderline personality disorder varied from a low of 0.2% to a high of 4.6%, with most studies indicating a prevalence around 1.5%. Borderline personality disorder is more common in women than men (Kroll et al., 1981; Kroll, Carey, Sines, & Roth, 1982; Weissman, 1993). Weissman (1993) also found that the rates of antisocial personality disorder clustered around 2% to 3%, and were five times higher in men than women.

STABILITY OF AGGRESSIVENESS ACROSS SITUATIONS

A number of investigators have demonstrated that aggressive behavior is stable across situations. Spouse assaulters are more likely than others also to be child physical abusers and to be violent outside the family (Farrington, 1994). Dinwiddie (1992) finds that, of spouse batterers among male relatives of alcoholics, 95% report other physical fighting in adulthood, compared with 40% of nonbatterers. Self-identified child batterers have an increased prevalence, compared with controls, of physical fighting, physical violence against a spouse, property destruction, many juvenile conduct disorder symptoms, and many other impulsive behaviors, such as promiscuity and marital infidelity (Dinwiddie & Bucholz, 1993). Lucker, Kruzich, Holt, and Gold (1991) found that soldiers arrested for driving while under the influence were more likely to have also been arrested for other offenses and antisocial behaviors. A special case of the stability of aggressiveness across situations is the association of aggressive behavior toward others with suicidal behaviors, which has been demonstrated by numerous studies (DeJong, Virkkunen, & Linnoila, 1992; Dinwiddie, 1992; Garrison, McKeown, Valois, & Vincent, 1993; Hawton & Fagg, 1992; Hillbrand, Krystal, Sharpe, & Foster, 1994; Martunnen, Aro, Henrikkson, & Lonnqvist, 1994).

STABILITY OF AGGRESSIVENESS OVER TIME

There is substantial evidence of temporal stability of the personality trait of aggressiveness, in that there is evidence of its stability from childhood to young adulthood. However, there is also substantial evidence of its temporal instability, in that there is evidence of substantial reduction in aggressiveness with advancing age in adults.

Many authors have demonstrated that childhood aggressive behavior of a sort that would make a child qualify for the diagnoses of oppositional-defiant disorder or conduct disorder prospectively predicts adult aggressive behavior of the sort that might make an adult qualify for the diagnoses of IED, BPD, or ASPD. Peer-rated aggression at age 8 predicts self-reported aggression, criminal violence, and spouse assault at age 30 in males (Farrington, 1994; Huesmann, & Eron, 1992). Pulkkinen and Pitkanen (1993) found that ratings of aggression at age 8 predicted self-reported aggressive behavior at age 26 for both males and females. Olweus (1994) has shown that 60% of boys who are characterized as bullies in Grades 6 through 9 have a criminal conviction by age 24; 40% of the former bullies have three or more convictions. Satterfield, Swanson, Schell, and Lee (1994) found that high teacher ratings of boys with attention-deficit hyperactivity disorder on the items "temper outburst," "irritable," "quick-tempered," "quarrelsome," "speaks out in a rude or sassy way to adults," "chip on shoulder attitude," and "acts smart" predicted serious antisocial behavior (i.e., arrests for assault with a deadly weapon, robbery, burglary, grand theft, and grand theft auto) 9 years later. Thus, childhood aggressiveness is associated with aggressiveness in young adulthood.

On the other hand, there is a substantial diminution of aggressiveness from young to middle adulthood. Data from the Epidemiologic Catchment Area study (ECA; Swanson et al., 1990) show that, in the general population, aggressiveness declines substantially with age; 7.3% of 18–29-year-olds, 3.6% of 30–44-year-olds, 1.2% of 45–64-year-olds, and fewer than 1% of persons over age 65 had committed at least one act of violence in the preceding year (abused a child, repeatedly hit a spouse, gotten into physical fights, or used a weapon in a fight).

Aggressiveness declines with advancing age in persons who meet criteria for ASPD and BPD. ASPD tends to remit by the fourth decade of life (American Psychiatric Association, 1994). Only 18% of female felons are still engaging in criminal behavior on 6-year follow-up (Martin, Cloninger, & Guze, 1982). Perry (1993) concludes that antisocial personality disorder remits substantially with advancing age in women. Robins et al. (1984) and Ames & Molinari (1994) found that ASPD is less common in older persons than in young adults. Weissman (1993) reviewed epidemiologic studies showing that the rates of prevalence of antisocial personality disorder are lower in persons over 45, than in those under that age.

BPD also appears not to be stable over time in adulthood. The most common course for BPD is chronic instability in early adulthood, with better vocational functioning, greater stability in relationships, decreased impairment, and less frequent parasuicidal behavior in the 30s and 40s (APA, 1994). Several studies have found that borderline personality disorder often remits over an interval of a few years (McGlashan, 1986; Paris, Brown, & Nowlis, 1987; Pope, Jonas, Hudson, Cohen, & Gunderson, 1983). McGlashan (1986) found that the typical borderline patient was a woman who had been hospitalized for 2½ years during her 20s, but who, in her 40s, was stably employed, socially involved, relatively free of symptoms, and seldom required hospitalization. McGlashan did not report specifically about the long-term stability of anger and aggressive behavior, but these symptoms are presumably among those that had by and large remitted. Perry (1993) concluded, on the basis of numerous studies, that only 52% and 33% of patients still have borderline personality disorder 10 and 15 years after intake, and that BPD is rare after age 40. Ames and Molinari (1994) also report that BPD is less common in older persons than in young adults.

The data regarding the tendency of ASPD and BPD to remit on long-term follow-up constitutes a serious challenge to the conceptualization of these disorders as personality disorders, which DSM-IV states are "an enduring pattern of inner experience and behavior [that is] stable and of long duration and [whose] onset can be traced back at least to adolescence or early adulthood" (APA, 1994, p. 633).

BIOLOGICAL THEORIES OF AGGRESSIVENESS

There is intriguing evidence that abnormalities in brain neurotransmitter functioning play a role in an individual's vulnerability to engage in aggressive behavior. Inverse relationships have been demonstrated between various indexes of brain serotonin function (5-hydroxytryptamine; i.e., 5-HT) and aggressive behavior. A direct correlation has been observed between aggressiveness, as measured by the Irritability subscale of the Buss-Durkee Hostility Inventory and the Externally Directed Hostility subscale of the Hostility and Direction of Hostility Questionnaire, and indexes of reduced central 5-HT system function have been reported in many studies (Brown, Goodwin, Ballenger, Goyer, & Major, 1979; Coccaro, Siever, Klar et al., 1989; Coccaro, Siever, Kavoussi et al., 1989; Coccaro, Gabriel, & Siever, 1990; Roy et all., 1988). In a study of 58 violent offenders and impulsive fire setters, 33 of whom met criteria for IED, Virkunnen, De Jong, Bartko, and Linnoila (1989) and Linnoila et al. (1983) found lower CSF concentrations of 5-hydroxyindoleacetic acid than in normal controls and nonviolent offenders. Brown et al. (1989) reported that the mean platelet [^{3}H] serotonin uptake was significantly lower in 15 male outpatients with episodic aggression than in 15 nonaggressive comparison subjects. Behavioral irritability also displays an inverse relationship with other measures of brain serotonin functioning, for example, the prolactin response to challenge with central 5-HT agents such as fenfluramine (Coccaro, Siever, Klar et al., 1989).

Abnormalities in the brain's noradrenergic system may also play a role in vulnerability to aggression. Growth hormone responses to the alpha-2 adrenergic agonist clonidine are significantly greater in personality-disordered patients than in remitted depressives or controls, and these responses correlate positively with self-report measures of lifetime irritability (but not assaultiveness) in both personality-disordered patients and normal controls (Coccaro et al., 1991). This suggests that the more irritable a patient is, the greater the sensitivity of the alpha-2 receptor and the greater sensitivity of the noradrenergic system to respond to novel or aversive stimuli.

GENETIC STUDIES OF AGGRESSIVENESS

Family history studies, direct interview family studies, twin studies, and adoption studies have demonstrated the heritability of aggressiveness and/or of antisocial or borderline personality disorder, and a few preliminary studies have identified a genetic polymorphism that may be associated with aggressiveness.

Adult men who assault their spouses or frequently engage in fights involving groups are more likely than other men to have had fathers who had criminal convictions, and men who have criminal convictions for violent acts tend to have sons who bully other children in school (Farrington, 1994). Family studies of patients with IED or episodic dyscontrol have shown elevated rates of IED, violence, depression, and drug and alcohol abuse in their first-degree relatives (McElroy, Hudson, Pope, Keck, & Aizley, 1992).

Data from twin, adoption, and family history studies suggest a heritable component to suicidal (Roy, Segal, Centerwell, & Robinette, 1991; Wender et al., 1986) and violent behavior (Bach-y-Rita, Lion, Climent, & Ervin, 1971; Mattes & Fink, 1987). Coccaro, Bergeman, and Mc-Clearn (1993) used mathematical modeling to demonstrate, in a sample of monozygotic and dizygotic twins, that self-reported "irritable impulsiveness" and "assertiveness/aggressiveness" show substantial genetic influences. Cates, Houston, Vavak, Crawfor, and Uttley (1993) have shown, in a twin study, that trait anger, verbal and indirect aggressiveness, and possibly irritability are significantly heritable in women.

An increased frequency of impulsive-aggressive behaviors in the family members of individuals with indexes of reduced central 5-HT system function (Coccaro, Silverman, Klar, Horvath, & Siever, 1994) suggests that an abnormality in central 5-HT and related psychopathology may be heritable in humans. The temporal stability of indexes of central 5-HT function (Coccaro, Astill, Herbert, & Schut, 1990) and of aggressiveness through childhood and young adulthood suggest that these two variables may represent biological and behavioral manifestations of a stable psychobiological trait in humans, which might be partially heritable. Nielsen et al. (1994) have shown a significant association between 5-HIAA concentration in cerebrospinal fluid (CSF) and tryptophan hydroxylase (TPH) genotype in impulsive violent offenders. Nielsen et al. also showed an association of TPH genotype with a history of suicide attempts in violent offenders.

ENVIRONMENTAL FACTORS IN AGGRESSIVENESS

Although environmental factors probably account for a significant proportion of predisposition to aggression, there have been few well-designed studies to explore the relationship between life experiences and aggression. There is some evidence of an association between childhood abuse and neglect and adult antisocial personality disorder (Luntz & Widom, 1994; Widom, 1989), but this relationship may be merely an artifact of the genetic relationship between parental and offspring antisocial personality disorder (Cloninger, Christiansen, Reich, & Gottesman, 1978; DiLalla & Gottesman, 1991; Mednick, Gabrielli, & Hutchings, 1987; Widom, 1991).

TREATMENT OF AGGRESSIVENESS

There is widening interest in the use of psychopharmacological agents to treat disorders of impulse control and aggression. Various psychopharmacological treatments of aggressive behavior have been reported to be effective in patients with BPD, ASPD, and IED. Lithium, anticonvulsants such as carbamazepine, antidepressants such as fluoxetine and sertraline, beta-noradrenergic receptor antagonists, buspirone, and antipsychotic medications all appear to have some usefulness in reducing aggression (Kaplan, Sadock, & Greb, 1994).

Neuroleptic agents have been widely used to treat impulsive aggressive behavior. However, it is not clear whether the antiaggressive effects of these agents are simply due to nonspecific sedation. Open-label thioridazine decreased impulse action scores on the Diagnostic Interview for Borderlines in patients with borderline personality disorder (Teicher et al., 1989). Similarly, treatment with low-dose haloperidol significantly improved ratings of hostility and impulsivity, compared with amitriptyline and placebo, in patients with borderline and/or schizotypal personality disorder (Soloff et al., 1989). This finding was not replicated, however, in two other double-blind, placebo-controlled studies of personality-disordered patients treated with thiothixine (Goldberg et al., 1986) or trifluroperazine (Cowdry & Gardner, 1988). These mixed findings and the risk of significant side effects (such as tardive dyskinesia) suggest caution in the use of neuroleptics in aggressive patients.

Although antidepressants and antianxiety medicines have often been used to treat aggressive individuals, controlled studies seem to suggest that these medications sometimes lead to increased aggressive behavior. Tricyclic antidepressants have been associated with increased impulse dyscontrol in subgroups of personality-disordered patients, particularly those prone to impulse dyscontrol (Soloff et al., 1986). In addition, Cowdry and Gardner (1988) reported that alprazolam, compared with placebo, increased the frequency of behavioral dyscontrol in borderline patients. Thus, these agents should also be used with caution in this population.

Several types of medication show promise in the reduction of aggressive behavior. Beta-adrenergic receptor blockers have been used effectively to treat aggressive behavior in certain psychiatric populations. High doses of propranolol decrease aggressive behavior in patients with temper outbursts and residual attention deficit disorder (Mattes, 1986). Lithium reduces impulsive aggression in prison inmates in both open (Tupin et al., 1973) and blinded placebo-controlled trials (Sheard et al., 1976). Carbamazepine selectively decreased behavioral dyscontrol in a double-blind crossover study of women with borderline personality disorder (Cowdry & Gardner, 1988). Mattes (1990) also found that carbamazepine was preferentially effective for rage outbursts in patients with intermittent explosive disorder.

The benefits of central 5-HT agents on aggressive behavior has, despite a strong theoretical rationale, received only limited study to date. In an open study, fluoxetine treatment was specifically associated with substantial reductions in overt aggressive behavior and irritability in three nondepressed personality-disordered outpatients with histories of impulsive aggressive behavior (Coccaro, Astill, et al., 1990). Similarly, sertraline reduced aggression in a series of 10 patients with various personality disorders (Kavoussi, Liu, & Coccaro, 1994). Fava, Rosenbaum et al. (1993) reported that fluoxetine completely eliminated anger attacks in 71% of the depressed patients who had reported them, and reduced patients' scores on the Cook-Medley Hostility scale, and on the Hostility and Irritability scale of the Kellner Symptom Questionnaire.

Nonpharmacological treatments have also shown promise in the treatment of impulsive behavior. Linehan, Heard, and Armstrong (1994) have shown that dialectical behavioral psychotherapy results in greater reductions in suicidal behavior, anger, psychiatric inpatient days, and psychosocial impairment than "treatment as usual" for chronically parasuicidal borderlines, and that these gains are maintained for up to one year. Unfortunately, Linehan et al.'s study (1994) did not include a measure of overt aggressive behavior toward others.

FUTURE RESEARCH DIRECTIONS

Despite the complexity of the taxonomy of aggressiveness in DSM-IV, there is no adequate diagnosis for adults who have a heightened disposition to aggressive behavior but do not perform "serious assault or property destruction," as specified in criteria for IED, and do not qualify for a diagnosis of BPD or ASPD. We have found, as did Felthous (1991) that such persons readily seek clinical treatment when it is made available, and reveal histories of substantial consequent psychosocial impairment. Preliminary evidence suggests, as discussed earlier, that this condition is responsive to treatment. It is therefore desirable to apply an Axis I diagnosis that indicates the focus of psychiatric treatment of these patients. Fava's use of the term anger attacks and the use by other authors of terms such as rage outbursts, temper outbursts, and episodic dyscontrol show the need for a clearly defined diagnostic term that can be applied to these individuals, especially given the expanding interest in this area. The diagnosis of IED might apply to some of these patients but is seldom used and rarely seems to be considered. We suggest strongly that the diagnosis of IED be considered in psychiatric evaluations, and that IED sections be added to existing structured psychiatric interviews for research use. However, as Felthous noted, many patients who seek treatment for heightened aggressiveness do not meet criteria for IED because of the exclusion criteria. Such persons might currently be diagnosed as having Personality Disorder NOS, or Impulse-Control Disorder NOS, which is less than satisfying, because these are heterogenous categories, whose use does not facilitate clear communication between researchers or clinicians interested in aggressiveness. We therefore recommend that researchers and clinicians in this area adopt a new set of diagnostic criteria, for a diagnosis entitled "Aggression Disorder."

The criteria for Aggression Disorder would be similar to those for IED but would suspend the DSM-IV exclusion criterion for individuals with BPD or ASPD. The DSM-IV exclusion criterion arbitrarily forecloses the issue of the relationship between Axis I and Axis II pathology by asserting without data that the Axis I symptoms are "due to" the Axis II symptoms, rather than that the Axis II symptoms are caused by the Axis I disorder, or that the two are unrelated, or that they reciprocally influence each other. The criteria that we suggest for Aggression Disorder also drop the requirement for IED that the individual's aggressive behavior result in injury or property destruction.

We propose the following criteria for Aggression Disorder:

1. There are recurrent incidents of verbal or physical aggression toward property or other people.
2. The degree of aggression is out of proportion to the provocation and circumstances.
3. The aggressive outbursts occur at least twice a week for at least a month.
4. The aggressive behavior is not better accounted for by mania, major depression, or psychosis, and is not solely due to the direct physiological effects of a substance (e.g., a drug of abuse, a medication)

or of a general medical condition (e.g., head trauma, Alzheimer's disease).

5. The aggressive behavior causes impairment in occupational or interpersonal functioning or marked distress.

We believe that wider use of the IED criteria and adoption of these criteria for Aggression Disorder would facilitate future research and clinical work on aggressiveness in personality-disordered individuals and others.

REFERENCES

American Psychiatric Association. (1987). *Diagnostic and statistical manual of mental disorders* (3rd ed. rev.). Washington, DC: Author.

American Psychiatric Association. (1994). *Diagnostic and statistical manual of mental disorders* (4th ed.). Washington, DC: Author.

Ames, A., & Molinari, V. (1994). Prevalence of personality disorders in community-living elderly. *Journal of Geriatric Psychiatry and Neurology, 7,* 189–194.

Angst, J., & Clayton, P. (1986). Premorbid personality of depressive, bipolar and schizophrenic patients with special reference to suicidal issues. *Comprehensive Psychiatry, 27,* 511–532.

Bach-y-Rita, G., Lion, J. R., Climent, C. E., & Ervin, F. R. (1971). Episodic dyscontrol: A study of 130 violent patients. *American Journal of Psychiatry, 127,* 1473–1478.

Barefoot, J. C., Williams, R. B., Dahlstrom, W. G., & Dodge, K. A. (1987). Predicting mortality from scores on the Cook-Medley scale: A follow-up study of 118 lawyers. *Psychosomatic Medicine, 34,* 210.

Bland, R., & Orn, H. (1986). Family violence and psychiatric disorder. *Canadian Journal of Psychiatry, 31,* 129–137.

Brown, C. S., Kent, T. A., Bryant, S. G., Gevedon, R. M., Campbell, J. L., Felthous, A. R., Barrat, E. S., & Rose, R. M. (1989). Blood platelet uptake of serotonin in episodic aggression. *Psychiatric Research, 27,* 5–12.

Brown, G. L., Goodwin, F. K., Ballenger, J. C., Goyer, P., & Major, L. (1979). Aggression in humans correlates with cerebrospinal fluid metabolites. *Psychiatry Research, 1,* 131–139.

Buss, A. H., & Durkee, A. (1957). An inventory for assessing different kinds of hostility. *Journal of Counselling Psychology, 21,* 343–349.

Buss, A. H., & Perry, M. (1992). The aggression questionnaire. *Journal of Personality and Social Psychology, 63,* 452–459.

Cates, D. S., Houston, B. K., Vavak, C. R., Crawfor, M. H., & Uttley, M. (1993). Heritability of hostility-related emotions, attitudes and behaviors. *Journal of Behavioral Medicine, 16,* 237–256.

Cloninger, C. R., Christiansen, K. O., Reich, T., & Gottesman, I. I. (1978). Implications of sex differences in the prevalences of antisocial personality, alcoholism, and criminality for familial transmission. *Archives of General Psychiatry, 35,* 941–951.

Coccaro, E. F., Astill, J. L., Herbert, J. L., & Schut, A. G. (1990). Fluoxetine treatment of impulsive aggression in DSM-III-R personality disorder patients. *Journal of Clinical Psychopharmacology, 10,* 373–375.

Coccaro, E. F., Bergeman, C. S., & McClearn, G. E. (1993). Heritability of irritable impulsiveness: A study of twins reared together and apart. *Psychiatry Research, 48,* 229–242.

Coccaro, E. F., Gabriel, S., & Siever, L. J. (1990). Buspirone challenge: Preliminary evidence for a role of central 5-HT1a receptor function in impulsive aggressive behavior in humans. *Psychopharmacology Bulletin, 26,* 393–405.

Coccaro, E. F., Lawrence, T., Trestman, R., Gabriel, S., Klar, H. M., & Siever, L. J. (1991). Growth hormone responses to intravenous clonidine challenge correlate with behavioral irritability in psychiatric patients and healthy volunteers. *Psychiatry Research, 39,* 129–139.

Coccaro, E. F., Siever, L. J., Kavoussi, R., & Davis, K. L. (1989). Impulsive aggression in personality disorder: Evidence for involvement of 5-HT-1 receptors. *Biological Psychiatry, 25,* 86A.

Coccaro, E. F., Siever, L. J., Klar, H., Maurer, G., Cochrane, K., Cooper, T. B., Mohs, R. C., & Davis, K. L. (1989). Serotonergic studies in patients with affective and personality disorders: Correlates with suicidal and impulsive aggressive behavior. *Archives of General Psychiatry, 46,* 587–599.

Coccaro, E. F., Silverman, J. M., Klar, H. M., Horvath, T. B., & Siever, L. J. (1994). Familial correlates of reduced central serotenergic function in patients with personality disorders. *Archives of General Psychiatry, 54,* 318–324.

Convit, A., Isay, D., Otis, D., & Volavka, J. (1990). Characteristics of repeatedly assaultive psychiatric inpatients. *Hospital and Community Psychiatry, 41,* 1112–1115.

Cook, W., & Medley, D. (1954). Proposed hostility and pharasaic-virtue scales of the MMPI. *Journal of Applied Psychology, 38,* 414–418.

Cowdry, R. W., & Gardner, D. L. (1988). Pharmacotherapy of borderline personality disorder: Alprazolam, carbamazepine, trifluoperazine, and tranylcypromine. *Archives of General Psychiatry, 45,* 111–119.

Davis, B. A., Durden, D. S., Pease, K., Yu, P. H., Green, C., Gordon, A., Menzies, R., Templeman, R., & Boulton, A. A. (1993). A longitudinal study of the relationships between psychometric test scores, offence history, and the plasma concentrations of phenylacetic and 5-hydroxyindoleacetic acids in seven inmates of a prison for the psychiatrically disturbed. *Progress in Neuro-Psychopharmacology and Biological Psychiatry, 17,* 619–635.

DeJong, J., Virkkunen, M., & Linnoila, M. (1992). Factors associated with recidivism in a criminal population. *Journal of Nervous and Mental Disease, 180,* 543–550.

DiLalla, L. F., & Gottesman, I. I. (1991). Biological and genetic contributors to violence—Widom's untold tale. *Psychological Bulletin, 109,* 125–129.

Dinwiddie, S. H. (1992). Psychiatric disorders among wife batterers. *Comprehensive Psychiatry, 33,* 411–416.

Dinwiddie, S. H., & Bucholz, K. K. (1993). Psychiatric diagnoses of self-reported child abusers. *Child Abuse and Neglect, 17,* 465–476.

Else, L. T., Wonderlich, S. A., Beatty, W. W., Christie, D. W., & Staton, R. D. (1993). Personality characteristics of men who physically abuse women. *Hospital and Community Psychiatry, 44,* 54–58.

Famularo, R., Kinscherff, R., & Fenton, T. (1992). Psychiatric diagnoses of abusive mothers: A preliminary report. *Journal of Nervous and Mental Disease, 180,* 658–661.

Farrington, D. (1994). Childhood, adolescent and adult features of violent males. In L. R. Huesmann (Ed.), *Aggressive behavior: Current perspectives.* New York: Plenum.

Fava, G. A., Grandi, S., Rafanelli, C., Saviotti, F. M., Ballin, M., & Pesarin, F. (1993). Hostility and irritable mood in panic disorder with agoraphobia. *Journal of Affective Disorders, 29,* 213–217.

Fava, M., Anderson, K., & Rosenbaum, J. F. (1990). "Anger attacks": Possible variants of panic and major depressive disorders. *American Journal of Psychiatry, 147,* 867–870.

Fava, M., Anderson, K., & Rosenbaum, J. F. (1993). Are thymoleptic-responsive "anger attacks" a discrete clinical syndrome? *Psychosomatics, 34,* 350–355.

Fava, M., Rosenbaum, J. F., McCarthy, M., Pava, J., Steingard, R., & Bless, E. (1991). Anger attacks in depressed outpatients and their response to fluoxetine. *Psychopharmacology Bulletin, 27,* 275–279.

Fava, M., Rosenbaum, J. F., Pava, J. A., McCarthy, M. K., Steingard, R. J., & Bouffides, E. (1993). Anger attacks in unipolar depression, Part 1: Clinical correlates and response to fluoxetine treatment. *American Journal of Psychiatry, 150,* 1158–1163.

Felthous, A. R., Bryant, S. G., Wingerter, C. B., & Barratt, E. (1991). The diagnosis of intermittent explosive disorder in violent men. *Bulletin of the American Academy of Psychiatry and the Law, 19,* 71–79.

Gardner, D. L., Leibenluft, E., O'Leary, K. M., & Cowdry, R. W. (1991). Self-ratings of anger and hostility in borderline personality disorder. *Journal of Nervous and Mental Disease, 179,* 157–161.

Garrison, C. Z., McKeown, R. E., Valois, R. F., & Vincent, M. L. (1993). Aggression, substance abuse, and suicidal behaviors in high school students. *American Journal of Public Health, 83,* 179–184.

Goldberg, S. C., Schulz, S. C., Schulz, P. M., Resnick, R. J., Hamer, R. M., & Friedel, R. O. (1986). Borderline and schizotypal personality disorders treated with low-dose thiothixene versus placebo. *Archives of General Psychiatry, 43,* 680–686.

Haertzen, C. A., Hickey, J. E., Rose, M. R., & Jaffe, J. H. (1990). The relationship between a diagnosis of antisocial personality and hostility: Development of an Antisocial Hostility scale. *Journal of Clinical Psychology, 46,* 679–686.

Hart, S. D., Dutton, D. G., & Newlove, T. (1993). The prevalence of personality disorder among wife assaulters. *Journal of Personality Disorders, 7,* 329–341.

Hawton, K., & Fagg, J. (1992). Deliberate self-poisoning and self-injury in adolescents. A study of characteristics and trends in Oxford, 1976–1989. *British Journal of Psychiatry, 161,* 816–823.

Hillbrand, M., Krystal, J. H. G., Sharpe, K. S., & Foster, H. G. (1994). Clinical predictors of self-mutilation in hospitalized forensic patients. *Journal of Nervous and Mental Disease, 182,* 9–13.

Huesmann, L. R., & Eron, L. D. (1992). Childhood aggression and adult criminality. In J. McCord (Ed.), *Facts, frameworks and forecasts: Advances in criminological theory* (Vol. 3, pp. 137–156). New Brunswick, NJ: Transaction.

Hyler, S. E., & Rieder, R. O. (1987). *PDQ-R: Personality Disorder Questionnaire-Revised.* New York: New York State Psychiatric Institute.

Kaplan, H. I., Sadock, B. J., & Greb, J. A. (1994). *Synopsis of psychiatry* (7th ed.). Baltimore, MD: Williams and Wilkins.

Kavoussi, R., Liu, J., & Coccaro, E. (1994). An open trial of sertraline in personality disorders patients with impulsive aggression. *Journal of Clinical Psychiatry, 55,* 137–141.

Kellner, R. A. (1987). Symptom questionnaire. *Journal of Clinical Psychiatry, 48,* 268–273.

Kolb, J. E., & Gunderson, J. G. (1980). Diagnosing borderline patients with a semi-structured interview. *Archives of General Psychiatry, 37,* 37–41.

Kroll, J., Carey, K., Sines, L., & Roth, M. (1982). Are there borderlines in Britain? *Archives of General Psychiatry, 39,* 60–63.

Kroll, J., Sines, L., & Martin, K., Lavi, S., Pyle, P., & Zander, J. (1981). Borderline personality disorder: Construct validity of the concept. *Archives of General Psychiatry, 38,* 1021–1026.

Lindqvist, P. (1991). Homicides committed by abusers of alcohol and illicit drugs. *British Journal of Addiction, 86,* 321–326.

Linchan, M. M., Heard, H. L., & Armstrong, H. E. (1994). Naturalistic follow-up of a behavioral treatment for chronically parasuicidal borderline patients. *Archives of General Psychiatry, 50,* 971–974.

Linnoila, M., Virkunnen, M., Scheinin, M., Nuutila, A., Rimon, R., & Goodwin, F. K. (1983). Low cerebrospinal fluid 5-hydroxyindoleacetic acid concentration differentiates impulsive from nonimpulsive violent behavior. *Life Sciences, 33,* 2609–2614.

Lucker, G. W., Kruzich, D. J., Holt, M. T., & Gold, J. D. (1991). The prevalence of antisocial behavior among U.S. Army DWI offenders. *Journal of Studies on Alcohol, 52,* 318–320.

Luntz, B. K., & Widom, C. S. (1994). Antisocial personality disorder in abused and neglected children grown up. *American Journal of Psychiatry, 151,* 670–674.

Martunnen, M. J., Aro, H. M., Henrikkson, M. M., & Lonnqvist, J. K. (1994). Antisocial behavior in adolescent suicide. *Acta Psychiatrica Scandinavica, 89,* 167–173.

Martin, R. L., Cloninger, C. R., & Guze, S. B. (1982). The natural history of somatization and substance abuse in women criminals: A six-year follow-up. *Comprehensive Psychiatry, 23,* 528–537.

Mattes, J. A. (1986). Propranolol for adults with temper outbursts and residual attention deficit disorder. *Journal of Clinical Psychopharmacology, 6,* 299–302.

Mattes, J. A. (1990). Comparative effectiveness of carbamazepine and propranolol for rage outbursts. *Journal of Neuropsychiatry and Clinical Neurosciences, 2,* 159–164.

Mattes, J. A., & Fink, M. A. (1987). A family study of patients with temper outbursts. *Journal of Psychiatric Research, 21,* 249–255.

McElroy, S. L., Hudson, J. I., Pope, H. G., Keck, P. E., & Aizley, H. G. (1992). The DSM-III-R impulse control disorders not elsewhere classified: Clinical characteristics and relationship to other psychiatric disorders. *American Journal of Psychiatry, 149,* 318–327.

McGlashan, T. H. (1986). The Chestnut Lodge follow-up study, II: long-term outcome of borderline personalities. *Archives of General Psychiatry, 43,* 20–30.

Mednick, S. A., Gabrielli, W. F., & Hutchings, B. (1987). Genetic factors in the etiology of criminal behavior. In S. A. Mednick, T. E. Moffit, & S. A. Stack (Eds.), *The causes of crime: New biological approaches.* New York: Cambridge University Press.

Moreno, J. K., Fuhriman, A., & Selby, M. J. (1993). Measurement of hostility, anger and depression in depressed and nondepressed subjects. *Journal of Personality Assessment, 61,* 511–523.

Muntaner, C., Walter, D., Nagoshi, C., Fishbein, D., Haertzen, C. A., & Jaffe, J. H. (1990). Self-report vs. laboratory measures of aggression as predictors of substance abuse. *Drug and Alcohol Dependence, 25,* 1–11.

Nielsen, D. A., Goldman, D., Virkunnen, M., Tokola, R., Rawlings, R., & Linnoila, M. (1994). Suicidality and 5-hydroxyindoleatic acid concentration associated with a tryptophan hydroxylase polymorphism. *Archives of General Psychiatry, 51,* 34–38.

Olweus, D. (1994). Bullying at school: Long-term outcomes for the victims and an effective school-based intervention program. In L. R. Huesmann (Ed.), *Aggressive behavior: Current perspectives.* New York: Plenum.

Paris, J., Brown, R., & Nowlis, D. (1987). Long-term follow-up of borderline patients in a general hospital. *Comprehensive Psychiatry, 28,* 530–535.

Perry, J. C. (1993). Longitudinal studies of personality disorders. *Journal of Personality Disorders,* Spring, 63–85.

Pope, H. G., Jonas, J. M., Hudson, J. I., Cohen, B. M., & Gunderson, J. G. (1983). The validity of DSM-III borderline personality disorder: A phenomenologic, family history, treatment response, and long-term follow-up study. *Archives of General Psychiatry, 40,* 23–30.

Pope, M. K., Smith, T. W., & Rhodewalt, F. (1990). Cognitive, behavioral and affective correlates of the Cook and Medley Hostility scale. *Journal of Personality Assessment, 54,* 501–514.

Pulkkinen, L., & Pitkanen, T. (1993). Continuities in aggressive behavior from childhood to adulthood. *Aggressive Behavior, 19,* 249–263.

Raine, A. (1993). Features of borderline personality and violence. *Journal of Clinical Psychology, 49,* 277–281.

Rix, K. J. (1994). A psychiatric study of adult arsonists. *Medicine, Science and the Law, 34,* 21–34.

Robins, L., Helzer, J., Wiessman, M. M., Orvaschel, H., Gruenberg, E., Burke, J. D., & Regier, D. A. (1984). Lifetime prevalence of specific psychiatric disorders in three sites. *Archives of General Psychiatry, 41,* 949–959.

Romanov, K., Hatakka, M., Keskinen, E., Laaksonen, H., Kaprio, J., Rose, R. J., & Koskenvuo, M. (1994). Self-reported hostility and suicidal acts, accidents, and accidental deaths: Prospective study of 21,443 adults aged 25 to 59. *Psychosomatic Medicine, 56,* 328–336.

Roy, A., Adinoff, B., & Linnoila, M. (1988). Acting out hostility in normal volunteers: Negative correlation with CSF 5HIAA levels. *Psychiatry Research, 24,* 187–194.

Roy, A., Segal, N. L., Centerwell, B. S., & Robinette, C. D. (1991). Suicide in twins. *Archives of General Psychiatry, 48,* 29–32.

Satterfield, J., Swanson, J., Schell, A., & Lee, F. (1994). Prediction of antisocial behavior in attention-deficit hyperactivity disorder boys from aggression/defiance scores. *Journal of the American Academy of Child and Adolescent Psychiatry, 33,* 185–190.

Schill, T., Ramanaiah, N., & Conn, S. R. (1990). Development of covert and overt hostility scales from the Buss-Durkee Inventory. *Psychological Reports, 67,* 671–674.

Schill, T., & Wang, S. (1990). Correlates of the MMPI-2 anger content scales. *Psychological Reports, 67,* 800–802.

Sheard, M. H., Marini, J. L., Bridges, C. I., & Wagner, E. (1976). The effect of lithium on impulsive aggressive behavior in man. *American Journal of Psychiatry, 133,* 1409–1413.

Smith, T. W., Sanders, J. D., & Alexander, J. F. (1990). What does the Cook and Medley hostility scale measure? Affect, behavior and attributions in the marital context. *Journal of Personality and Social Psychology, 58,* 699–708.

Soloff, P. H., George, A., Nathan, S., Schulz, P. M., Cornelius, J. R., Herring, J., & Perel, J. (1989). Amitriptyline versus haloperidol in borderlines: Final outcomes and predictors of response. *Journal of Clinical Psychopharmacology, 9,* 238–246.

Soloff, P. H., George, A., Nathan, R. S., Schulz, P. M., & Peril, J. M. (1986). Paradoxical effects of amitriptyline in borderline patients. *American Journal of Psychiatry, 143,* 1603–1605.

Spielberger, C. D., Jacobs, G., Russell, S., & Crane. (1983). Assessment of anger: The State-Trait Anger Scale. In J. N. Butcher & C. D. Spielberger (Eds.), *Advances in personality assessment* (Vol. 2, pp. 159–187). Hillsdale, NJ: Erlbaum.

Spielberger, C. D., Johnson, E. H., Russell, S. F., Crane, R. J., Jacobs, G. A., & Worden, T. J. (1985). The experience and expression of anger: Construction and validation of an anger expression scale. In M. A. Chesney & T. J. Worden (Eds.), *Anger and hostility in cardiovascular and behavioral disorders.* New York: Hemisphere/McGraw-Hill.

Swanson, J. W., Holzer, C. E., Ganju, V. K., & Jono, R. T. (1990). Violence and psychiatric disorder in the community: Evidence from the epidemiologic catchment area surveys. *Hospital and Community Psychiatry, 17,* 173–186.

Teicher, M. H., Glod, C. A., Aaronson, S. T., Gunter, P. A., Schatzberg, A. F., & Cole, J. O. (1989). Open assessment of the safety and efficacy of thioridazine in the treatment of patients with borderline personality disorder. *Psychopharmacological Bulletin, 25,* 535–549.

Tupin, J., Smith, D., Clanon, T., et al. (1973). The long term use of lithium in aggressive prisoners. *Comprehensive Psychiatry, 14,* 311–317.

Virkunnen, M., De Jong, J., Bartko, J., & Linnoila, M. (1989). Psychobiological concomitants of history of suicide attempts among violent offenders and impulsive firesetters. *Archives of General Psychiatry, 46,* 604–606.

Weissman, M. M. (1993). The epidemiology of personality disorders: A 1990 update. *Journal of Personality Disorders,* Spring, 44–62.

Wender, P. H., Kety, S. S., Rosenthal, D., Schulsinger, F., Ortmann, J., & Lunde, I. (1986). Psychiatric disorders in the biological and adoptive relatives of adopted individuals with affective disorders. *Archives of General Psychiatry, 43,* 923–929.

Widom, C. S. (1989). Does violence beget violence? A critical examination of the literature. *Psychological Bulletin, 106,* 3–28.

Widom, C. S. (1991). A tail on an untold tale: Response to "Biological and ge-netic contributors to violence—Widom's untold tale." *Psychological Bul-letin, 109,* 130–132.

Yarvis, R. M. (1990). Axis I and Axis II diagnostic parameters of homicide. *Bulletin of the American Academy of Psychiatry and the Law, 18,* 249–269.

Zelin, M., Adler, G., & Myerson, P. (1972). Anger self-report: An objective questionnaire for the measurement of aggression. *Journal of Consulting and Clinical Psychology, 39,* 340.

Zimmerman, M. (1994). Diagnosing personality disorders: A review of issues and research methods. *Archives of General Psychiatry, 51,* 225–245.

CHAPTER 3

Emotional Instability

MICHELE R. SPOONT

The construct of emotional instability, frequently called emotional liability or reactivity, has not been adequately defined. A number of related, but nonhomologous constructs have often been included in a definition of emotional instability (e.g., impulsivity, neuroticism, stress reactivity, irritability). Construct validity may be difficult to obtain for a trait of emotional instability because of the temporal feature inherent in the trait. One of the problems in generating a reliable definition of emotional instability is that it is essentially a clinical phenomenon being described by personality trait theory. Whereas trait approaches often focus on statistically independent dimensions or measures with homogeneous item content, clinical syndromes usually consist of overlapping trait dimensions that may show variability in their course over time. A comprehensive definition of emotional instability needs to accommodate the features of instability associated with clinical conditions.

On a behavioral level, emotional instability can be conceptualized as a form of impulsivity in the broad sense, in that behavior in individuals with this trait is relatively unpredictable; it shows a lack of constraint (Livesley, Jang, Jackson, & Vernon, 1993; Tellegen, 1982). Recent factor analytic studies of impulsivity reveal that the subtypes of impulsivity all load on the higher order factor that is most readily identified by Eysenck's Psychoticism (P) scale (Eysenck & Eysenck, 1985; Zuckerman, 1991). As noted by Zuckerman (1991), Eysenck's P scale comprises items assessing aggressiveness, impulsivity, psychopathy, irritability, moodiness, and sensation seeking. The definition of personality disorder in the *Diagnostic and Statistical Manual of Mental Disorders* (DSM-IV; American Psychiatric Association [APA], 1994) essentially incorporates the covariation of these traits, particularly within the Cluster B subtype of personality disorder. Factor analytic studies have delineated a more clearly defined dimension of "psychopathy-impulsive unsocialized sensation seeking" (P-ImpUss) to replace the ill-defined P dimension

(Zuckerman, 1991). A number of traits load on this higher order factor, but sensation seeking, aggression, disinhibition, and socialization (reversed) do so consistently (Tellegen, 1982; Zuckerman, 1991).

Hierarchical factor analytic solutions to personality structure provide a framework within which to understand the interrelationships of personality traits; however, the resulting solution can be quite variable across studies depending on where in the hierarchy the "cut" is made, the size and type of population used, and the method of item generation (Harkness & McNulty, in press). Thus, whereas the covariation of trait domains in factor analytic studies may represent behavioral correlates in the sample population, the interrelationships among traits within a clinical population may differ (Harkness & McNulty, in press). For example, most factor analytic solutions include orthogonal dimensions of negative emotionality and constraint (e.g., Tellegen & Waller, in press), a relationship that may not hold in certain personality disorders where low constraint and high negative affect appear to converge (Gray, 1987; Spoont, 1992; Zuckerman, 1991). Thus, another approach to elucidating the quality of emotional instability that characterizes the referent clinical population is required.

Emotional instability must be conceptualized as primarily a temporal trait. That is, it can only be conceptualized as the lack of stable behavior over time. Predictability would be one way of defining behavioral stability. In terms of behavior, predictability might refer to features of intensity, frequency, and quality. Four behavioral characteristics are proposed to describe emotional instability:

1. Unpredictability of responses to stimuli.
2. Increased lability of baseline.
3. Unusual intensity of responses.
4. Unusual responses.

Discrete events may be characterized by one or all of these features, yet a trait label of emotional instability would be inappropriate for a single instance of these behaviors. A pattern of these characteristics over time is required to identify emotional instability and to differentiate it from a situationally specific response.

The characteristics of increased baseline lability and increased response intensity are features of poorly constrained biobehavioral regulatory systems (Mandell, Knapp, Ehlers, & Russo, 1984; Spoont, 1992). In systems that are poorly constrained, the potential for a stimulus to influence the system's regulation is increased and the amplitude of the resulting system response is greater than would be expected in a well-regulated system.

There may be a lowered response threshold coupled with a tendency for increased response intensity. Irritability might be one behavioral manifestation of this kind of effect. Unpredictability of response may be another feature of such a system: The individual responds to stimuli that conspecifics typically either do not respond to or normally respond to by selecting a response from a different response repertoire. An example of an unpredictable response is a phobia. An individual who is phobic of grasshoppers responds to the insect with terror, whereas most people respond to grasshoppers with indifference or curiosity. The phobic individual gave an atypical response to the stimulus of grasshoppers by activation of the individual's fight/flight system. The last characteristic of emotional instability, unusual responses, includes those behaviors an individual engages in that are not part of the normal response set in the species; it is not a species-typical behavior (e.g., self-mutilation, suicidal behavior). The inclusion of unusual responses in a definition of emotional instability would imply that, in addition to dysfunctional regulation and abnormal learning contingencies, emotional instability may be a result of abnormal developmental organization of a biobehavioral system. Species-specific behaviors are organized during the natural course of development. Behavior that potentially compromises survival and/or fitness is not a manifestation of normal behavioral organization.

Cluster B personality disorders are not the only group associated with increased emotional instability. For example, affective disorders are also characterized by increased mood lability; however, the quality of mood shift between the conditions differs, with Cluster B disorders, such as borderline personality disorder (BPD), being associated with increased negative emotionality (e.g., rage) and affective disorders with dysregulation of positive affectivity (Depue & Spoont, 1986; Spoont, 1992; Tellegen, 1982). The distinction is important because negative and positive affect are thought to have different biological substrates (Depue & Spoont, 1986; Gray, 1987). This chapter will be limited to the instability associated with Cluster B personality disorders. Throughout this chapter, borderline personality will be used to represent Cluster B personality disorders because it is thought to be characterized by a more severe, yet easily recognized form of emotional instability that exists in the related personality disorders. BPD, therefore, may represent the end of a continuum of emotional instability.

The first section of this chapter will briefly review the relationship between altered serotonergic functioning and emotional instability. In the next section, the causes of emotional instability will be touched on, with specific reference to the effects of prolonged abuse during early childhood development. The biological impact of abuse will be explored, and a neurobehavioral model of emotional instability will be proposed.

THE ROLE OF 5-HYDROXYTRYPTAMINE IN EMOTIONAL INSTABILITY

The shared characteristics between the P or P-ImpUss dimensions and individuals who demonstrate low CNS (central nervous system) 5-hydroxytryptamine (5-HT) functioning is striking. A large number of studies have demonstrated relationships between low 5-HT activity and violence, suicidal behavior, impulsivity, and Cluster B personality disorders (Arango et al., 1990; Arora & Meltzer, 1989; Brent et al., 1993; Brown & Linnoila, 1990; Coccaro et al., 1989; Mann, Arango, & Underwood, 1990; Schalling, Asberg, Edman, & Levander, 1984; Virkkunen, Rawlings et al., 1994; Virkkunen, Kallio et al., 1994). Aggression and impulsivity appear to be integral parts of the personality structure of individuals who have low 5-HT functioning (as inferred from concentrations of cerebrospinal fluid 5-hydroxyindoleacetic acid, or CSF 5-HIAA, a metabolite of 5-HT). In suicide attempters and healthy controls, there is a negative correlation between CSF 5-HIAA levels and the personality dimension of P-ImpUss or P (Schalling, Asberg, Edman, & Levander, 1984). As previously stated, the P and P-ImpUss scales are correlated most strongly with measures of aggression, impulsivity, interpersonal alienation, and sensation seeking and tend to fall on the same higher order factors as other measures of these traits (Zuckerman, Kuhlman, & Camac, 1988; Zuckerman, 1991).

Alterations in 5-HT activity in suicidal and aggressive behavior are also demonstrated by increased cortical 5-HT2 receptor densities in the brainstems and frontal cortices of suicide completers (Arango et al., 1990; Arora & Meltzer, 1989; Mann, Arango, & Underwood, 1990). Increased 5-HT2 receptors may reflect a compensatory upregulation of postsynaptic receptors in response to decreased 5-HT synaptic transmission. This increase in 5-HT2 receptors in the frontal cortices of suicide victims has been demonstrated in five of seven studies investigating this relationship (Mann et al., 1990).

Evidence for the relationship between poor regulation of 5-HT and emotional instability can also be assessed through serotonergic modulation of prolactin. Enhanced 5-HT activity, such as that triggered by fenfluramine, stimulates prolactin release (Coccaro et al., 1989). Prolactin response to fenfluramine is blunted in individuals with BPD or a history of suicide attempts (Coccaro et al., 1989). Significant negative correlations have been found between Buss-Durkee Assault and Irritability scales and prolactin response, further supporting the association between aggression and decreased 5-HT activity (Coccaro et al., 1989; Siever & Trestman, 1993). Increased impulsivity, self-injurious behavior, and intense anger differentiate BPD individuals with and without blunted prolactin response to a fenfluramine challenge (Siever & Trestman, 1993). This suggests that altered 5-HT functioning is specifically related to suicidality and emotional instability, even within the BPD diagnostic group. Altered 5-HT functioning may reflect a temperament factor that appears to be preferentially associated with specific behavioral pathology (i.e., a vulnerability factor). Previously, decreased 5-HT activity was related to a lack of constraint of information flow through a significant biobehavioral system as a result of poor regulation (Spoont, 1992). Exploration of altered information flow due to decreased 5-HT may help to elucidate the nature of the vulnerability.

THE RELATIONSHIP OF CHILDHOOD ABUSE TO BORDERLINE PERSONALITY DISORDER

Decreased serotonergic functioning appears to be a contributing factor to the development of BPD, although it seems to be neither necessary nor sufficient. The phenomenological similarities between BPD and posttraumatic stress disorder (PTSD), suggest that trauma may also relate to the development of BPD (e.g., emotional lability, dissociations, irritability, depersonalization, reliving traumatic experiences, feelings of alienation, etc.; Herman, 1992). Histories of childhood abuse and trauma are very common among individuals with BPD (Gunderson & Sabo, 1993; Herman, 1992; Russ, Shearin, Clarkin, Harrison, & Hull, 1993) and with antisocial personality disorder (ASPD) (Emery, 1989; Patterson et al., 1989). Child abuse has been specifically linked to several features of these disorders, including self-destructive behavior, dissociations, suicide attempts, aggression, affective disturbance, poor peer relationships, poor social skills, diminished cognitive performance, and antisocial behaviors (Brent et al., 1993; Egeland, Sroufe, & Erickson, 1983; Emery, 1989; Gunderson & Sabo, 1993; Herman, 1992; Hoffman-Plotkin & Twentyman, 1984; Lewis, 1992; Luntz & Widom, 1994; Patterson, DeBaryshe, & Ramsey, 1989; van der Kolk & Fisler, 1993; Weiss, Dodge, Bates, & Pettit, 1992).

Individuals with BPD have more psychopathology in their first-degree relatives than a comparison outpatient sample (71% vs. 30%), and are more than six times more likely to have psychopathology in both parents (39% vs. 6%; Goldman, D'Angelo, & DeMaso, 1993). The families of the BPD probands are characterized by more major depression, substance abuse, and ASPD (Goldman et al., 1993; Gunderson & Sabo, 1993), suggesting a relationship between these conditions and BPD. Although there is evidence that some characteristics of BPD may be partially heritable, nonshared environmental variables still explain most of the variance

(Livesley, Jang, Jackson, & Vernon, 1993). In addition to direct abuse and trauma, other factors associated with the development of BPD and related disorders are those that adversely affect the formation of a healthy attachment. Parental variables associated with later development of BPD or related disorders include lack of positive parental interaction, parental neglect, parental hostility, parental inconsistency, and parental over-involvement (Bezirganian, Cohen, & Brooks, 1993; Gunderson & Sabo, 1993; Hoffman-Plotkin & Twentyman, 1984; Lewis, 1992; Lyons-Ruth, Connell, Zoll, & Stahl, 1987; Patterson et al., 1989). This appears to indicate that in addition to direct abuse, the development of BPD is associated with compromised attachment.

Attachment is essentially focused around increasing the proximity of the child to the primary caregiver so that the needs of the child can be attended to (Bowlby, 1982). Two forms of behavior that mediate the maintenance of proximity are signaling behavior (which brings the mother to the child) and approach behavior (which brings the child to the mother) (Bowlby, 1982). Parental hostility, neglect, or inappropriate interactions (e.g., inconsistency) work directly against either behavior associated with the child being in proximity to the caregiver. The result is an incomplete and poorly organized pattern of attachment that often fosters further isolation from caregivers and peers (Bowlby, 1982; Egeland & Sroufe, 1981). Abuse occurs more frequently in homes where attachment is compromised resulting in an increase in the impact of trauma on individuals who are more likely to experience it (Bowlby, 1982; Egeland & Sroufe, 1981; Herman, 1992). Thus, children with neglectful parents and poor attachment histories are both more likely to experience trauma and to have no buffer against its effects. This renders them especially vulnerable to enduring effects of trauma on their developmental process, which, in turn, increases the likelihood of developing a personality disturbance (Gunderson & Sabo, 1993; Herman, 1992; van der Kolk & Fisler, 1993).

The development of PTSD in response to a trauma occurs in only about one fourth of the individuals exposed to traumatic events, indicating that some individuals are more prone to develop PTSD (although with a sufficiently severe trauma, almost everyone will develop symptoms of PTSD) (Gunderson & Sabo, 1993; Herman, 1992). Identified risk factors include a previous history of trauma, poor coping mechanisms, family history of antisocial behavior, and childhood separations—characteristics often associated with BPD (Gunderson & Sabo, 1993). Attenuated 5-HT activity may be another risk factor.

Posttraumatic stress disorder is associated with a number of indicators of autonomic hyperarousal in response to stimuli that appear to be or represent threats to the individual's survival or equilibrium. Chronic hypothalamic-pituitary-adrenocortical axis (HPA) abnormalities are common in PTSD (Krystal et al., 1989; van der Kolk & Fisler, 1993). For example, PTSD is associated with a low basal 24-hour urinary cortisol excretion rate, but an exaggerated cortisol response during stress relative to normals (Yehuda, Giller, & Mason, 1993). This suggests that PTSD is associated with a sensitization of the HPA axis to stressful events. There is some evidence indicating that norepinephrine (NE) activity may be chronically high in PTSD, resulting in blunted stress-induced NE responses (Krystal et al., 1989; van der Kolk, Greenberg, Orr, & Pittman, 1989; Yehuda et al., 1993). Of interest, suicide has also been associated with a downregulation of alpha1-noradrenergic receptors, which also points to hyperactivity in NE systems, although this may not be true in all cortical regions (Arango et al., 1990; Gross-Isseroff, Dillon, Fieldust, & Biegon, 1990). Enhanced neurophysiological stress responses are thought to result in inappropriate "alarm" responses that preclude the ability of the individual to differentiate between dangerous and neutral events (Krystal et al., 1989; van der Kolk & Fisler, 1993). Alarm responses are mediated by the fight/flight system, which appears to be inappropriately modulated in PTSD.

Inescapable shock or stress in animals has been proposed as an animal model for PTSD (Foa, Zinbarg, & Rothbaum, 1992). Inescapable stress or shock are both associated with an adaptive analgesic response (i.e., stress-induced analgesia), that has been associated with the activity of endorphins, or endogenous opioid neuropeptides (Bandler & Depaulis, 1991; Beckett, Lawrence, Marsden, & Marshall, 1992; Faneslow, 1991; Herman & Panksepp, 1981; Kitchen, Crook, Muhammed, & Hill, 1994; Morgan, 1991; Spear, Enters, Aswad, & Louzan, 1985). This model is a useful analog to the human response to stress and trauma because humans also demonstrate stress-induced analgesia. The stress-induced release of endogenous opioids is mediated by sympathetic arousal (van der Kolk, 1987). Individuals with chronic PTSD have been found to develop stress-induced analgesia (SIA) in response to stressful events, an effect that can be blocked by naloxone (van der Kolk, et al., 1989). The development of SIA has also been found in BPDs who self-mutilate (Russ, Shearin, Clarkin, Harrison, & Hull, 1993). Relative to the BPDs who do not develop SIA, those who do develop SIA have significantly more dysphoria, dissociations, emotional lability, impulsivity, sensation seeking, and suicidal behavior, and are more likely to have histories of sexual abuse (Russ et al., 1993).

It has been postulated that the emotional numbing and dissociative experiences so often seen in traumatized individuals are a function of endogenous opioid activity (van der Kolk, 1987; van der Kolk et al., 1989;

van der Kolk & Fisler, 1993). Emotional numbing is experienced as aversive (van der Kolk et al., 1989). Because pain (or naloxone) diminishes emotional numbness, self-mutilation is viewed as a means of attenuating opiate-mediated emotional numbness (van der Kolk et al., 1989; van der Kolk & Saporta, 1993). Similarly, sensation seeking is conceptualized as another avenue in which traumatized individuals attempt to alter emotional numbness by exposing themselves to high levels of stimulation (van der Kolk & Fisler, 1993). The covariation of SIA, dissociations, and sensation seeking in BPDs who self-mutilate supports this relationship (Russ et al., 1993). Of interest, yohimbine combined with naloxone in normal volunteers results in an exponential increase in anxiety and plasma cortisol concentrations over what would be predicted on the basis of the drugs administered individually (Charney & Heninger, 1986). This suggests that the relative balance of NE and endorphin activity may underlie the affective extremes seen in BPD (van der Kolk & Fisler, 1993).

In summary, BPD is related to decreased 5-HT activity and shows phenomenological similarities with PTSD. Borderline personality disorder is associated with poor attachment, neglect, and abuse during childhood. In vulnerable individuals, trauma affects the responsivity of the individual's fight/flight system, resulting in a dysregulated HPA axis and augmented noradrenergic activity. Of interest, 5-HT has a primarily inhibitory modulation of NE (Chiang & Aston-Jones, 1993). Traumatized individuals also readily develop SIA, which is an adaptation to pain or stress. Notably, those traumatized individuals who develop SIA show the most characteristics of the trait of emotional instability. Both SIA and emotional numbing are thought to be mediated by endogenous opiates.

It is proposed here that dysregulation of the fight/flight system underlies emotional instability in BPD. More specifically, altered inhibitory modulation of the fight/flight system results in a biased sensitivity to cues of threat. This increased sensitivity contributes to the increased baseline lability of mood, increased response intensity, and some of the unpredictability of responses. The notion that P-ImpUss-type behaviors are related to a disinhibited fight/flight system is not new (Depue & Spoont, 1987; Fowles, 1987; Gray, 1987; van der Kolk & Saporta, 1993). What is proposed is that trauma during development (or in extremely vulnerable individuals) has a unique constellation of effects that result in developing greater emotional instability. This chapter attempts to integrate more of the distal factors associated with the development of BPD with proximal factors eliciting symptom increases that may be characterized as increased emotional instability. Some neurobiological mechanisms underlying these factors are proposed.

ORGANIZATION OF DEFENSIVE BEHAVIOR IN THE FIGHT/FLIGHT SYSTEM

There are three possible responses of the organism to threatening stimuli: flight behavior, freezing, or aggression (i.e., fight behavior). These defensive behaviors are largely coordinated in the periaqueductal gray of the midbrain (PAG). Specific regions of the PAG underlie different components of the animal's defense responses (Bandler & Depaulis, 1991; Faneslow, 1991). For example, feline threat displays are elicited by application of excitatory amino acids (EAA) in the intermediate third of the PAG lateral to the aqueduct; whereas immobility is elicited by EAA stimulation in ventrolateral sites of the caudal third of the PAG (Bandler & Depaulis, 1991).

Flight

A number of studies demonstrate that PAG neurons mediate an SIA response to nociceptive and aversive stimuli (Bandler & Depaulis, 1991; Beckett, et al., 1992; Faneslow, 1991; Morgan, 1991). A number of aversive stimuli can evoke SIA including tactile pain, restraint, excessive handling, electric shock, cold, conflict with a conspecific, isolation, deprivation of food intake, and parasitic infection (Pieretti, d'Amore, & Loizzo, 1991; Rodgers, Shepherd, & Donat, 1991; Spear, Enters, Aswad, & Louzan, 1985; Thorn, Applegate, & Johnson, 1989). There are two types of SIA: opioid-sensitive and nonopioid-sensitive analgesia. These forms of antinociception are subserved by different anatomic regions of the PAG. Opioid-sensitive analgesia is mediated by the ventral region of the PAG and nonopioid SIA by stimulation of the dorsolateral PAG (Faneslow, 1991; Morgan, 1991). Specific defense behaviors can also be localized within these subdivisions of the PAG. Stimulation of the ventral PAG produces freezing, hyporeactivity, and depressor responses; whereas dorsolateral PAG stimulation elicits fight-or-flight responses such as running, jumping, howling, increases in blood pressure and respiration, muscle vasodilation, and pupillary dilation (Bandler & Depaulis, 1991; Beckett et al., 1992; Faneslow, 1991; Morgan, 1991). The bidirectional influences on blood pressure are mediated by projections from the PAG to the rostral ventrolateral medulla (Shipley, Ennis, Rizi, & Behbehani, 1991). Thus, behavioral, autonomic, and antinociceptive components of defense activity are organized in the PAG according to different kinds of defense responses.

The SIA associated with stimulation of dorsal and lateral PAG regions may be a secondary effect of the stimulation (Besson, Fardin, & Oliveras, 1991). Dorsal and lateral PAG stimulation have been associated with hyperalgesia (Besson et al., 1991). Analgesia elicited by stimulation of these PAG regions is thought to arise from the extreme aversiveness of the experience (Besson et al., 1991). The resulting nonopioid analgesia associated with dorsolateral PAG stimulation appears to be primarily modulated by 5-HT. Analgesia in neonate rats is elicited by 5-HT agonism, an effect that cannot be attenuated by naloxone (Spear et al., 1985). The modulatory effect of 5-HT on dorsal PAG behaviors is also inhibitory. For example, 5-HT agonists dose-dependently increase the threshold of escape behaviors and attenuate defensive explosive behaviors resulting from localized dorsal PAG stimulation, indicating 5-HT modulation of all the defense responses elicited by stimulation of the dorsolateral PAG (Beckett et al., 1992; Besson et al., 1991; Graeff, 1984; Schutz, DeAguir, & Graeff, 1985). More specifically, the dorsal PAG-mediated explosive behaviors can be attenuated by 5-HT1A receptor activation, which, in turn, inhibits dorsal PAG neurons, probably by an increased K+ hyperpolarization (Beckett et al., 1992; Behbehani, Liu, Jiang, Pun, & Shipley, 1993).

Infusion of methylnaloxonium (an opiate antagonist) into the PAG of morphine-dependent animals elicits a withdrawal syndrome that is associated with intense agitation, escape behavior, increased reactivity, and increased vocalization. That opioid withdrawal is associated with escape behaviors suggests that endogenous opiate activity in the PAG may normally inhibit active defense behaviors (Stinus, LeMoal, & Koob, 1990). Similar to its effects on aversive stimulation, increased 5-HT activity decreases opiate withdrawal-dependent explosive behavior, and attenuates the hyperactivity of neurons in the locus coeruleus (LC) that occurs during opiate withdrawal (Akaoka & Aston-Jones, 1993; Cervo, Rochat, Romandini, & Saminin, 1981). Because the LC NE neurons are thought to mediate many withdrawal behaviors, 5-HT functionally limits the release of NE behaviors stimulated by opiate withdrawal. This may occur through the tonic activation of inhibitory gamma aminobutyric acid (GABA) input to the LC (Chiang & Aston-Jones, 1993). LC neurons increase firing in response to stressful or other potentially salient stimuli (Rasmussen & Jacobs, 1986; Rasmussen, Strecker, & Jacobs, 1986). The increased activity of LC neurons during opiate withdrawal is also found with administration of yohimbine, an alpha2 agonist that has anxiogenic properties (Rasmussen & Jacobs, 1986). Thus, opiate withdrawal induces an activation of LC nuerons, an effect that is associated with increased anxiety. Also, 5-HT modulates LC responses to sensory information. For example, 5-HT inhibits glutamate-induced excitation of LC neurons by 5-HT1A receptors and increases LC responding to sensory-induced excitatory amino acid (EAA) excitation by 5-HT2 receptor activity (Chiang & Aston-Jones, 1993).

Immobility

The PAG organizes defense behaviors for both unconditioned stimuli (UCS) and conditioned stimuli (CS) of threat. In general, the defense response to a CS of an aversive or threatening stimulus is immobilization, whereas the response to an UCS is flight or fight (Faneslow, 1991; Gray, 1987). However, an animal may respond to a threatening UCS with immobilization if the spatial and temporal relationship of the danger requires this response (Faneslow, 1991). A system such as the fight/flight system that is so crucial to survival requires some degree of flexibility because environmental conditions require ongoing evaluations and new adaptations. One example of how the system demonstrates flexible adaptation is that pain will disrupt the freezing response to a CS and facilitates a replacement of opioid analgesia with nonopioid analgesia (Faneslow, 1991). An immobility response to pain in a situation where danger has already been signaled is clearly maladaptive. The shift to active defense responding is accomplished by an inhibitory connection from the lateral PAG to the ventral PAG (Faneslow, 1991). The cessation of emotional numbing or dissociation by self-injurious behavior in BPD may be a capitalization on this mechanism. Thus, the likelihood of an immobilization response depends, in part, on the adaptive quality of the response in the given context and the changing adaptive demands of the contextual conditions.

The immobilization response pattern in response to a CS of threat formed the basis for the concept of a behavioral inhibition system (BIS; Depue & Spoont, 1987; Fowles, 1987; Gray, 1982, 1987). The BIS was initially predicated on the activity of the septo-hippocampal system where the salience of the stimulus was evaluated and compared with memory (Gray, 1982). Although the septo-hippocampal formation may be involved in the encoding of contextual cues associated with aversive or novel stimuli (Depue & Spoont, 1987; Gray, 1982), the affective "tag" that is attached to the once neutral contextual cues is likely integrated in the amygdala (Aggleton, 1993; LeDoux, Cicchetti, Xagoraris, & Romanski, 1990; LeDoux, 1992a; Stinus et al., 1990).

Facilitation of the opiate system (e.g., with morphine) in the ventral PAG elicits opioid SIA, inhibits fight/flight behaviors, and induces immobility (Spear et al., 1985; Thorn et al., 1989). Small doses of morphine only produce SIA if injected into the ventral PAG, indicating clear regional functional specificity (Besson et al., 1991). Like an addiction to an exogenous source of opioids, opioid SIA shows tolerance effects that can be inhibited by naloxone (Morgan, 1991). Opioid SIA appears to be mediated by mu receptors, as naltrexone (a fairly selective mu-receptor antagonist) can reverse the analgesic response (Faneslow, 1991). This may be important because SIA occurs in PTSD and BPD, and opioid mu-receptors have been found to be upregulated in the brains of suicide victims (Gross-Isseroff, Dillon, Israeli, & Biegon, 1990; Steklis & Kling, 1985).

The time course of 5-HT modulated and opioid-mediated analgesias may parallel their effect on other components of defense responding (Rodgers et al., 1991). It appears that 5-HT and opioids act in a synergistic fashion in defense behavior. For example, there is an increase in sensitivity of 5-HT receptors following prolonged immobilization stress that is abolished by naloxone and enhanced by beta-endorphin or morphine (Cancela, Volosin, & Molina, 1990). This suggests that prolonged stress is associated with a decrease of 5-HT activity in the PAG and a concomitant shift from 5-HT modulated nonopioid SIA to opioid SIA. This is further supported by the association of morphine-dependence with an increase in 5-HT metabolism and a decrease in 5-HT receptor binding in the brainstem (Cervo, Rochat, Romandini, & Saminin, 1981). Morphine increases 5-HT turnover, probably by mu-receptor activation (Narita et al., 1993). Thus, 5-HT alterations in the PAG response to stress are likely modulated by endorphin activity.

A great deal of evidence indicates that the activation of PAG defense behavior originates in the central nucleus of the amygdala (CeA) (Applegate, Kapp, Underwood, & McNall, 1982; Davis, 1992; Faneslow, 1991; Huang, Besson, Bernard, 1993; LeDoux, 1992a; Ottersen, 1981; Price, Russchen, & Amaral, 1987). The amygdala is important in the acquisition and expression of conditioned fear (Davis, 1992; Helmstetter, 1992; LeDoux, 1992a). For example, the pairing of a neutral stimulus with an aversive stimulus will alter neural firing in the amygdala (Davis, 1992). Furthermore, the amygdala demonstrates the synaptic plasticity required for induction of memories because long-term potentiation can be induced in this region, and N-methyl-D-aspartatic acid (NMDA) antagonists infused in the amygdala block the acquisition and extinction of conditioned fear (Davis, 1992; LeDoux, 1992a).

Electrical stimulation of the CeA elicits behavioral inhibition and ablation attenuates both behavioral inhibition and cardiovascular responses to a CS (Davis, 1992). Importantly, CeA lesions do not inhibit startle, but do block potentiated startle responses demonstrating the importance of the CeA in associative operations (Davis, 1989). Opiate agonists infused into the CeA block the acquisition of potentiated startle, suggesting an inhibitory role for opioids in the processing of conditioned fear associations (Davis, 1992).

The CeA inhibits affective defense behavior in the dorsal PAG by the stimulation of mu opioid receptors (Shaikh, Lu, & Siegal, 1991). The CeA appears to be involved in a direct nociceptive pathway extending from lamina I nociceptive-specific neurons in the spinal cord that innervate external portions of the parabrachial area, which, in turn, project back to the CeA (Huang et al., 1993). Access by the CeA to nociceptive information allows for the integration of this information in the formation of a conditioned emotional response.

Of the steps involved in the formation of conditioned emotional responses, the CeA region appears to be particularly important in response formation, for both aversive and nonaversive CSs (LeDoux, 1992b). That is, the CeA may be important for the expression of specific emotional response systems that accompany the development of a conditioned emotional response (LeDoux, 1992a). Thus, the CeA may be the last site of integration of response-independent information in the learning circuit of conditioned emotional responses (LeDoux, Cicchetti, Xagoraris, & Romanski, 1990).

The proposed functions of the amygdala in processing emotionally relevant stimuli have all included the ability of the amygdala to provide the "tag" for encoding the affective salience of stimuli in memory (Aggleton, 1993; Davis, 1992; Sarter & Markowitsch, 1985). It is likely the site for the synaptic plasticity required for the formation of emotional memories (LeDoux, 1992b). For example, the opiate antagonist, methylnaloxonium, when infused into the amygdala of a morphine-dependent animal elicits significant aversive place preference but not any apparent behavioral change (Stinus et al., 1990). This indicates a role for the amygdala in the consolidation of affective stimuli prior to response selection. Of interest, of the amygdaloid nuclei, only the CeA has significant enkephalin-containing cells (Sarter & Markowitsch, 1985). Endorphins impair fear conditioning. Opiate agonists (e.g., morphine, beta-endorphin) impair retention, whereas opiate antagonists (e.g., naloxone, naltrexone) enhance retention (McGaugh, 1992; McGaugh & Introini-Collison, 1987). The effects of endorphins on memory may occur through modulation of central NE neurons (McGaugh, 1992; McGaugh & Introini-Collison, 1987). The enhanced retention associated with naloxone can be blocked by a beta-adrenergic antagonist or the destruction of NE fibers (McGaugh & Introini-Collison, 1987). Naloxone also potentiates the memory-enhancing effects of beta-agonists (McGaugh, 1992; McGaugh & Introini-Collison, 1987). These effects are likely due to the activity of NE in the amygdala, because NE activiation in the amygdala enhances learning and retention, whereas NE depletions impair it (McGaugh, 1992; McGaugh & Introini-Collison, 1987). Moreover, amygdaloid infusion of the beta-adrenergic antagonist, propanolol, inhibits the memory-enhancing effect of naloxone (Mc-Gaugh, 1992). Norepinephrine may play a specific and important role in the tagging of salient environmental stimuli. For example, NE unit activity in the LC decreases during the repetition of irrelevant stimuli and increases in response to a neutral stimulus paired with a noxious stimulus (Rasmussen & Jacobs, 1986; Rasmussen, Strecker, & Jacobs, 1986).

Morphine withdrawal conditioned place aversion is actually greatest when infused into the nucleus accumbens (NAcc; Stinus et al., 1990). Infusion of methylnaloxonium into the NAcc produces agitation and a clear and sensitive aversive place preference (Stinus et al., 1990). Consistent with its relationship to structures involved in defense responding, VTA (ventral tegmental area) infusion was also associated with intense agitation and increased escape behaviors (Stinus et al., 1990). Neuroanatomic studies suggest that the CeA and the bed nucleus of the stria terminalis may be considered striatal-like structures and therefore share functional similarities with the NAcc. Portions of these structures receive innervation from the same fiber bundle originating in the basolateral amygdala and are innervated by dopamine (DA) neurons originating in the VTA (McDonald, 1991). Because opiate antagonism in morphine-dependent animals decreases dopamine (DA) release in the VTA-NAcc nuclei, the aversive emotional effects of the opioid antagonism may be partially due to the loss of DA-mediated reward (Duvauchelle, Levitin, MacConell, Lee, & Ettenberg, 1992; Tidey & Miczek, 1992).

The CeA likely receives sensory information for a conditioned emotional response (CER) from the lateral amygdaloid nucleus (LA; LeDoux, 1992a). The LA is integrally connected to sensory-relay thalamic nuclei (Davis, 1992; Edeline & Weinberger, 1992; LeDoux et al., 1990; LeDoux, 1992a; Price et al., 1987). The LA neurons respond to acoustic, visual and somatic stimuli, suggesting that the LA may be the sensory interface of the amygdala (LeDoux et al., 1990). Lesions of the LA attenuated conditioned immobilization, stress-related elevations in arterial pressure, and lick suppression in response to an acoustic CS of threat (LeDoux et al., 1990). Electrical stimulation of the acoustic thalamus is associated with excitatory action potentials in the LA (LeDoux et al., 1990). Activation of mu opioid receptors hyperpolarizes LA neurons and inhibits the release of GABA (Sugita & North, 1993). Hyperpolarization of local interneurons may excite pyramidal cells through disinhibition (Sugita & North, 1993). Thus, LA neurons are excited by opioid activation.

The connections between the LA and the medial region of the medial geniculate body (MGB) must be intact for auditory fear conditioning

(Edeline & Weinberger, 1992; LeDoux, 1992a). Cells in the medial MGB that receive projections from the inferior colliculus, themselves project to the LA and the auditory cortex (Edeline & Weinberger, 1992; LeDoux, 1992a). In this way, an aversive stimulus could elicit a defense response (escape or aggression) before higher cortical processing has taken place, increasing the chances for survival in an emergent context. Of interest, the cells in the MGB that demonstrate plasticity to a fear stimulus and respond to auditory CSs of that stimulus are broadly tuned (Edeline & Weinberger, 1992). This suggests that the features of the CS that are encoded are less specific, which the authors suggest could result in generalization of the CER to stimuli that are similar to, but not the same as, the CS.

In general, an immobility response is elicited by a CS of threat. Formation of conditioned associations appears to involve the amygdala in general and the CeA in particular. The amygdala is functionally and anatomically connected to the orbital frontal cortex, which is involved in the modulation of affective states (Stuss & Benson, 1986). Of interest, individuals with the dual diagnoses of PTSD and substance abuse have been found to have hyperactivation of the orbital frontal cortex (Semple et al., 1993). Whether this relates to PTSD or substance abuse is unclear, but it may support the role of the amygdala and associated limbic and cortical regions in emotional instability.

Aggression

As mentioned earlier, the animal's response selection to a threatening stimulus will vary depending on qualitative features of the stimulus and the animal's prior experience with comparable stimuli. Aggression (i.e., fight) is often the best and sometimes the only defense strategy available. The fight or aggressive response to threat appears to involve activation of the area of the hypothalamus beginning in the ventrolateral lobe of the ventromedial hypothalamus (VMH), extending to the ventral part of the lateral hypothalamus (LH), and including the VMH areas to the arcuate and anterior hypothalamic nuclei (Kruk, 1991). Aggressive responses are readily and reliably produced by stimulation of this zone. Notably, even stimulated aggressive responses do not occur at random and require specific environmental stimuli to elicit attack behaviors (Kruk, 1991). Stimulation of this hypothalamic region may enhance the salience to cues of threat, thereby lowering the threshold for stimuli to elicit an aggressive response (Kruk, 1991).

Simultaneous stimulation of aggressive and flight zones in the hypothalamus always results in only one of the behaviors being manifest (Kruk, 1991). This is consistent with the adaptive context within which these behaviors are activated (ambivalence would be maladaptive). The

CeA projects to the LH, which allows for integration of the autonomic aspects of aggressive and fear behaviors (Aalders & Meek, 1993; Davis, 1992; Price et al., 1987). Stimulation-induced hypothalamic aggression can be partially inhibited by 5-HT uptake inhibitors, quipazine, and the use of antianxiety agents such as propanolol and benzodiazepines (Kruk, 1991). Of interest, the attenuation effect is not found with the 5-HT1A agonist 8-OH-DPAT. The amygdala modulates 5-HT activity in the hypothalamus, as CeA lesions result in increased 5-HT activity in the hypothalamus (Beaulieu, Dipaolo, & Barden, 1985). Enhancement of 5-HT activity in the amygdala, especially the MA, decreases aggression, whereas diminished 5-HT functioning enhances it (File, James, & Macleod, 1981; Kruk, 1991; Sarter & Markowitsch, 1985). Thus, 5-HT modulates aggressive responses throughout the hypothalamic, amygdaloid, and PAG regions.

Stimulation of dopamine (DA) by l-dihydroxyphenylalanine (l-DOPA), amphetamine, or apomorphine increases defensive aggressive behavior, an effect that can be inhibited by DA antagonism, enhancement of NE activity, or enhancement of 5-HT activity (Antelman & Caggiula, 1977; Antelman & Chiodo, 1984; Spoont, 1992; Valzelli, 1981; Wang, Consolo, Vinci, Forloni, & Ladinsky, 1985; Winslow & Miczek, 1983). As with the induction of explosive behavior, opiate withdrawal facilitates aggression (Tidey & Miczek, 1992). Many behaviors associated with aggression during morphine withdrawal are mediated by DA because DA augmentation with d-amphetamine, apomorphine, cocaine, methylphenidate, or l-DOPA potentiates the aggressive effect (Tidey & Miczek, 1992). Release of DA is increased by opiate agonism via mu and delta opioid receptors and decreases during morphine withdrawal (Tidey & Miczek, 1992). The DA decrease during the withdrawal phase results in compensatory supersensitivity at postsynaptic receptors (Tidey, & Miczek, 1992). The DA involvement in withdrawal-induced aggression appears to be modulated primarily by D1 receptors, which inhibits aggression in morphine-withdrawal animals (Tidey & Miczek, 1992). However, when D1 and D2 receptors are stimulated simultaneously during morphine withdrawal, D1 receptors appear to attenuate D2 agonist-induced decreases in aggressive behavior (Tidey & Miczek, 1992).

Increased DA activity in the NAcc facilitates some forms of aggression (Depue & Spoont, 1986; Oades, 1985). Attack by a conspecific is associated with increased DA turnover in the NAcc and increased 5-HT turnover in the amygdala (Haney, Noda, Kream, & Miczek, 1990). Defeat in a conflict with a conspecific, on the other hand, was associated with decreased DA turnover in the amygdala (Haney et al., 1990). Although repeated experiences with conspecific attack and defeat were not associated with alterations in 5-HT or DA activity, it is associated with an enhanced sensitivity to amphetamine-induced escape behavior (Haney et al., 1990). This may be associated with conditioning of defense responses since the CeA and the LA have the greatest DA concentrations in the amygdala (Sarter & Markowitsch, 1985). Thus, DA modulation of morphine-withdrawal induced aggression may be mediated by the simultaneous release of the dorsal PAG and the NAcc.

The CeA has a moderate density of D1 and a greater density of D2 receptors, and is innervated by A8, A9, and A10 (VTA) DA cell groups in the ventral mesencephalon (Scibilia, Lachowicz, & Kilts, 1992). The CeA receives a large projection from the basolateral amygdala and the VTA, and projects to the NAcc (as does the VTA) (Scibilia et al., 1992; Wallace, Magnuson, & Gray, 1992). The amygdaloid innervation of the NAcc can be modulated by dopaminergic VTA projections to the NAcc (Beninger, 1983). The integrity of DA innervation of the CeA is important for proper functioning of the CeA and for protection against gastric ulceration (Wallace et al., 1992). Stimulation of the medial amygdaloid nucleus (MA) appears to facilitate affective defense behaviors, an action that is not mediated by enkephalinergic mechanisms but may be due to DA mechanisms (Shaikh et al., 1991; Wallace et al., 1992). The MA projects to the VMH, which projects to the PAG via an intermediary synaptic connection in the anteromedial hypothalamus (Aalders & Meek, 1993; Fuchs, Edinger, & Siegel, 1985a, 1985b). The VMH also sends projections to both the CeA and the MA, allowing for a modulatory loop (Price et al., 1987). Like the CeA, the MA receives projections from the LA and projects to the LH (Price et al., 1987), which permits integrated affective aggression.

The reciprocal modulatory influences of DA and endorphins depend on the receptors involved and the brain region being evaluated. For example, mu agonists enhance, whereas kappa agonists suppress, the activity of mesolimbic DA (Narita, Suzuki, Funada, Misawa, & Nagase, 1993). Although both kappa and mu receptor stimulation are associated with analgesia, activation of kappa receptors can inhibit mu agonist-induced enhancement of DA release and inhibit the reinforcing effects of opioid activation (Narita et al., 1993). Most of the modulation of DA by enkephalins, however, is through delta receptors, which are found primarily in the caudate-putamen, NAcc, olfactory tubercle, paleocortex, and neocortex (Angulo & McEwen, 1994; Petney & Gratton, 1991). Opioid agonists in the ventral tegmental area (VTA) stimulate DA release in the NAcc and facilitate DA-dependent behaviors such as spontaneous motor activity (Angulo & McEwen, 1994; Petney & Gratton, 1991). The interaction between midbrain enkephalin and DA neurons, at least in the NAcc and striatum, is one of reciprocal modulation because DA activation tonically inhibits the transcription of proenkephalin mRNA, most likely through D2 receptors (Angulo & McEwen, 1994). Of interest, D1 receptor activity is necessary for the expression of basal levels of proenkephalin mRNA, for the release of dynorphin in the striatum, and for the inhibitory effect of D2 receptors (Angulo & McEwen, 1994).

In summary, fight/flight system disinhibition includes the release of the PAG, the amygdala, and hypothalamic nuclei. Endorphins in the ventromedial portion of the PAG mediate a stress-induced analgesic state that accompanies immobilization and inhibits active defense behaviors. There is also a nonopioid stress-induced analgesia that accompanies defense behaviors organized in the dorsal and lateral aspects of the PAG. The 5-HT modulates the expression of active defense behaviors, with increased 5-HT activity associated with decreases in these behaviors. Both active and immobilization responses to threat are elicited by the CeA nucleus, which is involved in the development of conditioned emotional responses. Active defense behaviors involve projections from the CeA to the hypothalamic aggression zone and the VTA, both of which project directly to the PAG. The LA acts as the sensory interface of the amygdala for the formation of conditioned emotional responses. Aggression or escape behaviors can be enhanced by opiate withdrawal, DA facilitation, or 5-HT reduction. However, appropriate environmental stimuli are still required for the specific expression of the defense response. Biases toward employing one defense response over another may also occur as a result of other factors modulating the overall system, such as testosterone levels (Lewis, 1992). In general, enkephalins in limbic regions facilitate DA activity and attenuate 5-HT activity. These modulatory relationships allow for appropriate organization of behavior required by the environmental demand.

Repeated trauma and compromised attachment contribute to the development of BPD. As noted earlier, the trauma history results in a number of symptoms that are also associated with PTSD, including increased reactivity to stimuli (particularly stimuli that are associated with threat), a propensity to be emotionally numb (especially in response to stress), increased suicidality, increased likelihood of dissociative experiences, and often increased tendency toward sensation seeking. There is a strong overlap between symptoms associated with Cluster B personality disorders and those associated with decreased 5-HT functioning. Low 5-HT activity may predispose to the development of BPD or PTSD, or may be a concomitant of those conditions. Evaluation of the impact of trauma or stress on the monoaminergic and enkephalinergic systems may elucidate these relationships.

STRESS, TRAUMA, AND
NEUROPHYSIOLOGICAL ADAPTATION

The reactivity of endorphin-containing neurons to stress is well documented (Borsook et al., 1994). For example, mild chronic stress is associated with an induction of proenkephalin (the precursor of enkephalinergic peptides) gene expression within neurons of the paraventricular and supraoptic hypothalamic nuclei (Borsook et al., 1994).

Norepinephrine activation is also associated with acute stress (Inoue, Koyama, & Yamashita, 1993). As has been noted previously, chronic stress is associated with sensitization of NE response to stress (Adell, Garcia-Marquez, Armario, & Gelpi, 1988; Krystal et al., 1989; van der Kolk, 1987; Yehuda et al., 1993). NE activity appears to increase the amplitude of salient signals in the CNS, thereby increasing the signal-to-noise ratio (Oades, 1985). Activation of sensory processing areas is associated with increases in NE activity in the LC (Chiang & Aston-Jones, 1993; Marks, Speciale, Cobbey, & Roffwarg, 1987). This results in increased reactivity to subsequent stressful stimuli. Thus, individuals with chronic stress may have signal overresponsivity when a stress-related stimulus is presented.

The activity of 5-HT neurons during stressful or noxious conditions is varied depending on the state of the individual, the type of stressor, duration and intensity of the stimulus, and brain region evaluated. For example, 5-HT turnover increased in several cortical regions (i.e., NAcc, amygdala, and medial prefrontal cortex) in response to acute shock, but only increased in the medial frontal cortex (mPFC) during a CS to shock (Inoue et al., 1993). As would be expected of a CS of shock, the mPFC increased 5-HT turnover was accompanied by immobilization.

Dopamine turnover is also increased in the mPFC after presentation of the CS of shock or after having witnessed other animals receive shock (Inoue et al., 1993; Kaneyuki et al., 1991). The increased DA turnover in the mPFC was accompanied by concomitant DA activation in the VTA, NAcc, and/or striatum (Inoue et al., 1993; Kaneyuki et al., 1991). The increase in DA turnover in mPFC in response to witnessing conspecifics receive shock can be reversed by benzodiazepine administration (Kaneyuki et al., 1991). Thus, the mPFC in rodents is particularly important in the response to CSs of threat. The mPFC appears to be important for the negative feedback effects of increased glucocorticoid activity on stress-induced HPA activation (Diorio, Viau, & Meaney, 1993; Kaneyuki et al., 1991).

Chronic stress appears to have different effects on the 5-HT system than acute stress. The 5-HT turnover may be altered in specific brain regions in response to chronic stress or a CS of threat or stress. Chronic restraint stress, but not acute restraint, appears to increase both 5-HT and 5-HIAA levels in most brain regions and sensitizes the frontal cortex, midbrain, hypothalamus, hippocampus, and striatum to enhanced 5-HT turnover effects to an additional acute stressor (Adell et al., 1988). The sensitization effect suggests that the increased 5-HT levels may be associated with decreased 5-HT turnover. Thus, individuals experiencing chronic stress have a compensatory enhancement of 5-HT activity in response to an acute stress, indicating a potential protective function of 5-HT activity in the associated brain regions.

Of interest, 5-HT1A agonists cause a time-dependent disruption of retrieval for conditioned fear responses (Quartermain, Clemente, & Shemer, 1993). The 5-HT1A effect appears to be related to the encoding of retrieval cues, as the impairment occurred only if the 5-HT1A agonist were given preconditioning and not pretest. The impaired retrieval could be antagonized by d-amphetamine (Quartermain et al., 1993) indicating that 5-HT1A activation could contribute to impaired recall of aversive and/or fearful events. Acute restraint stress is associated with an increase in 5-HT1A receptors in the hippocampus (Watanabe, Sakai, McEwen, & Mendelson, 1993). Repeated restraint stress, on the other hand, has been associated with a decrease in 5-HT1A binding in the CA3, CA4, and dentate gyrus of the hippocampus (Watanabe et al., 1993). This is likely due to the downregulatory effect of high levels of stress-released cortisol over time (Watanabe et al., 1993).

The CA3 and dentate gyrus receive projections from the entorhinal cortex (Gray, 1982). Integrity of the entorhinal cortex and hippocampal formation are necessary for a functional memory system (Squire, 1987). The 5-HT and NE inputs to the hippocampus affect the signal-to-noise ratio of hippocampal signals (Gray, 1982; Squire, 1987). Norepinephrine suppresses weak inputs and enhances strong inputs to the hippocampus, whereas 5-HT raises the threshold of signal propagation (McNaughton, Azmitia, Williams, Buchan, & Gray, 1980; McNaughton et al., 1977; Oades, 1985; Spoont, 1992). For example, NE activity enhances long term potentiation (LTP) in CA3 region by activation of beta-adrenergic receptors and enhances synaptic efficiency in the dentate gyrus (Berridge, Arnsten, & Foote, 1993). Thus, stress can diminish the signal-to-noise ratio in the hippocampus by altering modulatory inputs.

To summarize, stress significantly alters the sensitivity of the fight/flight system to signals of threat. Imminent threat elicits an escape or aggressive response depending on the adaptive context. These behaviors are primarily supported by increased NE activity in the LC, and increased DA in the NAcc and prefrontal cortex (PFC), whereas 5-HT has an inhibitory modulation of these behaviors and facilitates the associated non-opioid analgesia. Signals of threat or chronic stress usually result in immobility through the activation of endorphins. Enhanced glucocorticoid secretion and DA activity, and attenuated NE and 5-HT activity also occur during chronic stress. These responses are not invariant; however, they provide an illustration of how the sensitivity of several systems can be altered at once, biasing the overall sensitivity to particular environmental cues and altering the overall processing of information. Chronic stimulation of the fight/flight system appears to result in an overall decline in 5-HT and NE activity, but an increased sensivity to subsequent stressors. Thus, the threshold to elicit a defense response is lowered with repeated stress. Moreover, compensatory postsynaptic supersensitivity and deficient inhibitory modulation can result in greater intensity of responses to subsequent stressors. These factors contribute greatly to the manifestation of the emotional instability trait.

ISOLATION: AN ANIMAL MODEL FOR A TRAUMATIC CHILDHOOD

Isolation is a specific class of stressor or trauma. Isolation rearing can be conceptualized as a model for the impoverished and traumatizing environments of children in homes with poor attachment figures and abuse. Isolation rearing affects behavior by its impact on attachment behavior and sensory experience, the extent of the damage being determined by age of the animal and duration of the isolation period. For example, monkeys isolated during the first 6 months of life show persistant abnormal social and sexual behavior, whereas monkeys isolated during the second 6 months of life show abnormal conspecific aggression (Kraemer, 1985). Isolation rearing as practiced in animal experimentation is not homologous to childhood abuse and deprivation. The impact of deprivation, however, must be conceptualized within the context of the sensitivity of the underlying biobehavioral system (Kraemer, 1985). This suggests that even though isolation rearing is an extreme condition, it may provide useful information about developmental deprivation conditions in humans. In contrast, repetitive acute isolation is fairly common among children—particularly neglected and abused children. This too provides a useful framework within which to consider the effects of maltreatment on children.

Prolonged isolation produces a consistent, aimless aggressive behavior in rodents (Valzelli, 1981). In mice, the enhanced aggression that occurs in response to isolation is polygenically inherited (Schicknick, Hoffman, Schneider, & Crusio, 1993). Induction of irritable aggression by prolonged isolation appears to occur only in those rodent strains that react to the isolation with decreased 5-HT neurotransmission (Valzelli, 1981). Similarly, enhanced 5-HT activity inhibits aggression most readily in rat strains that are trait-wise nonaggressive, indicating some specificity in the genetic 5-HT modulation of aggression (Valzelli, 1981). This implies that certain individuals are predisposed to react to the deprivational effects of isolation rearing with deficient 5-HT activity and increased aggressiveness. Thus, vulnerability in individual animals to the impact of deprivation differs as it does in humans.

In addition to increased aggression, isolation rearing has also been associated with hyperactivity, impaired response inhibition, and a shift to the left in the response curve of *d*-amphetamine (Jones, Hernandez, Kendall, Marsden, & Robbins, 1992). These effects appear to be due to a decrease in 5-HT turnover in the nucleus accumbens (NAcc), which is accompanied by a concomitant decrease in dopamine (DA) turnover in the prefrontal cortex (Jones et al., 1992). Both of these effects likely release DA in the NAcc (Jones, Mogenson, & Wu, 1981). The DA receptors appear to be upregulated because there is an enhanced DA release in response to amphetamine in both the NAcc and caudate (Jones et al., 1992). Thus, the increased aggression associated with decreased 5-HT activity during isolation rearing is also associated with changes in DA activity and increases in impulsivity (i.e., impaired response inhibition).

Isolation rearing has also been associated with hyperalgesia and increases in opiate ligand binding (Panksepp, 1981). Hyperalgesia could result from low 5-HT activity or deficient opioid activity. The increase in opiate ligand binding is thought to be secondary to the lack of endorphin occupancy of opioid-sensitive receptors in isolates (i.e., there is decreased endorphin activity) (Panksepp, 1981). The activity of 5-HT is facilitatory in the expression of prodorphin mRNA (Angulo & McEwen, 1994), and chronic 5-HT depletion could attenuate dynorphin levels. It may be significant that dynorphin is found primarily in the hypothalamus, CeA, and striatum (Angulo & McEwen, 1994). Thus, unlike prolonged restraint stress or inescapable shock, isolation rearing is associated with decreased endorphin activity. This may be related to the specific relationship between the function of endorphins in attachment that will be described in this chapter.

In primates, DA and NE depletion with AMPT increases the despair response associated with separation, whereas selective NE depletion with fusaric acid or 5-HT synthesis inhibition does not (McKinney, 1985). Notably, intensity of despair was inversely correlated with CSF 5-HIAA and homovanillic acid (HVA) levels (McKinney, 1985). This suggests that although changes in endorphins and all monamines occur as a consequence of separation and isolation, DA depletion, when it occurs, may be more associated with the experiental aspect of the despair response. As with humans, the traumatic impact of separation on primates is diminished with peer interaction and predictability of the separation (Coe, Wiener, Rosenberg, & Levine, 1985).

Isolation rearing results in low social status as an adult (Kraemer, 1985). In primates, social potency is associated with enhanced 5-HT activity and social submission with decreased 5-HT functioning (Raleigh, Brammer, & McGuire, 1983). Additionally, alterations in 5-HT activity are associated with changes in social status (Raleigh et al., 1983). Thus, low social status, low 5-HT activity, and isolation rearing are all interrelated. Animals with lesions in brain regions thought to underlie attachment behavior are largely rejected by peers and tend to prefer the company of other lesioned animals (Steklis & Kling, 1985). Similarly, there is an enhanced fear response to peers, but not to younger animals (Steklis & Kling, 1985).

Acute isolation stress produces a transient decrease in proenkephalin mRNA in the caudate and NAcc that may be reversed by stress-induced increases in corticosterone (Angulo & McEwen, 1994). Low endorphin activity during acute isolation appears to contribute to the elicitation of distress vocalizations (DV) (Carden & Hofer, 1990; Panksepp, 1981; Panksepp, Siviy, & Normansell, 1985). The DVs are significantly attenuated with the administration of opiate agonists or clonidine, and somewhat attenuated with facilitation of 5-HT transmission (Carden & Hofer, 1990; Panksepp, 1981; Panksepp et al., 1985; Steklis & Kling, 1985). Of interest, only agonists of mu and delta opioid receptors reduce DVs in rodents, whereas kappa agonism, which is aversive, increases DVs (Carden, Davachi, & Hofer, 1994). DVs can be elicited by stimulation of the dorsolateral PAG, dorsomedial thalamus, areas near the anterior commisure, or some amygdaloid and hypothalamic sites (Panksepp et al., 1985). Stimulation of opiate-mediated analgesic-producing sites in the PAG (i.e., ventral PAG) results in an inhibition of DVs elicited from stimulating other DV-sensitive sites (e.g., dorsomedial thalamus) (Herman & Panksepp, 1981). Stimulation of the nonanalgesic sites in the PAG (i.e., dorsolateral regions), results in "pain-like" screams and potentiation of septal-preoptic stimulated DVs (Herman & Panksepp, 1981). Thus, the developmentally immature distress response, DV, is organized in the PAG in a similar manner as other active threat responses.

In addition to their association with defense responding, the importance of DVs is their relationship to attachment. DVs are proximity-enhancing behaviors that support attachment formation (Panksepp et al., 1985). It has been postulated that endorphins contribute to the formation of attachment by elaborating socially based affects (Panksepp, 1981). The relationship appears to be complex. For example, decreased endorphin activity results in increases in social solicitation and affiliative tendencies, which can be blocked by morphine administration (Panksepp, 1981; Panksepp et al., 1985). In fact, high levels of opiate agonism may actually attenuate social interaction (Panksepp, 1981). Play, however, appears to require a certain level of endorphin activity to be supported, because it is decreased by naloxone in normal animals and enhanced by morphine in isolation-reared animals who have attenuated endorgenous opioid activity (Panksepp et al., 1985). As with low 5-HT activity, naloxone-treated animals are less dominant and prefer a social reward to a nonsocial one (Panksepp, 1981). Furthermore, animals treated with morphine become dominant over naloxone-treated animals over time (Panksepp et al., 1985). Thus, endorphin activity appears to modulate social behaviors, perhaps particularly those related to attachment. Repetitive acute isolation is associated with an increase in the pain threshold and a decrease in DVs over time suggesting enhanced endorphin response to isolation stress (Goodwin, Molina, & Spear, 1994; Pieretti, d'Amore, & Loizzo, 1991). Naltrexone can inhibit this effect on DVs, but only if given after the first isolation period (Goodwin et al., 1994). This indicates that attenuation of DVs during repeated isolation is indeed related to increased endorphin activity; but, once the attenuation of DVs in response to stress is established, endorphins are not necessary for expression of this (Goodwin et al., 1994). Thus, endorphin activity during the initial isolation phase may effectively "tag" the adaptive reduction in DVs. Isolation-induced distress and pain sensitivity can be reduced by ingestion of a polysaccharide, which can be blocked by naltrexone (Shide & Blass, 1989). Similarly, the calming effect of a conspecific on isolation distress also appears to be modulated by endorphins (Carden & Hofer, 1990). Thus, the endorphin system also underlies modulation of pain and distress through behavior.

As would be expected in a biological system that modulates attachment, the functional features of endorphin receptors show a developmental course. For example, the development of the kappa receptor system is important for the expression of the fetal stretch response, which is related to suckling (Andersen, Robinson, & Smotherman, 1993). Activation of the kappa receptor system during suckling is thought to diminish the neonate's responsivity to extraneous stimuli (Smotherman & Robinson, 1993). Opioid SIA in rodents is mediated by mu-opioid receptors prior to weaning and delta-opioid receptors after weaning (Kitchen et al., 1994). Weaning appears to be the stimulus for the expression of the delta 2 receptors, since a forced delay in weaning also delays the switch of receptor type underlying opioid SIA (Kitchen et al., 1994). Thus, behavior also modulates biology.

Endorphins are evidently associated with the organization of a number of attachment behaviors. Because the reactivity of the endorphin system is known to be altered in BPD and PTSD (Russ et al., 1993; van der Kolk & Saporta, 1993), the reactivity may occur as a consequence of either exposure to trauma, compromised attachment, or both. That the endorphin system is important in attachment, and that BPD and abuse are associated with disturbed attachment, suggests that poor modulation of endorphin reactivity in BPD may be partially due to improperly organized attachment.

PERCEPTION AND THE PROCESSING OF CUES

Recent formulations of the development of PTSD in response to trauma show that the formation of symptom intensity is partially a result of the cognitive meaning of the trauma and the coping strategies employed to deal with it (Creamer, Burgess, & Pattison, 1992; Foa, Steketee, & Rothbaum, 1989; Foa et al., 1992). Both uncontrollability and unpredictability increase the level of generalized fear in threatening contexts for both humans and animals (Foa et al., 1989; Foa et al., 1992). In animals, a CS for inescapable shock is associated with a repetitive intense fear response, whereas the fear response to controllability (escapable shock) decreases over time (Foa et al., 1992). Uncontrollability and unpredictability appear to facilitate the development of opioid SIA and impair escape responses (Foa et al., 1992). The escape deficit has been interpreted within the framework of an increased experience of fear (Foa et al., 1992). Although this may be true, the neurobiology of the fight/flight system predicts escape deficits once the stress is severe or chronic enough to result in endorphin release. In humans, intensity of fear evoked by trauma is associated with the formation of intrusive thoughts (Creamer et al., 1992). Intrusive thoughts may act as internal CSs to the trauma, resulting in increased fight/flight-mediated responses and greater affective instability. Of interest, signals of shock cessation or previous experiences of shock controllability reduce the escape deficits seen with inescapable shock (Foa et al., 1992). Thus, in addition to specific features of the trauma, prior experience with similar stressors can mediate the impact of the trauma.

Although adults may have learning histories that provide some inoculation against trauma or may have developed coping strategies that help to protect them from the impact of trauma, children's coping strategies are less developed. They must rely on the coping capabilities of their caregivers to protect them from trauma and to help them mitigate the impact of trauma should it occur. As noted earlier, childhood victimization is associated with the development of personality disorder symptoms that overlap considerably with symptoms of PTSD. Child abuse has been associated with self-destructive behavior, dissociations, suicide attempts, aggression, affective disturbance, poor peer relationships, poor social skills, diminished cognitive performance, and antisocial behaviors (Brent et al., 1993; Emery, 1989; Gunderson & Sabo, 1993; Herman, 1992; Lewis, 1992; Luntz & Widom, 1994; Patterson et al., 1989; van der Kolk & Fisler, 1993; Weiss et al., 1992). Similar symptoms have been associated with what had been conceptualized as borderline symptoms in children (but now are primarily conceptualized as childhood manifestations of PTSD). These "borderline" symptoms include appearance of stress-induced psychotic withdrawal into fantasy that can be terminated by reassurance; anxiety that is rooted in fears of self-annihilation, body mutilation, or world catastrophe; inability to control the progression of thinking from neutral themes to thoughts of death and repetitious themes in play; cognitive deficits, particularly those related to focusing attention, poor coordination, poor perceptual-motor skills, and nonspecific abnormal EEG tracings; a tendency to torment younger children and to fear peers; and a lack of control of anger, delaying gratification, panic, and impulsive behavior (Bemporad, Smith, Hanson, & Cicchetti, 1982). The fear of self-annihilation, preoccupation with morbid thoughts, repetition in play, and poor modulation of affect are classic symptoms of PTSD that parallel closely the adult variant. Stress-induced micropsychotic episodes and withdrawal into fantasy, neurological soft signs, and quality of peer interactions are notable because of their developmental specificity and potential developmental ramifications.

That childhood abuse or maltreatment frequently results in increased aggressiveness, hypervigilance, misinterpretation of surroundings, and a tendency to lash out when something is perceived as threatening suggests that the perception of threat appears to be altered in abused and maltreated children (Lewis, 1992). In fact, physical abuse of children results in a more hostile attributional bias (Quiggle, Garber, Panak, & Dodge, 1992; Rieder & Cicchetti, 1989; Weiss, Dodge, Bates, & Pettit, 1992). Maltreated children display a relative inattention to important social cues, an increased tendency to generate aggressive responses, and an increased tendency to predict positive outcomes of aggressive behavior (Weiss et al., 1992). Aggressive children tend to use fewer social cues before making attributions about another person's intent (Quiggle et al., 1992). Thus, physical abuse results in an increased sensitivity to cues of threat, an impairment in the processing of social information, and an increased likelihood of selecting an aggressive response. Importantly, the degree of skewedness in social information toward aggression and threat is related to the severity of physical abuse (Weiss et al., 1992).

A hostile attributional bias in aggressive children appears to extend to social information that is ambiguous or benign (Quiggle et al., 1992). Moreover, it also occurs when social cues specifically indicate that the other person's behavior was accidental or made with prosocial intent (Quiggle et al., 1992). This implies that not only do these children have a lowered threshold for the perception of threat in their environment, but that they are also more likely to perceive threat where none exists. This bias in information processing has a number of implications. First, the increased frequency of perception of threat increases the likelihood of a defensive response. Because such children are deficient in skills required to make a socially competent response to adverse circumstances, the likelihood of a defense response increases further (Quiggle et al., 1992). Second, the likelihood of a defense response increases even in neutral contexts because of altered information processing that results in misperceptions of threat. This may contribute to the increase in fear of peers and the tormenting of younger children that has been observed (Bemporad et al., 1982). Third, increased defensive responses in abused children (e.g., aggression) contribute to rejection by normal peer groups, which results in an increased probability of deviant peer group membership (Patterson et al., 1989). Specific social skill deficits, such as peer group entry, may exacerbate the social isolation (Patterson et al., 1989). Because social support can mitigate the likelihood of cognitive distortions and withdrawal into fantasy in these children (Bemporad et al., 1982), rejection by peers results in an increased propensity to use these cognitive mechanisms. Thus, a self-perpetuating system is created in which children who are symptomatic from abuse alienate peers, which, in turn, results in increased impact of the trauma on the child.

The information-processing errors that occur in abused children may be conceptualized as resulting from alterations in the child's cognitive-affective balance (Rieder & Cicchetti, 1989). According to these authors, cognitive-affective balance refers to the ability of the child to use cognition to coordinate demands from the external environment and internal affects so as to arrive at an adaptive response. In this context, cognition refers to an organizational framework within which information is processed, interpreted, and a response selected. Such organizational frameworks, called cognitive controls, follow a developmental course (Rieder & Cicchetti, 1989). These authors also note that maltreated children have greater difficulty tuning in to task-relevant stimuli and are more attendant to distracting stimuli when the distractions are aggressively toned (but not threatening) in nature. This is particularly notable because all children show a significant shift toward avoidance of aggressive stimuli (Rieder & Cicchetti, 1989). Maltreated children appear to shift away more from external stimuli regardless of stimulus content relative to nonmaltreated children. The result is that maltreated children have a greater difficulty constructing stable, undifferentiated memory images and show a failure to maintain discreteness of information. On the other hand, maltreated children assimilate aggressive stimuli more accurately and more free of distortions than nonmaltreated children (Rieder & Cicchetti, 1989). Thus, maltreated children selectively attend to and assimilate aggressive stimuli whether or not it is relevant to the task at hand. This occurs even though they use an overall cognitive control that turns attention away from the external world. The original adaptive significance of this cognitive organization is evident.

In social primates, such as humans, all behavioral patterns associated with fitness and survival are integrated within the context of ongoing social behavior (Kraemer, 1985). Alterations in defense behaviors, therefore, must also be integrated into the individual's social behavior. Research on the increased perception of threat in abused children demonstrates this relationship. Although it could be interpreted as a learned response (i.e., people are threatening), the misinterpretation of benign social cues, use of developmentally immature cognitive controls, the extensive social skills deficits, and intellectual deficiencies indicate that the impact of abuse affects the overall cognitive organization of the child. Other behaviors associated with abuse such as self-destructive behavior, tendency to withdraw into fantasy, poor modulation of affect, and increased likelihood of neurological soft signs also support the premise that the alteration in cognitive organization is profound. Behaviors that are necessary for survival or fitness are not expressed in an organized manner without adequate attachment (Kraemer, 1985). Thus, significant attachment problems may also be a vulnerability factor in the development of the extreme emotional instability associated with BPD.

CONTRIBUTIONS TO ALTERED COGNITIVE ORGANIZATION

Thus far, emotional instability (or in its extreme, BPD) has been associated with poor modulation of the fight/flight system and improper processing of social cues. In part, this appears to result from a combination of vulnerability factors, such as poor attachment and genotype, and the impact of stress or trauma. In this section, the vulnerability factor of decreased 5-HT activity will be used as an example of how alterations in one transmitter system can influence information processing at different cortical levels. Although there is some indication that 5-HT is dysfunctional in certain characterological conditions, alterations in other modulatory systems may result in similar behavioral changes. Thus, this section must be viewed merely as an illustration of how a biological vulnerability could contribute to the development of emotional instability.

The impact of reduced 5-HT on fight/flight systems is multifaceted. Low 5-HT is associated with a release of spontaneous LC NE activity (Chiang & Aston-Jones, 1993). This effect both increases the underlying baseline lability of fight/flight activity resulting in a greater frequency of defense responses, and increases the likelihood that any given stimulus will elicit a defense response. There are other probable effects of decreased 5-HT activity on fight/flight behavior. For example, decreased 5-HT activity may also result in attenuated nonopioid-sensitive SIA and a lack of modulation of the effects of reduced endorphin states (Akaoka & Aston-Jones, 1993; Spear et al., 1985). A greater propensity for the activation of opioid activation may also occur (Cancela et al., 1990). Other possible effects include a disinhibition of the NAcc, a decrease in NAcc DA release, and sensitization of postsynaptic DA receptors (Ferre & Artigas, 1993; Haney et al., 1990; Jones et al., 1992). These effects would likely have significant effects on mood, impulsivity, and propensity for aggression (Beninger, 1983; Depue & Spoont, 1986; Oades, 1985; Tidey & Miczek, 1992). Endorphin-stimulated DA release during stress could result in the stimulation of unregulated DA receptors, thereby intensifying these effects (Angulo & McEwen, 1994). Thus, alterations in only one modulatory system can greatly influence the responsivity and functional organization of the underlying system.

It was noted earlier that BPD and suicidality are associated with decreased 5-HT functioning. Suicidality in particular has been associated with an upregulation of 5-HT2 receptors in the prefrontal cortex (Arango et al., 1990; Arora & Meltzer, 1989; Mann et al., 1990). The upregulation may be specific to particular regions of the prefrontal cortex (Brodmann's Areas 8 and 9) because the two studies that did not find this difference used Area 10, and another study failed to show this effect in the temporal pole (Mann et al., 1990). It has been postulated that alterations in 5-HT-mediated aggression may result from the instigation of incorrectly tuned sensory control, allowing either inappropriate stimuli or distorted perceptual inputs to produce abnormal aggressive responses (Valzelli, 1981). The excitatory properties of a CS are invariably altered by modulatory changes that affect associative processes (Harvey, 1987). Thus, in addition to its potential effects on information processing, 5-HT alterations will also have an impact on the threshold for system responsivity.

The primary source of cortical 5-HT is from the dorsal and medial raphe nuclei (Azmitia 1976; Azmitia & Gannon, 1986). Of interest, descending cortical afferents to the midbrain raphe nuclei may only come from the dorsomedial and dorsolateral prefrontal cortex (Arnsten & Goldman-Rakic, 1984; Goldman-Rakic, 1987). This means that the prefrontal cortex and the raphe nuclei are reciprocally organized (Azmitia & Gannon, 1986). Because the dorsolateral and dorsomedial prefrontal regions may be the only source of highly processed information to affect serotonergic transmission, the PFC has a unique capacity to affect all regions innervated by the raphe nuclei.

Brodmann's Area 8 corresponds to the frontal eye fields (FEF), and Area 9 to the principal sulcal area (PSA). Because activation of frontal 5-HT2 receptors inhibit spontaneous activity in prefrontal cells and reduce measures of regional cerebral metabolic rates for glucose in those regions (Ashby, Jiang, Kasser, & Wang, 1990; Freo, Soncrant, Holloway, & Rapoport, 1991), it is likely that enhancement of 5-HT activity in these regions will effectively inhibit, or at least attenuate, activity of these brain regions. The type of deficits often associated with prefrontal damage are poor attention and planning, difficulty in grasping the essence of a situation, difficulty in using past experience to regulate behavior, loss of initiative and spatial orientation, loss of behavioral constraint, and abnormal social affect (Goldman-Rakic, 1987). The FEF is considered to be part of the transitional cortex and is thought to be involved in the control of voluntary eye movements. There is also some evidence that this region may be involved in the ability to select between different visual stimuli on conditional tasks (Petrides, 1992). That is, dysfunction would be related to difficulties forming an association between a particular stimulus and a specific response option (Petrides, 1992; Squire, 1987). This function may be particularly important in interpersonal interactions where there is a multiplicity of social cues and response options.

The principal sulcal area (PSA) is believed to be involved in control of executive functions for guiding voluntary behavior by representational memory, and lesions in the PSA are associated with difficulty in tasks relying on representational memory (Goldman-Rakic, 1987). This, in turn, may result in an overreliance on external cues and prepotent response patterns. In humans, such a behavioral pattern may be manifest as impulsivity. Another result of PSA lesions is perseveration of incorrect responses (Goldman-Rakic, 1987). This is thought to be due to the adventitious pairing of stimuli and responses (Goldman-Rakic, 1987). In this sense, the PSA may be needed to override the tendency to respond only to reinforcement contingencies. Activation of the PSA appears to be specifically required when there is a need for short-term storage of spatial information or for maintenance of an ongoing record of self-generated responses (Petrides, 1992; Squire, 1987). Both of these functions may be related to the more fundamental task of ordering information both spatially and temporally (Kesner, 1990; Malloy, Bihrle, & Duffy, 1993; Squire, 1987).

In addition to upregulated 5-HT2 receptors in these prefrontal regions in suicide, there is also some evidence for alterations in NE and endorphin functioning (Arango et al., 1990; Gross-Isseroff et al., 1990a; Gross-Isseroff et al., 1990b; Mann, McBride, & Stanley, 1987). PTSD has been specifically associated with altered NE functioning (Krystal et al., 1989; van der Kolk, et al., 1989; Yehuda et al., 1993). The 5-HT modulation of NE release from the LC is inhibitory for the spontaneous discharge of NE neurons, but facilitatory for NE neural firing in response to a significant stimulus (Chiang & Aston-Jones, 1993). Thus, 5-HT and NE act in tandem to increase the signal-to-noise ratio in neural systems responding to salient stimuli.

Alterations of any modulatory system will necessarily bias information processing at the locus of modulation. For example, clonidine, an alpha2-noradrenergic agonist infused into the PFC of primates improves their performance on a delayed response task—a task that requires the functioning of the PSA (Berridge et al., 1993). Decreased 5-HT may not impair functioning on tasks requiring the PSA unless there are distractions because 5-HT activation attenuates signal perturbation and 5-HT turnover is known to be increased on tasks requiring a functional PSA (Spoont, 1992; Vachon & Roberge, 1981). NE depletion is also associated with difficulty on tasks if distractions are involved, and NE turnover is also increased during tasks requiring the PSA (Berridge et al., 1993; Oades, 1985; Vachon & Roberge, 1981). Since 5-HT depletion releases the spontaneous firing of NE but attenuates the NE response to salient stimuli, decreased 5-HT activity would be associated with an increased tendency toward reliance on prepotent response patterns and an increased likelihood of adventitious pairing of stimuli and responses. Thus, whereas altered modulation does not result in the impairments associated with lesioning, the functioning of the modulated region may be significantly biased.

The integrity of neurotransmitter or neuropeptide systems is partially dependent on developmental factors. For example, in rodents maternal stress during gestation affects the 5-HT receptor binding in several brain regions of adult offspring and alters the intensity of the receptor response to 5-HT agonists (Peters, 1990). The endogenous opioid system also shows a developmental course in that the receptors that subserve the opioid SIA differ pre- versus postweaning (Kitchen et al., 1994). Notably, impaired attachment (as through isolation) alters both the 5-HT and opioid systems (Jones et al., 1992; Panksepp, 1981). Both 5-HT and endorphins have neurotrophic properties that can potentially regulate neural growth (Whitaker-Azmitia, Lauder, Shemmer, & Azmitia, 1987). In humans, PFC Regions 9 and 10 lack complete pyramidalization, which does not occur until puberty (Stuss & Benson, 1986). Limbic regions (including dorsomedial thalamus, amygdala, hippocampus, etc.) begin myelinization after birth and finish just before puberty (Stuss & Benson, 1986). More recently, it has been demonstrated that myelination can continue even into adulthood, as in the superior medullary lamina of the parahippocampal gyrus (Benes, Turtle, Khan, & Farol, 1994).

Research on the impact of developmental factors on neurobiology is only beginning. Greater understanding of how systems operate and interact during development will elucidate the biological mechanisms involved in temperament, vulnerability to disorder, and disorder itself. All disorder may be a combination of modulatory disturbances and poor developmental organization. Understanding that all behavior is purposeful, even if it is not properly organized or adaptive, can help to clarify what our patients are trying to tell us. Lowered thresholds for defense behavior coupled with a social information processing bias will result in extreme behavior patterns. Fight/flight behavior is about survival—even if the threat is perceived versus actual. Treatment approaches can be preventive, as in minimizing child abuse, or ameliorative. Tertiary treatment approaches can seek to raise the threshold for defense behavior (e.g., with 5-HT reuptake inhibitors), address the processing of social cues and appropriate social responses, or both. When dealing with these patients, who have a greater propensity for perceptions of threat and for using defense responses, clinicians must understand that it will be difficult to establish trust. Without such a foundation, however, perceptions of threat are only reinforced.

REFERENCES

Aalders, T. T. A., & Meek, J. (1993). The hypothalamic aggression region of the rat: Observations on the synaptic organization. *Brain Research Bulletin, 31,* 229–232.

Adell, A., Garcia-Marquez, C., Armario, A., & Gelpi, E. (1988). Chronic stress increases serotonin and noradrenaline in rat brain and sensitizes their responses to a further acute stress. *Journal of Neurochemistry, 50,* 1678–1681.

Aggleton, J. P. (1993). The contribution of the amygdala to normal and abnormal emotional states. *Topics in Neuroscience, 16,* 328–333.

Akaoka, H., & Aston-Jones, G. (1993). Indirect serotonergic agonists attenuate neuronal opiate withdrawal. *Neuroscience, 54,* 561–565.

American Psychiatric Association. (1994). *Diagnostic and statistical manual of mental disorders* (4th ed.). Washington, DC: Author.

Andersen, S. L., Robinson, S. R., & Smotherman, W. P. (1993). Ontogeny of the stretch response in the rat fetus: Kappa opioid involvement. *Behavioral Neuroscience, 107,* 370–376.

Angulo, J. A., & McEwen, B. S. (1994). Molecular aspects of neuropeptide regulation and function in the corpus striatum and nucleus accumbens. *Brain Research Reviews, 19,* 1–28.

Antelman, S. M., & Caggiula, A. R. (1977). Norepinephrine-dopamine interactions and behavior. *Science, 195,* 646–653.

Antelman, S. M., & Chiodo, L. A. (1984). Stress: Its effect on interactions among biogenic amines and role in the induction and treatment of disease. In L. Iversen, S. Iversen, & S. Snyder (Eds.), *Handbook of psychopharmacology. Vol. 18: Drugs, neurotransmitters, and behavior* (pp. 279–342). New York: Plenum.

Applegate, C. D., Kapp, B. S., Underwood, M. D., & McNall, C. L. (1982). Autonomic and somatomotor effects of amygdala central n. stimulation in awake rabbits. *Physiology and Behavior, 31,* 353–360.

Arango, V., Ernsberger, P., Marzuk, P. M., Chen, J., Tierney, H., Stanley, M., Reis, D. J., & Mann, J. J. (1990). Autoradiographic demonstration of increased serotonin 5-HT2 and β-adrenergic receptor binding sites in the brain of suicide victims. *Archives of General Psychiatry, 47,* 1038–1047.

Arnsten, A. F., & Goldman-Rakic, P. S. (1984). Selective prefrontal cortical projections to the region of the locus coeruleus and raphe nuclei in the rhesus monkey, *Brain Research, 306,* 9–18.

Arora, R. C., & Meltzer, H. Y. (1989). Serotonergic measures in the brains of suicide victims: 5-HT2 binding sites in the frontal cortex of suicide victims and control subjects. *American Journal of Psychiatry, 146,* 730–736.

Ashby, C. R., Jiang, L. H., Kasser, R. J., & Wang, R. Y. (1990). Electrophysiological characterization of 5-hydroxytryptamine2 receptors in the rat medial prefrontal cortex. *Journal of Pharmacology and Experimental Therapeutics, 252,* 171–178.

Azmitia, E. C. (1978). The serotonin-producing neurons of the midbrain median and dorsal raphe nuclei. In L. Iverson, S. Iverson, & S. Snyder (Eds.), *Handbook of psychopharmacology, Vol. 9: Chemical pathways in the brain* (pp. 233–314). New York: Plenum.

Azmitia, E. C., & Gannon, P. J. (1986). The primate serotonergic system: A review of human and animal studies and a report on Macaca fascicularis. In S. Fahn et al. (Eds.), *Advances in neurology, Vol. 43: Myoclonus* (pp. 407–468). New York: Raven.

Bandler, R., & Depaulis, A. (1991). Midbrain periaqueductal gray control of defense behavior in the cat and the rat. In A. Depaulis & R. Bandler (Eds.), *The midbrain periaqueductal gray matter* (pp. 175–198). New York: Plenum.

Beaulieu, S., Dipaolo, T., & Barden, N. (1985). Implication of the serotonergic system in the decreased ACTH response to stress after lesion of the amygdaloid central nucleus. *Progress in Neuropsychopharmacology & Biological Psychiatry, 9,* 665–669.

Beckett, S. R., Lawrence, A. J., Marsden, C. A., & Marshall, P. W. (1992). Attenuation of chemically induced defence response by 5-HT1 receptor agonists administered into the periqueductal gray. *Psychopharmacology, 108*, 110–114.

Behbehani, M. M., Liu, J., Jiang, M., Pun, R. Y. K., & Shipley, M. T. (1993). Activation of serotonin 1A receptors inhibits midbrain periaqueductal gray neurons of the rat. *Brain Research, 612*, 56–60.

Bemporad, J. R., Smith, H. F., Hanson, G., & Cicchetti, D. (1982). Borderline syndromes in childhood: Criteria for diagnosis. *American Journal of Psychiatry, 139*, 596–602.

Benes, F. M., Turtle, M., Khan, Y., & Farol, P. (1994). Myelination of a key relay zone in the hippocampal formation occurs in the human brain during childhood, adolescence, and adulthood. *Archives of General Psychiatry, 51*, 477–484.

Beninger, R. J. (1983). The role of dopamine in locomotor activity and learning. *Brain Research Reviews, 6*, 173–196.

Berridge, C. W., Arnsten, A. F. T., & Foote, S. L. (1993). Noradrenergic modulation of cognitive function: Clinical implications of anatomical, electrophysiological and behavioural studies in animal models. *Psychological Medicine, 23*, 557–564.

Besson, J. M., Fardin, V., & Oliveras, J. L. (1991). Analgesia produced by stimulation of the periaqueductal gray matter: True atinociception versus stress effects. In A. Depaulis & R. Bandler (Eds.), *The midbrain periaqueductal gray matter* (pp. 121–138). New York: Plenum.

Bezirganian, S., Cohen, P., & Brook, J. S. (1993). The impact of mother-child interaction on the development of borderline personality disorder. *American Journal of Psychiatry, 150*, 1836–1842.

Brent, D. A., Johnson, B., Bartle, S., Bridge, J., Rater, C., Matta, J., Connolly, J., & Constantine, D. (1993). Personality disorder, tendency to impulsive violence, and suicidal behavior in adolescents. *Journal of the American Academy of Child and Adolescent Psychiatry, 32*, 69–75.

Borsook, D., Falkowski, O., Burstein, R., Strassman, A., Konradi, C., Dauber, A., Comb, M., & Hyman, S. E. (1994). Stress-induced regulation of a human proenkephalin-beta-galactosidase fusion gene in the hypothalamus of transgenic mice. *Molecular Endocrinology, 8*, 116–125.

Bowlby, J. (1982). *Attachment*, (2nd ed.). New York: Basic Books.

Brown, G. L., Goodwin, F. K., & Bunney, W. E., Jr. (1982). Human aggression and suicide: Their relationship to neuropsychiatric diagnoses and serotonin metabolism. In B. T. Ho et al. (Eds.), *Serotonin in biological psychiatry.* New York: Raven.

Brown, G. L., & Linnoila, M. I. (1990). CSF serotonin metabolite (5-HIAA) studies in depression, impulsivity, and violence. *Journal of Clinical Psychiatry, 51* [4, Suppl], 31–41.

Cancela, L., Volosin, M., & Molina, V. A. (1990). Opioid involvement in the adaptive change of 5-HT1 receptors induced by chronic restraint. *European Journal of Pharmacology, 176*, 313–319.

Carden, S. E., Davachi, L., & Hofer, M. A. (1994). U50,488 increases ultrasonic vocalizations in 3-, 10-, and 18-day-old rat pups in isolation and the home cage. *Developmental Psychobiology, 27,* 65–83.

Carden, S. E., & Hofer, M. A. (1990). Socially mediated reduction of isolation distress in rat pups is blocked by naltrexone but not by Ro 15-1788. *Behavioral Neuroscience, 104,* 457–463.

Cervo, L., Rochat, C., Romandini, S., & Saminin, R. (1981). Evidence of a preferential role of brain serotonin in the mechanisms leading to naloxone-precipitated compulsive jumping in morphine-dependent rats. *Psychopharmacology, 74,* 271–274.

Charney, D. S., & Heninger, G. R. (1986). Alpha2-adrenergic and opiate receptor blockade: Synergistic effects on anxiety in healthy subjects. *Archives of General Psychiatry, 43,* 1037–1041.

Chiang, C. & Aston-Jones, G. (1993). A 5-hydroxytryptamine2 agonist augments gamma-aminobutyric acid and excitatory amino acid inputs to noradrenergic locus coeruleus neurons. *Neuroscience, 54,* 409–420.

Coccaro, E. F., Siever, L. J., Klar, H. M., Maurer, G., Cochrane, K., Cooper, T. B., Mohs, R. C., & Davis, K. L. (1989). Serotonergic studies in patients with affective and personality disorders. *Archives of General Psychiatry, 46,* 587–599.

Coe, C. L., Wiener, S. G., Rosenberg, L. T., & Levine, S. (1985). Endocrine and immune responses to separation and maternal loss in nonhuman primates. In M. Reite & T. Field (Eds.), *The psychobiology of attachment and separation* (pp. 163–199). New York: Academic Press.

Creamer, M., Burgess, P., & Pattison, P. (1992). Reaction to trauma: A cognitive processing model. *Journal of Abnormal Psychology, 101,* 452–459.

Davis, M. (1984). The mammalian startle response. In R. C. Eaton (Ed.), *Neural mechanisms of startle behavior* (pp. 287–351). New York: Plenum.

Davis, M. (1989). Neural systems involved in fear-potentiated startle. *Annals of the New York Academy of Sciences, 563,* 165–183.

Davis, M. (1992). The role of the amygdala in fear and anxiety. *Annual Review of Neuroscience, 15,* 353–375.

Depue, R. A., & Spoont, M. R. (1986). Conceptualizing a serotonin trait: A behavioral dimension of constraint. *Annals of the New York Academy of Sciences, 487,* 47–62.

Diorio, D., Viau, V., & Meaney, M. J. (1993). The role of the medial prefrontal cortex (cingulate gyrus) in the regulation of the hypothalamic-pituitary-adrenocortical responses to stress. *The Journal of Neuroscience, 13,* 3839–3847.

Duvauchelle, C. L., Levitin, M., MacConell, L. A., Lee, L. K., & Ettenberg, A. (1992). Opposite effects of prefrontal cortex and nucleus accumbens infucions of flupenthixol on stimulant-induced locomotion and brain stimulation reward. *Brain Research, 576,* 104–110.

Edeline, J. M., & Weinberger, N. M. (1992). Associative retuning in the thalamic source of input to the amygdala and auditory cortex: Receptive field plasticity in the medial division of the medial geniculate body. *Behavioral Neuroscience, 106,* 81–105.

Egeland, B., & Sroufe, L. A. (1981). Developmental sequellae of maltreatment in infancy. *New Directions for Child Development, 11,* 77–92.

Egeland, B., Sroufe, L. A., & Erickson, M. (1983). The developmental consequence of different patterns of maltreatment. *Child Abuse & Neglect, 7,* 459–469.

Emery, R. E. (1989). Family violence. *American Psychologist, 44,* 321–328.

Eysenck, H. J., & Eysenck, M. W. (1985). *Personality and individual differences: A natural science approach.* New York: Plenum.

Faneslow, M. S. (1991). The midbrain periaqueductal gray as a coordinator of action in response to fear and anxiety. In A. Depaulis & R. Bandler (Eds.), *The midbrain periaqueductal gray matter* (pp. 151–173). New York: Plenum.

Ferre, S., & Artigas, F. (1993). Dopamine D2 receptor-mediated regulation of serotonin extracellular concentration in the dorsal raphe nucleus of freely moving rats. *Journal of Neurochemistry, 61,* 772–775.

File, S., James, T. A., & Macleod, N. K. (1981). Depletion in amygdaloid 5-hydroxytryptamine concentration and changes in social and aggressive behavior. *Journal of Neural Transmission, 50,* 1–12.

Foa, E. B., Steketee, G., & Rothbaum, B. O. (1989). Behavioral/cognitive conceptualizations of post-traumatic stress disorder. *Behavior Therapy, 20,* 155–176.

Foa, E. B., Zinbarg, R., & Rothbaum, B. O. (1992). Uncontrollability and unpredictability in post-traumatic stress disorder: An animal model. *Psychological Bulletin, 112,* 218–238.

Fowles, D. C. (1987). Application of a behavioral theory of motivation to the concepts of anxiety and impulsivity. *Journal of Research in Personality, 21,* 417–435.

Freo, U., Soncrant, T. T., Holloway, J. W., & Rapoport, S. I. (1991). Dose- and time-dependent effects of 1-(2,5-dimethoxy-4-iodophenyl)-2-aminopropane (DOI), a serotonergic 5-HT2 receptor agonist, on local cerebral glucose metabolism in awake rats. *Brain Research, 541,* 63–69.

Fuchs, S. A., Edinger, H. M., & Siegel, A. (1985a). The organization of the hypothalamic pathways mediating affective defense behavior in the cat. *Brain Research, 330,* 77–92.

Fuchs, S. A., Edinger, H. M., & Siegel, A. (1985b). The role of the anterior hypothalamus in affective defense behavior elicited from the ventromedial hypothalamus of the cat. *Brain Research, 330,* 93–107.

Goldman, S. J., D'Angelo, E. J., & DeMaso, D. R. (1993). Psychopathology in the families of children and adolescents with borderline personality disorder. *American Journal of Psychiatry, 150,* 1832–1835.

Goldman-Rakic, P. S. (1987). Circuitry of primate prefrontal cortex and regulation of behavior by representational memory. In F. Plum (Ed.), *Handbook of Physiology* (pp. 373–417). Baltimore: American Physiology Society.

Goodwin, G. A., Molina, V. A., & Spear, L. P. (1994). Repeated exposure of rat pups to isolation attenuates isolation-induced ultrasonic vocalization rates: Reversal with naltrexone. *Developmental Psychobiology, 27,* 53–64.

Graeff, F. G. (1984). The anti-aversive action of minor tranquilizers. *Trends in Neuroscience,* June, 230–233.

Gray, J. A. (1982). *The neuropsychology of anxiety: An enquiry into the functions of the septo-hippocampal system.* New York: Oxford University Press.

Gray, J. A. (1987). Perspectives on anxiety and impulsivity: A commentary. *Journal of Research in Personality, 21,* 493–509.

Gross-Isseroff, R., Dillon, K. A., Fieldust, S. J., & Biegon, A. (1990). Autoradiographic analysis of alpha1-noradrenergic receptors in the human brain postmortem. *Archives of General Psychiatry, 47,* 1049–1053.

Gross-Isseroff, R., Dillon, K. A., Israeli, M., & Biegon, A. (1990). Regionally selective increases in mu opioid receptor density in the brains of suicide victims. *Brain Research, 530,* 312–316.

Gunderson, J. G., & Sabo, A. N. (1993). The phenomenological and conceptual interface between borderline personality disorder and PTSD. *American Journal of Psychiatry, 150,* 19–27.

Harkness, A. R., & McNulty, J. L. (in press). The personality psychopathology five (PSY-5): Issue from the pages of a diagnostic manual instead of a dictionary. In S. Strack & M. Lorr (Eds.), *Differentiating normal and abnormal personality.* New York: Springer.

Harvey, J. A. (1987). Effects of drugs on associative learning. In H. Y. Meltzer (Ed.), *Psychopharmacology: The third generation of progress* (pp. 1485–1491). New York: Raven Press.

Haney, M., Noda, K., Kream, R., & Miczek, K. A. (1990). Regional serotonin and dopamine activity: Sensitivity to amphetamine and aggressive behavior in mice. *Aggressive Behavior, 16,* 259–270.

Herman, B., & Panksepp, J. (1981). Ascending endorphin inhibition of distress vocalization. *Science, 211,* 1060–1062.

Herman, J. L. (1992). *Trauma and recovery.* New York: Basic Books.

Helmstetter, F. J. (1992). Contribution of the amygdala to learning and performance of conditioned fear. *Physiology and Behavior, 51,* 1271–1276.

Hoffman-Plotkin, D., & Twentyman, C. T. (1984). A multimodal assessment of behavioral and cognitive deficits in abused and neglected children. *Child Development, 55,* 794–802.

Huang, G. F., Besson, J. M., & Bernard, J. F. (1993). Intravenous morphine depresses the transmission of noxious messages to the nucleus centralis of the amygdala. *European Journal of Pharmacology, 236,* 449–456.

Inoue, T., Koyama, T., & Yamashita, I. (1993). Effect of conditional fear stress on serotonin metabolism in the rat brain. *Pharmacology, Biochemistry and Behavior, 44,* 371–374.

Jones, G. H., Hernandez, T. D., Kendall, D. A., Marsden, C. A., & Robbins, T. W. (1992). Dopaminergic and serotonergic function following isolation rearing in rats: Study of behavioural responses and postmortem and in vivo neurochemistry. *Pharmacology, Biochemistry, and Behavior, 43,* 17–35.

Jones, D. L., Mogenson, G. J., & Wu, M. (1981). Injections of dopaminergic, cholinergic, serotonergic and gabaergic drugs into the nucleus accumbens: Effects on locomotor activity in the rat. *Neuropharmacology, 20,* 29–37.

Kaneyuki, H., Yokoo, H., Tsuda, A., Yoshida, M., Mizuki, Y., Yamada, M., & Tanaka, M. (1991). Psychological stress increases dopamine turnover selectively in mesoprefrontal dopamine neurons of rats: Reversal by diazepam. *Brain Research, 557,* 154–161.

Kesner, R. P. (1990). Memory for frequency in rats: Role of the hippocampus and medial prefrontal cortex. *Behavioral and Neural Biology, 53,* 402–410.

Kitchen, I., Crook, T. J., Muhammed, B. Y., & Hill, R. G. (1994). Evidence that weaning stimulates the developmental expression of a δ-opioid receptor subtype in the rat. *Developmental Brain Research, 78,* 147–150.

Kraemer, G. K. (1985). Effects of differences in early social experience on primate neurobiological-behavioral development. In M. Reite & T. Field (Eds.), *The psychobiology of attachment and separation* (pp. 135–161). New York: Academic Press.

Kruk, M. R. (1991). Ethology and pharmacology of hypothalamic aggression in the rat. *Neuroscience & Biobehavioral Reviews, 15,* 527–538.

Krystal, J. H., Kosten, T. R., Southwick, S., Mason, J. W., Perry, B. D., & Giller, E. L. (1989). Neurobiological aspects of PTSD: Review of clinical and preclinical studies. *Behavior Therapy, 20,* 177–198.

LeDoux, J. E. (1992a). Brain mechanisms of emotion and emotional learning. *Current Opinion in Neurobiology, 2,* 191–197.

LeDoux, J. E. (1992b). Emotion as memory. In S. A. Christianson (Ed.), *The handbook of emotion and memory: Theory and research* (pp. 169–288). Hillsdale, NJ: Erlbaum.

LeDoux, J. E., Cicchetti, P., Xagoraris, A., & Romanski, L. M. (1990). The lateral amygdaloid nucleus: Sensory interface of the amygdala in fear conditioning. *The Journal of Neuroscience, 10,* 1062–1069.

Lewis, D. O. (1992). From abuse to violence: Psychophysiological consequences of maltreatment. *Journal of the American Academy of Child and Adolescent Psychiatry, 31,* 383–391.

Livesley, W. J., Jang, K. L., Jackson, D. N., & Vernon, P. A. (1993). Genetic and environmental contributions to dimensions of personality disorder. *American Journal of Psychiatry, 150,* 1826–1831.

Luntz, B. K., & Widom, C. S. (1994). Antisocial personality disorder in abused and neglected children grown up. *American Journal of Psychiatry, 151,* 670–674.

Lyons-Ruth, K., Connell, D. B., Zoll, D., & Stahl, J. (1987). Infants at social risk: Relations among infant maltreatment, maternal behavior, and infant attachment behavior. *Developmental Psychology, 23,* 223–232.

Mandell, A., Knapp, S., Ehlers, C., & Russo, P. V. (1984). The stability of constrained randomness: Lithium prophylaxis at several neurobiological levels. In R. Post & J. C. Ballenger (Eds.), *Neurobiology of mood disorders* (pp. 744–776). Baltimore, MD: Williams & Williams.

Mann, J. J., Arango, V., & Underwood, M. D. (1990). Serotonin and suicidal behavior. *Annals of the New York Academy of Sciences, 600,* 476–485.

Mann, J. J., McBride, P. A., & Stanley, M. (1987). Postmortem monoamine receptor and enzyme studies in suicide. *Annals of the New York Academy of Sciences, 487,* 114–121.

Marks, G. A., Speciale, S. G., Cobbey, K., & Roffwarg, H. P. (1987). Serotonergic inhibition of the dorsal lateral geniculate nucleus. *Brain Research, 418,* 76–84.

McGaugh, J. L. (1992). Affect, neuromodulatory systems, and memory storage. In S. A. Christianson (Ed.), *The handbook of emotion and memory: Theory and research* (pp. 245–268). Hillsdale, NJ: Erlbaum.

McGaugh, J. L., & Introini-Collison, I. B. (1987). Hormonal and neurotransmitter interactions in the modulation of memory storage: Involvement of the amygdala. *International Journal of Neurology, 21–22,* 58–72.

McKinney, W. T. (1985). Separation and depression: Biological markers. In M. Reite & T. Field (Eds.), *The psychobiology of attachment and separation* (pp. 201–222). New York: Academic Press.

McNaughton, N., Azmitia, E. C., Williams, J. H., Buchan, A., & Gray, J. A. (1980). Septal elicitation of hippocampal theta rhythm after localized deafferentation of serotonergic fibers. *Brain Research, 200,* 259–269.

McNaughton, N., James, D. T. D., Stewart, J., Gray, J. A., Valero, I., & Drewnowski, A. (1977). Septal driving of hippocampal theta rhythm as a function of frequency in the male rat: Effects of drugs. *Neuroscience, 2,* 1019–1027.

Morgan, M. M. (1991). Differences in antinociception evoked from dorsal and ventral regions of the caudal periaqueductal gray matter. In A. Depaulis & R. Bandler (Eds.), *The midbrain periaqueductal gray matter* (pp. 151–173). New York: Plenum.

Narita, M., Suzuki, T., Funada, M., Misawa, M., & Nagase, H. (1993). Blockade of the morphine-induced increase in turnover of dopamine on the mesolimbic dopaminergic system by k-opioid receptor activation in mice. *Life Sciences, 52,* 397–404.

Oades, R. D. (1985). The role of noradrenaline in tuning and dopamine in switching between signals in the CNS. *Neuroscience & Biobehavioral Reviews, 9,* 261–282.

Ottersen, O. P. (1981). Afferent connections to the amygdaloid complex of the rat with some observations in the cat. III. Afferents from the lower brainstem. *The Journal of Comparative Neurology, 202,* 335–356.

Panksepp, J. (1981). Brain opioids—A neurochemical substrate for narcotic and social dependence. In S. J. Cooper (Ed.), *Theory in psychopharmacology* (pp. 49–175). (Vol. 1, Chapter 5). London: Academic Press.

Panksepp, J., Siviy, S. M., & Normansell, L. A. (1985). Brain opioids and social emotions. In M. Reite & T. Field (Eds.), *The psychobiology of attachment and separation* (pp. 3–49). New York: Academic Press.

Patterson, G. R., DeBaryshe, B. D., & Ramsey, E. (1989). A developmental perspective on antisocial behavior. *American Psychologist, 44,* 329–335.

Petney, R. J., & Gratton, A. (1991). Effects of local delta and mu opioid receptor activation on basal and stimulated dopamine release in striatum and nucleus accumbens of rat: An in vivo study. *Neuroscience, 45,* 95–102.

Peters, D. A. V. (1990). Maternal stress increases fetal brain and neonatal cerebral cortex 5-hydroxytryptamine synthesis in rats: A possible mechanism by which stress influences brain development. *Pharmacology, Biochemistry & Behavior, 35,* 943–947.

Petrides, M. (1992). Functional specialization within the primate dorsolateral frontal cortex. *Advances in Neurology, 57,* 379–388.

Pieretti, S., d'Amore, A., & Loizzo, A. (1991). Long-term changes induced by developmental handling on pain threshold: Effects of morphine and naloxone. *Behavioral Neuroscience, 105,* 215–218.

Price, J. L., & Amaral, D. G. (1981). An autoradiographic study of the projections of the central nucleus of the monkey amygdala. *The Journal of Neuroscience, 1,* 1242–1259.

Price, J. L., Russchen, F. T., & Amaral, D. G. (1987). The Limbic region. II: The amygdalid complex. In A. Bjorklund, T. Hokfelt, and L. Swanson (Eds.), *Handbook of chemical neuroanatomy. Vol. 5: Integrated Systems of the CNS, Part I* (pp. 279–388). New York: Elsvier Science.

Quartermain, D., Clemente, J., & Shemer, A., (1993). 5-HT1a agonists disrupt memory of fear conditioning in mice. *Biological Psychiatry, 33,* 247–254.

Quiggle, N. L., Garber, J., Panak, W. F., & Dodge, K. A. (1992). Social information processing in aggressive and depressed children. *Child Development, 63,* 1305–1320.

Raleigh, M. J., Brammer, G. L., & McGuire, M. T. (1983). Male dominance, serotonergic systems, and the behavioral and physiological effects of drugs in vervet monkeys (Cercopithecus aethiops sabacus). In K. A. Miczek & A. R. Liss (Eds.), *Ethnopharmacology: Primate models of neuropsychiatric disorders.*

Rasmussen, K., & Jacobs, B. L. (1986). Single unit activity of locus coeruleus neurons in the freely moving cat. II. Conditioning and pharmacologic studies. *Brain Research, 371,* 335–344.

Rasmussen, K., Strecker, R. E., & Jacobs, B. L. (1986). Single unit response of noradrenergic, serotonergic and dopaminergic neurons in freely moving cats to simple sensory stimuli. *Brain Research, 369,* 336–340.

Rieder, C., & Cicchetti, D. (1989). Organizational perspective on cognitive control functioning and cognitive-affective balance in maltreated children. *Developmental Psychology, 25,* 382–393.

Rodgers, R. J., Shepherd, J. K., & Donat, P. (1991). Differential effects of novel ligands for 5-HT receptor subtypes on nonopioid defensive analgesia in male mice. *Neuroscience and Biobehavioral Reviews, 15,* 489–495.

Russ, M. J., Shearin, E. N., Clarkin, J. F., Harrison, K., & Hull, J. W. (1993). Subtypes of self-injurious patients with borderline personality disorder. *American Journal of Psychiatry, 150,* 1869–1871.

Sarter, M., & Markowitsch, H. J. (1985). Involvement of the amygdala in learning and memory: A critical review, with emphasis on anatomical relations. *Behavioral Neuroscience, 99,* 342–380.

Schalling, D., Asberg, M., Edman, G., & Levander, S. (1984). Impulsivity, nonconformity and sensation seeking as related to biological markers for vulnerability. *Clinical Neuropharmacology, 7*(Suppl. 1), s403–s404.

Schicknick, H., Hoffman, H. J., Schneider, R., & Crusio, W. E. (1993). Genetic analysis of isolation-induced aggression in the mouse. *Behavioral and Neural Biology, 59,* 242–248.

Scibilia, R. J., Lachowicz, J. E., & Kilts, C. D. (1992). Topographic nonoverlapping distribution of D1 and D2 dopamine receptors in the amygdaloid nuclear complex of the rat brain. *Synapse, 11,* 146–154.

Schultz, M. B., De Aguir, J. C., & Graeff, F. G. (1985). Anti-aversive role of serotonin in the dorsal periaqueductal gray matter. *Psychopharmacology, 85,* 340–345.

Semple, W. E., Goyer, P., McCormick, R., Morris, E., Compton, B., Muswick, G., Nelson, D., Donoan, B., Leisure, G., Berridge, M., Mirali, F., & Schulz, S. C. (1993). Preliminary report: Brain blood flow using PET in patients with posttraumatic stress disorder and substance-abuse histories. *Biolgoical Psychiatry, 34,* 115–118.

Shaikh, M. B., Lu, C. L., & Siegel, A. (1991). An enkephalinergic mechanism involved in amygdaloid suppression of affective defence behavior elicited from the midbrain periaqueductal gray in the cat. *Brain Research, 559,* 109–117.

Shide, D. J., & Blass, E. M. (1989). Opioidlike effects of intraoral infusions of corn oil and polcose on stress reactions in 10-day-old rats. *Behavioral Neuroscience, 6,* 1168–1175.

Shipley, M. T., Ennis, M., Rizi, T. A., & Behbehani, M. M. (1991). Topographical specificity of forebrain inputs to the midbrain periaqueductal gray: Evidence for discrete longitudinally organized input columns. In A. Depaulis & R. Bandler (Eds.), *The midbrain periaqueductal gray matter* (pp. 417–448). New York: Plenum.

Siever, L., & Trestman, R. L. (1993). The serotonin system and aggressive personality disorder. *International Clinical Psychopharmacology, 8*(Suppl. 2), 33–39.

Smotherman, W. P., & Robinson, S. R. (1993). Habituation of chemosensory stimuli in the rat fetus: Effects of endogenous kappa opioid activity. *Behavioral Neuroscience, 107,* 611–617.

Spear, L. P., Enters, E. K., Aswad, M. A., & Louzan, M. (1985). Drug and environmentally induced manipulations of the opiate and serotonergic systems alter nociception in neonatal rat pups. *Behavioral and Neural Biology, 44,* 1–22.

Spoont, M. R. (1992). Modulatory role of serotonin in neural information processing: Implications for human psychopathology. *Psychological Bulletin, 112,* 330–350.

Squire, L. (1987). *Mind and brain.* New York: Oxford University Press.

Steklis, H. D., & Kling, A. (1985). Neurobiology of affiliative behavior in nonhuman primates. In M. Reite & T. Field (Eds.), *The psychobiology of attachment and separation.* New York: Academic Press.

Stinus, L., LeMoal, M., & Koob, G. F. (1990). Nucleus accumbens and amygdala are possible substrates for the aversive stimulus effects of opiate withdrawal. *Neuroscience, 37,* 767–773.

Stuss, D. T., & Benson, D. F. (1986). *The Frontal Lobes.* New York: Raven.

Sugita, S., & North, R. A. (1993). Opioid actions on neurons of rat lateral amygdala in vitro. *Brain Research, 612,* 151–155.

Tellegen, A. (1982). *Brief Manual for the Differential Personality Questionnaire.* Unpublished Manuscript.

Tellegen, A., & Waller, N. G. (in press). Exploring personality through test construction: Development of the multidimensional personality questionnaire. In S. Briggs & J. M. Cheek (Eds.), *Personality measures: Development and evaluation (Vol. 1).* Greenwich, CN: JAI Press.

Thorn, B. E., Applegate, L., & Johnson, S. W., (1989). Ability of periaqueductal gray subdivisions and adjacent loci to elicit analgesia and ability of naloxone to reverse analgesia. *Behavioral Neuroscience, 103,* 1335–1339.

Tidey, J. W. & Miczek, K. A. (1992). Morphine withdrawal aggression: Modification with D1 and D2 receptor agonists. *Psychopharmacology, 108,* 177–184.

Vachon, L., & Roberge, A. G. (1981). Involvement of serotonin and catecholamine metabolism in cats trained to perform a delayed response task. *Neuroscience, 6,* 189–194.

Valzelli, L. (1981). *Psychobiology of Aggression and Violence.* New York: Raven.

Van der Kolk, B. (1987). *Psychological trauma.* Washington, DC: American Psychiatric Press.

Van der Kolk, B., & Fisler, R. (1993). The biologic basis of posttraumatic stress. *Primary Care, 20,* 417–432.

Van der Kolk, B. A., Greenberg, M. S., Orr, S. P., & Pittman, R. K. (1989). Endogenous opioids, stress induced analgesia, and posttraumatic stress disorder. *Psychopharmacology Bulletin, 25,* 417–421.

Van der Kolk, B. A., & Saporta, J. (1993). Biological response to psychic trauma. In J. P. Wilson & B. Raphael (Eds.), *International handbook of traumatic stress syndromes* (pp. 25–33). New York: Plenum.

Virkkunen, M., Rawlings, R., Tokola, R., Poland, R. E., Guidotti, A., Nemroff, C., Bissette, G., Kalogeras, K., Karonen, S. L., & Linnoila, M. (1994). CSF biochemistries, glucose metabolism, and diurnal activity rhythms in alcoholic, violent offenders, fire setters, and healthy volunteers. *Archives of General Psychiatry, 51,* 20–27.

Virkkunen, M., Kallio, E., Rawlings, R., Tokola, R., Poland, R. E., Guidotti, A., Nemroff, C., Bissette, G., Kalogeras, K., Karonen, S. L., & Linnoila, M. (1994). Personality profiles and state aggressiveness in Finnish Alcoholic, violent offenders, fire setters, and healthy volunteers. *Archives of General Psychiatry, 51,* 28–33.

Wallace, D. M., Magnuson, D. J., & Gray, T. S. (1992). Organization of amygdaloid projections to brainstem dopaminergic, noradrenergic, and adrenergic cell groups in the rat. *Brain Research, 28,* 447–454.

Wang, J., Consolo, S., Vinci, R., Forloni, G., & Ladinsky, H. (1985). Characterization of the alpha adrenergic receptor population in hippocampus upregulated by serotonergic raphe deafferentiation. *Life Sciences, 36,* 255–270.

Watanabe, Y., Sakai, R. R., McEwen, B. S., & Mendelson, S. (1993). Stress and antidepressant effects on hippocampal and cortical 5-HT1A and 5-HT2 receptors and transport sites for serotonin. *Brain Research, 615,* 87–94.

Weiss, B., Dodge, K. A., Bates, J. E., & Pettit, G. S. (1992). Some consequences of early harsh discipline: Child aggression and a maladaptive social information processing style. *Child Development, 63,* 1321–1335.

Whitaker-Azmitia, P. M., Lauder, J. M., Shemmer, A., & Azmitia, E. C. (1987). Postnatal changes in serotonin 1 receptors following prenatal alterations in serotonin levels: Further evidence for functional fetal serotonin 1 receptors. *Developmental Brain Research, 33,* 285–289.

Winslow, J. T., & Miczek, K. A. (1983). Habituation of aggression in mice: Pharmacological evidence of catecholaminergic and serotonergic mediation. *Psychopharmacology, 81,* 286–291.

Yehuda, R., Giller, E. L., & Mason, J. W. (1993). Psychoneuroendocrine assessment of posttraumatic stress disorder: Current progress and new directions. *Progress in Neuropsychopharmacology and Biological Psychiatry, 17,* 541–550.

Zuckerman, M. (1991). Basic Dimensions of Personality. In M. Zuckerman (Ed.), *Psychobiology of personality.* New York: Cambridge University Press.

Zuckerman, M., Kuhlman, D. M., & Camac, C. (1988). What lies beyond E and N? Factor analysis of scales believed to measure basic dimensions of personality. *Journal of Personality and Social Psychology, 54,* 96–107.

CHAPTER 4

Impulsiveness

ERNEST S. BARRATT and MATTHEW S. STANFORD

OVERVIEW AND BACKGROUND

Impulsiveness as a personality trait relates to the *control* of thoughts and behavior. It interacts with other personality traits to impact everyday behaviors that are classified as "normal, pathological, or marginal" within the context of a social definition of mental health. This classification of behaviors can be based on several different procedures including the use of cutoff points on a measurement scale that separates normal from pathological behaviors. A profile of several personality trait measures or categories of symptoms or signs postulated a priori may be used to describe pathological states. Regardless of the procedure used, "categories" variously defined ultimately guide therapeutic interventions. Impulsivity in combination with other personality traits produces a wide range of profiles that can be related to normal or pathological behaviors. Does impulsiveness have the same effect on thoughts and behaviors in all combinations? What role does impulsiveness play in psychopathology? These are the main questions to be addressed in this chapter.

The approach taken here to answering these questions is based on the assumption that measures of impulsiveness reflect the theory that led to their development and refinement. Various self-report and other measurement techniques will be reviewed by comparing them with the Barratt Impulsiveness Scale (BIS). This self-report measure is the first one developed specifically to measure impulsiveness that was not part of an omnibus test battery like the Thurstone Temperament Schedule (Thurstone, 1953). The BIS has been correlated with a wide range of impulsiveness and other personality measures and has formed the basis for a research program on impulsiveness covering over three decades. The BIS has been revised to achieve a more specific measure of impulsiveness with many item analyses leading to changes in its subfactor structure. The total scores on all forms of the BIS have been significantly correlated with each other ranging from .65 to .98, even though the sub-factors on the various forms have changed. The significant intercorre-lations among the total scores on the different forms of the BIS along with the significant correlations of the BIS with other selected self-report measures of "control" led Barratt and Patton (1983) to hypothe-size that impulsiveness is part of a higher order personality dimension that they labeled "action-oriented." Their spectrum of action-oriented personality traits included risk taking, sensation seeking, extroversion, and other control traits.

There are many measures and definitions of impulsiveness based on a wide range of models including psychosocial development (L'Abate, 1993), arousal (Eysenck & Eysenck, 1985), information processing (Dickman, 1993), learning theory (Wallace & Newman, 1990), and bio-logical substrates (Gray, 1987; Stein, Hollander, & Liebowitz, 1993). The Barratt and Patton (1983) approach assumes that there is some truth in all these theories of impulsiveness because data consistent with the construct defined by each theory have been explicated. Barratt (1991; Barratt, Kent, & Stanford, 1995) has proposed that data derived within the dif-ferent models using different measurements and searching for different correlates in construct validity studies should be examined for conver-gence in defining impulsiveness in an approach similar to the multitrait-multimethod technique outlined by Campbell and Fiske (1959). Barratt (1991; Barratt et al., 1995) further proposed that a "theory-neutral" model that allows for synthesizing data from various research programs and different disciplines should be developed. He used a general systems approach as a theory-neutral model to define impulsiveness and other personality traits separately and in combination.

Barratt (Barratt et al., 1995) has also indicated that restricting the mea-surement of impulsiveness to self-report, rating scale, or structured in-terview techniques is an incomplete approach to measuring impulsiveness. The use of biological measures as well as environmental (primarily so-cial stimuli) or milieu measures of impulsiveness will add significantly to the predictive value of self-report measures. This suggestion involves a shift in thinking about the construct validity of impulsiveness and other personality traits. For example, instead of searching for the biological cor-relates of impulsiveness, biological measures that are not correlated with self-report measures will be used along with self-report measures to as-sess impulsiveness in predictive validity studies. Apter and colleagues (1990) for example, suggest that a cluster of psychopathological dimen-sions is related to serotonin abnormalities including anxiety, depressed mood, impulsivity, and aggression dysregulation. The correlation of sero-tonin with these personality traits varies. Where it has a low correlation, the serotonin measures per se may be useful as a predictor measure of personality in validity studies. As noted, this involves a shift in thinking from the more traditional approaches to defining personality traits. Barratt (Barratt et al., 1995) and others (Rorer & Widiger, 1983) propose that to significantly increase the ability to predict criterion measures such as categories of psychopathology, a major change has to be made in measuring personality traits. Although the search for biological correlates of personality traits is important in construct validity studies, the higher the correlations between the self-report and biological measures, the less valuable will the two types of measurements be as independent predictors of the same criterion measures.

Impulsiveness as a personality trait is important because it relates to self-control and volition within the social context. Social norms for behavior are codified in mores and laws. Persons are expected to behave within socially defined behavioral limits. Conformity often involves "overcoming human nature" in learning to be civilized. Some persons appear to be more genetically predisposed than others to have problems in conforming. Research (Forzano & Logue, 1992; Gray, 1987; Klinteberg et al., 1992; Linnoila et al., 1983; Stein et al., 1993) indicates that impulsiveness is part of a system that is involved in controlling impulses that lead to being "civilized," especially from a biological and genetic viewpoint. Impulsiveness will be reviewed in this chapter within this broader context.

This chapter will be divided into three parts:

1. A review of measurements and related definitions and theories.
2. A brief overview of impulsiveness within Barratt's general systems theory approach to defining personality traits.
3. Suggestions for future research.

In evaluating theories, it is important to appreciate that they are evolving and are not complete at any one point in time. As new data accumulate, theories change. Within this context, Barratt's current theory includes the concept of temporal information processing as being important in locating impulsiveness within a spectrum of personality traits and related behaviors that define selected personality disorders. We will review data indicating that temporal information processing is related to language development, selected measures of psychomotor performance, impulsiveness, and socialization.

No predictive studies have compared the relationship of differing impulsiveness measures with a common set of criterion measures. Convergence of data related to defining impulsiveness has involved many construct or concurrent validity studies, but predictive validity studies have been neglected in general. Speculations that can lead to further predictive validity studies will be made throughout this chapter.

Impulsiveness has recently been reviewed in depth in McCown, Johnson, and Shure's (1993) book, *The Impulsive Client: Theory, Research, and Treatment*. There are extensive reviews of techniques and theories in this book, and these will not be repeated here. The divergent theories of impulsiveness discussed in their book and elsewhere indicate the need for a model that integrates data in a theory-neutral synthesis.

MEASURING AND DEFINING IMPULSIVENESS: FROM THE NORMAL TO THE PATHOLOGICAL

Self-Report Measures

The relationship of self-report measures of impulsiveness to criterion measures depends primarily on the item content of the scales. The Barratt Impulsiveness Scale (BIS) has been formally revised 11 times (BIS-11) to achieve a more "pure" measure of impulsiveness with many nonpublished item analyses intervening between the published analyses. The purposes of these revisions will not be reviewed in depth because that has been discussed elsewhere (Barratt, 1965, 1994; Barratt & Patton, 1983; Patton, Stanford, & Barratt, in press). The original and current BIS items will be contrasted and related to other self-report measures to better understand how impulsiveness, as measured by the BIS, relates to other measures of impulsiveness and other personality traits.

The BIS was first used along with measures of anxiety in psychophysiological and psychomotor performance studies (Barratt, 1959; 1963b). From a theoretical viewpoint, it was developed within the Hull-Spence learning theory to measure the construct of "oscillation" in contrast to "habit strength," which Taylor had shown was related to anxiety (Taylor & Spence, 1952; Taylor, 1958). The Taylor Manifest Anxiety Scale (TMAS; Taylor, 1953) did not correlate significantly with the BIS (Barratt, 1959). Many early item analyses were done not only to arrive at internal consistency within the BIS but also to eliminate items that correlated with anxiety measures. The first published revision of the BIS (Barratt, 1965) indicated that a pool of BIS items was orthogonal to a pool of anxiety items. A rotated varimax solution of the BIS-5 items produced four factors that were labeled speed of cognitive response, impulsiveness, adventure seeking (extroversion), and risk taking (Table 4.1). There were some suggestions in this study that "restraint" and "impulsiveness" may be a bipolar dimension. In summarizing the results, Barratt (1965) noted:

TABLE 4.1   Rotated Varimax Solution of BIS-5 Items

No.	Item	I	II	III	IV	Item Scored	Phi with Total Score
4	In the morning I usually bound out of bed energetically.	20	34	01	−08	T	15
9	I usually think before I act.	−20	37	01	−06	F	42
20	I make up my mind quickly.	89	−03	−03	−05	T	−37
57	I make up my mind easily.	86	02	−02	01	T	−27
75	I like to do things on the spur of the moment.	27	−09	05	26	T	−36
10	I like mathematics.	01	30	00	09	F	28
13	I like to work crossword puzzles.	06	30	24	02	F	13
14	I like classical music.	03	30	−06	05	F	24
17	I like detailed work.	−01	77	01	−01	F	30
24	I like to solve complex problems.	15	54	−01	28	F	26
27	I consider myself always careful.	03	29	−03	−05	F	31
38	I don't like to wait for traffic lights to change.	−02	−34	−04	11	T	−26
43	I like work requiring patience and carefulness.	03	84	−08	02	F	39
48	I easily become impatient with people.	−08	−45	−03	15	T	−30
68	It is easy for me to concentrate on my work.	01	51	15	04	F	31
72	My interests tend to change quickly.	01	−40	−05	03	T	−36
3	I like to take a chance just for the excitement.	07	−05	24	67	T	−30
46	I like work involving competition.	14	13	31	06	T	−19
51	In watching games, I often yell along with others.	11	00	41	05	T	−20
54	I don't like to eat outdoors.	−04	−08	−34	05	F	18
55	I don't enjoy meeting relatives at family reunions.	−09	−17	−30	10	F	−10
63	I like work that has lots of excitement.	07	06	48	38	T	−23
78	My friends consider me to be happy-go-lucky.	15	−13	36	03	T	−41
84	I like being where there is something going on all the time.	04	−07	74	−11	T	−16
21	As a youngster I rarely took part in risky stunts.	−17	13	−08	−54	F	35
39	I frequently feel on top of the world.	14	−03	10	38	T	−24

Note: Factors are: I, Speed of cognitive response; II, Impulsiveness (lack of impulse control); III, Adventure seeking (extroversion); and IV, Risk taking. From Barratt, 1965.

London and Rosenhan (1964) observed that "delay of gratification can be considered an explanation in search of a phenomenon. Since Dewey and Freud, impulse control or delay of gratification has been evoked as a critical explanatory concept for the development of the socialized self and its absence as an explanation of psychopathy, delinquency and such." The writer suggests that the invariant second-order factor of impulsiveness presented in this study is a basic element in the phenomenon needed for this explanation. (p. 533)

This item analysis of the BIS was followed by a long series of unpublished analyses aimed at developing not only a scale orthogonal to anxiety but also an item pool that more specifically measured impulsiveness in contrast to sensation seeking, extroversion, risk taking, and other action-oriented traits.

As research on impulsiveness progressed, Barratt continued to look for a convergence of data that would more clearly define impulsiveness. Based on these analyses, clinical experiences, and a review of the literature, he defined on an a priori basis three facets of impulsiveness: (a) *motor impulsiveness,* or "acting without thinking"; this is similar to the Eysencks' impulsiveness subfactor that they labeled "impulsiveness narrow" (Eysenck & Eysenck, 1977); (b) *cognitive impulsiveness,* which involves making up one's mind quickly; in Barratt's 1965 factor analysis, a cognitive impulsiveness factor had been identified that was similar to the Eysencks' (1977) liveliness factor; (c) *nonplanning* impulsiveness, or a "lack of futuring"; this was similar to Mezey and Cohen's (1961) and Cottle's (1976) time zone measures involving the ability to plan ahead. On the basis of the preceding a priori analysis the BIS-10 items were divided into the three categories. Items typical of each subfactor were (a) *motor impulsiveness:* "I do things without thinking," "I act on the spur of the moment"; (b) *cognitive impulsiveness:* "I have extraneous thoughts when thinking," "I make up my mind quickly"; (c) *nonplanning impulsiveness:* "I am more interested in the present than in the future," "I plan tasks carefully." In the initial empirical test of the BIS-10 factor structure, the three subsets of items were confirmed as oblique factors with an average factor intercorrelation of .34. Subsequent empirical analyses by Barratt (1994) and others (Luengo, Carrillo-de-la-Peña, & Otero, 1991) confirmed the motor and nonplanning factors but did not confirm the cognitive impulsiveness factor.

In a recent analysis of the factor structure of the BIS-11 (Patton et al., in press) six first-order and three second-order factors were identified. The first-order (Table 4.2) factors were labeled as follows:

1. *Attention,* or "focusing on the task at hand."
2. *Motor impulsiveness,* or "acting on the spur of the moment."
3. *Self-control,* or "planning and thinking carefully."
4. *Cognitive complexity,* or "enjoying challenging mental tasks."
5. *Perseverance,* or a consistent life style.
6. *Cognitive instability,* or "thought insertions and racing thoughts."

TABLE 4.2   Principal Components Analysis of BIS-11 Items (Oblique Rotation)

BIS-11 Items	First-Order Factors						
	1	2	3	4	5	6	h^2
11. I "squirm" at plays or lectures.	**0.84**	0.17	−0.08	−0.03	0.03	0.02	0.78
32. I am restless at the theater or lectures.	**0.84**	0.19	−0.12	−0.06	0.00	−0.03	0.76
5. I don't "pay attention."	**0.57**	0.04	0.16	−0.02	0.27	0.02	0.49
9. I concentrate easily.*	**0.55**	−0.28	0.26	0.01	0.12	0.26	0.55
21. I am a steady thinker.*	**0.45**	−0.04	0.37	0.17	−0.02	−0.06	0.54
17. I act "on impulse."	0.15	**0.74**	0.08	−0.02	−0.20	0.06	0.65
20. I act on the spur of the moment.	0.12	**0.72**	0.19	−0.10	−0.19	0.01	0.65
23. I buy things on impulse.	−0.08	**0.59**	−0.04	0.28	0.10	0.11	0.47
3. I make up my mind quickly.	0.11	**0.48**	−0.14	0.04	0.11	0.06	0.41
2. I do things without thinking.	0.04	**0.42**	0.29	0.15	0.16	0.06	0.47
28. I spend or charge more than I earn.	0.02	**0.37**	0.04	0.20	0.35	−0.02	0.38
4. I am happy-go-lucky.	0.12	**0.32**	0.01	−0.10	0.17	0.11	0.21
12. I am a careful thinker.*	0.17	−0.13	**0.64**	0.17	−0.18	0.05	0.55
1. I plan tasks carefully.*	−0.05	0.16	**0.64**	−0.04	0.11	−0.10	0.47
8. I am self-controlled.*	0.10	0.00	**0.63**	−0.24	0.08	−0.17	0.40
7. I plan trips well ahead of time.*	−0.13	0.17	**0.57**	−0.17	0.29	0.02	0.50
13. I plan for job security.*	−0.32	0.06	**0.49**	0.22	0.16	−0.06	0.43
14. I say things without thinking.	0.21	0.16	**0.45**	0.00	−0.17	0.17	0.44
15. I like to think about complex problems.*	0.10	0.06	0.03	**0.71**	−0.06	−0.10	0.54
33. I like puzzles.*	−0.10	−0.09	−0.05	**0.68**	0.01	−0.06	0.46
10. I save regularly.*	−0.18	0.34	0.18	**0.46**	−0.07	0.14	0.43
31. I am more interested in the present than the future.	−0.01	0.16	−0.12	**0.36**	0.04	0.24	0.21
18. I get easily bored when solving thought problems.	0.29	0.20	−0.05	**0.34**	0.26	−0.15	0.36
22. I change residences.	0.22	−0.02	−0.07	−0.05	**0.69**	−0.05	0.51
16. I change jobs.	−0.05	0.06	0.13	−0.16	**0.54**	0.18	0.39
34. I am future oriented.*	0.03	−0.11	0.26	0.15	**0.53**	−0.06	0.42
24. I can only think about one problem at a time.	0.15	−0.21	−0.13	0.31	**0.38**	0.20	0.33
30. I often have extraneous thoughts when thinking.	0.12	0.05	−0.14	0.20	−0.06	**0.77**	0.68
6. I have "racing" thoughts.	0.08	0.18	−0.05	−0.21	0.14	**0.58**	0.46
25. I change hobbies.	−0.17	0.29	−0.05	−0.10	0.19	**0.35**	0.28
% Total Variance	18.3	7.6	6.5	5.3	5.1	4.5	

Note: Items scored on 4–point scale: Rarely/Never (1), Occasionally (2), Often (3), Almost Always/Always (4). Bold numbers indicate items used to define factors. From Patton, Stanford, & Barratt, in press.
* Item scored 4, 3, 2, 1.

A second-order factor analysis produced three factors (Table 4.3):

1. *Attentional impulsiveness,* combining the first-order factors of attention and cognitive instability.
2. *Motor impulsiveness,* combining first-order factors motor impulsiveness and perseverance.
3. *Nonplanning impulsiveness,* combining first-order factors self-control and cognitive complexity.

Three similar second-order impulsiveness factors have been found in other studies (Gerbing, Ahadi, & Patton, 1987; Luengo et al., 1991; Parker, Bagby, & Webster, 1993). Cronbach's alpha for the internal consistency of the BIS-11 total score was .82. The BIS-11 total score correlated .98 with the BIS-10 total score.

In this study and recent past studies, the motor impulsiveness and nonplanning subscales were clearly defined by separate oblique factors. Cognitive impulsiveness per se was not defined clearly. Cognitive items were evident on all the second-order factors although the *attentional* impulsiveness factor was heavily weighted toward cognitive impulsiveness. The authors (Patton et al., in press) noted:

> In the current study, cognitive items loaded on all the factors suggesting that cognitive processes underlie impulsiveness in general. There are several possible reasons for not identifying a cognitive impulsiveness factor per se. The first and most obvious reason would be that a cognitive impulsiveness factor does not exist and, as noted above, "thought processes" in general underlie the personality trait of impulsiveness. It is also possible that subjects cannot independently assess thought processes that characterize impulsiveness.

TABLE 4.3   Second-Order Factor Structure of the BIS-11

First-Order Factor	Factor I	Factor II	Factor III	h^2
Factor 6	**0.74**	−0.16	0.07	0.55
Factor 1	**0.66**	0.02	0.03	0.44
Factor 5	−0.30	**0.84**	0.14	0.75
Factor 2	0.39	**0.65**	−0.21	0.67
Factor 4	0.00	−0.06	**0.91**	0.82
Factor 3	0.39	0.25	**0.50**	0.54
% Total Variance	28.0	18.9	17.1	

Note: Bold numbers indicate first-order factors used to define second-order factors. From Patton, Stanford, & Barratt, in press.

The correlations among second-order factors in this study ranged from .46 to .53 ($p < .0001$), which indicates that the item pool is a general measure of the personality trait of impulsiveness.

In a study of aggression among male inmates, the BIS-10 total score correlated .32 ($p < .001$) with the Neuroticism, Extroversion, Openness to Excellence Personality Inventory (NEO-PI) (Costa & McCrae, 1985) facet scale of impulsiveness. The BIS-10 motor impulsiveness and non-planning subscales were also significantly correlated with the NEO impulsiveness facet score, but the BIS-10 cognitive impulsiveness subscale was not. The NEO impulsiveness facet scale does not contain cognitive items or items that relate to planning ahead. The items primarily involve "the inability to resist cravings and temptations." Within the NEO-PI, the impulsiveness facet loads on the second-order Neuroticism factor, one of the "Big Five" personality dimensions (Digman, 1994). Other facet scales that load on the NEO-PI Neuroticism dimension are anxiety, hostility, and depression, which are part of what Barratt and Patton (1983) termed the "feeling" personality dimensions. Feeling and action-oriented have been orthogonal dimensions in Barratt's research as indicated by the early studies on impulsiveness and anxiety (Barratt, 1959, 1965). Thus, even though the BIS-10 total score and NEO-PI impulsiveness facet score correlated at a significant level, they are not factorially comparable, which substantiates the point made earlier in this chapter and emphasized by Barratt and Patton (1983)—all tests labeled as measures of impulsiveness do not necessarily measure the same personality trait.

Within the Eysencks' original personality model, impulsiveness and socialization were subscales within the second-order personality dimension of extroversion (E; Eysenck & Eysenck, 1963). They later revised their model to include a psychoticism (P) dimension, and impulsiveness then loaded on P. The BIS correlated .68 with the Eysencks' E dimension in the Eysenck Personality Inventory (EPI) (Barratt & Patton, 1983). After the Eysencks' shifted impulsiveness items to the P factor, the BIS-10 correlated .66 with the P and .08 with the E among inpatient substance abuse patients (O'Boyle & Barratt, 1993). The BIS-10 also correlated significantly with the Eysencks' impulsiveness questionnaire (Luengo et al., 1991).

The important point, again, is that not all self-report measures of impulsiveness measure the same personality trait. Thus, in construct validity studies in which behavioral, cognitive, biological, and environmental (social) variables are related to self-report measures of impulsiveness, it is important to be sensitive to the item content of the self-report measures being used.

In studying the interrelationships of personality traits and the relationship of trait profiles to criterion measures, the wording of items can produce unexpected results. In Barratt's current study of aggression, the

BIS-10 total score correlated significantly (.35, p < .0001) with the *anger-out* score on Spielberger's AX-24 scale (Spielberger, Jacobs, Russell, & Crane, 1983) and *negatively* with the anger-control score ($-.41, p$ < .0001). Although we could hypothesize that aggression was related to both anger and impulsiveness, one would not expect these two personality traits to be correlated if the feeling dimensions and acting-out dimensions are independent. It is probable that these self-report measures are significantly correlated in part due to the specific content variance of the items and not to the true variance of anger or impulsiveness per se. To develop a self-report measure of anger-out, items that measure "self-control of behavior" are often used. For example, "I do things like slam doors" is a self-control item as well as an anger item. On the basis of some biological theories of personality, however, one would expect anger and impulsiveness to be separate personality dimensions (e.g., within Gray's theory; Gray, 1987). This also emphasizes the importance of reviewing the item analyses of various measures. One could for example arrive at a second-order "impulsive/hostility" dimension, based on self-report measures, that is an epiphenomenon and not a true impulsive/hostility dimension. If one then proceeds to get biological correlates of the impulsive/hostility dimension, it could be misleading because the self-report factor itself is not a meaningful measure of a specific construct within nature.

Other Measures of Impulsiveness

Beyond self-report measures, a wide range of behavioral and other assessment techniques have been used to measure impulsiveness (Barratt & Patton, 1983; Oas, 1985; Wallace & Newman, 1990). Within the early clinical literature, especially among psychoanalysts, impulsiveness and impulse control were important clinical concepts that were assessed by clinical interviews. This section will be limited to a brief discussion of impulse control in psychoanalysis. The main reason for briefly discussing the analytic approach is that the distinction between cognitive and motor impulsiveness has been discussed at length in the analytic literature in attempting to differentiate between acting-out and impulse disorders (Frosch & Wortis, 1954; Frosch, 1977). The relationship of impulsiveness to antisocial disorders and psychopathy will be discussed later, and the analytic literature provides a historical perspective for better understanding these relationships.

Impulsiveness is defined in this chapter in the broader context of the control of behavior and thoughts in society in contrast to the place of impulsiveness within the *structure* of personality per se. This broader approach is helpful in defining both criterion measures and predictors within a "natural system" as Fiske (1971) discussed in his guidelines for conceptualizing a variable. Both predictor and criterion measures are developed from what were originally informal observations of natural events. As informal observations of behavior were studied more rigorously, more formal measurement tools such as self-report inventories or behavioral performance measures were developed. Within the writings of the psychoanalysts, the references to impulsiveness include more general personality attributes than the constructs measured by most current psychometric instruments. This occurred because assessments were made primarily by interviewing persons, not by using measures that were scientifically developed. It is interesting that concepts of the impulse control disorders that were common in the analytic literature are being reexamined within the "cognitive revolution" of the past few decades, especially within the domain of cognitive neuroscience. The concepts of conscious control of behavior, volition, and the development of language are part of this current attempt to correlate cognitive and biological measures (Baars, 1988).

Within the psychoanalytic tradition, the concept of impulsiveness has had a varied history. The traditional Freudian approach focused on "the etiology and nature of impulsive thoughts" (McCown & DeSimone, 1993). Frosch and Wortis (1954) proposed a "nosology of the impulse disorders" primarily within an analytic framework but recognizing the role of genetic or biological correlates. They defined an impulse as "the sudden unpremeditated welling-up of a drive toward some action, which usually has the quality of hastiness and a lack of deliberation" (p. 132). "Acting-out and its relation to impulse disorders" was explored in a panel at the annual meeting of the American Psychoanalytic Association in 1956 (Kanzer, 1957). The distinction between cognitive and motor aspects of impulsiveness were pervasive in the panel presentations. Fenichel, for example, discussed the role of memory in acting-out. Frosch discussed a hierarchy of delay mechanisms and Greenson discussed the role of language and speech in developing impulse control. In a later paper, Frosch (1977) drew a distinction between patients with impulse control disorders and psychopaths, the latter lacking a conscience and the experience of guilt with regard to their antisocial behaviors. Frosch noted that patients with impulse control disorders are "intolerant" of tension and frustration" and "whatever they need, they must have immediately. They cannot postpone reactions; they generally act instead of think" (p. 300). Consistent with the "multi-impulsive personality disorder" discussed later in this chapter, he noted that "such impulsivity may reflect itself in many spheres, and may be reflected in a life-style characterized by restlessness and a constant need to be on the go, a running from one activity to another. These patients are rarely able to be by themselves or to concentrate on anything in a sustained fashion" (p. 300). Thus, it is clear in the analytic literature that there is both a cognitive and motor component to impulsiveness in a broad sense.

Monroe (1970), in his book *Episodic Behavioral Disorders,* integrated psychoanalytic and biological concepts into a complex dyscontrol theory. He substituted the concept of episodic dyscontrol for impulsiveness and acting-out. Episodic dyscontrol was defined as:

> An abrupt single act or short series of acts with a common intention car-
> ried through to completion with at least a partial relief of tension or grat-
> ification of a specific need. As a subclass of the episodic behavioral
> disorders it also has the characteristic of a maladaptive, precipitous in-
> terruption in the life style or life flow of the individual. (p. 26)

Monroe anticipated current theories (e.g., Gray, 1987) that explicate separate control and impulse systems. He noted that "episodic dyscontrol is
an imbalance between drives and controls wherein the drives overwhelm
inhibiting control mechanisms" (p. 26).

These theories have more than a historical interest. They define impulsiveness within a broad social framework and impart a broad role to
it in coping with everyday life problems. The concepts of unconscious
motivation, the use of language in controlling behavior, the perceptual
synthesis of stimuli, and motor output had special roles in analytic theory and were partly instrumental in providing the bases for interpreting
the responses of projective tests which are still used to measure impulsiveness related to psychopathy, antisocial behaviors, and other disorders
(Gacono & Meloy, 1992, 1994).

Biological Theories

As noted previously, most biological studies of impulsiveness involve the
search for correlates of self-report measures. It would be equally logical to
start with biological measures and search for self-report measures of
various personality traits including impulsiveness, similar to Cloninger's
(1987) approach in developing the Tridimensional Personality Questionnaire. Barratt (1994; Barratt et al., 1995) also has suggested that biological and behavioral measures that do not correlate with self-report measures
could be used as predictor measures of impulsiveness and other personality measures. This section will briefly review one example of a biological
substrate that appears to relate to a spectrum of personality measures.

Serotonin levels have been inversely correlated with self-report measures of impulsiveness (Brown et al., 1989; Kent et al., 1988) and impulsive behavior (Candito, Askenazy, Myquel, Chambon, & Darcourt, 1993;
Linnoila et al., 1983). As noted earlier, Van Praag and his colleagues (Apter

et al., 1990) suggest that there is a serotonergically linked cluster of personality traits that include anxiety, depressed mood, impulsivity, and aggression dysregulation. As noted earlier, Barratt (1965) has shown that self-report measures of anxiety and impulsiveness define orthogonal factors that would be inconsistent with Apter et al.'s suggestion. In contrast, Costa and McCrae (1985) found impulsiveness to load on a second-order Neuroticism dimension, which would be consistent with the proposed serotonergically linked cluster. This is a confusing picture with regard to impulsiveness, and factor analyses of large pools of items similar to Parker et al.'s (1993) will not resolve this issue without including other than self-report measures.

Siever and Davis (1991) outlined a heuristic model for taking a psychobiological perspective to personality disorders. Their approach, however, also emphasized biological correlates of personality factors and disorders and not a search for biological and behavioral measures that can be combined with self-report and rating scale instruments as independent measures of a trait. Concentrating on the self-report measures of personality may actually have been misleading and masked "the true personality dimensions that exist in nature." Widiger, Trull, Clarkin, Sanderson, and Costa (1994) have recently discussed in depth the relationships of personality traits to personality disorders.

Impulsiveness Combined with Other Personality Traits

What effect does impulsiveness have on behavior when it is combined with other personality traits? Barratt (1959, 1965, 1972) studied the effects of impulsiveness and anxiety on performance in a wide range of laboratory tasks, psychophysiological measures, and everyday life experiences. As noted, Barratt (1965) developed a pool of impulsiveness items that was orthogonal to a pool of anxiety items. Because the two item pools were not significantly correlated, the four quadrants of a scatter diagram had an approximately equal number of subjects in each. Thus, four groups of subjects could be compared; high impulsive-high anxiety (HIHA); low impulsive-low anxiety (LILA); high impulsive-low anxiety (HILA); and low impulsive-high anxiety (LIHA).

Comparing the performance of these four groups on perceptual-motor tasks, Barratt (1967b) found that HILA subjects (Ss) performed significantly less efficiently than the other three groups across a wide range of laboratory tasks. For some tasks, the interactive effects of anxiety and impulsiveness were less obvious than on others. Barratt (1967b) noted, "The measurements reflecting primarily a motor response as opposed to the sensory processing measurements appear to be more affected by impulsiveness." In studies involving the Porteus mazes, the high impulsiveness Ss had significantly more "tremors" evident in their tracings than did the low impulsiveness Ss. High impulsive Ss were often significantly more variable in their performance in selected tasks than were low impulsiveness Ss. These results led Barratt to conduct a series of studies in lower animals of neural structures involved in motor control and seizure discharges that he hypothesized to be related to impulsiveness (Barratt, 1963a, 1967a, 1972). The early animal studies were aimed at uncovering neural mechanisms that were related to controlling "variability" of motor performance. The results of the animal studies indicated that selected neural structures (e.g., amygdala and cerebellum) were related to intraindividual variability of performance on complex operant tasks (McDiarmiad & Barratt, 1969). These same neural substrates have also been implicated in seizure disorders. Based on both the human and lower animal research results, Barratt (1972) hypothesized that in general, impulsiveness appeared to be related more to variability of psychomotor performance and anxiety more to the mean level of performance. In some instances, the two personality traits and related biological substrates interacted to influence performance, especially as previously noted, when impulsiveness is high and anxiety is low.

Barratt and White (1969) studied the relationship of impulsiveness and anxiety to academic performance and attitudes among medical students. Four medical students in each of the four quadrants of a scatter diagram interrelating impulsiveness and anxiety were studied ($N = 16$) over the first three years of medical school. The N was small because the purpose of the study was to assess these students "in depth." A wide range of measurements including personality measures, semistructured psychiatric interviews, academic grades, social ratings from fraternity members, spouses and professors' description of the students' social skills, and Q sort ratings to determine the students' concepts of their "ideal selves," "true selves," and a typical medical student were obtained. The goal of this study was to provide the bases for studying the interrelationships of impulsiveness and anxiety in everyday life coping. From a "social adjustment" viewpoint, all the HIHA Ss sought psychiatric help or counseling during the first three years of medical school while only one other subject (LIHA) sought help. The HILA Ss had many "sociopathic" tendencies: "They were not well integrated into their fraternities . . . they expressed dislike for fraternity affairs and their fraternity officers considered them to be trouble makers." In contrast to their peers' evaluations, professors who were not involved with the HILA Ss as extensively as their peers had a much more positive view of them. These findings are not surprising since high impulsiveness and low anxiety are two characteristics of psychopaths (Cleckley, 1976). What is important is the relationship of the psychomotor performance data to high and low impulsiveness. The HILA Ss were consistently less efficient and more variable than the other three groups in performing psychomotor tasks. As previously noted, impulsiveness and motor performance may also involve the same neural substrates as those involved in seizure disorders. At a subseizure threshold, the activity of these neural substrates may be manifest in more variable behavior. This will be pursued later in this chapter in the discussion of temporal information processing related to impulsiveness and impulsive aggression. These early observations also led to our using anticonvulsants in the study of impulsive aggression.

As noted earlier, Van Praag and his colleagues (Apter et al., 1990) proposed a "serotonergically linked" cluster of personality characteristics. Their research suggested that selected biological measures may be more related to the psychological characteristics of patients than to diagnostic categories. That is, biological measures may be more related to symptoms and signs than to diagnostic categories per se. In their study of 60 acute psychiatric patients, they found that impulsivity as measured by self-report correlated .48 ($p < .001$) with trait anxiety and .43 ($p < .001$) with anger. All three of these personality traits were significantly correlated with suicide risk.

The Apter et al. (1990) study raises an important point in studying the place of selected personality traits within personality structure and also the relationship of personality traits to clinical criterion measures. Many studies of personality traits have been done using "normal" Ss. Although it is important to describe personality structure among normals, especially from a dimensional view of psychopathology, the personality structures of patients and other "non-normal" Ss are often different and the relative role of selected personality traits in combination (profiles) may be different in normals and non-normals. An analogy is the relationships of various medications on physiological measures such as the EEG or heart rate. The uptake of medication in a non-normal system may cause different changes in these peripheral physiological measures than it causes in a normal system due to metabolic differences or deficiencies. Barratt found the factor structure of the BIS to be different between college students and psychiatric inpatients (Barratt, 1994), comparable to the metabolic system being different. Caution then is warranted in generalizing the relationships between personality traits and criterion measures found in normals to non-normal populations. The role of impulsiveness in a non-normal person may be different in relationship to personality traits in a normal individual. This further emphasizes the need for a "theory-neutral" model to search for convergence across modality different measures to define personality traits.

Zuckerman (1993) has recently speculated about common biological bases that may explain the positive relationships between sensation seeking measures and impulsiveness. He discusses neurotransmitter systems that he feels may be related to behavioral inhibition and impulse or reward systems. He noted that the neurotransmitters involved in reward and impulse control systems are not clear. Probably one of the most replicated findings in relating biological substrates to personality is the inverse relationships of serotonin to impulsiveness and other action-oriented personality traits. Yet, Huang, Stanford, and Barratt (1994) found a significant positive relationship between the frequency of spontaneous eye blinks and impulsiveness. Eye blinks are a putative dopaminergic-related behavior (Karson, 1983).

The effects of different personality traits including impulsiveness in combination with other personality traits have not been studied extensively and such studies are badly needed. As Zuckerman (1993) notes, "A broad theoretical and practical perspective is needed to encompass the biological and behavioral complexities of impulsiveness" (p. 87).

Impulsiveness and Psychiatric Disorders

In addition to the contribution of psychoanalytic theory to an understanding of impulsiveness in psychopathology as previously discussed, several psychiatric disorders include impulsiveness as a symptom. These and the multi-impulsive personality disorder will be discussed below.

The concept of the "impulsivist: multi-impulsive personality disorder" was first proposed by Lacey and Evans (1986). They noted that impulsivity has been related to a wide range of disorders involving impulse control. They also noted that among patients in each of these clinic populations there were some patients who had a poor prognosis and who engaged in a wide range of different types of abuses within the general patterns of abuses for a specific disorder or across disorders. How does impulsiveness relate to the "multi-impulsive" personality?

Stanford and Barratt (1992) studied the role of impulsiveness in the multi-impulsive personality disorder among prison inmates. Using the BIS-10, they found that the motor impulsiveness subscale ("I act without thinking") was significantly related to the total number of impulse disorders an individual displayed. Age, education achievement, crime committed, and intelligence were controlled in the study. It was also found that inmates who exhibited three or more impulse disorders formed a markedly different subgroup of multi-impulsive Ss who scored significantly higher on the BIS. It was suggested that these Ss may suffer from a true generalized lack of impulse control. The clinical importance of these findings was summarized by Stanford and Barratt:

These observations have important implications for diagnosing selected impulse control disorders. For example, in DSM-III-R (American Psychiatric Association [APA], 1987) the diagnosis of intermittent explosive disorder (IED) has one criteria that "there are no signs of generalized impulsiveness or aggressiveness between episodes." Our data indicates that this is accurate if IED occurs in conjunction with two or less impulsive disorders. If it occurs as part of three or more impulse control disorders, generalized impulsiveness is probably present." (pp. 833–834)

The multi-impulsive disorder has been studied among adolescent psychiatric patients (Stanford, Ebner, Patton, & Williams, 1994), alcoholic women (Evans & Lacey, 1992), substance abusers (McCown, 1988; O'Boyle & Barratt, 1993) and prisoners (Kennedy & Grubin, 1990). Parenthetically, O'Boyle and Barratt (1993) also studied the relationship of the BIS-10 to DSM-III-R personality disorders. They found that the P dimension in the Eysencks' EPQ and the BIS-10 significantly differentiated between single and multiple substance abuse.

Impulsiveness has been related to a wide range of other psychiatric disorders and socially unacceptable behaviors including anorexia nervosa/bulimia nervosa (Sohlberg, Norring, Holmgren, & Rosmark, 1989), violent recidivism among criminals (De Jong, Virkkunen, & Linnoila, 1992), parole violation (Heilbrun, Heilbrun, & Heilbrun, 1978; Heilbrun, Knopf, & Bruner, 1976) and borderline personality disorder (Kruedelbach, McCormick, Schulz, & Grueneich, 1993; Russ, Shearin, Clarkin, Harrison, & Hull, 1993). McElroy, Hudson, Pope, Keck, and Aizley (1992) reviewed the literature on a wide range of impulse control disorders to search for common elements. They concluded that the impulse control disorders listed in DSM-III-R may represent forms of "affective spectrum disorders" that have common underlying biological substrates.

Research related to obsessive-compulsive disorders (OCD; Hollander, 1993) provides some possible further insight into impulsiveness. Common sense would indicate that the underlying biological substrates for compulsive and impulsive disorders would be different either in terms of biochemical or neural systems involved or in terms of concentrations of a single biochemical. Serotonin has been implicated in both impulsiveness and OCD although the results with OCD have been equivocal (Stein, Hollander, DeCaria, & Trungold, 1991; Pandey, Kim, Davis, & Pandey, 1993). Stein, Hollander, Simeon, & Cohen (1994) studied impulsivity among patients with OCD using the BIS-10R. They found that cognitive and nonplanning impulsivity were significantly positively correlated with severity of OCD symptoms on the Yale-Brown Obsessive-Compulsive Scale (Y-BOCS; Goodman, Price, & Rasmussen, 1989). The correlations in this study were small but did represent an interesting pattern.

The BIS-10R motor impulsivity subscale was not significantly related to the obsessive-compulsive disorders but the cognitive and nonplanning subscales were. The most consistent significant relationships were found between the Y-BOCS and the BIS-10R nonplanning subscale. As will be discussed, one possible explanation of the underlying "cause" of impulsiveness relates to temporal information processing in the central nervous system. It is possible that there are two types of OCD patients, one of whom is characterized by poor temporal information processing. Studies have implicated common brain structures (e.g., frontal lobes) that relate to behavioral control and temporal information processing in OCD (Calabrese, Colombo, Bonfanti, Scotti, & Scarone, 1993; Prichep et al., 1993; Insel, 1992; Towey et al., 1990). Developmental considerations are important here also, as Hoehn-Saric and Barksdale (1983) noted in a study of OCD patients who also had impulse control disorders. They noted the impulse control problems were evident in childhood, but the OCD symptoms were "superimposed at a later date." It is possible that a genetic predisposition is common to both impulsiveness and OCD but the predisposition comes into play at different developmental stages, possibly related to different social stressors. The relationship of impulsiveness to OCD is not clear at this point but presents an interesting research challenge that could add substantially to our understanding of both.

A GENERAL SYSTEMS THEORY APPROACH TO DEFINING IMPULSIVENESS AND OTHER PERSONALITY TRAITS

How can the divergent research results from the construct validity studies aimed at defining and measuring impulsiveness be assessed for convergence? Barratt (1991; Barratt et al., 1995) has suggested that there are two necessary conditions: (a) A theory-neutral model must be used; (b) impulsiveness measures other than self-report or rating scale procedures must be used. In this section, these two suggestions will be briefly explained.

What is a theory-neutral model? Much has been written in both philosophy and science about what constitutes a model from a scientific viewpoint. Definition of models, theories, paradigms, and hypothetical constructs have been extensively discussed without universal agreement. Barratt (Barratt, 1993, 1994; Barratt et al., 1995) has proposed the concept of a theory-neutral model to help synthesize findings from personality research to define personality traits and related functions. An example of using such a model will be briefly reviewed here to indicate how Barratt and his colleagues arrived at the importance of "temporal information processing" in conceptualizing impulsiveness as a personality trait.

Barratt (Barratt & Patton, 1983; Barratt, 1991) divides concepts and measurements of natural phenomena that are used to describe persons into four categories:

1. *Biological.* Especially, but not restricted to, the nervous system.
2. *Behavioral.* Body movements through time and space.
3. *Environmental.* From physical stimuli through social mores to characteristics of culture.
4. *Cognitive.* Thought processes including feelings, covert problem solving, and conscious and unconscious memories.

Research and theories related to these four classes of measurements and concepts are integrated by him using a negative feedback general systems theory model. Convergence of data and concepts *within* the model are sought as a basis for defining personality traits including impulsiveness. The model is always changing as new data accumulate. Data and concepts are reviewed with the model without being biased by theories or hypotheses that led to the data being gathered. Thus, a "theory-neutral" assessment. Why have a model at all?

A model may not be necessary. For Barratt (Barratt et al., 1995), it is a heuristic device that allows a wealth of data to be reviewed in a systematic way. The use of the model may lead to a theory. For example, the use of the construct of "temporal information processing" as a theoretical explanation that integrates impulsiveness with other personality characteristics of antisocial, impulsively aggressive persons is an example of arriving at a theoretical position using the model.

The model is based on the assumption that a personality trait can only be fully described by considering all four categories of data. The interrelationships of basic data used to describe the traits change over time. Criterion data are also described using the four basic categories in the model. Thus, it is important to distinguish construct validity and concurrent validity studies from predictive validity studies. As noted previously, the latter type of validity studies will answer many questions about constructs like impulsiveness that cannot be answered in construct validity studies.

The construct of impulsiveness as assessed with this model has been presented elsewhere (Barratt & Patton, 1983; Barratt, 1994) and will not be repeated in depth here. What will be presented is an overview of the early results in Barratt's study of impulsiveness along with the more recent data that has led to viewing temporal information processing as important in defining impulsiveness.

As noted earlier, Barratt's early research indicated that impulsivity was related to psychomotor efficiency (Barratt, 1959, 1967b). There were also indications that intraindividual variability of performance (behavior) on the psychomotor tasks was related to impulsiveness. Cognitive processes involving time judgments and planning ahead (Barratt, 1981, 1985) were related to the BIS and other impulsiveness measures. Psychophysiological (Barratt, 1963b) and cognitive psychophysiological studies (Barratt, 1981; Barratt & Patton, 1983) implicated the autonomic nervous system and frontal lobes in impulsiveness (e.g., using techniques such as visual augmenting/reducing: Barratt, Pritchard, Faulk, & Brandt, 1987; Carrillo-de-la-Peña & Barratt, 1993).

Barratt (Barratt & Patton, 1983) had proposed a number of different theoretical bases for these overall results. However, in recent studies of impulsive aggression, a review of the data against the background of the earlier studies revealed an interesting suggestion. Barratt (1991) had hypothesized that the personality traits of impulsiveness and anger/hostility would be significantly related to aggression and would distinguish between Ss with nonimpulsive and impulsive aggression. To test this hypothesis, three groups of Ss were obtained: matched noninmate controls, nonimpulsive aggressive inmates, and impulsive aggressive inmates. Inmates were selected for this study using correctional officers' reports of aggressive acts while in prison. Aggressive acts were reliably classified using a semistructured interview into impulsive aggressive versus nonimpulsive aggressive acts. An impulsive aggressive act involved a "hair trigger" response that was spontaneous and not premeditated. Both groups of inmates were significantly higher on impulsiveness and anger/hostility personality trait measures than were the noninmate controls. The two groups of inmates, all of whom met the criteria for antisocial personality disorder (PDI-R; Othmer, Penick, Powell, Read, & Othmer, 1989), were not significantly different from one another on impulsiveness and anger/hostility. Parenthetically, the concept of impulsive aggression has been used in the literature for many years but our results indicate that "impulsive" may not be an appropriate label because both groups of inmates were both high on impulsiveness and not significantly different in their impulsiveness scores. The two groups of inmates were different in several other ways however: (a) the impulsive aggressive inmates were significantly lower in verbal skills; for example their prorated verbal IQs, reading scores, and verbal memory scores were significantly lower than those of the nonimpulsive aggressive prisoner group; (b) the cognitive psychophysiological measures implicated differences in cortical areas that were consistent with the differences in verbal skills; the left anterior frontal cortex especially was shown to be the focus for differences in information processing in a P300 event related potential study involving verbal stimuli. Other differences in reaction time and cognitive psychophysiological differences consistent with past studies were also found. If one considers the verbal deficits and related cognitive psychophysiological findings within the context of past impulsiveness studies, an important convergence is evident. Current research by Tallal and others (Tallal, Galaburda, Llinas, & Von Euler, 1993) has shown that reading and reading disorders are related to temporal information processing in the brain. Barratt's earlier research suggested that both psychomotor, cognitive processing of time duration and "cognitive tempo" were related to impulsiveness. The factor analysis of the BIS-11 items indicated an attention factor and the cognitive psychophysiological data from the aggression study implicated "attention" areas of the brain as outlined by Posner (1992) and others (Nakagawa, 1991). Could temporal information processing be a key factor in impulsiveness? Stanford and Barratt (1994) analyzed data from 150 male adolescents that included verbal, motor, and impulsiveness measures (see Figure 4.1).

Three first-order factors (verbal skills, cognitive tempo, and finger tapping) combined to produce a second-order factor of temporal information processing. The BIS had a negative loading on the verbal skills

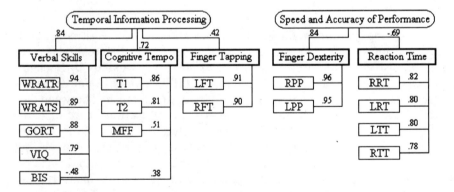

Figure 4.1 *Second-Order Temporal Information Processing Factor.* First-order factors in bold-lined boxes, second-order factors in rounded-end boxes. WRATR— Wide Range Achievement Test: Reading; WRATS—Wide Range Achievement Test: Spelling; GORT—Gray Oral Reading Test; VIQ—WISC-R Verbal IQ; BIS— Barratt Impulsiveness Scale (7B); T1—Time Reproduction (1 minute); T2—Time Reproduction (2 minutes); MFF—Matching Familiar Figures Test: Latency; LFT— Finger Tapping: Left Hand; RFT—Finger Tapping: Right Hand; RPP—Purdue Pegboard: Right Hand; LPP—Purdue Pegboard: Left Hand; RRT—Reaction Time: Right Hand; LRT—Reaction Time: Left Hand; LTT—Transport Time: Left Hand; RTT—Transport Time: Right Hand.

factor and, along with the Matching Familiar Figures Test (Kagan, Rosman, Day, Albert, & Phillips, 1964), a positive loading on the cognitive tempo factor. Thus, impulsiveness is negatively related to verbal skills and positively related to poor judgments of time duration. Finger tapping is a continuous performance task. Subjects with a steady rhythm perform better on this task than those who exhibit fits and starts in tapping. Barratt had shown in previous studies that timing and rhythm measures of motor and cognitive tasks were related to impulsiveness (Barratt, Patton, Olsson, & Zucker, 1981; Barratt, 1983). Reaction time and the Purdue Pegboard were not related to temporal information processing in the current study. In contrast to the continuous performance required in finger tapping, both reaction time and the Purdue Pegboard require segmented discontinuous motor responses. Reaction time was correlated with impulsiveness as in past studies, but in the factor analyses it did not load on the temporal information processing factor.

As discussed in the previous section, in the long history of the concept of impulsiveness from William James through psychoanalysis to current theories, both motor and cognitive dimensions of impulsiveness were evident. Barratt's current theory suggests that temporal information processing underlies these two aspects of impulsiveness.

FUTURE RESEARCH

Considering the large number of theories and related measurements of impulsiveness, it is obvious that research relating the different measures of impulsiveness to criterion measures is necessary. A study by Luengo, Carrillo-de-la-Peña, Otero, and Romero (1994) which found that the Eysencks' impulsiveness questionnaire better distinguished between antisocial and nonantisocial Ss than did Barratt's BIS-10 is an example of this. As they noted, the BIS-10 cognitive items probably led to its not being as good a predictor as the impulsiveness questionnaire. This leads to the next suggestion for research, mentioned several times in this chapter. Impulsiveness and other personality traits need to be measured by other than self-report or rating scale techniques. Behavioral and biological measures that may measure characteristics of impulsiveness that are not measured by self-report measures should be developed to complement self-report measures as predictors. Rather than only seeking biological correlates of self-report measures of personality traits for the purposes of construct validation, measures should be sought that don't correlate with the self-report measures. Long-term studies with well-defined criterion measures are needed to compare predictor measures, within each of the four basic categories suggested by Barratt.

REFERENCES

American Psychiatric Association. (1987). *Diagnostic and statistical manual of mental disorders* (3rd ed., rev.). Washington, DC: Author.

Apter, A., Van Praag, H. M., Plutchik, R., Sevy, S., Korn, M., & Brown, S. L. (1990). Interrelationships among anxiety, aggression, impulsivity, and mood: A serotonergically linked cluster? *Psychiatry Research, 32,* 191–199.

Baars, B. J. (1988). *A cognitive theory of consciousness.* Cambridge, MA: Cambridge University Press.

Barratt, E. S. (1959). Anxiety and impulsiveness related to psychomotor efficiency. *Perceptual and Motor Skills, 9,* 191–198.

Barratt, E. S. (1963a). Behavioral variability related to stimulation of the cat amygdala. *Journal of the American Medical Association, 186,* 113–115.

Barratt, E. S. (1963b). Intra-individual variability of performance: ANS and psychometric correlates. *Texas Reports on Biology and Medicine, 21,* 496–504.

Barratt, E. S. (1965). Factor analysis of some psychometric measures of impulsiveness and anxiety. *Psychological Reports, 16,* 547–554.

Barratt, E. S. (1967a). The effects of thiazesim, LSD-25, and bilateral lesions of the amygdala on the release of a suppressed response. *Recent Advances in Biological Psychiatry, 9,* 229–240.

Barratt, E. S. (1967b). Perceptual-motor performance related to impulsiveness and anxiety. *Perceptual and Motor Skills, 25,* 485–492.

Barratt, E. S. (1972). Anxiety and impulsiveness: Toward a neuropsychological model. In C. D. Spielberger (Ed.), *Current trends in theory and research: Vol. 1.* New York: Academic Press.

Barratt, E. S. (1981). Time perception and cortical evoked potentials among male juvenile delinquents, adolescent psychiatric patients, and normal controls. In K. Roberts, R. Hays, & L. Soloway (Eds.), *Violence and the violent individual.* New York: Spectrum.

Barratt, E. S. (1983). The biological basis of impulsiveness: The significance of timing and rhythm disorders. *Personality and Individual Differences, 4,* 387–391.

Barratt, E. S. (1985). Impulsiveness subtraits: Arousal and information processing. In J. T. Spence & C. E. Izard (Eds.), *Advances in personality assessment: Vol. 5.* Hillsdale, NJ: Erlbaum.

Barratt, E. S. (1991). Measuring and predicting aggression within the context of a personality theory. *Journal of Neuropsychiatry and Clinical Neurosciences, 3,* S35–S39.

Barratt, E. S. (1993). Impulsivity: Integrating cognitive, behavioral, biological and environmental data. In W. G. McCown, J. L. Johnson, & M. B. Shure (Eds.), *The impulsive client: Theory, research, and treatment.* Washington, DC: American Psychological Association.

Barratt, E. S. (1994). Impulsiveness and aggression. In J. Monahan & H. J. Steadman (Eds.), *Violence and mental disorder: Developments in risk assessment.* Chicago, IL: University of Chicago Press.

Barratt, E. S., Kent, T., & Stanford, M. S. (1995). The role of biological variables in defining and measuring personality. In J. Ratey (Ed.), *Neuropsychiatry of personality disorders.* Cambridge, MA: Blackwell Scientific Publications.

Barratt, E. S., & Patton, J. H. (1983). Impulsivity: Cognitive, behavioral, and psychophysiological correlates. In M. Zuckerman (Ed.), *Biological bases of sensation seeking, impulsivity, and anxiety.* Hillsdale, NJ: Erlbaum.

Barratt, E. S., Patton, J. H., Olsson, N. G., & Zucker, G. (1981). Impulsivity and paced tapping. *Journal of Motor Behavior, 13,* 286–300.

Barratt, E. S., Pritchard, W. S., Faulk, D. M., & Brandt, M. E. (1987). The relationship between impulsiveness subtraits, trait anxiety, and visual N100 augmenting/reducing: A topographic analysis. *Personality and Individual Differences, 8,* 43–51.

Barratt, E. S., & White, R. (1969). Impulsiveness and anxiety related to medical student's performance and attitudes. *Journal of Medical Education, 44,* 604–607.

Brown, C. S., Kent, T. A., Bryant, S. G., Gevedon, R. M., Campbell, J. L., Felthous, A. R., Barratt, E. S., & Rose, R. M. (1989). Blood platelet uptake of serotonin in episodic aggression. *Psychiatry Research, 27,* 5–12.

Calabrese, G., Colombo, C., Bonfanti, A., Scotti, G., & Scarone, S. (1993). Caudate nucleus abnormalities in obsessive-compulsive disorder: Measurements of MRI signal intensity. *Psychiatry Research: Neuroimaging, 50,* 89–92.

Campbell, D. T., & Fiske, D. W. (1959). Convergent and discriminant validation by the multitrait-multimethod matrix. *Psychological Bulletin, 56,* 81–105.

Candito, M., Askenazy, F., Myquel, M., Chambon, P., & Darcourt, G. (1993). Tryptophanemia and tyrosinemia in adolescents with impulsive behavior. *International Clinical Psychopharmacology, 8,* 129–132.

Carrillo-de-la-Peña, M. T., & Barratt, E. S. (1993). Impulsivity and ERP augmenting/reducing. *Personality and Individual Differences, 15,* 25–32.

Cleckley, H. (1976). *The mask of sanity.* St. Louis, MO: Mosby.

Cloninger, C. R. (1987). A systematic method for clinical description and classification of personality. *Archives of General Psychiatry, 44,* 573–588.

Costa, P. T., Jr., & McCrae, R. R. (1985). *The NEO personality inventory manual.* Odessa, FL: Psychological Assessment Resources.

Cottle, T. (1976). *Perceiving time.* New York: Wiley.

De Jong, J., Virkkunen, M., & Linnoila, M. (1992). Factors associated with recidivism in a criminal population. *Journal of Nervous and Mental Disease, 180,* 543–550.

Dickman, S. J. (1993). Impulsivity and information processing. In W. G. McCown, J. L. Johnson, & M. B. Shure (Eds.), *The impulsive client: Theory, research, and treatment.* Washington, DC: American Psychological Association.

Digman, J. M. (1994). Historical antecedents of the five-factor model. In P. T. Costa, Jr. & T. A. Widiger (Eds.), *Personality disorders and the five-factor model of personality.* Washington, DC: American Psychological Association.

Evans, C. D. H., & Lacey, J. H. (1992). Multiple self-damaging behavior among alcoholic women: A prevalence study. *British Journal of Psychiatry, 161,* 643–647.

Eysenck, H. J., & Eysenck, M. W. (1985). *Personality and individual differences: A natural science approach.* New York: Plenum.

Eysenck, S. B. G., & Eysenck, H. J. (1963). On the dual nature of extraversion. *British Journal of Social and Clinical Psychology, 2,* 46–55.

Eysenck, S. B. G., & Eysenck, H. J. (1977). The place of impulsiveness in a dimensional system of personality description. *British Journal of Social and Clinical Psychology, 16,* 57–68.

Fiske, D. W. (1971). *Measuring the concepts of personality.* Chicago, IL: Aldine.

Forzano, L. B., & Logue, A. W. (1992). Predictors of adult humans' self-control and impulsiveness for food reinforcers. *Appetite, 19,* 33–47.

Frosch, J. (1977). The relation between acting out and disorders of impulse control. *Psychiatry, 40,* 295–314.

Frosch, J., & Wortis, S. B. (1954). A contribution to the nosology of the impulse disorders. *American Journal of Psychiatry, 111,* 132–138.

Gacono, C. B., & Meloy, J. R. (1992). The Rorschach and the DSM-III-R antisocial personality: A tribute to Robert Linder. *Journal of Clinical Psychology, 48,* 393–405.

Gacono, C. B., & Meloy, J. R. (1994). *The Rorschach assessment of aggressive and psychopathic personalities.* Hillsdale, NJ: Erlbaum.

Gerbing, D. W., Ahadi, S. A., & Patton, J. H. (1987). Toward a conceptualization of impulsivity: Components across the behavioral and self-report domains. *Multivariate Behavioral Research, 22,* 357–379.

Goodman, W. K., Price, L., & Rasmussen, S. (1989). The Yale-Brown Obsessive-Compulsive scale (Y-BOCS): Past development, use and reliability. *Archives of General Psychiatry, 46,* 1006–1016.

Gray, J. A. (1987). *The psychology of fear and stress.* Cambridge, MA: Cambridge University Press.

Heilbrun, A. B., Heilbrun, L. C., & Heilbrun, K. L. (1978). Impulsive and premeditated homicide: An analysis of subsequent parole risk of the murderer. *Journal of Criminal Law and Criminology, 69,* 108–114.

Heilbrun, A. B., Knopf, I. J., & Bruner, P. (1976). Criminal impulsivity and violence and subsequent parole outcome. *British Journal of Criminology, 16,* 367–377.

Hoehn-Saric, R., & Barksdale, V. C. (1983). Impulsiveness in obsessive-compulsive patients. *British Journal of Psychiatry, 143,* 177–182.

Hollander, E. (Ed.). (1993). *Obsessive-compulsive related disorders.* Washington, DC: American Psychiatric Press. '

Huang, Z., Stanford, M. S., & Barratt, E. S. (1994). Blink rate related to impulsiveness and task demands during performance of event-related potential tasks. *Personality and Individual Differences, 16,* 645–648.

Insel, T. R. (1992). Toward a neuroanatomy of obsessive-compulsive disorder. *Archives of General Psychiatry, 49,* 739–744.

Kagan, J., Rosman, B. L., Day, D., Albert, J., & Phillips, W. (1964). Information processing in the child: Significance of analytic and reflective attitudes. *Psychological Monographs, 78,* Whole No. 578.

Kanzer, M. (1957). Acting out and its relation to impulse disorders. *Journal of the Psychoanalytic Association, 5,* 136–145.

Karson, C. N. (1983). Spontaneous eye-blink rates and dopaminergic systems. *Brain, 106,* 643–653.

Kennedy, H. G., & Grubin, D. H. (1990). Hot-headed or impulsive? *British Journal of Addiction, 85,* 639–643.

Kent, T. A., Brown, C. S., Bryant, S. G., Barratt, E. S., Felthous, A. R., & Rose, R. M. (1988). Blood platelet uptake of serotonin in episodic aggression: Correlation with red blood cell proton T_1 and impulsivity. *Psychopharmacology Bulletin, 24,* 454–457.

Klinteberg, B., Hallman, J., Oreland, L., Wirsen, A., Levander, S. E., & Schalling, D. (1992). Exploring the connections between platelet monoamine oxidase activity and behavior: II. Impulsive personality without neuropsychological signs of disinhibition in air force pilot recruits. *Neuropsychobiology, 26,* 136–145.

Kruedelbach, N., McCormick, R. A., Schulz, S. C., & Grueneich, R. (1993). Impulsivity, coping styles, and triggers for craving in substance abusers with borderline personality disorder. *Journal of Personality Disorders, 7,* 214–222.

L'Abate, L. (1993). A family theory of impulsivity. In W. G. McCown, J. L. Johnson, & M. B. Shure (Eds.), *The impulsive client: Theory, research, and treatment.* Washington, DC: American Psychological Association.

Lacey, J. H., & Evans, C. D. H. (1986). The impulsivist: A multi-impulsive personality disorder. *British Journal of Addiction, 81,* 641–649.

Linnoila, M., Virkkunen, M., Scheinin, M., Nuutila, A., Rimon, R., & Goodwin, F. K. (1983). Low cerebrospinal fluid 5-hydroxyindoleacetic acid concentration differentiates impulsive from nonimpulsive violent behavior. *Life Sciences, 33,* 2609–2614.

London, P., & Rosenhan, D. (1964). Personality dynamics. *Annual Review of Psychology, 15,* 447–492.

Luengo, M. A., Carrillo-de-la-Peña, M. T., & Otero, J. M. (1991). The components of impulsiveness: A comparison of the I.7 impulsiveness questionnaire and the Barratt impulsiveness scale. *Personality and Individual Differences, 12,* 657–667.

Luengo, M. A., Carrillo-de-la-Peña, M. T., & Otero, J. M., & Romero, E. (1994). A short-term longitudinal study of impulsivity and antisocial behavior. *Journal of Personality and Social Psychology, 66,* 542–548.

McCown, W. G. (1988). Multi-impulsive personality disorder and multiple substance abuse: Evidence from members of self-help groups. *British Journal of Addiction, 83,* 431–432.

McCown, W. G., & DeSimone, P. A. (1993). Impulses, impulsivity, and impulsive behaviors: A historical review of a contemporary issue. In W. G. McCown, J. L. Johnson, & M. B. Shure (Eds.), *The impulsive client: Theory, research, and treatment.* Washington, DC: American Psychological Association.

McCown, W. G., Johnson, J. L., & Shure, M. B. (Eds.). (1993). *The impulsive client: Theory, research, and treatment.* Washington, DC: American Psychological Association.

McDiarmiad, C., & Barratt, E. S. (1969). Techniques for psychophysiological research with squirrel monkeys. *Proceedings of the Second International Congress of Primatology, 1,* 10–16.

McElroy, S. L., Hudson, J. I., Pope, H. G., Keck, P. E., & Aizley, H. G. (1992). The DSM-III-R impulse control disorders not elsewhere classified: Clinical characteristics and relationships to other psychiatric disorders. *American Journal of Psychiatry, 149,* 318–327.

Mezey, A., & Cohen, S. (1961). The effect of depressive illness on time judgement and time experience. *Journal of Neurology, Neurosurgery, and Psychiatry, 24,* 269–270.

Monroe, R. R. (1970). *Episodic behavioral disorders: A psychodynamic and neurophysiological analysis.* Cambridge, MA: Harvard University Press.

Nakagawa, A. (1991). Role of anterior and posterior attention networks in hemispheric asymmetries during lexical decisions. *Journal of Cognitive Neuroscience, 3,* 313–321.

Oas, P. (1985). The psychological assessment of impulsivity: A review. *Journal of Psychoeducational Assessment, 3,* 141–156.

O'Boyle, M., & Barratt, E. S. (1993). Impulsivity and DSM-III-R personality disorders. *Personality and Individual Differences, 14,* 609–611.

Othmer, E., Penick, E. C., Powell, B. J., Read, M. R., & Othmer, S. C. (1989). *Psychiatric Diagnostic Interview—Revised: Manual.* Los Angeles, CA: Western Psychological Services.

Pandey, S. C., Kim, S. W., Davis, J. M., & Pandey, G. N. (1993). Platelet serotonin-2 receptors in obsessive-compulsive disorder. *Biological Psychiatry, 33,* 367–372.

Parker, J. D. A., Bagby, R. M., & Webster, C. D. (1993). Domains of the impulsivity construct: A factor analytic investigation. *Personality and Individual Differences, 15,* 267–274.

Patton, J. H., Stanford, M. S., & Barratt, E. S. (in press). Factor structure of the Barratt impulsiveness scale. *Journal of Clinical Psychology.*

Posner, M. I. (1992). Attention as a cognitive and neural system. *Current Directions in Psychological Science, 1,* 11–14.

Prichep, L. S., Mas, F., Hollander, E., Liebowitz, M., John, E. R., Almas, M., DeCaria, C. M., & Levine, R. H. (1993). Quantitative electroencephalographic subtyping of obsessive-compulsive disorder. *Psychiatry Research: Neuroimaging, 50,* 25–32.

Rorer, L. G., & Widiger, T. A. (1983). Personality structure and assessment. *Annual Review of Psychology, 34,* 431–463.

Siever, L. J., & Davis, K. L. (1991). A psychobiological perspective on the personality disorders. *American Journal of Psychiatry, 148,* 1647–1658.

Sohlberg, S., Norring, C., Holmgren, S., & Rosmark, B. (1989). Impulsivity and long-term prognosis of psychiatric patients with anorexia nervosa/bulimia nervosa. *Journal of Nervous and Mental Disease, 177,* 249–258.

Spielberger, C. D., Jacobs, G., Russell, S., & Crane, R. S. (1983). Assessment of anger: The state-trait anger scale. In J. N. Butcher & C. D. Spielberger (Eds.), *Advances in personality assessment: Vol. 2.* Hillsdale, NJ: Erlbaum.

Stanford, M. S., & Barratt, E. S. (1992). Impulsivity and the multi-impulsive personality disorder. *Personality and Individual Differences, 13,* 831–834.

Stanford, M. S., & Barratt, E. S. (1994). Verbal skills, finger tapping, and cognitive tempo define a second-order factor of temporal information processing. Manuscript submitted for publication.

Stanford, M. S., Ebner, D., Patton, J. H., & Williams, J. (1994). Multi-impulsivity within an adolescent psychiatric population. *Personality and Individual Differences, 16,* 395–402.

Stein, D. J., Hollander, E., DeCaria, C., & Trungold, S. (1991). OCD: A disorder with anxiety, aggression, impulsivity and depressed mood. *Psychiatry Research, 36,* 237–239.

Stein, D. J., Hollander, E., & Liebowitz, M. R. (1993). Neurobiology of impulsivity and the impulse control disorders. *Journal of Neuropsychiatry and Clinical Neurosciences, 5,* 9–17.

Stein, D. J., Hollander, E., Simeon, D., & Cohen, L. (1994). Impulsivity scores in patients with obsessive-compulsive disorder. *Journal of Nervous and Mental Disease, 182,* 240–241.

Tallal, P., Galaburda, A. M., Llinas, R. R., & Von Euler, C. (Eds.). (1993). *Temporal information processing in the nervous system: Special reference to dyslexia and dysphasia.* New York: New York Academy of Sciences.

Taylor, J. A. (1953). A personality scale of manifest anxiety. *Journal of Abnormal and Social Psychology, 48,* 285–290.

Taylor, J. A. (1958). The effects of anxiety level and psychological stress on verbal learning. *Journal of Abnormal and Social Psychology, 57,* 55–60.

Taylor, J. A., & Spence, K. W. (1952). The relationship of anxiety level to performance in serial learning. *Journal of Experimental Psychology, 44,* 61–64.

Thurstone, L. (1953). *Examiner's manual for the Thurstone Temperament Schedule.* Chicago, IL: Science Research Associates.

Towey, J., Bruder, G., Hollander, E., Friedman, D., Erhan, H., Liebowitz, M., & Sutton, S. (1990). Endogenous event-related potentials in obsessive-compulsive disorder. *Biological Psychiatry, 28,* 92–98.

Wallace, J. F., & Newman, J. P. (1990). Differential effects of reward and punishment cues on response speed in anxious and impulsive individuals. *Personality and Individual Differences, 11,* 999–1009.

Widiger, T. A., Trull, T. J., Clarkin, J. F., Sanderson, C., & Costa, P. T., Jr. (1994). A description of the DSM-III-R and DSM-IV personality disorders with the five-factor model of personality. In P. T. Costa, Jr. & T. A. Widiger (Eds.), *Personality disorders and the five-factor model of personality.* Washington, DC: American Psychological Association.

Zuckerman, M. (1993). Sensation seeking and impulsivity: A marriage of traits made in biology? In W. G. McCown, J. L. Johnson, & M. B. Shure (Eds.), *The impulsive client: Theory, research, and treatment.* Washington, DC: American Psychological Association.

CHAPTER 5

Dependency

ROBERT F. BORNSTEIN

Dependency in adults has long been regarded as a flaw or deficit in functioning. As Ainsworth (1969, p. 970) noted, the overt expression of dependent traits and behaviors in adults invariably "implies immaturity." Similarly, Siegel (1988) argued that dependency is "linked with symbiosis, weakness [and] passivity . . . and is attributed to women, children, and persons perceived as inadequately functioning" (p. 113). Guntrip (1961) was even more direct in his assertion that "the root cause of all personality disturbance is the unconscious persistence within the adult personality of too strong an element of infantile dependence" (p. 381). Birtchnell (1988), Millon (1981), and others (e.g., McLemore & Brokaw, 1987) also discussed the negative effects of exaggerated dependency strivings on inter- and intrapersonal functioning. As these writings make clear, clinicians, researchers, and laypersons alike view high levels of dependency in adults as a pathognomic sign, especially among men (Bornstein, 1992, 1993).

Not surprisingly, a great deal of research has focused on uncovering the relationships between dependency and various forms of psychopathology. Most of this research examined hypothesized links between high levels of dependency and risk for psychological disorders such as depression (Blatt, D'Afflitti, & Quinlan, 1976), schizophrenia (Jackson, Rudd, Gazis, & Edwards, 1991), alcoholism (Weiss & Masling, 1970), tobacco addiction (Fisher & Fisher, 1975), eating disorders (Bornstein & Greenberg, 1991), and anxiety disorders (Reich, Noyes, & Troughton, 1987). In general, these studies found that elevated levels of dependency are associated with increased risk for theoretically related psychopathologies. Moreover, preliminary findings suggest that dependency may act as a diathesis which—when coupled with high levels of interpersonal stress—places an individual at increased risk for an array of Axis I disorders (see Bornstein, 1993).

Just as studies of the dependency/pathology relationship in clinical subjects have tended to focus on the deleterious effects of strong underlying dependency needs on psychological adjustment and risk for psychopathology, studies of exaggerated dependency strivings in normal (i.e., nonclinical) subjects have tended to emphasize the negative impact of exaggerated dependency needs on social and interpersonal functioning. These investigations demonstrated that high levels of dependency are associated with suggestibility (Tribich & Messer, 1974), help-seeking tendencies (Shilkret & Masling, 1981), an inclination to yield to others in interpersonal negotiations (Bornstein, Masling, & Poynton, 1987), fear of negative evaluation (Goldberg, Segal, Vella, & Shaw, 1989), jealousy and insecurity (Buunk, 1982), low self-efficacy and feelings of powerlessness (Bornstein, Leone, & Galley, 1988), performance anxiety (Devito & Kubis, 1983), strong needs for intimacy and affiliation (Masling, Price, Goldband, & Katkin, 1981), fears of abandonment (Sperling & Berman, 1991), and a desire to be nurtured, protected, and cared for by others (Hollender, Luborsky, & Harvey, 1970).

Although the majority of studies assessing the interpersonal correlates of dependency in adults have emphasized the maladaptive consequences of exaggerated dependency strivings in various situations and settings, in recent years a number of contradictory findings have emerged from these investigations. These findings suggest that high levels of dependency can be associated with adaptive as well as maladaptive traits, attitudes, and behaviors (Bornstein, 1994). The adaptive correlates of dependency include relationship-strengthening skills, health-promoting behaviors, and behaviors that facilitate performance in academic settings.

For example, studies have shown that high levels of dependency are associated with increased skill at decoding subtle verbal and nonverbal cues exhibited by acquaintances, teachers, therapists, and strangers (Juni & Semel, 1982; Masling, Johnson, & Saturansky, 1974). To the extent to which a dependent person is able to infer accurately the attitudes, preferences, and beliefs of other people, he or she will be in a better position to develop and maintain ties to potential nurturers and protectors.

Other investigations have demonstrated that dependent persons (a) seek medical help more quickly than do nondependent persons when physical symptoms appear (Greenberg & Fisher, 1977); and (b) are particularly conscientious in following prescribed medical and psychotherapeutic regimens (Bornstein, Krukonis, Manning, Mastrosimone, & Rossner, 1993). Both of these "medical help-seeking" tendencies are associated with enhanced treatment efficacy and with an increased likelihood of recovery from illness or disease (Greenberg & Bornstein, 1988).

Finally, studies have shown that high levels of dependency are associated with strong academic performance among elementary school and high school students, in part because students who have pronounced dependency needs are particularly concerned with performing well academically in order to please parents and teachers (Bornstein & Kennedy, 1994; Flanders, Anderson, & Amidon, 1961). Studies of the dependency/academic performance relationship represent an important example of the ways in which the dependent person's fear of negative evaluation can lead to adaptive behavior in the academic setting.

Although research has demonstrated that exaggerated dependency strivings may be associated with adaptive as well as maladaptive traits, attitudes, and behaviors, there have been no attempts to examine systematically the factors that determine whether an individual's dependency strivings will be associated with positive or negative consequences. No researchers have examined individual difference variables that may play a role in determining whether a person's underlying dependency needs are expressed in an adaptive, function-enhancing manner or in a maladaptive, self-defeating manner. Put another way, researchers have not identified variables that mediate the dependency/adaptivity relationship, even though identifying such variables may have important implications for researchers' conceptualization of the interpersonal and intrapsychic dynamics of dependency (see Bornstein, 1993).

A factor that potentially mediates the dependency/adaptivity relationship is the presence (versus absence) of personality pathology superimposed on strong underlying dependency needs. Considerable indirect evidence has accumulated suggesting that dependency-related traits, attitudes, and behaviors are expressed in a more adaptive manner by normal (non-personality-disordered) persons than by personality-disordered individuals. The purpose of this chapter is to describe clinical and empirical findings which indicate that the way in which an individual's underlying dependency needs are expressed is partly a function of that person's overall level of personality adjustment.

Specifically, I argue that both normal and personality-disordered individuals sometimes exhibit strong dependency-related strivings, but that the ways in which underlying dependency needs are expressed by normals are quite different from the ways that these dependency needs are expressed by personality-disordered individuals. Because personality-disordered individuals utilize less effective ego defenses and coping strategies than do normals when attempting to cope with internal impulses and external stressors (Ihilevich & Gleser, 1986; Johnson & Bornstein, 1992; McLemore & Brokaw, 1987; Millon, 1981; Vaillant, 1994), they cannot modulate and attenuate the expression of underlying dependency strivings as effectively as do non-personality-disordered persons. Thus, whereas nonclinical subjects tend to express underlying

dependency needs in relatively subtle—even adaptive—ways, personality-disordered subjects tend to express underlying dependency needs
in a more uncontrolled, unmodulated, maladaptive manner.

Before discussing the ways in which the overt expression of underlying dependency needs differ in personality-disordered and normal individuals, it is important to place the ensuing discussion into an appropriate
context. Although many writers have discussed the characteristics that
distinguish normal from personality-disordered individuals (e.g.,
Frances & Widiger, 1987; Livesley & Jackson, 1992; McLemore &
Brokaw, 1987; Millon, 1981; Vaillant, 1994; Widiger, 1992), one of the
most influential frameworks used by clinicians and researchers to distinguish normal from disordered personality functioning is that described in the fourth edition of the *Diagnostic and Statistical Manual of
Mental Disorders* (DSM-IV; American Psychiatric Association [APA],
1994). According to the DSM-IV, the general criteria that distinguish
personality-disordered functioning from normal personality functioning include:

> An enduring pattern of inner experience and behavior that deviates
> markedly from the expectations of the individual's culture, [which is re-
> flected in difficulties in] cognition (i.e., ways of perceiving and inter-
> preting self, other people and events), affectivity (i.e., the range, intensity,
> lability and appropriateness of emotional response), interpersonal func-
> tioning and impulse control. (p. 633)

These difficulties must be "inflexible and pervasive across a broad range
of personal and social situations," must lead to "clinically significant distress or impairment," and must represent a pattern of relating to others
that is "stable and of long duration . . . [which] can be traced back at least
to adolescence or early adulthood" (APA, 1994, p. 633).

With the DSM-IV definition of personality pathology in mind, it is
possible to (a) explore in detail the ways in which underlying dependency
needs are expressed differently by normal and personality-disordered
persons, and (b) elucidate the impact of these contrasting manifestations
of underlying dependency needs on an individual's adjustment and psychological functioning. To address these issues, I first discuss research
examining the etiology and dynamics of dependent personality traits in
normal and personality-disordered individuals. I then contrast the ways
in which underlying dependency strivings are expressed in normal and
personality-disordered persons. Finally, I discuss the theoretical and clinical implications of research on the expression of underlying dependency
needs in normal and personality-disordered individuals.

THE ETIOLOGY AND DYNAMICS OF DEPENDENCY: EMPIRICAL FINDINGS

Early studies examining the etiology of dependent personality traits focused primarily on events associated with breastfeeding and weaning, testing the psychoanalytic hypothesis that high levels of dependency result primarily from frustration or overgratification experienced during the infantile, oral phase of psychosexual development (Bornstein, 1992; Masling, 1986). Investigations in this area ultimately produced inconsistent and inconclusive results, and furthermore were associated with many conceptual and methodological difficulties (Bornstein, 1993). Consequently, researchers began to explore other factors that potentially play a role in the etiology and dynamics of dependency in various subject groups. Studies assessing the heritability of dependent personality traits suggest that genetic factors account for a relatively small portion of the variability in dependency levels in children, adolescents, and adults (see Dworkin, Burke, Maher, & Gottesman, 1976; Livesley, Jang, Jackson, & Vernon, 1993). The most robust findings in this area have come from studies of the parent/child relationship as a causal factor in the acquisition and development of dependent personality traits during infancy and early childhood.

Studies of the dependency/parenting style relationship suggest that two parenting styles in particular lead to high levels of dependency in offspring. First, there is strong evidence that authoritarian parenting leads to high levels of dependency, in part because authoritarian parenting prevents the child from engaging in the kinds of trial-and-error learning that facilitate the development of autonomy and feelings of self-efficacy (McCranie & Bass, 1984). Second, studies indicate that overprotective parenting can also lead to high levels of dependency in offspring, for much the same reason that authoritarian parenting produces increases in dependency. Overprotective parenting—like authoritarian parenting—instills in the child a belief that he or she cannot function without the help, guidance, and support of others, especially figures of authority (Parker & Lipscombe, 1980).

Finney's (1961) investigation of the parental overprotectiveness/dependency link illustrates nicely the pattern of results typically obtained in this area. Finney interviewed the mothers of 31 boys enrolled in a child guidance clinic, obtaining information regarding a variety of dimensions related to the infant/mother relationship (e.g., maternal protectiveness, rigidity of discipline, expression of affection). Clinicians' ratings of the mothers on these same dimensions were also obtained. Clinicians' and teachers' ratings were used to assess level of dependency in the child subjects. As predicted, the mothers of dependent boys were significantly more protective of their child than were the mothers of nondependent boys. Specifically, significant correlations were obtained between maternal protectiveness ratings and the child's dependency score ($r = .37$), and between ratings of a mother's tendency to reinforce dependent behavior and her child's dependency score ($r = .40$). Similar results were subsequently obtained by Baumrind (1967, 1971), Berg and McGuire (1974), and Head, Baker, and Williamson (1991).

Although a number of studies found parental overprotectiveness to be associated with increased dependency in children, adolescents, and adults, several studies also found parental authoritarianism to predict later dependency. For example, Vaillant (1980) found that memories of the parents as harsh and demanding during childhood were associated with increased levels of dependency in a sample of male undergraduates who were first studied around age 20 and then reassessed at age 50. Similarly, McCranie and Bass (1984) found that ratings of parental authoritarianism were positively correlated with Depressive Experiences Questionnaire (DEQ) dependency scores (Blatt et al., 1976) in a sample of female undergraduates. Consistent with these findings, Baumrind (1967, 1971), Bhogle (1983), Whiffen and Sasseville (1991), and others found that parental authoritarianism and authoritarian parenting styles were associated with increased dependency during early, middle, and late childhood.

What are the links between overprotective, authoritarian parenting and the subsequent emergence of dependent traits, attitudes, and behaviors in offspring? As I have pointed out elsewhere (Bornstein, 1993), the most immediate consequences of overprotective, authoritarian parenting are (a) the construction of particular mental representations of the self and other people; and (b) the acquisition of particular kinds of beliefs about one's own self-efficacy and about the power and potency of others. Because early relationships with the parents play a central role in the construction of the self-concept, the children of overprotective parents will come to believe that they cannot function without the guidance and protection of others, especially figures of authority (Parker, 1983). Furthermore, because early relationships with the parents create particular expectations for future interpersonal relationships, parental overprotectiveness will lead to an expectation on the part of children that they will be nurtured and cared for by others (Baumrind, 1973). Similarly, parental authoritarianism will lead children to believe that the way to maintain good relationships with others is to acquiesce to their requests, expectations, and demands (Vaillant, 1980).

Thus, cognitive structures (self- and object-representations) that are formed in response to early experiences within the family influence the motivations, behaviors, and affective responses of the dependent person in predictable ways. A perception of oneself as powerless and ineffectual will, first and foremost, have motivational effects: A person with such a self-concept will be motivated to seek guidance, support, nurturance, and protection from other people. This self-concept-based motivation will in turn produce particular patterns of dependent behavior: The person who is motivated to seek the guidance and support of others will behave in ways that maximize the probability that they will obtain the guidance and support that they desire. Finally, a representation of the self as powerless and ineffectual will have important affective consequences (e.g., fear of abandonment, fear of negative evaluation by others).

A detailed discussion of the ways in which the cognitive, motivational, behavioral, and affective components of dependency interact to produce dependency-related traits, attitudes, and behaviors is provided by Bornstein (1993). For the time being, it is sufficient to note that such behaviors exhibited by dependent persons in various circumstances and settings can invariably be traced to (a) the dependent individual's perception of the self as weak and ineffectual, coupled with his or her belief that other people are comparatively powerful and in control of the outcome of situations; and (b) the dependent person's strong desire to obtain and maintain nurturant, supportive relationships.

Studies assessing the behaviors of dependent persons in different situations and settings illustrate the ways in which the cognitive and motivational components of dependency ultimately lead to the overt expression of dependency-related behaviors. For example, Jakubczak and Walters (1959) examined the dependency/suggestibility relationship by pre-screening a sample of 9-year-old boys for level of dependency, and then having subjects participate in a standard autokinetic effect experiment wherein erroneous judgments regarding the movement of a stationary light source were provided by either a high-status confederate (an adult male), or a same-sex peer. Jakubczak and Walters found that dependent subjects were more susceptible than nondependent subjects to the autokinetic effect, regardless of the status of the confederate. Moreover, subject dependency and confederate status interacted to predict susceptibility to the autokinetic effect, with the influence of confederate status being significantly greater for dependent than nondependent boys. These results not only suggest that dependency is associated with increased suggestibility, but further indicate that this effect is particularly pronounced when the source of information is a high-status person rather than a peer. Similar findings were subsequently reported by Tribich and Messer (1974), and Ojha (1972).

The results of Weiss's (1969) study of the dependency/compliance relationship dovetail with Jakubczak and Walters' (1959) findings regarding the dependency/suggestibility link. Weiss preselected groups of dependent and nondependent undergraduates, and informed the subjects that they were participating in a study of perceptual processes in normal college students. She then presented a series of slides containing different numbers of dots and asked the subjects to estimate the number of dots on each slide. Half the subjects were told that "college students like you typically overestimate the number of dots on these slides," and the remaining subjects were told that college students typically underestimate the number of dots on the slides. As predicted, Weiss found that dependent subjects over- or underestimated the number of dots in accordance with the perceived expectations of the experimenter, whereas nondependent subjects showed relatively little compliance with the experimenter's expectations. Similar findings were subsequently obtained by Agrawal and Rai (1988) in a laboratory study involving a frustrating problem-solving task, and by Bornstein and Masling (1985) in a naturalistic study of the dependency/compliance relationship in Psychology 101 students.

Using a very different procedure and subject sample than has been used in most laboratory and field studies of dependency, Keinan and Hobfall (1989) obtained results that parallel closely those obtained by Jakubczak and Walters (1959), Weiss (1969), and others. In Keinan and Hobfall's study, a sample of pregnant Israeli women was divided into dependent and nondependent groups based on their scores on a self-report measure of dependency. Twelve hours postdelivery, each woman reported whether or not her husband had been present in the delivery room and provided a rating of the amount of anxiety that she had experienced during her delivery. Keinan and Hobfall found that dependent women were significantly more anxious during delivery when the husband was absent than when he was present. Nondependent women reported comparable levels of anxiety whether or not the husband was present during delivery. Similar findings were obtained by Masling et al. (1981). The results of these studies offer strong support for the hypothesis that the presence of a nurturer/protector acts as a stress-reducer in dependent individuals.

The picture of the dependent person that emerges from these (and other) investigations is that of a suggestible, compliant individual who looks to others for protection, guidance, nurturance, and support rather than taking a more active, assertive approach to meeting his or her needs. These results illustrate the ways in which the cognitive and motivational components of dependency influence the dependent individual's behavior in the laboratory and the field (for discussions of this issue, see also Bornstein, 1993, 1994). In addition, these studies provide a context within which it is possible to contrast the dependency-related behaviors exhibited by normal and personality-disordered subjects. As the ensuing review of

the literature will show, the ways in which these dependency-related behaviors are expressed differ substantially in personality-disordered and
normal individuals.

THE EXPRESSION OF UNDERLYING DEPENDENCY NEEDS IN NORMAL AND PERSONALITY-DISORDERED PERSONS

Everyone experiences needs for nurturance, guidance, support, and approval from others, especially in times of stress. In other words, everyone shows some degree of dependency on others. Although studies
suggest that certain forms of personality pathology are associated with
particularly strong dependency strivings (Frances & Widiger, 1987; Millon, 1981), perhaps the most important difference between normal and
personality-disordered persons with respect to underlying dependency
needs has to do with the ways in which the individual copes with and ex-
presses these needs. As noted earlier, because personality-disordered individuals have less effective ego defenses than normals (Ihilevich &
Gleser, 1986; Vaillant, 1994), and furthermore utilize less effective
coping strategies when attempting to deal with internal impulses and external stressors (McLemore & Brokaw, 1987; Millon, 1981), personality-
disordered individuals typically express underlying dependency needs in
a more direct, unmodulated manner than do normals. Thus, although in
many instances normal and personality-disordered persons experience
similar kinds of dependency-related impulses (e.g., need for guidance
and support from others), these impulses typically are expressed in a
more adaptive way by normals than by those with personality pathology.

In the following sections, I discuss the ways in which normal and
personality-disordered persons express similar underlying dependency
needs, focusing on differences in the adaptivity of expressed dependency-
related strivings in personality-disordered and non-personality-disordered
subjects. Three sets of dependency-related behaviors are discussed:
(a) help-seeking tendencies; (b) affiliative behaviors; and (c) sensitivity to
interpersonal cues.

Help-Seeking

Although help-seeking behaviors exhibited by normals occasionally elicit
negative reactions from others (Blatt et al., 1976; Simpson & Gangestad,
1991), research suggests that in general, dependency-related help-seeking
behaviors exhibited by normals are effective in obtaining guidance, nurturance, and support (Bornstein, 1994). Moreover, studies suggest that the

non-personality-disordered dependent individual is able to utilize this support and guidance to enhance his or her autonomous, independent functioning, at least temporarily. This finding has been obtained in children, adolescents, and adults, regardless of the type of dependency measure used to select subjects for study or the way in which help-seeking behavior was operationalized in a particular investigation.

In one of the earliest studies in this area, Flanders et al. (1961) examined the dependency/help-seeking relationship in a mixed-sex sample of children in elementary school. Dependent children in this study sought—and obtained—reassurance, approval, and positive feedback from the teacher more frequently than did nondependent children, and were able to utilize these periodic reassurances to enhance their performance in various classroom activities. In other words, although dependent children in Anderson et al.'s investigation showed higher levels of help-, approval-, and reassurance-seeking than did nondependent children, the dependent children in this study were able to utilize the teacher's feedback in an adaptive, performance-enhancing manner. Just as securely attached children are able to utilize the primary caretaker as a "secure base" (Ainsworth, 1969; Bowlby, 1980), obtaining periodic "doses" of maternal or paternal affection in order to function autonomously between reassurance-seeking episodes, the dependent children in Anderson et al.'s investigation were able to utilize the teacher as a source of security and reassurance that facilitated autonomous performance in various classroom projects and activities. Similar results were subsequently obtained by Sroufe, Fox, and Pancake (1983), and Yasunaga (1985) in samples of American and Japanese nursery-school children.

Studies of the dependency/help-seeking relationship in normal adolescents and adults produced findings similar to those obtained by Flanders et al. (1961), Sroufe et al. (1983), and Yasunaga (1985). For example, Bernardin and Jessor (1957) found that dependent men sought help from an experimenter significantly more often than did nondependent men during a laboratory problem-solving task, and were able to utilize this help to facilitate problem-solving performance. Similar findings were subsequently obtained by Cairns (1961) and Sinha and Pandey (1972) in samples of American and Indian adolescents. Shilkret and Masling (1981) also found that dependent college students exhibited more direct (verbal) and indirect (nonverbal) requests for help than did nondependent college students during laboratory problem-solving tasks. Along somewhat different lines, Bornstein and Kennedy (1994) found that various help- and reassurance-seeking behaviors were used effectively by high school students to facilitate academic performance: In this investigation, dependent students of both sexes sought help from teachers more often than did nondependent students, and also obtained higher overall grade-point averages than did nondependent students, even when scholastic aptitude was controlled for statistically.

Taken together, the results of studies assessing the dependency/help-seeking relationship in normal children, adolescents, and adults confirm that these subjects are able to express their dependency-related help-seeking behaviors in a relatively subtle, adaptive manner, obtaining help and support from figures of authority (teachers and experimenters) and using this assistance and reassurance to facilitate their performance in classroom and laboratory tasks. A very different pattern of results emerges in studies of the dependency/help-seeking relationship in personality-disordered subjects. In these investigations, personality-disordered subjects have often been found to express their desire for help and reassurance in a manipulative, maladaptive manner, inadvertently subverting their efforts to obtain guidance and support from others.

Two sets of findings illustrate the maladaptive aspects of the personality-disordered individual's dependency-related help-seeking behaviors. In a recent study of this issue, O'Neill and Bornstein (1990) derived an index of help-seeking response set from the MMPI validity scales ($F - K$) of a mixed-sex sample of psychiatric inpatients who completed the MMPI as part of a standard psychological test battery administered on admission to the hospital. Dependency scores were obtained from patients' Rorschach protocols, using Masling, Rabie, and Blondheim's (1967) Rorschach Oral Dependency (ROD) scale. O'Neill and Bornstein found that, as predicted, dependency was associated with a help-seeking response set on the MMPI (high F and low K score), in both men and women. The correlation between ROD scores and $F - K$ scores was quite substantial ($r = .52$) in this investigation, and many of the dependent patients' F scale scores were so elevated that the validity of their MMPI profiles was questionable.

Similar results were reported by Lorr and McNair (1964) and Emery and Lesher (1982), who found that dependency-related help-seeking behaviors exhibited by psychiatric outpatients (Lorr & McNair) and inpatients (Emery & Lesher) interfered with therapeutic progress. In both of these studies, dependent patients were found to make excessive demands on the therapist, including reporting numerous "pseudo-emergencies" that, on scrutiny, turned out to be relatively mundane events. In addition, in both investigations the dependent patients: (a) attempted to shift responsibility for therapeutic progress to the therapist; (b) expressed strong doubts regarding their ability to function independently outside therapy; and (c) resisted termination. Greenberg and Bornstein (1989) also found that dependent psychiatric inpatients resisted leaving the hospital, so that the typical dependent patient in Greenberg and Bornstein's study spent an average of 40 days longer in the inpatient unit that did a matched non-dependent patient with a similar disorder.

The second set of findings that illustrates the maladaptive aspects of the personality-disordered person's dependency-related help-seeking behaviors involves suicide. Several investigations have demonstrated that dependent individuals make a significantly greater number of suicidal gestures and nonlethal suicide attempts than do nondependent persons (Berman, 1992; Canetto & Feldman, 1993; Pallis & Birtchnell, 1976; Tabachnick, 1961). Moreover, Berman (1992) reported that such suicidal gestures and attempts often followed periods of interpersonal conflict or experiences of rejection (see also Canetto & Feldman, 1993). Apparently, personality-disordered individuals with strong underlying dependency strivings sometimes express their needs for help and support by acting out suicidal, self-destructive impulses, especially in those situations wherein they believe that they have exhausted other potential avenues of help-, nurturance-, and reassurance-seeking.

Affiliative Behavior

Dependent individuals almost invariably obtain higher scores than do nondependent individuals on self-report and projective measures of need for affiliation (Bornstein, 1992, 1993; Masling, 1986). In normal subjects, however, dependency-related affiliative needs are generally expressed in a relatively subtle and indirect manner. For example, researchers have shown that dependent children (Sroufe et al., 1983), adolescents (Juni, Masling, & Brannon, 1979), and adults (Keinan & Hobfall, 1989) initiate physical contact with other people more frequently than do nondependent children, adolescents, and adults. Similarly, investigators have found that dependent subjects make eye contact with peers and experimenters significantly more often than do nondependent subjects (Exline & Messick, 1967; Libby & Yanklevich, 1973). Dependent children also provide nurturance and support to peers at significantly higher rates than do nondependent children (Hartup & Keller, 1960).

In one of the most creative and well-designed studies of the dependency/affiliation relationship in normals, Simpson and Gangestad (1991) tested the hypothesis that dependency-related affiliative tendencies would result in increased commitment in romantic relationships, because the dependent person's affiliative needs should be associated with concerns regarding the availability and accessibility of a nurturing, caretaking figure. The participants in this study were 241 unmarried monogamous couples. Each subject was prescreened for level of dependency via Berscheid and Fei's (1977) self-report dependency measure and provided ratings of (a) his or her degree of commitment to the relationship; and (b) his or her partner's degree of commitment. Two noteworthy findings emerged from this investigation. First, there was a significant positive relationship between level of dependency and degree of commitment to the relationship in both men ($r = .59$) and women ($r = .49$). Second, there was a significant positive relationship between level of dependency and subjects' estimates of the partner's degree of commitment to the relationship ($r = .29$) in subjects of both sexes.

These results not only confirm that dependency is associated with increased commitment in romantic relationships, but further suggest that level of dependency predicts subjects' perceptions of the partner's degree of commitment to the relationship. There are at least two plausible explanations for this latter finding. First, it is possible that dependent individuals are able to identify—and develop relationships with—romantic partners who are highly committed to the relationship. This is an adaptive behavior on the part of the dependent person, in that developing relationships with committed romantic partners will help to gratify the dependent person's strong needs for support, protection, and nurturance.

Alternatively, it may be that there is no real relationship between level of dependency and the degree of commitment of one's romantic partner, but that dependent persons tend to perceive greater commitment in their romantic partners than actually exists. Although such a misperception certainly entails some costs and risks (Bornstein, 1993), it also plays an important role in helping the dependent person modulate anxiety and cope with fears of abandonment and rejection: Dependent persons' overestimates of their partners' degree of commitment may represent a kind of self-serving bias in perception wherein the dependent individual allays fears of rejection and abandonment by perceiving greater commitment in the romantic partner than the romantic partner perceives in him- or herself. Such a misperception—although inaccurate—can serve an important defensive, self-protective function for the dependent person.

In personality-disordered individuals, dependency-related affiliative needs are often expressed in less adaptive ways, primarily because these needs are expressed in a more direct, overt manner in personality-disordered individuals than in normals. Among the pathological manifestations of dependency-related affiliative needs that have been reported by researchers are (a) intense fears of abandonment and "clinging dependency" in close interpersonal relationships (Sperling & Berman, 1991); (b) adoption of a passive, helpless stance in intimate relationships in order to force significant others (e.g., parents, siblings, romantic partners) to enter into a caretaking role (Hollender et al., 1970); and (c) the development of phobic symptoms in an effort to minimize separation between the dependent person and his or her spouse or parent (Kleiner & Marshall, 1985).

The majority of investigations assessing maladaptive aspects of dependency-related affiliative strivings have focused on school phobia in children and agoraphobia in adults. For example, in a series of studies conducted during the late 1960s and early 1970s, Berg and his colleagues (Berg, 1974; Berg & McGuire, 1974; Berg, Nichols, & Pritchard, 1969) found that dependency was associated with elevated rates of school phobia among elementary school and junior high school students. Comparable dependency/school phobia relationships were found in boys and girls in these studies. Furthermore, Berg et al. (1969) found that "chronic" school phobics—those children who showed clinically significant school phobia for three consecutive years—obtained significantly higher dependency scores than did "acute" school phobics, whose phobic reactions were less intense and of shorter duration.

Findings regarding the dependency/agoraphobia relationship in adults parallel those obtained in studies of the dependency/school phobia relationship in schoolchildren. Studies in this area have shown that agoraphobic psychiatric patients obtain significantly higher scores than do nonphobic control patients on various dependency measures (Reich et al., 1987; Shafar, 1970; Torgerson, 1979). Moreover, agoraphobic patients show higher levels of dependency than do patients with other types of phobias (Bornstein, 1993; Reich et al., 1987). As Kleiner and Marshall (1985, p. 582) noted, agoraphobic behavior allows the phobic person to "regress emotionally to infantile dependence," by expressing directly the needs for nurturance and protection. However, such overt expressions of infantile dependency strivings interfere with the phobic person's social and occupational functioning (Reich et al., 1987), and may also damage—or even destroy—the close relationships with nurturing figures that the dependent person so strongly desires (Symonds, 1971).

Sensitivity to Interpersonal Cues

If obtaining support from others is important to the dependent person, high levels of dependency should be associated with increased sensitivity to verbal and nonverbal cues emitted by others. After all, to the extent that dependent individuals are able to infer accurately the attitudes, beliefs, and feelings of other people, they should be better able to obtain the help, nurturance, and support that they desire. In this context, researchers have examined the dependency/interpersonal sensitivity relationship in both laboratory (Masling, O'Neill, & Katkin, 1982) and naturalistic settings (Juni & Semel, 1982; Masling et al., 1974).

Masling et al. (1982) assessed the dependency/interpersonal sensitivity relationship in college students by investigating whether dependent subjects would be more strongly affected than nondependent subjects by warm versus cold treatment by a confederate. In this experiment, dependent and nondependent subjects were selected via scores on Masling et al.'s (1967) ROD scale. They were informed that they were taking part in a study of "how people get to know each other," and then were asked to interact for 10 minutes with a confederate subject who treated them either in a warm, friendly manner or in a cold, aloof manner. Subjects' electrodermal responses (EDRs) were recorded before, during, and after the interaction period. Masling et al. found that dependent subjects' EDRs increased significantly from baseline (preinteraction) to postconversation period only in the "cold" condition. In the "warm" condition, dependent subjects' EDRs remained unchanged from baseline to postconversation period. Nondependent subjects showed no differential responding to warm versus cold treatment by the confederate. These results suggest that dependent persons are particularly sensitive to how they are being treated by others, and show increased physiological arousal in situations wherein they anticipate interpersonal conflict or rejection.

An earlier study by Masling et al. (1974) produced results consistent with Masling et al.'s (1982) investigation, and further indicated that dependent persons are more accurate social perceivers than are nondependent persons. This study comprised two experiments. In the first, a mixed-sex sample of undergraduates was divided into dependent and nondependent groups based on scores on Masling et al.'s (1967) ROD scale. Each subject was then randomly paired with another subject, and the two members of each dyad were given 15 minutes to "get acquainted" with each other. Following the conversations, subjects individually completed a questionnaire that asked about their attitudes, beliefs, and preferences. Finally, each subject was given an identical questionnaire and was asked to complete it as he or she thought his or her partner would. The measure of interpersonal sensitivity used in this study was the concordance of the subject's guesses with is or her partner's self-ratings. As expected, dependent subjects in this investigation showed greater predictive accuracy than did nondependent subjects. Masling et al. (1974, Experiment 2) replicated this experiment on a sample of Peace Corps volunteers who provided estimates of their roommates' attitudes and personal beliefs after a series of brief interactions. Virtually identical results were obtained.

Further information regarding the dependency/interpersonal sensitivity relationship in normal subjects was provided by Juni and Semel (1982), who performed a modified replication of Masling et al.'s (1974) experiments. In Juni and Semel's study, undergraduate students participating in a psychology seminar were asked to make judgments regarding the attitudes, interests, and personal beliefs of the female seminar leader after a brief (10-minute) discussion period. Consistent with Masling et al.'s earlier results, Juni and Semel found that level of dependency predicted accuracy of subjects' perceptions of the seminar leader, although somewhat stronger results were obtained for men than women in this study.

The results obtained by Masling et al. (1974, 1982) and Juni and Semel (1982) confirm that in normals, high levels of dependency are associated with increased sensitivity to subtle interpersonal cues emitted by others. Moreover, it is clear that subjects in these studies were able to use the information that they had gleaned to make accurate inferences regarding other peoples' internal states (attitudes, preferences, etc.). As one might expect, studies suggest that personality-disordered dependent subjects also show increased sensitivity to verbal and nonverbal cues (Bornstein, 1992, 1993). However, because personality-disordered subjects show deficits in their ability to cope with anxiety and modulate internal impulses (Millon, 1981), their increased interpersonal sensitivity sometimes results not in accurate inferences regarding others' internal states, but rather in jealousy and suspiciousness on the part of the dependent person. In other words, studies conducted to date suggest that an increased sensitivity to interpersonal cues can cause the personality-disordered dependent person to become preoccupied with real or imagined "clues" which suggest that an important relationship with a nurturing, protecting figure may be at risk.

Not surprisingly, several investigations have demonstrated that personality-disordered dependent persons show high levels of jealousy and suspiciousness in close interpersonal relationships (Berscheid & Fei, 1977; Buunk, 1982; Mathes, Roter, & Joerger, 1982). In those dependent persons for whom personality pathology is particularly pronounced, suspiciousness and jealousy can become more severe, resulting in paranoid ideation and rumination (Aronson, 1953; Sacks, 1988). Thus, although they do in fact show increased sensitivity to subtle interpersonal communications, it appears that personality-disordered individuals with strong underlying dependency needs focus primarily on the negative, anxiety-producing aspects of others' verbal and nonverbal communications, with the end result being increases in jealousy, insecurity, and suspiciousness.

The personality-disordered individual's underlying dependency needs can, in certain circumstances, lead to such upsetting and disruptive jealousy and insecurity that he or she engages in abusive behavior directed toward children, spouses, and elder family members. Moreover, dependency-related jealousy and insecurity is most likely to result in abusive behavior when other stressors (e.g., financial pressures, substance abuse problems) have already resulted in interpersonal conflict and tension within the dependent person's family. Several studies have shown that among families at risk for spousal abuse, high levels of dependency and personality pathology in the husband are associated with jealousy, insecurity, and increased probability of spousal battering

(Beasley & Stoltenberg, 1992; Hart, Dutton, & Newlove, 1993; Ponzetti, Cate, & Koval, 1983). Similar results are obtained in studies of the dependency/child abuse (Kertzman, 1980; Melnick & Hurley, 1969) and dependency/elder abuse (Pillemer & Finkelhor, 1989) relationships.

DISCUSSION AND CONCLUSIONS

Individuals with personality pathology express underlying dependency needs in less adaptive ways than do normals. Consequently, personality-disordered persons are less likely than normals to obtain and maintain the nurturant, supportive relationships that they so strongly desire. Instead, the maladaptive dependency-related behaviors exhibited by personality-disordered persons often lead to interpersonal conflict, rejection, and isolation, exacerbating dependency-related strivings and increasing feelings of helplessness, loneliness, and abandonment in the personality-disordered individual. These differences in personality-disordered and normal persons' ability to gratify underlying dependency needs through the development and maintenance of nurturant, supportive relationships with others turn out to have some noteworthy theoretical and clinical implications.

In most cases, the relatively high level of functioning exhibited by the non-personality-disordered person with strong underlying dependency needs should be associated with success in eliciting social support, and with success in developing and maintaining nurturant, supportive relationships. In fact, the high levels of interpersonal sensitivity exhibited by the non-personality-disordered dependent person will lead to adaptive, relationship-strengthening behavior in at least three ways. First, sensitivity to interpersonal cues may help the dependent person to identify those individuals who are most likely to meet his or her needs for nurturance, guidance, and support. Second, interpersonal sensitivity should enable the dependent person to develop relationships with these potential nurturers and protectors. Third, sensitivity to interpersonal cues will enable the dependent person to anticipate stress and conflict in close interpersonal relationships, and to adopt strategies for dealing with stress and conflict that strengthen—rather than weaken—these important relationships. Simply put, the high-functioning dependent person should be able to use social skills and sensitivity to interpersonal cues to obtain and maintain good relationships with nurturers, caretakers, and protectors.

To the extent that dependent persons are able to obtain and maintain the supportive relationships that they desire, anxiety and stress will be minimized. In a sense, this represents the best possible long-term outcome of high levels of dependency in adults. However, two less-than-positive consequences of this long-term outcome are worth mentioning in this context.

First, the dependent person in this situation has, in effect, recapitulated the earlier parent-child dynamic that led to the dependency in the first place. In other words, the high-functioning dependent person in this situation actually has sought out a guide and protector who functions much like the overprotective, authoritarian parent of infancy and childhood. Second, insofar as the presence of a nurturant, supportive other serves as an anxiety and stress reducer for the dependent person, the presence of such a nurturer and protector will reinforce the dependent person's helpless self-concept. To the extent that he or she continues to rely on a significant other for guidance, protection, and support, the dependent person will continue to believe that he or she cannot function autonomously, without the protection and help of others.

The personality-disordered individual with strong underlying dependency needs will not be as successful in obtaining and maintaining supportive, protective relationships as is the non-personality-disordered dependent individual. This will lead to a very different—and much less positive—outcome in personality-disordered persons relative to normals. The inflexibility and dysfunctional interpersonal behavior that is characteristic of personality pathology will result in a paucity of nurturant, supportive relationships in the personality-disordered dependent person (see Frances & Widiger, 1987; McLemore & Brokaw, 1987), which in turn will lead to increased anxiety and stress for that person. This increased anxiety and stress has implications for both physical and psychological functioning. With respect to psychological functioning, high levels of anxiety and stress will lead to increased risk for various forms of Axis I psychopathology in the dependent individual (Bornstein, 1992, 1993). With respect to physiological functioning, high levels of anxiety and stress will lead to diminished immunocompetence in the dependent person, ultimately leading to increased susceptibility to various illnesses and diseases that are mediated by immune system functioning (Greenberg & Bornstein, 1988).

The onset of physical or psychological pathology will also have implications for the dependent person's behavior and self-concept. Research confirms that the onset of physical or psychological illness is often followed by increases in dependent, help-seeking behavior, especially in those individuals who previously had high levels of underlying dependency needs (Alsop, 1984; Colton, 1980). Moreover, to the extent that the dependent person assumes the "sick role" following the onset of physical or psychological illness, his or her self-perception as powerless, ineffectual, and dependent on others for support and protection is likely to increase (Booth, 1986; Rosenberg, 1970).

Thus, it is ironic that—although an individual's overall level of personality pathology appears to play a key role in determining the long-term consequences of exaggerated dependency needs in adults—both the long-term outcomes just described ultimately lead to the same end: reinforcement of the dependent person's "helpless" self-concept. In a sense, this conclusion is not surprising. Numerous studies have demonstrated that individuals typically behave (and process social information) in such a way as to protect and reinforce preexisting beliefs about the self and other people (see Kihlstrom & Cantor, 1984). In this context, Caspi, Bem, and Elder (1989) suggested:

> Dependency as an individual interactional style may well be even more self-perpetuating than [other personality styles] because dependent individuals are motivated to select and recruit environments that sustain their dependency. . . . Dependent persons recruit and attach themselves to others who will continue to provide the nurturance and support that they seek. [Moreover], these individuals become increasingly skilled at evoking from others those nurturing responses that reinforce their dependency.

Caspi et al.'s (1989) speculations regarding the self-propagating nature of dependency in adults are most directly applicable to those dependent persons who do not show significant personality pathology (and who therefore have developed the interpersonal sensitivity and social skills necessary to obtain and maintain nurturant, supportive relationships). Nonetheless, the results of this review confirm that regardless of their overall level of personality pathology, dependent persons behave in ways that reinforce and maintain the helpless self-concept that plays a key role in the etiology and dynamics of dependency. Not surprisingly, psychotherapy with dependent persons typically focuses on changing the dependent individual's dysfunctional beliefs regarding self and others (see, e.g., Crowder, 1972; Emery & Lesher, 1982; Overholser, 1987; Snyder, 1963). The present results suggest that although changing beliefs regarding self and others may play an important role in psychotherapy with dependent persons, somewhat different therapeutic approaches are warranted when working with personality-disordered dependent persons and those dependent persons with no underlying personality pathology.

As Overholser (1987) and others (e.g., Crowder, 1972) have noted, psychotherapy with high-functioning dependent individuals ultimately must focus on increasing feelings of internal control and self-efficacy, countering (either subtly or directly) the dependent person's belief that other people must be looked to for protection and support. Such a therapeutic goal may be too ambitious for the personality-disordered individual with strong underlying dependency needs, because the personality-disordered person does not have the skills and resources needed to develop a sense of independent, autonomous functioning (see Frances & Widiger, 1987).

Thus, psychotherapy with such individuals must begin by helping them strengthen social skills, modulate dependency-related feelings and impulses, and enhance their ability to perceive accurately the subtle verbal and nonverbal cues emitted by others. Only when these basic goals have been achieved can psychotherapy with personality-disordered patients begin to address issues related to increasing independent, autonomous functioning. Although a number of psychotherapeutic approaches to working with personality-disordered dependent persons have been described (see Bornstein, 1993, for a review), none of these therapeutic approaches have been shown to influence dependency-related motivations and behaviors in consistent, predictable ways.

Questions regarding the efficacy of different psychotherapeutic approaches notwithstanding, recognition of the relationship-strengthening effects of dependency in high-functioning persons, and of the relationship-hindering effects of dependency in personality-disordered individuals will be extremely important for the therapist who works with dependent patients. This information will not only help the therapist gain a better understanding of the ways in which dependency in adults affects the dynamics of important interpersonal relationships, but in addition, this information can help the therapist to (a) understand the interpersonal and environmental contingencies that propagate dependent behavior in vivo; and (b) deal with patient dependency in a manner that takes into account the myriad effects—both positive and negative—that dependency can have on other important individuals in the patient's life.

REFERENCES

Ainsworth, M. D. S. (1969). Object relations, dependency and attachment: A theoretical review of the infant-mother relationship. *Child Development, 40,* 969–1025.

Alsop, A. E. (1984). Purley Day Hospital: An appraisal with special reference to institutionalized behavior and dependence. *Occupational Therapy, 47,* 306–310.

American Psychiatric Association. (1994). *Diagnostic and statistical manual of mental disorders* (4th ed.). Washington, DC: Author.

Aronson, M. L. (1953). A study of the Freudian theory of paranoia by means of the Blacky pictures. *Journal of Projective Techniques, 17,* 3–19.

Baumrind, D. (1967). Child care practices anteceding three patterns of preschool behavior. *Genetic Psychology Monographs, 75,* 43–88.

Baumrind, D. (1971). Current patterns of parental authority. *Developmental Psychology Monograph, 4,* (No. 1, Pt. 2).

Baumrind, D. (1973). The development of instrumental competence through socialization. In A. D. Pick (Ed.), *Minnesota symposium on child psychology* (Vol. 7, pp. 3–46). Minneapolis: University of Minnesota Press.

Beasley, R., & Stoltenberg, C. D. (1992). Personality characteristics of male spouse abusers. *Professional Psychology, 23,* 310–317.

Berg, I. (1974). A self-administered dependency questionnaire for use with mothers of schoolchildren. *British Journal of Psychiatry, 124,* 1–9.

Berg, I., & McGuire, R. (1974). Are mothers of school-phobic adolescents over-protective? *British Journal of Psychiatry, 124,* 10–13.

Berg, I., Nichols, K., & Pritchard, C. (1969). School phobia: Its classification and relationship to dependency. *Journal of Child Psychology and Psychiatry, 10,* 123–141.

Berman, A. L. (1992). Suicidal behavior and marital interaction. *Suicide and Life-Threatening Behavior, 22,* 268–277.

Bernardin, A., & Jessor, R. (1957). A construct validation of the Edwards Personal Preference Schedule with respect to dependency. *Journal of Consulting Psychology, 21,* 63–67.

Berscheid, E., & Fei, J. (1977). Romantic love and sexual jealousy. In G. Clanton & L. G. Smith (Eds.), *Jealousy* (pp. 101–109). Englewood Cliffs, NJ: Prentice-Hall.

Bhogle, S. (1983). Antecedents of dependency behavior in children of low social class. *Psychological Studies, 28,* 92–95.

Birtchnell, J. (1988). Defining dependence. *British Journal of Medical Psychology, 61,* 111–123.

Blatt, S. J., D'Afflitti, J. P., & Quinlan, D. M. (1976). Experiences of depression in normal young adults. *Journal of Abnormal Psychology, 85,* 383–389.

Booth, T. (1986). Institutional regimes and induced dependency in homes for the aged. *The Gerontologist, 26,* 418–423.

Bornstein, R. F. (1992). The dependent personality: Developmental, social and clinical perspectives. *Psychological Bulletin, 112,* 3–23.

Bornstein, R. F. (1993). *The dependent personality.* New York: Guilford.

Bornstein, R. F. (1994). Dependency as a social cue: A meta-analytic review of research on the dependency—helping relationship. *Journal of Research in Personality, 28,* 182–213.

Bornstein, R. F. (1994). Adaptive and maladaptive aspects of dependency: An integrative review. *American Journal of Orthopsychiatry, 64,* 622–635.

Bornstein, R. F., & Greenberg, R. P. (1991). Dependency and eating disorders in female psychiatric inpatients. *Journal of Nervous and Mental Disease, 179,* 148–152.

Bornstein, R. F., & Kennedy, T. D. (1994). Interpersonal dependency and academic performance. *Journal of Personality Disorders, 8,* 240–248.

Bornstein, R. F., Krukonis, A. B., Manning, K. A., Mastrosimone, C. C., & Rossner, S. C. (1993). Interpersonal dependency and health service utilization in a college student sample. *Journal of Social and Clinical Psychology, 12,* 262–279.

Bornstein, R. F., Leone, D. R., & Galley, D. J. (1988). Rorschach measures of oral dependence and the internalized self-representation in normal college students. *Journal of Personality Assessment, 52,* 648–657.

Bornstein, R. F., & Masling, J. M. (1985). Orality and latency of volunteering to serve as experimental subjects. *Journal of Personality Assessment, 49,* 306–310.

Bornstein, R. F., Masling, J. M., & Poynton, F. G. (1987). Orality as a factor in interpersonal yielding. *Psychoanalytic Psychology, 4,* 161–170.

Bowlby, J. (1980). *Loss: Sadness and depression.* New York: Basic Books.

Buunk, B. (1982). Anticipated sexual jealousy: Its relationship to self-esteem, dependency and reciprocity. *Personality and Social Psychology Bulletin, 8,* 310–316.

Cairns, R. B. (1961). The influence of dependency inhibition on the effectiveness of social reinforcement. *Journal of Personality, 29,* 466–488.

Canetto, S. S., & Feldman, L. B. (1993). Covert and overt dependence in suicidal women and their male partners. *Omega, 27,* 177–194.

Caspi, A., Bem, D. J., & Elder, G. H. (1989). Continuities and consequences of interactional styles across the life course. *Journal of Personality, 57,* 375–406.

Colton, S. I. (1980). Instrumental dependency in institutionalized schizophrenics. *Psychosocial Rehabilitation Journal, 4,* 9–18.

Crowder, J. E. (1972). Relationship between therapist and client interpersonal behaviors and psychotherapy outcome. *Journal of Counseling Psychology, 19,* 68–75.

Devito, A. J., & Kubis, J. K. (1983). Actual and recalled test anxiety and flexibility, rigidity and self-control. *Journal of Clinical Psychology, 39,* 970–975.

Dworkin, R. H., Burke, B. B., Maher, B. A., & Gottesman, I. I. (1976). A longitudinal study of the genetics of personality. *Journal of Personality and Social Psychology, 34,* 510–518.

Emery, G., & Lesher, E. (1982). Treatment of depression in older adults: Personality considerations. *Psychotherapy, 19,* 500–505.

Exline, R. V., & Messick, D. (1967). The effects of dependency and social reinforcement upon visual behavior during an interview. *British Journal of Social and Clinical Psychology, 6,* 256–266.

Finney, J. C. (1961). Some maternal influences on children's personality and character. *Genetic Psychology Monographs, 63,* 199–278.

Fisher, J. M., & Fisher, S. (1975). Response to cigarette deprivation as a function of oral fantasy. *Journal of Personality Assessment, 39,* 381–385.

Flanders, N. A., Anderson, J. P., & Amidon, E. J. (1961). Measuring dependence proneness in the classroom. *Educational and Psychological Measurement, 21,* 575–587.

Frances, A., & Widiger, T. A. (1987). A critical review of four DSM-III personality disorders. In G. L. Tischler (Ed.), *Diagnosis and classification in psychiatry* (pp. 269–289). New York: Cambridge University Press.

Goldberg, J. O., Segal, Z. V., Vella, D. D., & Shaw, B. F. (1989). Depressive personality: MCMI profiles of sociotropic and autonomous subtypes. *Journal of Personality Disorders, 3,* 193–198.

Greenberg, R. P., & Bornstein, R. F. (1988). The dependent personality: Risk for physical disorders. *Journal of Personality Disorders, 2,* 126–135.

Greenberg, R. P., & Bornstein, R. F. (1989). Length of psychiatric hospitalization and oral dependency. *Journal of Personality Disorders, 3,* 199–204.

Greenberg, R. P., & Fisher, S. (1977). The relationship between willingness to adopt the sick role and attitudes toward women. *Journal of Chronic Disease, 30,* 29–37.

Guntrip, H. (1961). *Personality structure and human interaction.* London: Hogarth Press.

Hart, S. D., Dutton, D. G., & Newlove, T. (1993). The prevalence of personality disorder diagnoses among wife assaulters. *Journal of Personality Disorders, 7,* 329–341.

Hartup, W. W., & Keller, E. D. (1960). Nurturance in preschool children and its relation to dependency. *Child Development, 31,* 681–689.

Head, S. B., Baker, J. D., & Williamson, D. A. (1991). Family environment characteristics and dependent personality disorder. *Journal of Personality Disorders, 5,* 256–263.

Hollender, M. C., Luborsky, L., & Harvey, R. (1970). Correlates of the desire to be held in women. *Journal of Psychosomatic Research, 14,* 387–390.

Ihilevich, D., & Gleser, G. C. (1986). *Defense mechanisms.* Owosso, MI: DMI Associates.

Jackson, H. J., Rudd, R., Gazis, J., & Edwards, J. (1991). Using the MCMI to diagnose personality disorders in inpatients: Axis I/Axis II associations and sex differences. *Australian Psychologist, 26,* 37–41.

Jakubczak, L. F., & Walters, R. H. (1959). Suggestibility as dependency behavior. *Journal of Abnormal and Social Psychology, 59,* 102–107.

Johnson, J. G., & Bornstein, R. F. (1992). Utility of the Personality Diagnostic Questionnaire—Revised in a nonclinical sample. *Journal of Personality Disorders, 6,* 450–457.

Juni, S., Masling, J. M., & Brannon, R. (1979). Interpersonal touching and orality. *Journal of Personality Assessment, 43,* 235–237.

Juni, S., & Semel, S. R. (1982). Person perception as a function of orality and anality. *Journal of Social Psychology, 118,* 99–103.

Keinan, G., & Hobfall, S. E. (1989). Stress, dependency and social support: Who benefits from husband's presence in delivery? *Journal of Social and Clinical Psychology, 8,* 32–44.

Kertzman, D. (1980). *Dependency, frustration tolerance and impulse control in child abusers.* Saratoga, CA: Century Twenty-One.

Kihlstrom, J. F., & Cantor, N. (1984). Mental representations of the self. In L. Berkowitz (Ed.), *Advances in experimental social psychology* (Vol. 17, pp. 1–47). New York: Academic Press.

Kleiner, L., & Marshall, W. L. (1985). Relationship difficulties and agoraphobia. *Clinical Psychology Review, 5,* 581–595.

Libby, W. L., & Yanklevich, D. (1973). Personality determinants of eye contact and direction of gaze aversion. *Journal of Personality and Social Psychology, 27,* 197–206.

Livesley, W. J., & Jackson, D. N. (1992). Guidelines for developing, evaluating and revising the classification of personality disorders. *Journal of Nervous and Mental Disease, 180,* 609–618.

Livesley, W. J., Jang, K. L., Jackson, D. N., & Vernon, P. A. (1993). Genetic and environmental contributions to dimensions of personality disorder. *American Journal of Psychiatry, 150,* 1826–1831.

Lorr, M., & McNair, D. M. (1964). The interview relationship in therapy. *Journal of Nervous and Mental Disease, 139,* 328–331.

Masling, J. M. (1986). Orality, pathology and interpersonal behavior. In J. Masling (Ed.), *Empirical studies of psychoanalytic theories* (Vol. 2, pp. 73–106). Hillsdale, NJ: Erlbaum.

Masling, J. M., Johnson, C., & Saturansky, C. (1974). Oral imagery, accuracy of perceiving others and performance in Peace Corps training. *Journal of Personality and Social Psychology, 30,* 414–419.

Masling, J. M., O'Neill, R. M., & Katkin, E. S. (1982). Autonomic arousal, interpersonal climate and orality. *Journal of Personality and Social Psychology, 42,* 529–534.

Masling, J. M., Price, J., Goldband, S., & Katkin, E. S. (1981). Oral imagery and autonomic arousal in social isolation. *Journal of Personality and Social Psychology, 40,* 395–400.

Masling, J. M., Rabie, L., & Blondheim, S. H. (1967). Obesity, level of aspiration, and Rorschach and TAT measures of oral dependence. *Journal of Consulting Psychology, 31,* 233–239.

Mathes, E. W., Roter, P. M., & Joerger, S. M. (1982). A convergent validity study of six jealousy scales. *Psychological Reports, 50,* 1143–1147.

McCranie, E. W., & Bass, J. D. (1984). Childhood family antecedents of dependency and self-criticism. *Journal of Abnormal Psychology, 93,* 3–8.

McLemore, C. W., & Brokaw, D. W. (1987). Personality disorders as dysfunctional interpersonal behavior. *Journal of Personality Disorders, 1,* 270–285.

Melnick, B., & Hurley, J. R. (1969). Distinctive personality attributes of child-abusing mothers. *Journal of Consulting and Clinical Psychology, 33,* 746–749.

Millon, T. (1981). *Disorders of personality.* New York: Wiley.

Ojha, H. (1972). The relation of prestige suggestion to rigidity and dependence proneness. *Journal of Psychological Research, 16,* 70–73.

O'Neill, R. M., & Bornstein, R. F. (1990). Oral dependence and gender: Factors in help-seeking response set and self-reported psychopathology in psychiatric inpatients. *Journal of Personality Assessment, 55,* 28–40.

Overholser, J. C. (1987). Facilitating autonomy in passive-dependent persons: An integrative model. *Journal of Contemporary Psychotherapy, 17,* 250–269.

Pallis, D. J., & Birtchnell, J. (1976). Personality and suicidal history in psychiatric patients. *Journal of Clinical Psychology, 32,* 246–253.

Parker, G. (1983). *Parental overprotection.* New York: Grune and Stratton.

Parker, G., & Lipscombe, P. (1980). The relevance of early parental experiences to adult dependency, hypochondriasis and utilization of primary physicians. *British Journal of Medical Psychology, 53,* 355–363.

Pillemer, K., & Finkelhor, D. (1989). Causes of elder abuse. *American Journal of Orthopsychiatry, 50,* 179–187.

Ponzetti, J. J., Cate, R. M., & Koval, J. E. (1983). Violence between couples: Profiling the male abuser. *Personnel and Guidance Journal, 61,* 222–224.

Reich, J., Noyes, R., & Troughton, E. (1987). Dependent personality disorder associated with phobic avoidance in patients with panic disorder. *American Journal of Psychiatry, 144,* 323–326.

Rosenberg, S. (1970). Hospital culture as collective defense. *Psychiatry, 33,* 21–35.

Sacks, M. (1988). Folie a deux. *Comprehensive Psychiatry, 29,* 270–277.

Shafar, S. (1970). Aspects of phobic illness. *British Journal of Medical Psychology, 49,* 211–236.

Shilkret, C. J., & Masling, J. M. (1981). Oral dependence and dependent behavior. *Journal of Personality Assessment, 45,* 125–129.

Siegel, R. J. (1988). Women's dependency in a male-centered value system. *Women and Therapy, 7,* 113–123.

Simpson, J. A., & Gangestad, S. W. (1991). Individual differences in sociosexuality: Evidence for convergent and discriminant validity. *Journal of Personality and Social Psychology, 60,* 870–883.

Sinha, J. B. P., & Pandey, J. (1972). The processes of decision making in dependence prone persons. *Journal of Psychological Research, 16,* 35–37.

Snyder, W. U. (1963). *Dependency in psychotherapy.* New York: MacMillan.

Sperling, M. B., & Berman, W. H. (1991). An attachment classification of desperate love. *Journal of Personality Assessment, 56,* 45–55.

Sroufe, L. A., Fox, N. E., & Pancake, V. R. (1983). Attachment and dependency in developmental perspective. *Child Development, 54,* 1615–1627.

Symonds, A. (1971). Phobias after marriage: Women's declaration of dependence. *American Journal of Psychoanalysis, 31,* 144–152.

Tabachnick, N. (1961). Interpersonal relations in suicide attempts. *Archives of General Psychiatry, 4,* 16–21.

Torgerson, S. (1979). The nature and origin of common phobic fears. *American Journal of Psychiatry, 134,* 343–351.

Tribich, D., & Messer, S. (1974). Psychoanalytic character type and status of authority as determiners of suggestibility. *Journal of Consulting and Clinical Psychology, 42,* 842–848.

Vaillant, G. E. (1980). Natural history of male psychological health, VIII: Antecedents of alcoholism and orality. *American Journal of Psychiatry, 137,* 181–186.

Vaillant, G. E. (1994). Ego mechanisms of defense and personality psychopathology. *Journal of Abnormal Psychology, 103,* 44–50.

Weiss, L. R. (1969). Effects of subject, experimenter and task variables on compliance with the experimenter's expectation. *Journal of Projective Techniques and Personality Assessment, 33,* 247–256.

Weiss, L. R., & Masling, J. (1970). Further validation of a Rorschach measure of oral imagery: A study of six clinical groups. *Journal of Abnormal Psychology, 76,* 83–87.

Whiffen, V. E., & Sasseville, T. M. (1991). Dependency, self-criticism and recollections of parenting: Sex differences and the role of depressive affect. *Journal of Social and Clinical Psychology, 10,* 121–133.

Widiger, T. A. (1992). Categorical versus dimensional classification: Implications from and for research. *Journal of Personality Disorders, 6,* 287–300.

Yasunaga, S. (1985). The effects of dependency and strategy patterns on modeling. *Japanese Journal of Psychology, 55,* 374–377.

CHAPTER 6

Narcissism

PAUL WINK

The second half of this century has witnessed an unprecedented interest in narcissism. From its obscure origins, the legend of Narcissus has become the myth for our times. Although the reasons for the recent rise in popularity of narcissism are complex and overdetermined, two developments are noteworthy. From the 1960s onward, the construct of narcissism has played a vital role in metapsychological debates within the psychoanalytic community. At stake was the primacy of the self or the whole person over the tripartite structure comprising the id, ego, and superego (Stolorow, 1975). The debate was simultaneously fueled by the development of new therapeutic techniques that made it possible to treat, hitherto deemed untreatable, patients with narcissistic personality disorders (Adler, 1986).

Although the psychoanalysts may have provided the necessary tools for the understanding of narcissism, its popularity within the mainstream culture was aided by a growing perception after World War II that, for better or worse, Americans were becoming more and more self-oriented. According to Kohut (1977), the beginning of this century was marked by the centrality of the "Guilty Individual," a person who was typically brought up in an extended family system and who, because of overstimulation in childhood, had to struggle as an adult with unresolved oedipal feelings and conflicts between the id, ego, and the superego. In contrast, the contemporary "Tragic Individual"—a product of the nuclear family—is more susceptible to understimulation as a child and consequently in adulthood faces the ever-present danger of fragmentation of the self.

The writing of this chapter was supported in part by a Wellesley College Faculty Award. I would like to thank Ashley Hull for her help in researching the current literature on narcissism.

In analogous terms, Masterson (1990) depicts a historical shift in psychopathology from preoccupation with guilt and neuroses to a new concern with boredom, meaninglessness, and the search for a real or authentic sense of the self. Kohut's and Masterson's depiction of a person grappling with issues of fragmentation, authenticity, and meaning reflects well the plight of the postmodern individual. It challenges us with a vision of life in times when old truths are being decentered and where new meanings have to be actively constructed rather than accepted as a legacy of past generations.

In distinction to Kohut (1977), Lasch (1979) perceives the societal turn toward narcissism as a sad reflection on American culture in the age of diminished expectations. For Lasch, the contemporary emphasis on the self is a defense against the threat posed by a dying culture, which has become devoid of old meanings and depleted by the abandonment of communal values.

Irrespective of our ultimate explanation for the increase in preoccupation with the self, the rapid growth of interest in narcissism has resulted in a wealth of publications and review articles on the subject matter. Comprehensive reviews of psychoanalytic and psychiatric research on narcissism are provided by Akhtar (1989) and Volkan (1982). Ornstein (1978) and Baker and Baker (1987) offer excellent introductions to the, at times, daunting writings of Kohut, and Gunderson, Ronningstam, and Smith (1991) report on the recent psychiatric research on symptoms that differentiate narcissism from other personality disorders.

In distinction to past reviews, the focus of this chapter is on quantitative research into narcissism construed as a continuous dimension and a source of individual variation. Following a brief exposition of the commonly accepted, psychoanalytically based theory of narcissism and its development (the Received View), I will discuss issues of assessment and symptomatology and then survey the implications of narcissism for self-esteem, affect, real-life outcomes, childhood and adult development, and gender. Most of the work reviewed in this chapter comes from the field of psychology and relies on self-report narcissism scales to study group and individual differences primarily in college populations. Just as Freud assumed that the study of abnormal psychic processes would shed light on healthy functioning, so, conversely, the present review is based on the assumption that research on narcissism in the nonpsychiatric population will shed light on psychopathology. This chapter asks these questions: How much empirical support does mainstream academic psychology provide for the Received View? and, To what extent do quantitative studies of group and individual differences contribute to the broadening of our clinically based understanding of the narcissistic personality?

NARCISSISM: THE RECEIVED VIEW

Broadly defined, narcissism means a concentration of psychological interest on the self (Bursten, 1982). Construed in this way, narcissism is devoid of pathological significance and is an essential ingredient of healthy functioning. Self-oriented mental activity is necessary for robust self-esteem, personal cohesiveness, and stability (Stolorow, 1975). It is also a precursor to creativity, wisdom, and empathy (Kohut, 1966). The important question then is not who possesses narcissistic characteristics, because we all do, but rather when, and why does the process of self-investment go astray? Despite a history of heated theoretical debates, there appears to have emerged a relatively consensual psychoanalytic formulation of the origins and phenomenology of narcissistic pathology. I call this consensual characterization the *Received View*.

Pathological narcissism is the product of unempathic parenting (Kernberg, 1975; Kohut, 1971, 1977; Miller, 1981). In the case of narcissism, unlike the case of borderline personalities, the lack of attunement is not catastrophic enough to prevent the development of a basic sense of self or identity. Nevertheless, it is serious enough to result in the child's, and subsequently the adult's, use of splitting (Kernberg, 1975). In other words, there is a lack of proper integration of positive and negative affect and a tendency toward self-fragmentation. Typically, the narcissistic individual has a history of being taken care of by a cold and vulnerable parent who uses the child to regulate his or her own fragile psychical functioning (Kohut, 1971). Alternatively, the child might identify strongly with a parent who is quite narcissistic in order to escape from the other parent who is even more psychologically disturbed (Masterson, 1990). In this instance, once again, the child has to renounce his or her own "true" self and succumb to being used by the other. Narcissistic individuals are frequently treated as "special" by their parents because of their being firstborn, having exceptional beauty or talent (Kernberg, 1975), or empathising with parental overt wishes and unconscious desires (Miller, 1981). The outcome of a prolonged (unmitigated by external sources such as grandparents or school teachers) history of lack of attunement to one's childhood needs, is the simultaneous development of a grandiose sense of the self and feelings of vulnerability and inferiority (Kohut, 1977).

Although a broad consensus exists regarding the central place of grandiosity in narcissistic pathology, there is disagreement concerning its origins. For Kohut (1977, 1984), it is a product of a developmental arrest and reflects an only partially transformed grandiosity of the young child. According to Kernberg (1975), however, the narcissistic grandiose self is a pathological amalgam of psychic representations of the real self, the ideal self, and the ideal object (other), which serves the defensive function of keeping at bay feelings of aggression and envy. Whichever way the grandiose self is construed, it is accompanied by split-off, or unintegrated, feelings of inferiority and vulnerability that correspond to the narcissist's awareness of a past history of misuse by the parent(s) (Kohut, 1971). Behind the grandiose facade, there is a deeply ingrained concern by the narcissistic individual of being ultimately responsible for his or her true self not being accepted and celebrated by the parents.

In adulthood, narcissistic grandiosity is typically accompanied by impaired empathy, exhibitionism, a sense of entitlement, and exploitativeness of others (Kernberg, 1975, 1986). In interpersonal relations, narcissism leads to the use of others to fulfill one's own psychological needs and maintain stability of the self. At times, others are used to affirm or mirror the actions of the narcissistic individual. On other occasions, narcissistic needs may be met through a merger with an "all powerful" idealized individual. In both instances, the other is related to as a self-object whose value is defined in terms of how well that person functions as a provider of comfort and emotional stability (Kohut, 1984). In addition, interactions with people may be detrimentally affected by projected feelings of envy and aggression that prevent the narcissistic individual from forming deep and close attachments, and may lead him or her to withdraw into "splendid isolation" (Kernberg, 1975).

In the area of work, the predominant feelings are boredom, dissatisfaction, and lack of fulfillment and meaning. This attitude may reflect a basic misalignment between what inspires true enthusiasm and the goals or ideals that are being actually pursued (Kohut, 1977). Alternatively, it may reflect the presence of a false self (Masterson, 1990; Winnicott, 1960/1965), or even a defensive need to devalue one's own achievement and those of others to avoid overwhelming feelings of envy (Kernberg, 1975).

A final central feature of narcissistic pathology is the tendency to oscillate between feelings of grandiosity and those of inferiority, depression, and depletion. Usually, the latter surface only as a result of failure or slight. When they do emerge, the feelings of inferiority remain quite separate from the feelings of grandeur and, hence, they cannot be integrated into a healthy and well modulated sense of self. For narcissistic individuals, healing of the split between positive and negative affect is too painful and threatening (Kernberg, 1975).

From a developmental perspective, narcissism has been associated with deterioration in midlife. The realization of mortality, physical aging, and the limits to accomplishments potentiate in narcissistic individuals feelings of envy and resentment (Kernberg, 1980), and also elicit feelings of shame and self-mortification at not having lived a life that was true to their inner hopes, wishes, and aspirations (Kohut, 1977). The resulting defensive devaluation of self and others and a sense of depletion means that the narcissistic individual inhabits a world that is progressively more hostile, lonely, and devoid of meaning and nourishment (Kernberg, 1980).

TYPOLOGIES

Several typologies of narcissism have been proposed in the past. Kohut and Wolf (1978), for example, distinguished between *merger-hungry* individuals, who must continually attach and define themselves through others; *contact-shunning* individuals, who avoid social contact because of a fear that their behaviors will not be admired or accepted; and *mirror-hungry* individuals, who tend to display themselves in front of others. In contrast, Bursten (1973) proposed four types of narcissistic personalities differentiated by the various strategies used in the process of self-regulation. The *craving* individuals are clinging, demanding, and needy; the *paranoid* individuals are critical and suspicious; the *manipulative* individuals derive satisfaction from conscious and deliberate deception of others; and the *phallic narcissists* are aggressive, exhibitionistic, reckless, and daring. This last group has been originally described by Wilhelm Reich (1949). Neither of the above two classifications has gained wide acceptance. Kohut's distinction is too embedded in self-psychology, and Bursten's schema seems overly inclusive of other types of pathology.

A much wider acceptance has been gained by the distinction between overt (exhibitionistic) and covert (closet) forms of narcissistic personality. This dichotomy draws on the aforementioned tendency of narcissists to hold contradictory views of the self (Akhtar & Thomson, 1982; Akhtar, 1989). The majority of narcissistic individuals "impress" others with their open display of grandiosity, exhibitionism, and entitlement. In their case, feelings of inferiority, depression, and depletion surface only infrequently. A smaller but nevertheless significant group of "closet narcissists" (Masterson, 1981) present as timid, shy, inhibited, and ineffective, only to reveal their exhibitionistic and grandiose fantasies on closer contact. Their core narcissistic pathology is hidden by a defensive posture of inhibition and passivity (Masterson, 1990). Interpersonally, such individuals may tend more toward relationships based on idealization than mirroring. Gabbard (1989) comments on the DSM-III's (American Psychiatric Association [APA], 1980) failure to include "the shy quietly grandiose narcissistic individual whose extreme sensitivity to slight leads to an assiduous avoidance of the spotlight" (p. 527). The presence of covertly narcissistic individuals has been acknowledged by both Kohut (1971) and Kernberg (1986).

A second classification of narcissism to gain wider acceptance is based on the severity of the condition. Both Kernberg (1975, 1986) and Masterson (1990) divide narcissistic individuals into high-, middle-, and low-functioning groups. High-functioning narcissists rarely seek treatment as they are well able to satisfy their needs through their professional careers and relations with others. Such individuals are frequently found in artistic and creative professions that allow them to sublimate their exhibitionism and use productively their intellectual interests and keen sense of empathy. The middle category consists of those narcissistic individuals whose grandiosity, impaired empathy, exploitativeness, hypersensitivity, and boredom lead them to serious difficulties at love and work. These individuals may benefit from psychotherapy, though their unique transferences and countertransferences need to be recognized by the therapist. At the bottom, are those narcissists whose pathology resembles that of borderline individuals.

ASSESSMENT

The recent growth of interest in narcissism has resulted in the development of a number of self-report measures of the construct. The majority of these scales were developed combining the DSM-III (APA, 1980) criteria for the narcissistic personality disorder and the internal consistency method of test construction. The internal consistency method produces scales with items that are highly intercorrelated with each other and with the total scale. The main advantage of measures developed in this way is clarity of interpretation. Their main disadvantage is an insensitivity to the potentially multifaceted nature of a construct.

The single most widely researched narcissism scale developed using the DSM-III criteria and the internal consistency method is the Narcissistic Personality Inventory (NPI; Raskin & Hall, 1979, 1981). Other scales developed using the same methodology are the Wink and Gough (1990) California Psychological Inventory (CPI) and MMPI Narcissism scales, Raskin and Novacek's (1989) MMPI Narcissism scale, and the Morey, Waugh, and Blashfield (1985) Narcissism scale. This last scale was developed as part of a battery of measures assessing all 11 DSM-III personality disorders. All the preceding scales are highly intercorrelated, with rs ranging from .50 to about .80 and each scale correlates significantly with observer ratings of narcissism (Raskin & Novacek, 1989; Raskin & Terry, 1988; Wink, 1991a).

Although in general little attention has been paid in developing narcissism scales to issues of discriminant validity, the Morey et al. (1985)

Narcissism scale and the NPI are only moderately correlated with measures of other personality disorders. Both measures show highest positive correlation with Morey's DSM-III Hysterical Personality Disorder scale and highest negative correlation with the Avoidant Personality Disorder scale. In addition, the Morey Narcissism scale correlates positively with the Antisocial Personality Disorder scale. On the MMPI (Hathaway & McKinley, 1940), the NPI, the two Narcissism scales of Wink and Gough, and Morey's scale all correlate positively with Hypomania, a measure of ego inflation and energy, and correlate negatively with the Depression and Social Introversion scales (Morey et al., 1985; Raskin & Novacek, 1989; Wink & Gough, 1990).

A second group of narcissism scales was developed using an empirical method of scale construction. In the case of Ashby, Lee, and Duke's (1979) Narcissistic Personality Disorder scale (NPDS), the criterion group consisted of diagnosed narcissists in treatment. Both Serkownek's (1975) Narcissism-Hypersensitivity scale and Pepper and Strong's (1958) Ego-Sensitivity scale were the result of a factor analysis of the MMPI Masculinity/Femininity scale, which in its turn, was developed using a criterion group of creative, artistic, and presumably narcissistic individuals in psychotherapy with the MMPI's author, Stark Hathaway. Once again, these three scales are highly intercorrelated (rs ranging from high 40s to low 50s) and are all significantly related to observer ratings of narcissism (Wink, 1991a; Wink & Gough, 1990). Nevertheless, several studies have shown them to be uncorrelated with the NPI and other narcissism measures developed using the internal consistency method (Emmons, 1987; Mullins & Kopelman, 1988; Watson, Grisham, Trotter, & Biderman, 1984; Wink & Gough, 1990). Furthermore, the NPDS has very different personality correlates to the NPI. The nature and meaning of these differences is discussed in the next section.

Two other narcissism self-report scales were developed from a theoretical perspective other than the DSM-III. The O'Brien (1987) Multiphasic Narcissism Inventory, which is based on Alice Miller's (1981) view of narcissism, includes a Poisonous Pedagogy subscale reflecting an unconscious need to control others, and a Narcissistically Abused Personality subscale measuring the tendency to derive self-validation from the approval of others. Millon's (1982) Narcissism scale, on the other hand, reflects the author's unique brand of social learning theory. Both these measures correlate with the NPI, and the O'Brien scale is also positively correlated with the NPDS (Auerbach, 1984; Hibbard, 1992). On the MMPI, Millon's scale shows the familiar pattern of a positive correlation with Hypomania and negative correlations with the Depression and Social Introversion scales (Auerbach, 1984).

In the observer domain, Wink (1992a) developed a California Q-set (CAQ) (Block, 1978) Narcissism prototype that allows for the scaling and aggregation of ratings made by judges and peers. The prototype allows for the scoring of three scales. The Willfulness scale includes items indicative of undercontrol of impulses, self-indulgence, self-dramatization, and condescension. Items included in the Hypersensitivity scale suggest the presence of hostility and irritability, sensitivity to criticism and demands, and self-defensiveness. High scores on the Autonomy scale are indicative of high aspirations, independence, wide interests, unusual thought processes, and sensitivity to aesthetic experiences. All three scales correlate significantly with observer ratings of narcissism, but only Willfulness and Hypersensitivity are positively associated with ratings of pathology (Wink, 1991b). The Willfulness scale is correlated with the NPI and the Hypersensitivity scale correlates positively with the NPDS (Wink, 1991a).

Also in the observer domain, Patton, Connor, and Scott (1982) developed 10 observer rating scales to measure Kohut's formulation of narcissism or self psychology. These scales were intended to measure therapeutic outcomes, but so far they have not been widely researched.

Finally, Harder (1979) reports on the construction of projective narcissism scales for the Early Memory Test, the Thematic Apperception Test, and the Rorschach. These three measures are significantly intercorrelated with each other and show preliminary evidence of criterion-related validity, but once again have not gained widespread acceptance.

Symptoms, Types, and Level of Pathology

As expected from scales developed using DSM-III criteria, the personality correlates of the NPI, the Wink and Gough CPI and MMPI Narcissism scales, and the MMPI Narcissism scale of Raskin and Novacek include ego expansiveness, desire for attention, and disesteem for others. Also evident are conceit, exhibitionism, self-centeredness, and impulsivity. These characteristics are present both in the self-report and observer domains (Raskin & Novacek, 1989; Raskin & Terry, 1988; Wink & Gough, 1990). In addition, the NPI is associated with daydreams and fantasies indicative of the need for power (Carroll, 1987; Raskin & Novacek, 1991). All the preceding findings support psychiatric research on the differential diagnosis of personality disorders suggesting that a grandiose sense of self-importance, fantasies of unlimited success, and need for attention and admiration are central to the construct of narcissism (Gunderson, Ronningstam, & Smith, 1991).

On the positive side, high scorers on the NPI and the two scales of Wink and Gough are characterized by assertiveness, social poise, and assurance (Wink, 1991a). The NPI is also associated with leadership potential and achievement orientation (Emmons, 1984; Raskin & Terry, 1988). Overall, the personality correlates of these reviewed self-report narcissism scales indicate that they measure overt narcissism.

In contrast to measures of overt narcissism, the personality correlates of Ashby, Lee, and Duke's (1979) NPDS, the second most widely researched narcissism scale, and of the MMPI Narcissism-Hypersensitivity (Serkownek, 1975) and Ego-Sensitivity (Pepper & Strong, 1958) scales indicate sensitivity to slight and a lack of social presence, sociability, and dominance (Graham, 1987; Graham, Schroeder, & Lilly, 1971; Wink, 1991a). In addition, the NPDS is associated with depression (Watson, Taylor, & Morris, 1987) and inadequacy, unhappiness, and worry (Mullins & Kopelman, 1988). All these characteristics are congruent with covert narcissism. Taken on their own, however, they may also be indicative of other personality disorders such as paranoid, avoidant, and schizoid. Because the NPDS and the two other narcissism scales related to it were developed either directly or indirectly using as a criterion patients in psychotherapy, it is also possible that they measure the sensitive and vulnerable side of overt narcissism that becomes activated in response to slight or injury to the self. Factors in favor of the NPDS and the MMPI scales of Serkownek (1975) and Pepper and Strong (1958) being measures of narcissism are that, just as the NPI, they are correlated with (a) observer ratings of narcissism, (b) spouse perceptions of being bossy, intolerant, cruel, conceited, arrogant, and demanding, and (c) hostility and undercontrol of aggressive and erotic impulses (Wink, 1991a). In addition, the lack of interpersonal poise and confidence associated with the NPDS is reflected in CPI (Gough, 1987) scales that measure stable personality traits rather than states. It is unlikely, therefore, that this scale reflects a transient response to slight or injury.

In summary, empirical research using the NPI, the NPDS, and narcissism scales associated with them offers support for the psychoanalytically based distinction between overt and covert narcissism. Although these two forms of the disorder share several underlying features, they remain uncorrelated or independent of each other in self-report and observer ratings.

In terms of level of pathology, covert narcissism appears to be more dysfunctional than the overt form of the disorder. Only covert narcissism is associated with lack of well-being, competence, and personal adjustment (Wink, 1991a), depression and low self-esteem (Watson, Taylor, & Morris, 1987), disturbed object-relations and masochism (Hibbard, 1992), and deterioration in the course of adult life (Wink, 1992b, in press) (see section on Childhood and Adult Development). It may be that internality associated with covert narcissism is indicative of a lack of ego strength, whereas the strong sense of agency associated with overt narcissism points to a well integrated, albeit grandiose, sense of the self.

Within the domain of overt narcissism, research on factor analytically based subscales of the NPI suggests that self-reported exploitativeness and entitlement have more pathological implications than a sense of leadership and authority, self-absorption, or vanity, and feelings of superiority. Only the Exploitativeness/Entitlement subscale of the NPI correlates with suspiciousness, anxiety, and neuroticism (Emmons, 1984), lack of empathy (Watson et al., 1984), depression, and the NPDS (Watson et al., 1987). Compared with the other factors of the NPI, it also shows a stronger relationship with presence of irrational beliefs (Watson & Morris, 1990) and cynicism (Watson, Sawrie, & Biderman, 1991).

In distinction to overt and covert narcissism, which in the observer domain are measured by the CAQ Willfulness and Hypersensitivity scales (Wink, 1992a), the CAQ Autonomy scale measures a healthy sense of self-directedness characterized by a sense of personal autonomy, high aspirations, and intellectual and aesthetic interests. As discussed in the following section, healthily self-directed individuals share with overt narcissists a sense of social poise and assurance, but in addition, their lives are characterized by success at work, creativity, and positive personal growth in adulthood (Wink, 1991b, 1992b).

Self, Self-Esteem, and Self-Enhancement

As expected, high scorers on the NPI are characterized by self-focus (Gramzow & Tangney, 1992) or "selfism" (Emmons, 1987); they believe that their needs are best met by adopting an egocentric orientation to life. They also show a self-referential attitude as exemplified by greater frequency in the use of the pronoun "I" (Raskin & Shaw, 1988).

On the Received View, narcissistic individuals are thought to possess a defensively inflated sense of self-esteem. Narcissistic grandiosity is both a sign of ego-inflation and an attempt to deny feelings of vulnerability and self-depreciation that result from the use of the child by primary care givers. From the point of view of empirical research, the preceding claim can be broken down into two questions: Is narcissism associated with high self-esteem? and, Is this high esteem the result of pathological self-enhancement?

Numerous studies report a positive relationship between overt narcissism, as measured by the NPI, and self-esteem (e.g., Emmons, 1984; Raskin & Terry, 1988; Watson et al., 1987). Understandably, the reverse is true of covert narcissism where the external manifestations of self-depletion are accompanied by report of lowered self-esteem (Watson et al., 1987) and feelings of inadequacy (Mullins & Kopelman, 1988).

As indicated by Raskin, Novacek, and Hogan (1991a), defensive self-esteem or self-enhancement can take the form of social desirability (self-validation through the extraction of favorable evaluations and approval from others) or, alternatively, it can be linked to grandiosity (a combination of exhibitionism and the expectation of being admired by others). Both overt (Raskin et al., 1991a) and covert (Watson et al., 1984) measures of narcissism correlated negatively with social desirability, which means that pathological narcissists generally have little regard for the impression they make on others. Self-ingratiation is not a narcissistic way of regulating self-esteem. The NPI is, however, associated with grandiosity (Raskin et al., 1991a). This suggests that self-display in the hope of being admired by others is important for the self-esteem of the overt narcissist. Additional evidence for self-enhancement bias associated with overt narcissism is provided by John and Robins (1994) who found the tendency among narcissistic individuals to overestimate, compared with ratings of observers, the quality of their performance in leaderless group discussion.

Just as not all forms of self-enhancement are maladaptive, so some forms of narcissistic self-biases appear related to healthy adjustment. In particular, the NPI subscales measuring leadership, self-absorption, and vanity are all associated with an adaptive, if somewhat exaggerated, expectation of personal control over events and a sense of invulnerability (Watson et al., 1991). The preceding components of the NPI retain a positive correlation with self-esteem even after social desirability and grandiosity have been partialed out (Raskin et al., 1991a). The same is not true, however, of the more pathological Entitlement/Exploitativeness dimension, which loses its positive association with self-esteem after grandiosity is controlled for. Entitlement/Exploitativeness is also related to an unadaptive sense of cynicism and perception of being victimized (Watson et al., 1991).

EMOTIONS AND FEELINGS

Hostility

Both overt and covert forms of narcissism have been associated with the undercontrol of hostile and negative impulses (Wink, 1991a). The expression of hostility is likely to take on, however, different forms in the two types of narcissistic individuals. In the case of overt narcissism, it tends to be expressed directly without particular concern for the setting or target. In support of this conjecture, Wink (1992b) found that high scorers on the observer-based CAQ Willfulness scale reported conflict in their relations with friends. In the case of covert narcissism, the hostile impulses are likely to be held back and may be more evident in marriage and family relations (see Life Implications section). Another factor that may affect the expression of hostility is gender. McCann and Biaggio (1989), for example, reported that the NPI was correlated with general, though possibly unacknowledged, feelings of anger in both men and women. In the case of men, however, the anger was expressed more in physical terms than was the case for women.

In his research on the NPI, Emmons (1987) found that whereas the overall score on the total scale correlated positively with negative affect, the more pathological Exploitativeness/Entitlement subscale correlated with both positive and negative affect and the intensity of affective experience. Emmons suggests that the extreme mood swings of overtly narcissistic individuals may be the result of their relatively simple self-representations. The tendency toward rapid oscillations in mood may also be indicative of the use of the defense mechanism of splitting, which is characteristic of narcissism.

How can overtly narcissistic individuals simultaneously report feelings of hostility and still maintain high self-esteem? According to Raskin, Novacek, and Hogan (1991b), the answer to this question once again involves a grandiose sense of self. Although hostility and self-esteem do not appear to be directly related, when grandiosity and narcissism are partialed out, their relationship becomes negative. In other words, in the absence of grandiosity and narcissism, people who express high hostility also report low self-esteem. In the presence of grandiosity as a moderator variable, the connection between hostility and self-esteem becomes positive.

Shame and Shyness

The connection between narcissism and shame can be construed in one of two ways. According to Lewis (1971), the entire narcissistic personality structure serves as a defense against profound feelings of shame that originate in childhood. For Lewis, narcissism is a consequence of shame. It could be argued, however, that the arrow of causality points the other way and that it is narcissistic exhibitionism and the tendency to set unrealistic goals that produces shame as a response to the experience of slight, injury, and disappointment (Morrison, 1989).

Initial empirical research using the NPI revealed, contrary to expectations, a negative rather than positive correlation between narcissism and shame (Wright, O'Leary, & Balkin, 1989). Gramzow and Tangney (1992) partialed out healthy subscales of the NPI from the Exploitativeness/Entitlement subscale and found a significant, but low, correlation between pathological overt narcissism and shame. Such a connection between

Exploitativeness/Entitlement and shame was not found by Hibbard (1992) who, however, reported a strong positive association between Ashby, Lee, and Duke's (1979) NPDS and O'Brien's (1987) Multiphasic Narcissistic Inventory and two measures of shame and a measure of masochism. The propensity toward feelings of shame appears to be confined to covertly narcissistic individuals, and it tends not to be consciously experienced by overt narcissists.

Since covert narcissists experience shame, are they also prone to shyness? Cheek and Melchior (1985) found this to be the case, although the relationship between narcissism as measured by Murray's (1938) Narcissism scale, and shyness, as measured by the Cheek and Buss Shyness scale (Cheek & Melchior, 1990), was stronger for women than men. In support of Cheek and Melchior, Wink (1991a) reports a strong negative association between self-reported covert narcissism and CPI (Gough, 1987) measures of social presence, externality, and assurance. If indeed there is a relationship between narcissism and shyness, this raises the possibility of there being two distinct types of shy individuals. In particular, narcissistically based shyness seems to be more ominous and different in its origins and implications compared with the more anxiety-driven shyness characteristic of social phobias and avoidant personality disorders.

Boredom and Sensation Seeking

Narcissistic feelings of boredom serve potentially two different functions. First, they serve as markers of a false sense of self (Svrakic, 1985). Not having been allowed as children to experience and develop their authentic sense of self (Masterson, 1990; Miller, 1981), narcissistic adults pursue life goals that feel alien and imposed, and that, therefore, lack meaning and fail to energize and vitalize. Second, boredom serves a defensive function of blocking intensive feelings of envy and aggression that threaten the narcissistic individual's equilibrium of the self (Kernberg, 1975). The reverse side of boredom is the propensity toward sensation-seeking undertaken in the hope of coming to life and revitalizing the self.

In a study using the NPI, Emmons (1981) found a relationship between narcissism and susceptibility to boredom and experience seeking, with men reporting greater feelings of boredom and women indicating a stronger sensation-seeking tendency. A risk-seeking factor was also uncovered by Wink and Gough (1990) in their principal components analysis of the CPI and MMPI Narcissism scales.

Similarly to their overt counterparts, covertly narcissistic individuals report feelings of boredom across the major adult social roles of partner, worker, parent, and friend (Wink, in press). These feelings of boredom do not reflect objective evidence of failure to maintain a work career or develop long-term relationships. Rather, they indicate feelings of hostility and resentment that are turned inward and that pervade the lives of covertly narcissistic individuals.

Empathy

Although an impaired sense of empathy is one of the symptoms of narcissism listed in the DSM-III (APA, 1980), its relationship to narcissism is far from straightforward. On the one hand, a grandiose sense of self inhibits genuine capacity for empathy and, parenthetically, elicits feelings of boredom in interactions with others. On the other hand, however, the narcissistic tendency toward merger with others and toward the regulation of self-esteem by eliciting admiration from others requires considerable empathy, even if it happens to be put to manipulative use. Further, Kohut (1966) argues that healthy empathy in adulthood has its roots in developmentally early relationships based on merger with, and idealization, of the other.

In my research on middle-aged women (Wink, 1992b), I found that across the first half of their adult life, hypersensitive or covertly narcissistic women were less empathic than other women. The autonomous or healthily narcissistic women were, however, consistently more empathic than others, and willful or overtly narcissistic women showed empathy in their late 20s. Gough and I (Wink & Gough, 1990) also found a positive correlation between overt narcissism and empathy. Watson et al. (1984), however, report the NPI to be negatively correlated with two of three empathy scales used in their study. The verdict on the relationship between overt narcissism and empathy is still open. It is likely though that overt narcissists possess the kind of empathy that allows them to manipulate and elicit admiration from others. In distinction, healthily narcissistic individuals are capable of mature empathy, which is used in the service of understanding self and others.

LIFE IMPLICATIONS

Because most of the empirical research on narcissism is performed on college students, relatively little is known about its effect on real-life outcomes such as the quality of interpersonal relations, success at work, and personal adjustment. In this and the next section, I will rely largely on my own research to flush out some concurrent and developmental implications of narcissism in a group of close to 100 Mills College women graduates (classes of 1958 and 1960) who were initially studied as seniors in college and then followed up at the average ages of 27, 43, and 52 (Helson, 1967;

Helson & Wink, 1992). I have investigated narcissism or self-directedness in these women with the three narcissism scales discussed earlier and scored from observer CAQ-ratings of the rich, open-ended questionnaire responses provided by the participants at age 43.

Among the Mills women, those who scored high on hypersensitivity showed signs of psychological distress at midlife, and lacked enjoyment and engagement in their work careers. They also reported home conflict, a lack of family cohesion, dissatisfaction as partner and parent, and problems with children (Wink, 1991b). Marital dissatisfaction was evident in follow-ups at both age 43 and age 52 (Wink, 1992b; in press). Problems of covertly narcissistic individuals in maintaining satisfactory love relationships have been also reported by Solomon (1982) in a study using Ashby, Lee, and Duke's NPDS. In sum, midlife covert narcissism appears to affect detrimentally both areas of work and love and leads to poor psychological adjustment.

In contrast, willful or overtly narcissistic women at midlife were characterized by high energy level and enjoyment of work (Wink, 1991b), and perceived themselves as stimulating and creative across major social roles (Wink, in press). This optimistic, if not grandiose, self-perception was not matched however, by any objective signs of success or achievement in the realm of work or interpersonal relations. Although women classified as willful at midlife showed signs of investment in their mid-20s in an upwardly mobile work career, these commitments were not sustained through to the early 40s. A low but significant correlation between willfulness and drug use (Wink, 1991b) suggests that the personal adjustment of the overtly narcissistic women at midlife may be more conflicted than it would appear at first glance.

High scorers on Autonomy or healthy narcissism were not correlated with any measures of interpersonal adjustment, but were associated positively with virtually all measures of success at work. The autonomous women who embarked on an upwardly mobile career in their mid to late 20s tended to achieve high status level at work by midlife. All the psychotherapists and most of the artists in the Mills sample scored high on the CAQ Autonomy scale. This finding supports Kohut's (1966) contention that empathy and creativity are the results of a healthy transformation of childhood narcissism and are, therefore, related to the self-directed line of development.

More direct evidence of a link between narcissism and creativity in the Mills study is that the Autonomy scale correlated positively with the CPI Creative Temperament scale (Gough, 1987) and two Adjective Check List (Gough & Heilbrun, 1983) creativity scales. In addition, Raskin (1980) found a positive relationship between the NPI and the Symbolic Equivalents Test, a measure of creativity developed by Frank Barron

(1974). Solomon (1985) noted a correlation between the NPDS and a self-report creativity scale. It may be that the connection between narcissism and creativity transcends the distinctions between healthy and pathological narcissism.

CHILDHOOD AND ADULT DEVELOPMENT

Empirical research on the origins and development of narcissism includes studies of family dynamics and early relations with parents, research on the special status of narcissistic adults as children, and inquiry into personality change in adulthood.

Childhood Origins

There is little direct description of narcissism in children. Most psychoanalytic work on childhood origins of narcissism, including the writings of Kernberg (1975) and Kohut (1971, 1977), are based on inferences drawn from the analysis of transference and regression of adults seen in treatment.

Clinical observations of children indicate that narcissistic vulnerability is already evident in children of 3 or 4 years of age (Noshpitz, 1984). Once in school, narcissistic children develop a posture of arrogant isolation (overt narcissism) or, alternatively, appear shy and awkward, and eager to please in order to avoid shame and humiliation. These covertly narcissistic children relegate their grandiosity and entitlement to the world of fantasy (Bleiberg, 1988). Clinical studies of severely disturbed and abused young children link narcissism to an unusual sensitivity, responsiveness, and ability to anticipate the needs of others, which, however, mask a core sense of aloofness and fear of dependency (Yates, 1981). Frequently, the precocious, and defensive in nature, empathic ability is used to obtain gratification through the self-serving manipulation of the outside world, which is perceived as threatening and hostile (Tooley, 1975).

In a retrospective study of early parenting styles among college undergraduates, Watson, Little, and Biderman (1992) found NPI's Exploitativeness/Entitlement subscale to be negatively correlated with the mature authoritative parenting style and positively correlated with parental permissiveness. In the Mills Longitudinal study, Wink (1992b) found that in midlife, hypersensitive or covertly narcissistic women characterized their early relations with both their mothers and fathers as lacking in warmth and caring. The mother was also reported as inspiring distrust and lack of security. Women with high scores on willfulness or overt narcissism expressed, on the other hand, a dislike of their mothers but indicated a liking and pride of their fathers, who themselves showed narcissistic personality traits (Wink, 1991b). Evidence of an early identification with a narcissistic father among overtly narcissistic women is also provided by Block (1971) in his analysis of data from two longitudinal studies. As argued by Masterson (1990), one route toward adult narcissism appears to involve an identification with a narcissistic parent in order to escape from the even more disturbed other parent.

In my research, I have found no relationship between Autonomy or healthy narcissism and retrospective accounts of early relations with parents. Mills women with high scores on Autonomy did, however, report being involved in artistic, creative, and agenetic childhood activities (Wink, 1992b).

Special Status

Do narcissistic adults possess special characteristics as children that predispose them to differential treatment by parents? Empirically, this question has been addressed primarily through research on the relationship between narcissism and birth order. The results are mixed. Joubert (1989) reports a positive relationship between birth order and scores on the NPI. Narayan (1990), however, failed to replicate this finding, and Watson and Biderman (1989) obtained no support for the hypothesis that being an only child relates to narcissism. It is likely that birth order on its own is not a sensitive enough criterion for the multiplicity of reasons why children may be selected as special by parents who need them to maintain their own frail psychological equilibrium.

Adult Development

As will be recalled, the Received View assumes that narcissism leads to deterioration in midlife. The signs of aging associated with middle adulthood and the growing realization that there are limits to one's accomplishments, are supposed to potentiate narcissistic feelings of envy and resentment that, in turn, result in depression and a sense of depletion.

In the Mills Longitudinal Study, the preceding pattern of adult development was evident in personality changes associated with Hypersensitivity. In their early 40s, hypersensitive women scored lower than the rest of the Mills women on CPI measures of social poise and assurance, normative control of impulse, and achievement (Wink, 1992b). When still in college, however, the same women were virtually indistinguishable from their classmates. Evidently, hypersensitivity at midlife is the product of deterioration that starts in the mid-20s as individuals confront the challenges of establishing a work career and maintaining long-term relationships. Although from early 40s to early 50s, the hypersensitive women gained somewhat in impulse control, they continued to be more troubled than the rest of the Mills women (Wink, in press).

A very different pattern of adult personality change was evident among the Mills women classified at midlife as willful. The willful women increased in social poise, confidence, and level of effective functioning during the first few years after graduation from college, a time of novelty and excitement associated with the formation of the first adult life-structure. In their early 40s, however, high scorers on Willfulness showed very little difference from college days. At both ages, they were more impulsive and self-indulgent than the other Mills women. The same findings continued to be true in the early 50s (Wink, 1992b, in press). The Mills findings regarding the long-term stability of personality in overtly narcissistic women agree with Block's (1971) account of personality development of the dominant narcissist.

From the early 20s to the early 50s, the autonomous or healthily narcissistic women scored higher than the rest of Mills women on CPI measures of tolerance, psychological mindedness, creativity, and intellectual achievement. Unlike high scorers on Willfulness, who were at their best in their late 20s, for the autonomous women the late 30s and early 40s were a time of growth in confidence, social poise, and understanding of self and others (Wink, 1992b). From the 40s to early 50s, autonomy was associated with increases in responsibility and the ability to maintain friction-free relationships with others that are characteristic of individuals in positions of social and personal dominance and power (Wink, in press).

The different patterns of change associated with Hypersensitivity, Willfulness, and Autonomy highlight, once again, the importance of the distinction between overt and covert and healthy and less healthy forms of narcissism.

GENDER

The main body of psychoanalytic research on narcissism does not take into account issues of gender. Although Kohut (1977, 1984) distinguishes between two types of narcissistic relationships, those based on mirroring and exhibitionism and those involving merger with the idealized other, they are not seen as gender specific. As early as the 1950s, however, the psychoanalyst Annie Reich (1953) argued that women narcissists, in contrast to their male counterparts, were much more likely to be involved in relationships based on idealization. Such relations take on either the form of dependent subservience to a strongly admired partner or, alternatively, involve short-lived infatuations that lead to inevitable disappointment.

More recently, Phillipson (1985) has applied Chodorow's (1978) theory of gender differences to narcissism. Because in our society women are the primary caregivers, girls tend to be brought up by a parent of the same gender, whereas boys are not. According to Phillipson, this produces very different kinds of faulty empathy in the mother-daughter and mother-son dyads. In the case of the boy, mother's lack of empathy leads to an exaggerated sense of otherness, and a need for admiration and mirroring that are characteristic of phallic narcissism. A daughter exposed to faulty maternal empathy, on the other hand, can gain self-worth through acting as an extension of her mother. In adulthood, this leads to merger relationships based on idealization that, according to Phillipson, should not be viewed as narcissistic. Similar considerations have led Haaken (1983) to postulate that early parental lack of empathy results in borderline symptomatology in women and narcissism in men.

Most researchers who have used the NPI to analyze gender differences report significantly higher mean scores for men than women (Carroll, 1987; Joubert, 1989; Watson et al., 1984; Watson et al., 1987), though there are some exceptions (Auerbach, 1984; Raskin & Hall, 1981). The presence of mean differences does not preclude, however, the possibility that high scores on measures of narcissism have similar implications for both genders. In fact, in the research on the Mills Longitudinal sample described earlier, I found that predictions drawn from a general, and gender undifferentiated theory of narcissism were applicable to women. Similarly, Wink and Gough (1990) found that although men scored significantly higher than women on both the CPI and MMPI Narcissism scales, the pattern of correlations between these two scales and other self-report personality measures were virtually identical for both genders.

Even though women and men with high scores on narcissism scales may have many characteristics in common, this does not mean that there are no important gender differences. As discussed earlier, the relationship between narcissism and shyness is stronger for women (Cheek & Melchior, 1985), and narcissistic women tend to be less prone to physical aggression than narcissistic men (McCann & Biaggio, 1989). In addition, in a study using the NPI and the Thematic Apperception Test (TAT, Murray, 1943), Carroll (1987) noted a positive correlation between overt narcissism and the need for power in men and a negative correlation between narcissism and the need for intimacy in women. Watson et al. (1987) report that femininity, as measured by the Bem (1981) Sex Role Inventory, was inversely related to exploitative narcissism.

The relationship between narcissism and gender obviously raises the issue of social and cultural influences on personality structure and psychopathology. We have no research data on how the changing role of women in our society impacts narcissism. We may expect, however, that as women begin to occupy positions of privilege and power in the workplace and as men become more involved in the care of children, gender differences in narcissism should gradually disappear.

IMPLICATIONS AND RECOMMENDATIONS

The quantitative research on narcissism reviewed in this chapter contributes in an important way to our understanding of the construct. It is quite evident that research on individual differences plays an important role in testing and extending theories of narcissism derived from qualitative, clinically based case studies. As has been amply documented, research using self-report scales such as the NPI and NPDS, and the three observer-based CAQ narcissism scales, confirms the psychoanalytically based hypothesis that grandiosity, egocentricity, and self-enhancement are central features of narcissistic pathology. The presence of negative affect, in particular hostility, feelings of boredom, problematic relationships with others, and a deterioration at midlife, at least in some forms of narcissism, have all been confirmed in studies of group and individual differences.

Perhaps the most salient insight into narcissism to emerge from this review pertains to the complexity and multidimensionality of the construct. An obvious manifestation of this complexity is the distinction between overt and covert narcissism. Although uncorrelated with one another, the self-report NPI and NPDS, as well as the observer-based Willfulness and Hypersensitivity scales, are all associated with external ratings of narcissism and underlying attitudes of arrogance and exploitativeness. Yet, on the surface, overtly narcissistic individuals present as domineering, assertive, and exhibitionistic, whereas covertly narcissistic persons strike us with their sense of shyness, inadequacy, and depletion. Both types of narcissism show important differences in terms of real-life outcomes and patterns of adult development.

Equally important as the distinction based on type, is the differentiation of narcissism according to level of pathology. Among the two more pathological forms of the disorder, only covert narcissism is linked to lack of empathy, poor personal adjustment in love and work, and deterioration in personality functioning at midlife. Within the domain of overt narcissism, the NPI's exploitativeness/entitlement dimension is related to cynicism, a fragile sense of self-esteem, and extremity of mood swings, whereas the self-reported sense of authority, superiority, and vanity is not. In distinction to pathological narcissism, healthy self-directedness is associated with creativity, empathy, an upwardly mobile work career, and personality growth in adulthood.

Another manifestation of the complexity surrounding narcissism has to do with the meaning of symptoms. For example, feelings of empathy characterize both healthy and more pathological overt narcissists. Yet, although feelings of empathy associated with healthy narcissism have their roots in altruism, the empathy related to pathological narcissism serves the purpose of manipulation and exploitation. Similarly, feelings of shyness associated with covert narcissism are probably quite different from the social anxiety found among individuals with an avoidant personality disorder.

Finally, gender provides an additional source of variation affecting narcissistic symptomatology. Narcissistic women have been reported, for example, to be less physically aggressive, less power oriented, and more prone to idealization than men. Although virtually no research exists on the relationship between narcissism and ethnicity and social class, they are also likely to affect narcissistic symptomatology. Smith (1990), for example, found Caucasian women to be more narcissistic than Asian women.

A model of narcissism that takes into account type, level of pathology, gender, ethnicity, and class has important implications for both the clinician and researcher. From a clinical perspective, narcissistic fantasies of power and grandeur, for example, can equally well lurk behind a bombastic and exhibitionistic facade as one of shyness, vulnerability, and depletion. Clinicians should also keep in mind that narcissistic clients have the potential to transform or channel their self-invested energy into creativity, empathy, and wisdom. Conversely, individuals who initially impress us with their sensitivity to others, and understanding of the world may turn out ultimately to be quite egocentric and grandiose.

From a research perspective, the different patterns of adult development associated with type and level of narcissistic pathology are important to the study of aging. Equally, the relationship between overt narcissism and self-enhancement and the self-concept in general should be of interest to both personality and social psychologists. In general, psychological research into the real-life implications of narcissism supplements psychiatric research into the construct that thus far has focused primarily on symptoms and differential diagnosis, and has neglected issues of construct, concurrent, and predictive validity (Gunderson et al., 1991).

More research is obviously needed into the relationship between the various types of narcissism and their concurrent and developmental implications. Direct research on childhood antecedents of narcissism is sadly lacking. In distinction to psychiatric research, psychological studies of narcissism have neglected the issue of differential diagnosis (discriminant validity). We need to study the relationship between measures of overt narcissism and those of histrionic and antisocial personality disorders. Research is also required on the relationship between self-reported covert narcissism and schizoid, avoidant, and passive-aggressive personality disorders. Both types of pathological narcissism need to be related to the borderline personality. Research efforts in all these areas need to be sensitive to issues of gender, ethnicity, and class, as well as to the impact of changing sociocultural contexts on the prevalence and manifestations of healthy and more pathological levels of self-investment.

REFERENCES

Adler, G. (1986). Psychotherapy of the narcissistic personality disorder patient: Two contrasting approaches. *American Journal of Psychiatry, 143,* 430–436.

Akhtar, S. (1989). Narcissistic personality disorder: Descriptive features and differential diagnosis. *Psychiatric Clinics of North America, 12,* 505–529.

Akhtar, S., & Thomson, J. A. (1982). Overview: Narcissistic personality disorder. *American Journal of Psychiatry, 139,* 12–20.

American Psychiatric Association. (1980). *Diagnostic and statistical manual of mental disorders* (3rd ed.). Washington, DC: Author.

Ashby, H. U., Lee, R. R., & Duke, E. H. (1979). *A narcissistic personality disorder MMPI scale.* Paper presented at the 87th Annual Convention of the American Psychological Association, New York.

Auerbach, J. (1984). Validation of two scales for narcissistic personality disorder. *Journal of Personality Assessment, 46,* 649–653.

Baker, S., & Baker, M. N. (1987). Heinz Kohut's self psychology: An overview. *American Journal of Psychiatry, 114,* 1–9.

Barron, F. X. (1974). *Basic research and aesthetic education.* Washington, DC: U.S. Office of Education.

Bem, S. L. (1981). *Bem sex role inventory: Professional manual.* Palo Alto, CA: Consulting Psychologists Press.

Bleiberg, E. (1988). Developmental pathogenesis of narcissistic disorders in children. *Bulletin of the Menninger Clinic, 52,* 3–15.

Block, J. (1971). *Lives through time.* Berkeley: Bancroft Books.

Block, J. (1978). *The Q-sort method in personality assessment and psychiatric research.* Palo Alto, CA: Consulting Psychologists Press.

Bursten, B. (1973). Some narcissistic personality types. *International Journal of Psychoanalysis, 54,* 287–300.

Bursten, B. (1982). Narcissistic personalities in DSM-III. *Comprehensive Psychiatry, 23,* 409–420.

Carroll, L. (1987). A study of narcissism affiliation, intimacy, and power motives among students in business administration. *Psychological Reports, 61,* 355–358.

Cheek, J. M., & Melchior, L. A. (1985). *Are shy people narcissistic?* Paper presented at the 93rd Annual Convention of the American Psychological Association, Los Angeles.

Cheek, J. M., & Melchior, L. A. (1990). Shyness, self-esteem, and self-consciousness. In H. Leitenberg (Ed.), *Handbook of social and evaluation anxiety* (pp. 47–82). New York: Plenum.

Chodorow, N. (1978). *The reproduction of mothering.* Berkeley, CA: University of California Press.

Emmons, R. (1981). Relationship between narcissism and sensation seeking. *Psychological Reports, 48,* 847–850.

Emmons, R. (1984). Factor analysis and construct validity of the NPI. *Journal of Personality Assessment, 48,* 291–299.

Emmons, R. (1987). Narcissism: Theory and measurement. *Journal of Personality and Social Psychology, 52,* 11–17.

Gabbard, G. (1989). Two subtypes of narcissistic personality disorder. *Bulletin of the Menninger Clinic, 53,* 527–532.

Gough, H. G. (1987). *California Psychological Inventory: Administrator's guide.* Palo Alto, CA: Consulting Psychologists Press.

Gough, H. G., & Heilbrun, A. B. (1983). *The Adjective Check List manual.* Palo Alto, CA: Consulting Psychologists Press.

Graham, J. R., Schroeder, H. E., & Lilly, R. S. (1971). Factor analysis of items on the social introversion and masculinity-femininity scales of the MMPI. *Journal of Clinical Psychology, 27,* 367–370.

Gramzow, T., & Tangney, J. P. (1992). Proneness to shame and the narcissistic personality. *Personality and Social Psychology Bulletin, 18,* 369–376.

Gunderson, J., Ronningstam, E., & Smith, L. (1991). Narcissistic personality disorder: A review of data on DSM-III-R descriptions. *Journal of Personality Disorders, 5,* 167–177.

Haaken, J. (1983). Sex differences and narcissistic disorders. *American Journal of Psychoanalysis, 43,* 315–324.

Harder, D. (1979). The assessment of ambitious-narcissistic character style with three projective tests: The Early Memories, TAT, and Rorschach. *Journal of Personality Assessment, 43,* 23–32.

Hathaway, S. R., & McKinley, J. C. (1940). A multiphasic personality inventory (Minnesota): I. Construction of the schedule. *Journal of Psychology, 10,* 249–254.

Helson, R. (1967). Personality characteristics and developmental history of creative college women. *Genetic Psychology Monographs, 76,* 205–256.

Helson, R., & Wink, P. (1992). Personality change in women from the early 40s to the early 50s. *Psychology and Aging, 7,* 46–55.

Hibbard, S. (1992). Narcissism, shame, masochism, and object relations: An exploratory correlational study. *Psychoanalytic Psychology, 9,* 489–508.

John, O. R., & Robins, R. W. (1994). Accuracy and bias in self-perception: Individual differences in self-enhancement and the role of narcissism. *Journal of Personality and Social Psychology, 66,* 206–219.

Joubert, C. (1989). Birth order and narcissism. *Psychological Reports, 64,* 721–722.

Kernberg, O. F. (1975). *Borderline conditions and pathological narcissism.* New York: Aronson.

Kernberg, O. F. (1980). *Internal world and external realities.* New York: Aronson.

Kernberg, O. F. (1986). Narcissistic personality disorder. In A. A. Cooper, A. J. Frances, & M. H. Sachs (Eds.), *The personality disorders and neuroses* (Vol. 1, pp. 219–231). New York: Basic Books.

Kohut, H. (1966). Forms and transformations of narcissism. *Journal of the American Psychoanalytic Association, 14,* 243–272.

Kohut, H. (1971). *The analysis of the self.* New York: International Universities Press.

Kohut, H. (1977). *The restoration of the self.* New York: International Universities Press.

Kohut, H. (1984). *How does analysis cure?* Chicago, IL: The University of Chicago Press.

Kohut, H., & Wolf, E. (1978). The disorder of the self and their treatment: An outline. *International Journal of Psychoanalysis, 59,* 413–425.

Lasch, C. (1979). *The culture of narcissism.* New York: Warner Books.

Lewis, H. (1971). *Shame and guilt in neurosis.* New York: International Universities Press.

Masterson, J. F. (1981). *The narcissistic and borderline disorders.* New York: Brunner/Mazel.

Masterson, J. F. (1990). *The search for the real self.* New York: Free Press.

McCann, J. T., & Biaggio, M. K. (1989). Narcissistic personality and self-reported anger. *Psychological Reports, 64,* 55–58.

Miller, A. (1981). *The drama of the gifted child.* New York: Basic Books.

Millon, T. (1982). *Clinical multiaxial inventory manual.* Minneapolis, MN: National Computer Systems.

Morey, L., Waugh, M. H., & Blashfield, R. K. (1985). MMPI scales for DSM-III personality disorders. Their derivation and correlates. *Journal of Personality Assessment, 49,* 245–251.

Morrison, A. P. (1989). *Shame; the underside of narcissism.* Hillsdale, NJ: Analytic Press.

Mullins, L. S., & Kopelman, R. E. (1988). Toward an assessment of the construct validity of four measures of narcissism. *Journal of Personality Assessment, 52,* 610–625.

Murray, H. (1938). *Explorations in personality.* New York: Oxford University Press.

Murray, H. (1943). *Thematic Apperception Test.* Cambridge, MA: Harvard University Press.

Narayan, C. (1990). Birth order and narcissism. *Psychological Reports, 67,* 1184–1186.

Noshpitz, J. D. (1984). Narcissism and aggression. *American Journal of Psychotherapy, 1,* 17–34.

O'Brien, M. (1987). Examining the dimensionality of pathological narcissism: Factory analysis and construct validity of the O'Brien Multiphasic Narcissism Inventory. *Psychological Reports, 61,* 499–510.

Ornstein, P. (1978). Introduction. In Heinz Kohut, *The search for the self* (Vol. 1, pp. 3–115). New York: International Universities Press.

Patton, M. J., Connor, G. E., & Scott, K. J. (1982). Kohut's psychology of the self: Theory and measures of counseling outcome. *Journal of Counseling Psychology, 29,* 268–282.

Pepper, L. J., & Strong, P. N. (1958). *Judgmental subscales for the Mf scale of the MMPI.* Unpublished manuscript.

Phillipson, I. (1985). Gender and narcissism. *Psychology of Women Quarterly, 9,* 213–228.

Raskin, R. (1980). Narcissism and creativity: Are they related? *Psychological Reports, 46,* 55–60.

Raskin, R., & Hall, C. S. (1979). A narcissistic personality inventory. *Psychological Reports, 45,* 590.

Raskin, R., & Hall, C. (1981). Narcissistic Personality Inventory: Alternate form reliability and further evidence of construct validity. *Journal of Personality Assessment, 45,* 159–162.

Raskin, R., & Novacek, J. (1989). An MMPI description of the narcissistic personality. *Journal of Personality Assessment, 53,* 66–80.

Raskin, R., & Novacek, J. (1991). Narcissism and the use of fantasy. *Journal of Clinical Psychology, 47,* 490–499.

Raskin, R., Novacek, J., & Hogan, R. (1991a). Narcissism, self esteem, and defensive self-enhancement. *Journal of Personality, 59,* 19–38.

Raskin, R., Novacek, J., & Hogan, R. (1991b). Narcissistic self-esteem management. *Journal of Personality and Social Psychology, 60,* 911–918.

Raskin, R., & Shaw, R. (1988). Narcissism and the use of personal pronouns. *Journal of Personality, 56,* 393–404.

Raskin, R., & Terry, H. (1988). A principal-components analysis of the Narcissistic Personality Inventory and further evidence of its construct validity. *Journal of Personality and Social Psychology, 54,* 890–902.

Reich, A. (1953). Narcissistic object choice in women. *Journal of American Psychoanalytic Association, 1,* 22–44.

Reich, W. (1949). *Character analysis* (3rd ed.). New York: Farrar, Straus, & Giroux.

Serkownek, K. (1975). *Subscales for scale 5 and 0 of the MMPI.* Unpublished manuscript.

Smith, B. M. (1990). The measurement of narcissism in Asian, Caucasian, and Hispanic women. *Psychological Reports, 67,* 779–785.

Solomon, R. (1982). Validity of the MMPI Narcissistic Personality Disorder Scale. *Psychological Reports, 50,* 463–466.

Solomon, R. (1985). Creativity and normal narcissism. *Journal of Creative Behavior, 19,* 47–55.

Stolorow, R. D. (1975). Toward a functional definition of narcissism. *International Journal of Psychoanalysis, 56,* 179–185.

Svrakic, D. M. (1985). Emotional features of narcissistic personality disorder. *American Journal of Psychiatry, 142,* 720–724.

Tooley, K. (1975). The small assassins. *Journal of the American Academy of Child Psychology, 14,* 306–318.

Volkan, V. D. (1982). Narcissistic personality disorder. In J. O. Cavenar & H. K. H. Brodie (Eds.), *Critical problems in psychiatry* (pp. 332–350). Philadelphia, PA: Lippincott.

Watson, P. J., & Biderman, M. D. (1989). Failure of only-child status to predict narcissism. *Perceptual and Motor Skills, 69,* 1346.

Watson, P. J., Grisham, S. O., Trotter, M. V., & Biderman, M. D. (1984). Narcissism and empathy: Validity evidence for the NPI. *Journal of Personality Assessment, 48,* 301–305.

Watson, P. J., Little, T., & Biderman, M. D. (1992). Narcissism and parenting style. *Psychoanalytic Psychology, 12,* 231–244.

Watson, P. J., & Morris, R. J. (1990). Irrational beliefs and the problem of narcissism. *Personality and Individual Differences, 11,* 1137–1140.

Watson, P. J., Sawrie, S. M., & Biderman, M. D. (1991). Personal control, assumptive worlds, and narcissism. *Journal of Social Behavior and Personality, 6,* 929–941.

Watson, P. J., Taylor, D., & Morris, R. J. (1987). Narcissism, sex roles, and self-functioning. *Sex Roles, 16,* 335–350.

Wink, P. (1991a). Two faces of narcissism. *Journal of Personality and Social Psychology, 61,* 590–597.

Wink, P. (1991b). Self and object-directedness in adult women. *Journal of Personality, 59,* 769–791.

Wink, P. (1992a). Three narcissism scales for the California Q-set. *Journal of Personality Assessment, 58,* 51–66.

Wink, P. (1992b). Three types of narcissism in women from college to midlife. *Journal of Personality, 60,* 7–30.

Wink, P. (in press). Transitions from early 40s to early 50s in self-directed women. *Journal of Personality.*

Wink, P., & Gough, H. G. (1990). New narcissism scales for the California Psychological Inventory and MMPI. *Journal of Personality Assessment, 54,* 446–462.

Winnicott, D. W. (1965). Ego distortions in terms of true and false self. In D. W. Winnicott (Ed.), *The maturational processes and the facilitating environment* (pp. 146–152). London: Hogarth. (Original work published 1960)

Wright, F., O'Leary, J., & Balkin, J. (1989). Shame, guilt, narcissism, and depression: Correlates and sex differences. *Psychoanalytic Psychology, 6,* 217–230.

Yates, A. (1981). Narcissistic traits in certain abused children. *American Journal of Orthopsychiatry, 51,* 55–62.

CHAPTER 7

Detachment

JOHN BIRTCHNELL

I would consider personality characteristics to be of two kinds: intrapersonal and interpersonal. Intrapersonal concern the individual's mental functioning, and interpersonal concern the individual's relating to others. Of the 10 classes of personality considered in this book, four are intrapersonal (Chapters 3, 4, 10, and 11) and six are interpersonal (Chapters 2, 5, 6, 7, 8, and 9). I have proposed (Birtchnell, 1993) that interpersonal characteristics are classifiable along two axes: a horizontal one, concerned with the regulation of distance between the self and others, and a vertical one concerned with the distribution of power between the self and others. My thesis is that every individual needs to be capable of functioning at each end of each axis and I have given each end a name. I have called the ends of the horizontal axis closeness and distance and those of the vertical axis upperness and lowerness. Closeness is the capacity or inclination to become closely involved with others, and distance is the capacity or inclination to function separately. Upperness is the capacity or inclination to relate from a position of relative strength, and lowerness is the capacity or inclination to relate from a position of relative weakness. Because it is possible to function on both axes at the same time, there are four intermediate positions called upper-close, lower-close, upper-distant and lower-distant. The characteristics of the four main positions and the four intermediate positions are fully described in Birtchnell (1993). Of the six types of interpersonal behavior covered in this book, I would categorize detachment, narcissism, peculiarity and paranoia as distant, dependence as lower close, and aggressiveness as upper distant.

NORMAL FORMS OF DISTANCE

There have to be normal and acceptable forms of interpersonal attitudes and behavior associated with each position, and it is necessary to be aware of and define these before considering the pathological forms. The following are the main forms of normal and acceptable distance.

Separation from Others

Physical separation is the most obvious and primitive form of distance. The survival of young animals in the wild is dependent on their becoming physically separate from their parents as soon as possible. For humans, there is less urgency to become separate and the process of separation is a more gradual process. Exploration, to seek more advantageous environments and sources of food, forms an essential part of much animal behavior. Exploration is a prominent feature of the activity of children and adolescents. In adults, it takes the form of curiosity, the quest for new and exciting experiences, and the accumulation of scientific knowledge. For many animals, speed is a necessary means of escape from rivals and predators. For humans, this is rarely so, but they do need to escape from the discomforting or disturbing relating of others, such as intrusive overinvolvement, clinging dependence, or controlling domination. By adopting distance relating strategies, humans are able to distance themselves from others without actually leaving the situation. In the setting of a long-term relationship, the adoption of certain strategies may create the impression that the person has a distant personality. Such distancing may however be entirely reactive and specific to the relationship. Eibl-Eibesfeldt (1989) maintained that we must accept that a child is phylogenetically programmed to act as though strangers are potentially dangerous. Waters, Matas, and Sroufe (1975) showed that, between 5 and 10 months, the pulse rate increases dramatically upon the approach of a stranger, even if the stranger speaks with a friendly voice, and Smith and Martinsen (1977) confirmed that a child selectively chooses his or her mother. Fear of strangers and fear of the unfamiliar extend into adult life and are factors that reinforce the distancing tendency.

Turning Inward

It is likely that the nervous system can become fatigued by incoming stimuli and that mechanisms exist for filtering and regulating them. Stimulus reduction procedures, such as flotation (Suedfeld & Kristeller, 1982) and meditation (West, 1987) can have a powerful anxiety-reducing effect. Almost all animals sleep, and one of the functions of sleep may be the temporary reduction of sensory input to enable the brain to catch up with and process the accumulated input of the day. Sleep is sometimes a means of escape, as was observed by Frankl (1967) in Nazi concentration camps. When external stimuli are reduced, the individual becomes more exposed to internal stimuli. Lilly (1956) observed that under conditions of sensory deprivation the inner life becomes vivid and intense. Dreams emerge during the external stimulus reduction of sleep. Such emergence may serve an important function because deprivation of dreaming time may have unpleasant consequences (Dement, 1960).

When people stop relating externally, they may start relating internally to what are called internal objects. There are two kinds of internal object: self-representations and the internal representations of others (Jacobson, 1964). Self-representations enable the person to interact with the self. The two most important forms of internalized other are the internalized close other and the internalized upper other (Birtchnell, 1993). The internalized close other provides the experience of closeness. The internalized upper other provides the experience of lowerness—of being protected or looked after, controlled or restricted, approved of or disapproved of. Internalized others sometimes assume the form of a god.

Distance and the Self

A feature of distance is a concern with the self. This involves such issues as self-preservation; self-interest, satisfying self-needs; introspection and curiosity about the self. This is linked with the concept of introversion, first introduced by Jung (1921/1971) and later developed and measured by Eysenck (1970). The introvert is quiet, imaginative, and more interested in ideas than in people. In humans, one of the most important functions of distance is the opportunity it affords for the development of a separate self. This was called by Blatt and Shichman (1983) the "introjective developmental line." It involves the attainment of a differentiated, consolidated, stable, realistic, and essentially positive identity. The earliest strivings toward this were termed by Mahler (1961) "separation-individuation." The process of absorbing parts of the fused mother-child identity into the self was called by Kohut (1971) "transmuting internalization." Bowen (1978) described a later developmental process that he called "the differentiation of self from the family of origin." When a person has a secure sense of self he or she has what Laing (1965) called "ontological security." An extension of self-development is autonomy (being driven from within rather than from without). Autonomous individuals are self-motivating; have a clear sense of what they want and where they want to go; operate according to their own standards and judgments, and are not excessively affected by the opinions of others. Beck (1983) considered that autonomy refers to the individual's investment in preserving and increasing independence, mobility, personal rights, and freedom of choice.

Solitude is a pleasurable state of distance in which people seek to be away from others, alone with their thoughts. One of the pleasures of solitude is establishing a connectedness with nature and the universe. Freud (1930/1939) used the term "oceanic feeling" to describe this. Religious people sometimes equate this with being alone with God. Individuation means becoming an individual, that is becoming recognizably distinct from others. Individuality can be disruptive, and a society made up of individuals would be chaotic. However, every generation needs its original thinkers who are able to introduce new ideas and new ways of doing things. To be this way, they have to allow themselves to become unconventional and idiosyncratic, and to function in what Fromm-Reichmann (1959) called constructive aloneness.

Once the self has been established, the individual becomes capable of developing feelings toward the self. This is called narcissism, from the Greek myth of the youth Narcissus, who fell in love with his reflection in a pool. Freud (1914/1957) proposed that, during early infancy, libido is directed entirely toward the mother. This he called primary narcissism. During the phase that Suttie (1935) called psychic weaning, the libido is withdrawn from the mother and directed on to the self. This Freud called secondary narcissism and Macdiarmid (1989) called self-cathexis. Jacobson (1964) maintained that it is the endopsychic representations of the self toward which the libido is directed. Freud believed that the major proportion of libido remains invested in the self, and this he called normal or healthy narcissism. Writers such as Fenichel (1945), Coopersmith (1967), Kohut (1971), and Storr (1983) considered that high self-esteem requires the additional ingredients of the parents showing total interest in and acceptance of the child. The child, and subsequently the adult, will be motivated to relate to others only if he or she feels worthy of their attention.

The Protection of Boundaries

Animals protect their territorial boundaries to ensure adequate supplies of food for themselves and their young. They protect their individual boundaries, as a means of controlling temperature and limiting infection. Humans also protect their territorial and individual boundaries (Hall, 1966). They surround themselves with protective layers, such as clothing, walls, doors, and fences. The preservation of personal space and the respect of the right to privacy are essential components of human social life (McBride, King, & James, 1965). People adjust their position from strangers in public places (Mazur, 1977) and avoid eye contact (Goffman, 1963). Altman (1975) observed that the more anxious a person is the less close he or she will allow others to become.

Psychoanalysts use the term "ego-boundary" to refer to the distinction between the subjective experience of self and not-self. A person is said to have a weak ego-boundary if his or her identity merges easily with that of someone else. The adjective permeable is sometimes applied to the ego-boundary to imply an inclination, either voluntary or involuntary, to merge or identify with another. The ego-boundary might also be considered to be a barrier against the penetration of others into the psychic interior. People need to feel that their psychic interior is a safe and private place where secrets are kept.

Distant Relating

Distance is not simply the avoidance of others. People relate to others from a position of distance. In fact, distant relating is more prevalent than close relating. A particular form of distant relating is formal relating. It is the kind of relating that people adopt in formal transactions such as occur with professional people, tradespeople, and the providers of services. Even people in close relationships spend a lot of time in distant relating. In it, there is a reduction of spontaneous expression, an absence of personal disclosure, and a suppression of the open show of emotion. Eibl-Eibesfeldt (1989) called this last feature "expression masking" and considered that it served to conceal feelings of which a stranger might take advantage. The wording is more precise and to the point, and the issues discussed are more practical. Suttie (1935) considered that all humans have a reluctance to become emotionally involved with others. Such reluctance he believed, originated at the time of what he called psychic weaning, when the child was compelled to relinquish the close tie to mother and move outward toward others. This he maintained was so painful that the child resolved never to get that close to another person again. He called this the taboo on tenderness, and whether his proposed origin is correct, the phenomenon exists.

Distancing in the Modern World

The capacity to be insensitive to the feelings of others is an aspect of normal distance. It is probably essential for survival in a world in which people are continuously confronted by the appalling hardship and suffering of others. Political parties committed to the relief of poverty do not get elected. Milgram (1974) observed that most acts of inhumanity are carried out by ordinary people doing what they are told. At times of war, people are capable of committing acts of extreme cruelty. Torture is currently practiced by one government in three (Moore, 1985).

A stage beyond distant relating is relating to things rather than to people. It is possible that the origin of relating to things is the transitional object, such as the blanket or soft toy that the young child relates to in the absence of the mother (Winnicott, 1953). People relate to animals and, less commonly, to plants. They also relate to inert objects—stars, mountains, volcanos, and rocks. In a technological age, relating to things is common. People relate to tools, musical instruments, vehicles, road signs, traffic lights, houses, clothing, machines, particularly vending machines, and computers. Much of art depends on the human ability to relate to things that represent people. Relating to characters on the cinema or television screen, the recorded voice, the voice on the telephone, or the written word is relating to people through things.

Berman (1982) was disturbed by the processes of modernization such as industrialization, urban growth, mass communication and an ever expanding, drastically fluctuating world market. Frosch (1991) maintained that modernity is characterized by the denial of relationships with others and an inclination toward narcissism, by which he meant an absence of interest in and empathy for others and a retreat from reality into a fantasy world. Lasch (1984) used the term narcissism to describe the superficiality, deep sense of emptiness, egocentricity, rampant individualism, and avoidance of intimacy that typify the consumerist culture. He considered that narcissistic types thrive in a society that rewards those who manipulate others and punishes those who show genuine care.

PATHOLOGICAL FORMS OF DISTANCE

Pathological forms of distance will be grouped under three headings:

1. Extreme manifestations of distancing functions.
2. The imperfect acquisition of closeness functions.
3. The imperfect acquisition of distancing functions.

Extreme Manifestations of Distancing Functions

The Shunning of Close Interpersonal Relationships

The well-adjusted individual has the capacity for both closeness and distance and draws on one or the other according to circumstance. Pathologically distant individuals consistently relate in a distant manner irrespective of circumstance. Their reason for doing so is not always the same, and this will be considered separately for each form of pathological distance.

Xenophobia and Racism

Bailey (1988) believed that our predecessors in phylogeny who failed to develop effective kinship strategies for distinguishing between familiars and strangers became extinct. Although such innate tendencies are significantly diminished by humane and moral considerations, there are circumstances under which they are exaggerated and lead to victimization, cruelty, and mass extermination.

Membership in an Outsider Group

It is a strange paradox that certain distant individuals are able to establish bonds with each other to form outsider groups. Such groups are common among adolescents and young adults but also among those with antisocial personalities.

Low Tolerance of Sensory Input

Stimulus overload theory (Baron & Byrne, 1991) proposes that individuals who receive too much stimulus information are unable to process it efficiently and are compelled to screen out redundant stimuli. There is probably considerable variation in the tolerance of individuals to sensory input. Introverts are less tolerant than extroverts (Eysenck, 1947) and autistic (Ornitz, 1983), schizoid, and schizotypal (Millon, 1981) individuals; and schizophrenics (Tsuang, 1982) are the least tolerant of all. It is possible that the low tolerance of sensory input is the primary dysfunction of these kinds of people and that many of their other characteristics follow from this.

High Tolerance of Sensory Deprivation

Solitary sailors (Slocum, 1948) and prisoners in solitary confinement (Grassian, 1983) may become deluded or hallucinated. In contrast, schizophrenics are particularly tolerant of isolation and, under such conditions, may even experience a reduction in hallucinatory experiences (Harris, 1959). It is probable that schizoid and schizotypal individuals also have a high tolerance.

Closeness Fatigue

This is a term introduced (Birtchnell, 1993) to describe the condition that results from prolonged or overexposure to closeness, particularly when it is imposed and there is no means of escape. Distant people are probably particularly prone to it. It gives rise to an increasingly compelling desire to break away. It was maintained by Feldman (1979) that the intermittent conflicts that break out between married partners have a closeness-reducing function. The aggressive outbursts of some antisocial individuals may serve a similar function, and are probably precipitated by the steady buildup of closeness fatigue.

Withdrawal

This is a characteristic of what will later be called introverted types. The person turns away from the world and turns in on the self. The preoccupation may be entirely with the inner self and the individual may become neglectful of appearance and physical condition. No attempt is made to communicate with others and no response is made to the communications of others. In such extreme states of withdrawal, the person is described as inaccessible.

The Splitting of the Self from the Body

This process, described by Laing (1965) as occurring in schizophrenia, is probably a feature of the schizoid personality. The disembodied self regards the body as though it were a thing. The self wishes to be wedded to and embedded in the body but is constantly afraid to lodge in the body for fear of the dangers that might befall it if it did.

Egocentricity

It is inevitable that, with the screening out of external stimuli, there will be a directing of attention onto the self. The egocentric person demonstrates to excess what Macdiarmid (1989) called self-cathexis; that is a preoccupation with and a curiosity about the self. The person talks about his or her own interests and pays little attention to the interests of others. This is probably a feature of all distant personalities, but particularly narcissists.

Hypochondria

This is a form of egocentricity in which attention is focused entirely onto the body. It may be so pervasive as to amount to a personality disorder. Unlike the narcissist, the hypochondriac feels insecure and worried about him- or herself (Barsky & Klerman, 1983). Typically, these individuals harbor an excessive concern about their bodies and fear they have or may develop a serious illness. They are constantly on the lookout for signs of illness and become excessively alarmed by minor symptoms.

Pathological Forms of Escape

People resort to a range of distancing devices for separating themselves from stressful situations. The most extreme of these is suicide. Durkheim (1897/1951) associated suicide with what he called egoism, that is having an absence of group ties and therefore carrying a responsibility for one's own fate. Suicide is an egocentric form of behavior, involving minimal concern for the effects it may have on other people. Sainsbury (1955) demonstrated a link between suicide and social isolation. It is common in avoidant personalities.

Humans have the capacity to reduce the effect of stress by inducing states of psychological distance without actual loss of consciousness. The term hysterical is sometimes applied to such behavior. Laing (1965) wrote, "The hysteric characteristically dissociates himself from much that he does" (p. 95). Avoidants are also prone to dissociation (Millon, 1981). In a dissociative state, the person feels unreal, detached, and not entirely in the situation. It may be as if the individual is separated from his or her body, or watching the self from outside. The person has the experience that "This is not really happening to me." Dissociation may occur in states of hypnosis, or self-hypnosis. In such states, some people are able to undergo surgical procedures without experiencing pain. An extreme form of dissociation is the stupor, in which the person, though conscious, remains mute and motionless. In the fugue (Stengel, 1941), the person, usually in a dissociative state, wanders, drives, or travels sometimes long distances from the place of stress and, on arrival, may be unaware of who he or she is and have no knowledge of a previous existence.

Eccentricity

Millon (1981) observed that the more individuals turn inward, the more they lose contact with the styles of behavior and thought of those around them. They lose their sense of behavioral propriety and suitability and gradually begin the process of acting, thinking, and perceiving in peculiar, unreal, and somewhat "crazy" ways. The term eccentricity is applied almost entirely to that type of personality disorder called schizotypal. In fact, the presence of eccentricity precludes a diagnosis of schizoid personality disorder.

Preoccupation with the Paranormal

Extending beyond eccentricity is a concern with and interest in so-called paranormal and mystical experiences. Claridge et al. (1990) observed that many of the questionnaires used in research on schizotypy in normal subjects contain items that probe a belief in and report of telepathy and other forms of extrasensory perception. Such beliefs may be a way of explaining the subjective experiences of apparent thought insertion and thought transference.

An Excessive Preoccupation with Things and Abstractions

There are those whose preoccupation with things is so great that it precludes, or greatly impairs, any involvement with people. For some, namely those described as schizoid and schizotypal, such preoccupation is primary, in that they have never shown an interest in people; for others, who are likely to belong to the avoidant category, some of whom may even be married, it appears to be secondary, though even for these, there may have been a preexisting disposition. Such interest extends beyond things to abstract thought such as mathematics, banking, economics, computing, philosophy, and music.

The Minimal Show of Emotion

In her description of the "detached" or "moving away from people" personality type, Horney (1945) referred to a general tendency to suppress all feeling, even to deny its existence. Here, it seems, she was referring to that form of personality disorder which is called avoidant. In this, the capacity to show emotion is presumed once to have existed but, in response to painful rejection was withdrawn to avoid further pain. In recent years (Sifneos, 1973), the condition alexithymia has been proposed as the factor that underlies many psychosomatic disorders. It is defined as the inability to express feelings verbally and the lack of discrimination between different feeling states. There is some evidence that it is a defensive response to repeated psychological traumatization (Zeitlin et al., 1993). Both schizoid and schizotypal personality disorders demonstrate an emotional flatness that is considered to have been present from an early age. However, Millon (1981) observed that many schizotypals have stored up, throughout their lives, intense, repressed anxieties and hostilities that they are capable of releasing in a "frenzied cathartic discharge," when subjected to, what are for them, intolerable social pressures.

The Imperfect Acquisition of Closeness Functions

Relating to Others as Though They Were Things

One aspect of being close is having an interest in and a curiosity about the other. This involves appreciating that the other is a separate being who has rights and expectations of his or her own. Only humans are capable of such closeness. Seyfarth and Cheney (1992) observed that monkeys see the world as things. People vary in the extent to which they are able to differentiate between, and therefore relate differently toward, things and people. Buber (1937) distinguished between what he called the I-Thou and the I-It way of relating. Persons who relate in an I-It way are incapable of imagining, or even caring, what the inner world of another might be like. They experience others as extensions of their own inner life. This is a feature of the antisocial personality, but it is also apparent in some schizotypals.

Minimal Sensitivity to the Feelings and Thoughts of Others

The person who experiences others as things, lacks the capacity to identify, sympathize, and empathize with them. Because of this, the individual is capable of performing acts of extreme cruelty without sign of remorse. This also is a feature of the antisocial personality. The sadistic personality, characterized by a pervasive pattern of cruel, demeaning, and aggressive behavior, is not exactly indifferent to the suffering of others, because awareness of their suffering gives the sadist pleasure.

Lack of Trust

Trust is a feature of two forms of relatedness (Birtchnell, 1993): in closeness, when it is necessary to trust that the other will not break off the relationship; and in lowerness, when it is necessary to trust that the other will not abuse power. Lack of trust of the first kind forms the basis of the avoidant personality. In this, the person is afraid of close involvement with others for fear of being hurt should the relationship break down. He or she acquires a "once bitten twice shy" attitude. The characteristic behavior of what Millon (1969) called avoidant schizophrenics is identical to that of people with avoidant personalities. Burnham, Gladstone, and Gibson (1969) referred to their need-fear dilemma, maintaining that the very extensiveness of their need for objects makes such objects inordinately dangerous and fearsome to them, because the object can destroy them through abandonment. Bannister (1987) referred to their enormous distrust, and observed that during psychotherapy, trust continues to be tested time and time again. A recovering patient of this kind reported on by Hayward and Taylor (1956) said, "The problem with schizophrenics is that they can't trust anyone. The doctor will have to fight to get in no matter how much the patient objects." A feature of what Kohut (1971) called the narcissistic personality is a defensive withdrawal into the self resulting from hurts experienced in childhood. This corresponds with Bartholomew's (1990) fearful avoidant personality, which will be described shortly.

Lack of trust of the second kind was included in Horney's (1945) detached type of personality. She considered that the resulting self-sufficiency assumed two forms: resourcefulness and the conscious or unconscious restriction of needs. By doing everything for themselves and doing without things that they cannot do for themselves, these individuals do not need to ask anything of anyone. This is the same as Parkes's (1973) compulsive self-reliance. Bowlby (1980) observed that the compulsively self-reliant individual chooses not to utilize available sources of social support at times of crisis. This corresponds with Bartholomew's (1990) dismissive avoidant personality, which also will be described shortly.

The Formation of Multiple, Superficial, Short-Term Relationships

This is a feature of a number of distant personality disorders (e.g., antisocials, hysterics, narcissists). By maintaining a range of superficial relationships, or by flitting from one relationship to another, it is possible to derive small amounts of closeness from each while avoiding commitment to any one of them. The distinction between this kind of behavior and intimate involvement is similar to that which Bowlby (1969) made between what Murray (1938) called affiliation and his concept of attachment. Many important features of long-term committed closeness are missing from multiple superficial relationships. The partners do not become caught up in each other's lives or get to know and understand each other to the same extent. The degree of self-revelation and mutual identification is limited, and there is no deep devotion, loyalty, or compassion.

The Imperfect Acquisition of Distancing Functions

The imperfect acquisition of many distancing functions leads to pathological closeness, not pathological distance. The person who finds it hard to be distant clings excessively to closeness. There is however a cluster of distancing functions that, if imperfectly acquired, lead to further distancing. These are concerned with the development of the self, the establishment and protection of firm boundaries around the self, and the acquisition of adequate self-esteem.

Ontological Insecurity

Laing (1965) introduced this term to cover the three related deficiencies of poor identity formation, ill-defined ego-boundaries, and low autonomy. Persons with a poorly formed identity lack a clear conception of who they are, what they like or dislike, and what things are important to them. They are insubstantial persons who do not feel real and who are not experienced as real by others. Persons with ill-defined ego-boundaries have no clear perception of where they end and others begin. They have difficulty determining which are their own thoughts, ideas, or emotions and which are someone else's. Individuals who lack autonomy have difficulty taking charge of themselves and organizing their own behavior. They are heavily dependent on the judgment and direction of others.

Without a firm sense of self, moving close to another person carries the risk of what Laing (1965) called engulfment and what Bowen (1978) called fusion, namely the complete loss of being by becoming absorbed into the identity of the other. Ontologically insecure persons have three possible choices: (a) to keep a safe distance from others in order to hold on to whatever frail identity they have; (b) to become what Laing called ontologically dependent, by becoming parasitic on the other person, assuming the other's identity, and allowing the other to make all the choices and decisions; or (c) to attempt to impose their own frail identity on the other, so that the other is required to become an extension of their insecure self. Ontological insecurity may lie behind some forms of what Kantor (1993) has called commitment phobia, namely the inability to stay committed to one person over a prolonged period of time. As each relationship deepens, the danger of becoming lost within the other's identity increases and the individual finds it necessary to terminate the relationship. Commitment phobia is also a consequence of closeness fatigue and a fear of being tied down.

The False Self

Winnicott (1956) described the process of creating what he called a false self, which is a pretended self through which the person lives in order not to be a part of what is going on. The true self contains the person's vulnerability and needfulness. The function of the false self is to protect the real self which hides behind it. Guntrip (1969) described a similar split between what he called the central ego and the withdrawn ego. The central ego is left to cope with the stresses of life while hiding the withdrawn ego, which is the equivalent of Winnicott's true self.

Fear of Intrusion

Others can intrude into the person's personal property, personal life, personal space, clothes, body, or mind. Fear of intrusion may be either a reaction to the intrusiveness of others (leading to its more neurotic forms) or a manifestation of ontological insecurity (leading to its more psychotic forms). Experiences of intrusion such as burglary, denial of privacy, parents wanting to know everything about the person, sexual abuse, and rape weaken the individual's sense of having a secure boundary and sensitize the individual to the possibility of intrusion. This may lead to caution about allowing others to become close and a reluctance to get close to them; it may extend to a fear of being touched, contaminated, or infected, or of being harmed by small animals and insects.

Laing (1965) wrote of the fear that others can see into the psychic interior and of seeming to be transparent. He wrote, "In psychotic conditions the gaze or scrutiny of the other can be experienced as an actual penetration into the core of the 'inner' self" (p. 106). Such a fear is likely to be present in those with schizoid and schizotypal disorders. It can take the form of a fear of being understood, of being known too well, or of not being able to keep things from others. A defense against this fear is telling lies, and this may account for the lying behavior of antisocials.

Low Self-Esteem

Persons with low self-esteem cannot believe that others would want to become involved with them. In fact such low self-esteem may be a consequence of the rejecting behavior of past significant others. McCranie

(1971) suggested that rejected children feel that they must be at fault, concluding that they are not accepted because they are somehow unacceptable. Beck (1990) observed that some people believe that others are superior to them and will reject them or think critically of them once they get to know them. Therefore, they are careful not to allow themselves to get too close to people or to reveal too much of themselves to them. This is an important feature of the avoidant personality.

THE CLINICAL FEATURES OF DISTANT FORMS OF PERSONALITY DISORDER

The five main classes of personality disorder associated with distance will be called:

1. Avoidant.
2. Paranoid.
3. Antisocial.
4. Narcissistic.
5. Introverted.

Classes 2, 3 and 4 will be dealt with in other chapters. The present chapter will be concerned with classes 1 and 5 and some aspects of 3. Blackburn (1989) presented a hypothesized distribution of personality disorders around his modification of the classical interpersonal circle, which was first proposed by Freedman, Leary, Ossorio, and Coffee (1951). The original circle was constructed around the two axes of hostile versus friendly and dominant versus submissive, and he has introduced the two additional axes of coercive versus compliant (coercive being placed between dominant and hostile) and sociable versus withdrawn (withdrawn being placed between hostile and submissive). Moving around the hostile side of the circle, from dominant to submissive, he has placed narcissistic between dominant and coercive, antisocial between coercive and hostile, paranoid between hostile and withdrawn and avoidant and introverted between withdrawn and submissive. This provides support for the proposal that these are indeed the disorders of distance.

Before considering the classes separately, some general points concerning the classification of personality disorders should be made. The *Diagnostic and Statistical Manual of Mental Disorders* (DSM-III; American Psychiatric Association [APA], 1980) assumes that personality disorders can be classified into discrete and mutually exclusive categories, even though the appropriateness of the categorical model has long been disputed (Kendell, 1975; Presley & Walton, 1973). Livesley, West, and Tanney (1985) concluded that membership of a category of disorder is not an all-or-none phenomenon, but a matter of degree. They observed that most patients show features of more than one disorder and many show some, but not all, the features of any particular category. Depending on the populations studied and the instruments used, researchers have reported mean numbers of disorders per patient extending to 5.6 (Hyler, Skodol, Kellman, Oldham, & Rosnick, 1990).

Of particular relevance to the present chapter is the possible overlap between the three classes (of distant disorders) considered here. Wolff and Cull (1986) observed that antisocial behavior sometimes develops in children with schizoid disorder and provided evidence of schizoid features among some adults with antisocial disorder. Tantam (1988a) observed that nearly half of a series of nonpsychotic, socially isolated, and eccentric psychiatric patients had been involved in antisocial behavior. Silverton (1988) found a familial association between criminal or antisocial behavior and schizophrenia. Millon (1981) maintained that avoidant personalities are especially prone to slip into a schizophrenialike state resembling a catatonic stupor. By blocking the flow of thoughts and memories, he wrote, they effectively distract themselves and dilute the impact of painful feelings and recollections. He also described what he called schizotypal-avoidant mixed personality disorders who learn that it is best to deny real feelings and aspirations. Although there are no reports of an overlap between avoidant and antisocial personality disorders, there do appear to be certain commonalities between the two conditions. Whereas avoidants resolve their fear of closeness by remaining distant, antisocials do so by restricting the length and depth of their relationships.

Avoidant Disorders

People with avoidant personality disorder appear to want closeness but are afraid of attaining it for fear of the painful consequences of losing it. Millon (1981) observed that "Desires for affection may be strong but are self-protectedly denied." In the DSM-III definition of the condition, it is stressed that closeness will be accepted by them providing that strong guarantees are given of uncritical acceptance. Consequently, they may have one or two close friends, but such friendships are contingent on their receiving unconditional approval. The descriptions included under the heading "Lack of trust" apply to the avoidant personality.

Essentially then, avoidant personalities are in a permanent state of approach-avoidant conflict. Their clinical picture depends on the extent to which they are prepared to continue the risk of approaching rather than adopting the safer stance of preferring to avoid. Their conflicts are identical to those of dependent personalities, but dependent personalities are prepared to get that much closer to their attachment objects. Whereas dependent personalities are classifiable as lower close, avoidant personalities belong more to the category of lower distant (Birtchnell, 1993). It is tempting to speculate that, at various times in their lives, they have experienced the pleasure of closeness but have subsequently suffered such pain, as a result of losing it, that they have resolved not to risk seeking it again.

Millon (1969) referred to them as being actively avoidant, to distinguish them from those with schizoid personalities whom he described as being passively avoidant. There is a striking similarity between them and those he called active or avoidant schizophrenics, which he described as being chronically overactive. Although such people present a facade of mistrustfulness, they appear to be inwardly hoping that others, particularly psychotherapists, are willing to work hard enough at gaining their trust.

Bowlby's (1969) attachment theory makes an important contribution to the understanding of such people. Bowlby maintained that, for the first 6 months of life, the infant remains relatively unattached. After this, as a result of repeated interactions between the child and his or her parent, a close bond develops that is called attachment. Bowlby has argued that the child's later confidence in the availability of an attachment figure is determined largely by the success with which this bond is established. Ainsworth, Blehar, Waters, and Wall (1978) proposed that the parents of securely attached infants tend to be consistently responsive to their infant's signals and show warmth in interactions.

Main, Kaplan, and Cassidy (1986) devised what they called the "Strange Situation Test" for determining the extent of the attachment between the child and mother. The child is left with a stranger, then left alone, then reintroduced to the mother. On the basis of the reunion behavior, the attachment is categorized as secure, ambivalent, or avoidant. The avoidant category is characterized by a turning away from the mother and a turning toward either someone else or an inert object. Sroufe and Waters (1977) observed that avoidant infants exhibit cardiac acceleration in response to separation, despite their overt lack of distress, but such acceleration is not diminished by reunion with the parent, as it is with secure infants. They concluded that this represented active avoidance rather than a form of secure distance.

A number of measures have been developed aimed at classifying the attachment styles of adults in a way which is comparable to that of infants. These include the Love-Experience Questionnaire (Hazan & Shaver, 1987), the Adult Attachment Interview (Main & Goldwyn, 1990), the Attachment Interview and the Relationship Questionnaire (Bartholomew & Horowitz, 1991), and the Adult Attachment Questionnaire (Shaver &

Hazan, 1993). Using the Love-Experience Questionnaire, Hazan and Shaver (1987) demonstrated, in romantic relationships, the adult equivalents of the three attachment styles observed in infants by Main et al. (1986), and in the same proportions.

Bartholomew (1990) distinguished between two types of avoidant personality: the fearful avoidant, who desires intimacy but fears rejection and is hypersensitive to social approval; and the dismissive avoidant, who appears to have given up on involvement, adopting a sour grapes attitude, maintaining that relationships are unimportant and placing value on independence. She maintained that the Love-Experience Questionnaire identifies her fearful avoidants and the Adult Attachment Interview identifies her dismissive avoidants. She constructed a two-by-two matrix of a positive and negative model of the self against a positive and negative model of the other. She considered that both types of avoidants experience the other as negative, but that dismissive avoidants experience themselves as positive and fearful avoidants experience themselves as negative. She proposed a third category of personality, which she called preoccupied, in which the person experiences the other as positive and him- or herself as negative. The description of the preoccupied personality corresponds with what would normally be called the dependent personality.

The minimal show of emotion, considered to be linked to the avoidant personality may be different for the fearful and dismissive types. Millon (1981) considered avoidants to be perceptually hypersensitive, vigilantly scanning for potential threats to self; exquisitely sensitive to rejection, humiliation, and shame; devastated by the slightest hint of disapproval; and inclined to overinterpret innocuous behaviors as signs of ridicule and humiliation. Such descriptions are more appropriate to the fearful type, who remain concerned about what people think of them and who continue to try to impress. The dismissive type, who attempt to deny the importance of close relationships, are more likely to exhibit Horney's (1945) proposed tendency to suppress all feeling, exhibiting what Bartholomew (1990) has called emotional numbness or what others (Sifneos, 1973) have called alexithymia.

Nonavoidant people approach others on the basis of a realistic appraisal of their attractiveness. Avoidant people consistently assume themselves to be unattractive. Like dependent people, they lack the ability to make objective judgments about themselves and rely heavily on the judgments of others. Their assumption of low self-worth probably stems from their interpretation of the attitudes and behavior of early influential others. This assumption is carried forward, unquestioningly, into adult life.

Kantor (1993) made the point that avoidant people are capable of bringing about their own rejection by the adoption of inappropriate or ill-judged approaches to others. Such clumsiness may be fueled by a lack of social confidence and the expectation that they are going to fail anyway. Kantor implied that their half-hearted approach may be an expression of their fear of success, for if they succeed, they have the added problem of worrying whether the relationship, once started, can be maintained. For these reasons, he believed that the behavior of some avoidants is directed toward driving others away.

Antisocial Disorders

The aggressive component of antisocial disorders has been dealt with in Chapter 2. The concern here is with the distant component. Despite its broad diversity of characteristics, Hare (1980) maintained that psychopathy, a term commonly applied to the antisocial disorders, is a unitary syndrome that can be measured by his checklist, originally derived from Cleckley's (1976) description. However, a factor analysis has revealed two distinct, but correlated factors (Harpur, Hare, & Hakstian, 1989). The first of these corresponds with the aggressive component, and the second corresponds with the distant component. Part of Eysenck's theory of criminality (Eysenck & Gudjonsson, 1989) is the linking of criminality with extroversion. Extroverts, it is argued, are less susceptible to the pain of punishment and form conditioned responses more slowly. They therefore will be less socialized than introverts. Blackburn (1993) found little support for Eysenck's theory and pointed out that there are probably two components to extroversion, which he called sociability and impulsiveness. He considered the impulsiveness component (an intrapersonal characteristic) to be the more relevant to criminality. The linking of extroversion with antisocial behavior is not necessarily a problem for the theoretical position adopted in this chapter, for the formation of multiple, superficial, short-term relationships is a feature of the behavior of many extroverts.

People with antisocial disorders, unlike those with avoidant disorders do form relationships with others, but such relationships are multiple, transient, and superficial. Also unlike avoidants, they are not concerned about what others think of them, they do not manifest low self-esteem, and they protect their self-esteem by blaming others rather than themselves (ICD-10, World Health Organization, 1992). Quoting from the DSM-III (APA, 1980), Millon (1981) observed that almost invariably there is a markedly impaired capacity to sustain lasting, close, warm, and responsible relationships with family, friends, or sexual partners. This is a manifestation of Kantor's (1993) commitment phobia. Antisocials are inclined to replace loving behavior with sexual behavior and to force sexual activity on others. Whereas sexual behavior between intimates can be tender and caring and an endorsement of closeness, that of antisocials is cold, sadistic, and self-gratifying. Among the ICD-10 criteria is "incapacity to maintain enduring relationships"; among the DSM-III-R (APA, 1987) criteria is "has never sustained a monogamous relationship for more than one year"; and two items from Hare's Revised Psychopathy Checklist (Hare, 1991) are "promiscuous sexual behavior," and "many short term marital relationships." This style of relating is partly explained by certain other characteristics such as "gross and persistent attitude of irresponsibility and disregard for social norms, rules and obligations" (ICD-10), "impulsive and failure to plan ahead" (DSM-III-R), "need for stimulation and proneness to boredom," and "lack of realistic, long term goals" (Hare's Checklist). Antisocials therefore, get their closeness in small doses, as, where, and when they can.

Whitely (1994) was at pains to dispel the romantic image that some people have of those with antisocial personalities. He cited the example of a cult pop idol, who later died of a surfeit of drink and drugs, who responded to a journalist, who had commented on his seemingly free and irresponsible lifestyle, by saying "You think I'm free, man? If I seem free it's because I'm always running." Antisocials move on not just because they are bored or in need of new stimulation, but also because they are afraid of becoming deeply involved, sinking their roots, settling down, and being accepted by conventional others.

Again, unlike avoidants, antisocials involve themselves with people, but only in a cold and manipulative manner. Hoffman (1987) stressed the importance of a capacity for empathy as a basis for prosocial behavior. It is the reduced or absent capacity for empathy of antisocial people that causes them to be indifferent to the feelings of others. They tend to treat them as though they were things, and to exploit and terrorize them. They steal their belongings and destroy their property. They are callous and cruel without experiencing guilt or remorse. They have no regard for the truth and they fail to honor financial obligations (DSM-III-R).

The taboo on tenderness is a prominent feature of antisocial behavior. Antisocials consider sentimentality to be a sign of weakness and hardness to be a virtue. They try to render themselves unhurtable. People who try to hurt, humiliate, or insult them are viciously punished. They are not kind to others and they cannot tolerate the acts of kindness of others. They pride themselves on not becoming emotionally dependent on others. They guard against relationships becoming serious by moving from one to another. Those who try to befriend them or to develop lasting relationships with them are met with hostility.

Antisocials are prepared to be members of groups but such groups are groups of outsiders. This enables them to be both close and distant at the same time. Within such groups, the members are united against conventional others and share a sense of bitterness, mistrust, and resentment toward those whom they consider have wronged them. There can be a loyalty to other group members, known as "honor among thieves," but, within the group, there is also a mutual mistrust and a pride that anyone who insults or deceives another will be severely dealt with.

Before leaving the antisocial disorders, some mention should be made of certain resemblances they bear to histrionic disorders. Like antisocials, histrionics are easily bored, intolerant of frustration, and crave novelty, stimulation, and excitement. They are also superficially charming, though shallow, irresponsible and lacking in genuineness. They can be manipulative, exploitative, and sometimes promiscuous, but unlike antisocials they are vain, egocentric, dramatic, exhibitionistic, seductive, and solicitous of praise. They are socially gregarious and not inclined to be cruel or aggressive (Millon, 1981).

A case could be made for including histrionics among those with distant personality disorders for, despite their proclivity for social interaction, they have difficulty in maintaining full, meaningful, and stable relationships with others. They have many acquaintances but few friends. Like narcissists, although they enjoy the attention of others, they show little interest in or concern for the well-being of others. Millon (1981) observed that they are inclined to shy away from prolonged contact with others for fear that their falseness and lack of inner substance will become apparent. Another distancing feature of hysterics is their capacity for dissociation. While remaining physically within an interpersonal situation, they are able to remain psychologically distant from it. They are also able to dissociate themselves from their intentions, particularly when indulging in sympathy-seeking behavior.

Introverted Disorders

People with introverted disorders appear either to avoid closeness altogether or to subsist on minimal amounts of it. Their central characteristic appears to be a low tolerance of sensory input, so that closeness fatigue sets in rapidly. Thereafter, involvement with others becomes painful and there is a growing compulsion to get away from them. Claridge (1987) observed, ". . . a unique feature of the psychotic nervous system might be its tendency to physiological 'dissociation,' demonstrable empirically as a grossly altered sensitivity to sensory stimulation, inappropriate to the individual's prevailing level of tonic arousal" (p. 738). It is highly probable that what Claridge was saying about psychosis applies equally to the introverted disorders. There is probably a series of stages of introversion, with each stage carrying the features of the previous stage plus additional features. The mildest form of introversion corresponds with the introvert personality (Eysenck, 1970; Jung, 1921/1971). People with such a personality form limited relationships and sometimes get married, most successfully to people of similar type. They tend to be more interested in things, objects, or abstractions than in people.

Those at the next level of introversion are called schizoid. They are considered (DSM-III) to have an intrinsic defect in the capacity to form social relationships, but they can be useful members of society, for they are able to work, often constructively and creatively, for long periods, under conditions of isolation. Suedfeld (1991) described men who had spent many years working in Arctic weather stations. He called them "deepeners" because they were prepared to probe ever more deeply into complex circumstances and situations. They have few, if any, close friends and prefer to be loners. They remain unobtrusive and have what Millon (1981) called an emotional blandness and an interpersonal imperceptiveness. Like antisocials, they show no evidence of warm, tender feeling toward others, but in addition, they are indifferent to praise or criticism and are often unable to express aggression or hostility. They have no interest in exploiting or humiliating others.

Schizoids have what Hoch (1910) called a "shut-in" personality. They do not make personal revelations to others and are not interested in the personal lives of others. They live in a world of fantasies and daydreams. Fairbairn's (1940/1952) schizoid personality was considered to be someone who is isolated and detached and preoccupied with inner reality, who experiences the self as artificial and unreal, as if separated from others by a sheet of glass. A number of writers have linked the schizoid personality with the presentation of a false self. Deutsch (1942) wrote of the "as if" personality, who lacks any genuine emotional relationship to the outside world but behaves as if he or she does.

Because of the low level of motivation of schizoid individuals, questionnaire measures are not likely to be very useful as a means of diagnosis. There are schizoid scales in the Millon Clinical Multiaxial Inventory (Millon, 1982) and the Personality Diagnosis Questionnaire (Hyler et al., 1990). The Rust Inventory of Schizoid Cognitions (Rust, 1987) is not a specific measure of the schizoid personality. It is more a general index of psychotic cognition and contains a number of items pertaining to schizotypy. Tantam (1988b) constructed what he called scale a of schizoid personality characteristics that was derived from a structured interview. It included the five subscales of emotional detachment, unsociability, rigidity, oversensitivity, and suspiciousness and secretiveness. On the basis of the interview, ratings were also made of oddity, magical thinking, and illusions. Like the Rust instrument then, it measures both schizoid and schizotypal features.

Tantam (1988a) described a minority of his series who were violent. The commonest type of assault was on members of the family, most often the mother, and frequently for some trivial grievance, such as a meal not being ready. The subjects in this violent minority often appeared to have no empathic grasp of their victim's distress; it was not uncommon for them to criticize the victim for making too much fuss. One of them had thought it "very funny" when he had seen, on the television news, a mother and three children burned to death.

Schizotypals represent a further stage still in the introversion process. In fact, they are too introverted to be useful members of society. Millon (1981) described them as leading meaningless, idle, and ineffectual existences, drifting from one aimless activity to another, remaining on the periphery of societal life, and rarely developing intimate attachments or accepting enduring responsibilities. A characteristic that distinguishes schizotypals from schizoids is their eccentricity. As Millon (1981) observed, "As they become progressively estranged from their social environment, they lose touch with the conventions of reality and with the checks against irrational thought and behavior that are provided by reciprocal relationships" (p. 400). Schizotypals exhibit a blurring of fantasy and reality (Millon, 1990). The fantasies and daydreams of schizoids become the illusions, ideas of reference (Millon, 1981), magical thinking (Eckblad & Chapman, 1983), and preoccupations with the paranormal (Williams & Irwin, 1991) of schizotypals. These features of schizotypals are further examined in the next chapter.

Claridge (1987) concluded that schizotypy is not a unitary dimension, but consists of several subcomponents that encompass personality traits of social nonconformity as well as more manifestly psychotic characteristics. In view of the large number of pathological forms of distance that have been described in this chapter, a statement such as this could reasonably be made about any one of the personality disorders considered. Tantam (1988a, 1988b) described a series of 60 adult psychiatric patients with schizotypal features, many of whom had had the symptoms of autism beginning in later childhood. He concluded that schizotypal disorder could be a final common pathway of a number of conditions and circumstances that restrict early emotional and social development.

The close association between schizotypy and the illness schizophrenia cannot be ignored. Stone (1993) observed that evidence for viewing schizotypy as a condition within the spectrum of schizophrenia has been presented from many sources. The term schizotypal was coined by Rado (1956) to be an abbreviation of schizophrenic phenotype, implying that it carries a hereditary disposition to schizophrenia. Almost all studies of the families of schizophrenic probands have found an excess of both schizophrenia and schizotypal personality disorder among relatives (Baron et al., 1983; Kendler et al., 1984), and adding schizotypy to schizophrenia produces a higher monozygous to dizygous concordance ratio in twin studies (Farmer, McGuffin, & Gottesman, 1987). Much that has been written about schizophrenia applies also to schizoid and schizotypal disorders. Bowen (1978) considered schizophrenia to be a failure of differentiation, and this may also be said of schizotypy. Blatt and Wild (1976) conceptualized schizophrenia as involving a malfunctioning of the self-other boundary, which also is a feature of schizotypy. Millon (1990) referred to the schizotypal as having permeable ego-boundaries, but this description, to a lesser degree, applies also to schizoids. It appears that the establishment of a secure sense of self and a firm distinction between self and not self requires an adequate amount of interaction with others. The turning away from others at an early stage, a characteristic of all introverts, seems to prevent this happening and results in ontological insecurity (Laing, 1965).

RECOMMENDATIONS FOR CLINICIANS AND RESEARCHERS

In writing this chapter, I have followed three principles:

1. It is useful to conceive distance as a generic construct and to determine the range of psychological processes that might be contained within it.
2. Before examining the pathological forms of distance, it is necessary to identify the normal forms.
3. Before defining the characteristics of specific personality disorders, it is necessary to describe the range of possible pathological processes that might be involved.

Of the five main classes of distant personality disorder listed, only three have been considered here. From both a clinical and a research point of view, it is useful to (a) conceive these three disparate conditions as having the unifying theme of distance and (b) identify those psychological processes that differentiate between them.

One way to differentiate between them is to locate each of them on the vertical axis. Antisocials are upper distant. They like to have power and to use it to their advantage. They do not respect, and are contemptuous toward, those in authority over them and they disregard rules and obligations (ICD-10). Millon (1981) maintained that they enjoy and gain satisfaction from derogating and humiliating others. He linked this with the idea that they consider themselves to have been victimized in their early lives and are determined (a) to prevent this happening again and (b) to even the score by heaping on to others the harm that was done to them. Introverts are what I have called neutral distant (Birtchnell, 1993); that is they are neither upper nor lower. They seem to have no need of others and simply wish to keep away from them. When others approach them, they find it intrusive. Avoidants are lower distant. They relate in an upwardly directed way, fearing that others will either reject them or take advantage of them. They resolve therefore never to put themselves in a position in which they might be dependent on others. What they cannot do for themselves, they deny that they have need of.

Focusing now on the horizontal axis, it would appear that the distinct differences between these three classes of disorder are largely to do with the mental and/or neurophysiological mechanisms that result in the individual becoming and remaining distant. Identifying these, and their possible origins, should be the main priorities for future research. It is only when advances in this direction have been made that it will be feasible to develop and test therapeutic interventions for modifying such mechanisms.

Antisocials are the least distanced from other people. In fact, their involvement with them is quite considerable. They relate to each other by forming outsider groups; they freely engage in sexual behavior; they have multiple marriages; they exploit people and they derive satisfaction from humiliating and hurting them. They appear to have three principal deficiencies:

1. They cannot tolerate being part of conventional society, of having expectations made of them, of other people needing them, of being tied down.
2. They cannot identify with the feelings of others, feel guilty or ashamed of what they do to them, which enables them to use, exploit, and be cruel to them.
3. They cannot allow others to get to them emotionally; the only emotion they are prepared to express toward others is anger.

Largely because of antisocials' criminal propensity, a great deal of research attention has been directed toward efforts to modify their behavior. Dolan and Coid (1993) reviewed over 80 studies and concluded that the quality of such studies has been generally poor. Because outcome was measured almost entirely in terms of the recurrence of criminal behavior, these studies have little to contribute to an understanding of factors that might contribute to the distancing processes of these kinds of individual. Dolan and Coid (1993) concluded that it is premature to invest resources in treatment programs before etiologic factors have been identified. A useful start in this direction might be to focus specifically on both the causes and methods of modifying the distancing behavior of antisocials. There is accumulating evidence that significant proportions of those who manifest conduct disorders in childhood, have poor peer relationships, or come from disordered or deprived family backgrounds are more likely to have antisocial disorders in adult life (McCord, 1982; Offord, 1982). It seems likely that there are certain similarities between the family backgrounds of avoidants and antisocials and many antisocials manifest the same self-reliance as some (dismissive) avoidants; but where avoidants are accepting of the treatment they received, antisocials are resentful of it. One objective of future research is to determine what, if anything, is different about the two types of family background. Why do antisocials blame others and avoidants blame themselves?

Avoidants appear to want involvement with others but are not prepared to risk getting it in case it goes wrong and they get badly hurt. This suggests that, at some time in their lives, they have experienced having it and then losing it. Kantor (1993) maintained that avoidants—but here presumably he was referring to Bartholomew's (1990) fearful avoidants— are much preoccupied with how they might achieve closeness and spend a great deal of time trying to achieve it. This suggests that the mental mechanisms necessary for achieving closeness are intact and that, with improvement in their self-esteem and assurances that they are acceptable and likable, avoidants can be helped to overcome their fears of rejection and risk getting closer to people. Kantor's (1993) therapeutic approach was largely a cognitive behavioral one. He listed a number of what he called avoidance-reducing techniques that the patient can be taught. A psychodynamic therapist would adopt a long-term approach during which the origins of the patient's fears of rejection would be explored and reexperienced within the safety of the session, and the patient's present assumptions concerning his or her acceptability would be tested in the setting of the relationship to the therapist.

The relevance of Bowlby's (1969) attachment theory to the understanding of avoidant disorders has already been discussed. Research interest into attachment processes in adults is gaining momentum (Bartholomew & Perlman, 1994). At present, the application of this work to avoidant disorders is lacking, but it is an obvious direction in which it should move. Although a genetic contribution to avoidant behavior cannot be ruled out, its determinants are more likely to lie in early deficiencies in relationships to parents. Bowlby (1980) proposed one possible psychophysiological mechanism that could be explored further. He said that when a child's approaches to its parents are frequently, over a prolonged period, not responded to, the system controlling its attachment behavior may ultimately become deactivated. This could be achieved by the defensive exclusion of sensory inflow of any and every kind that might activate attachment feelings or behavior. Main et al. (1986) were able to establish links between the detachment behavior of children and the behavior of their mothers. The mothers of anxious avoidant children were observed to be consistently undemonstrative and rejecting. Fonagy, Steele, and Steele (1991) observed that women with poor reported early attachments related less well to their own infants. This might equally point to a genetic predisposition to distance that was apparent in both mother and infant, though Fonagy (personal communication, 1992) has argued against this possibility.

The so-called avoidant schizophrenics (Millon, 1969) come closer to a personality disorder than a disease entity. They form a category of distance midway between the avoidants and the introverts. Like the avoidants, they are capable of achieving closeness, but the psychotherapeutic effort that may be required to enable them to do so is considerable. The therapist needs to be patient and expect only slow progress. Fromm-Reichmann (1959) quoted a patient who had recovered from such a condition as saying, "Hell is if you are frozen in isolation into a block of ice. That is where I have been" (p. 9).

Unlike antisocials and avoidants, those with purely introverted disorders demonstrate what is probably an innate, and largely genetically determined, aversion to closeness. A low tolerance of sensory input appears to be "hard-wired" into their central nervous systems. In time, it may be possible to locate those centers within the CNS that regulate closeness and distance-seeking behavior. It may not be unreasonable to expect that some day researchers may develop means for modifying these centers. It seems unlikely that any form of psychotherapeutic intervention will influence their relating behavior. A more profitable approach may be to train relatives and others who are in contact with them to respect their need for distance in the way that the relatives of schizophrenics have been trained (Kuipers, Leff, & Lam, 1992).

The fact that the international classifications of personality disorders are continually being updated suggests a degree of arbitrariness in them, and what appears to be lacking is a sound, theoretical framework on which to base such classifications. The evolutionary models of Millon (1990) and Birtchnell (1993) may provide such a framework. In some interesting work, recently reported on, Plutchik, Conte, & Karasu (1994) invited 16 clinicians to rate independently the degree of similarity between the descriptions of the DSM-III-R personality disorders to that of three "reference" descriptions. The mean ratings for the total group were then converted into angular locations on a circle. It was found that the 14 descriptions were more or less evenly distributed around a circle. This empirical and atheoretical approach helps to shed light on the interrelatedness of the personality disorders. It is left to further researchers to explain why some disorders are similar and others are different. The aspects of distance considered in this chapter should prove to be of value in this respect.

Although there may be advantages to examining the nature and characteristics of individual personality disorders, science works best when it is able to identify and focus on specific processes. A case can be made for taking as a starting point for research, and also perhaps for therapy, the separate forms of normal and pathological distance listed at the beginning of this chapter, rather than classes of personality disorder. Some of these forms of distancing may have similar origins and some may have different origins. Once the origins have been determined, means of modifying them can be devised.

REFERENCES

Ainsworth, M. D. S., Blehar, M. C., Waters, E., & Wall, S. (1978). *Patterns of attachment: A psychological study of the strange situation.* Hillsdale, NJ: Erlbaum.

Altman, I. (1975). *The environment and social behavior: Privacy, personal space, territory and crowding.* Monterey, CA: Brooks/Cole.

American Psychiatric Association. (1980). *Diagnostic and statistical manual of mental disorders* (3rd ed.). Washington, DC: Author.

American Psychiatric Association. (1987). *Diagnostic and statistical manual of mental disorders* (3rd ed., rev.). Washington, DC: Author.

Bailey, K. G. (1988). Psychological kinship: Implications for the helping professions. *Psychotherapy, 25,* 132–141.

Bannister, D. (1987). The psychotic disguise. In W. Dryden (Ed.), *Therapists' dilemmas.* London: Harper & Row.

Baron, M., Gruen, R., Asnis, L., & Kane, J. (1983). Familial relatedness of schizophrenic and schizotypal states. *American Journal of Psychiatry, 140,* 1437–1442.

Baron, R. A., & Byrne, D. (1991). *Social psychology.* London: Allyn & Bacon.

Barsky, A. J., & Klerman, G. L. (1983). Overview: Hypochondriasis, bodily complaints and somatic styles. *American Journal of Psychiatry, 140,* 273–283.

Bartholomew, K. (1990). Avoidance of intimacy: An attachment perspective. *Journal of Social and Personal Relationships, 7,* 147–178.

Bartholomew, K., & Horowitz, L. M. (1991). Attachment styles among young adults: A test of a four-category model. *Journal of Personality and Social Psychology, 61,* 226–244.

Bartholomew, K., & Perlman, D. (Eds.). (1994). *Attachment processes in adults: Advances in personal relationships* (Vol. 5). London: Jessica Kingsley.

Beck, A. T. (1983). Cognitive therapy of depression: New perspectives. In P. J. Clayton & J. E. Barrett (Eds.), *Treatment of depression: Old controversies and new approaches.* New York: Raven Press.

Beck, A. T. (1990). *Cognitive therapy of the personality disorders.* New York: Guilford.

Berman, M. (1982). *All that is solid melts into air.* London: Verso.

Birtchnell, J. (1993). *How humans relate: A new interpersonal theory.* Westport, CT: Praeger.

Blackburn, R. (1989). Psychopathy and personality disorder in relation to violence. In K. Howells & C. R. Hollin (Eds.), *Clinical approaches to violence.* Chichester: Wiley.

Blackburn, R. (1993). *The psychology of criminal conduct.* Chichester: Wiley.

Blatt, S. J., & Shichman, S. (1983). Two primary configurations of psychopathology. *Psychoanalysis and Contemporary Thought, 6,* 187–249.

Blatt, S. J., & Wild, C. M. (1976). *Schizophrenia: A developmental analysis.* New York: Academic Press.

Bowen, M. (1978). *Family therapy in clinical practice.* London: Aronson.

Bowlby, J. (1969). *Attachment and loss. Vol. 1: Attachment.* London: Hogarth Press/Institute of Psychoanalysis.

Bowlby, J. (1980). *Attachment and loss. Vol. 3: Loss, sadness and depression.* London: Hogarth Press/Institute of Psychoanalysis.

Buber, M. (1937). *I and thou.* Edinburgh: Clark.

Burnham, D. L., Gladstone, A. I., & Gibson, R. W. (1969). *Schizophrenia and the need-fear dilemma.* New York: International Universities Press.

Claridge, G. (1987). "The schizophrenias as nervous types" revisited. *British Journal of Psychiatry, 151,* 735–743.

Claridge, G., Pryor, R., & Watkins, G. (1990). *Sounds from the bell jar. Ten psychotic authors.* London: Macmillan.

Cleckley, H. (1976). *The mask of sanity.* St. Louis, MO: Mosby.

Coopersmith, S. (1967). *The antecedents of self-esteem.* San Francisco, CA: Freeman.

Dement, W. (1960). The effect of dream deprivation. *Science, 131,* 1705–1707.

Deutsch, H. (1942). Some forms of emotional disturbance and their relationship to schizophrenia. *Psychoanalytic Quarterly, 11,* 301–321.

Dolan, B., & Coid, J. (1993). *Psychopathic and antisocial personality disorders: Treatment and research issues.* London: Gaskell.

Durkheim, E. (1951). *Suicide.* New York: Free Press. (Original work published 1897)

Eckblad, M., & Chapman, L. J. (1983). Magical ideation as an indicator of schizotypy. *Journal of Clinical and Consulting Psychology, 52,* 215–225.

Eibl-Eibesfeldt, I. (1989). *Human ethology.* New York: Aldine de Gruyter.

Eysenck, H. J. (1947). *Dimensions of personality.* London: Routledge & Kegan Paul.

Eysenck, H. J. (1970). The structure of human personality (rev. ed.). London: Methuen.

Eysenck, H. J., & Gudjonsson, G. H. (1989). *The causes and cures of criminality.* New York: Plenum.

Fairbairn, W. R. D. (1952). Schizoid factors in the personality. In *Psychoanalytic Studies of the Personality*. London: Routledge & Kegan Paul. (Original work published 1940)

Farmer, A., McGuffin, P., & Gottesman, I. I. (1987). Twin concordance for DSM-III schizophrenia. Scrutinizing the validity of the definition. *Archives of General Psychiatry, 44,* 634–641.

Feldman, L. B. (1979). Marital conflict and martial intimacy: An integrative psychodynamic-behavioral-systemic model. *Family Process, 18,* 69–78.

Fenichel, O. (1945). *The psychoanalytic theory of neurosis*. New York: Norton.

Fonagy, P., Steele, H., & Steele, M. (1991). Maternal representations of attachment during pregnancy predict the organization of infant-mother attachment at one year of age. *Child Development, 62,* 891–905.

Frankl, V. E. (1967). *Psychotherapy and existentialism: Selected papers on logotherapy*. London: Souvenir.

Freedman, M. B., Leary, T., Ossorio, A. G., & Coffee, H. S. (1951). The interpersonal dimension of personality. *Journal of Personality, 20,* 143–161.

Freud, S. (1939). *Civilisation and its discontents* (J. Riviere Trans.). London: Hogarth Press. (Original work published 1930)

Freud, S. (1957). On narcissism: An introduction. In J. Strachey (Ed. and Trans.), *The standard edition of the complete psychological works of Sigmund Freud* (Vol. 14). London: Hogarth Press. (Original work published 1914)

Fromm-Reichmann, F. (1959). Loneliness. *Psychiatry, 22,* 1–25.

Frosch, S. (1991). *Identity crisis: Modernity, psychoanalysis and the self.* London: Macmillan.

Goffman, E. (1963). *Behavior in public places: Notes on the social organisation of gatherings*. New York: Free Press.

Grassian, S. (1983). Psychological effects of solitary confinement. *American Journal of Psychiatry, 140,* 1450–1454.

Guntrip, H. (1969). *Schizoid phenomena, object relations and the self.* London: Hogarth Press.

Hall, E. T. (1966). *The hidden dimension*. New York: Doubleday.

Hare, R. D. (1980). A research scale for the assessment of psychopathy in criminal populations. *Personality and Individual Differences, 1,* 111–119.

Hare, R. D. (1991). *The psychopathy checklist—Revised*. Toronto: Multi Health Systems.

Harpur, T. J., Hare, R. D., & Hakstian, A. R. (1989). Two-factor conceptualization of psychopathy: Construct validity and assessment implications. *Psychological Assessment: A Journal of Consulting and Clinical Psychology, 1,* 6–17.

Harris, A. (1959). Sensory deprivation and schizophrenia. *Journal of Mental Science, 105,* 237.

Hayward, M. L., & Taylor, J. E. (1956). A schizophrenic patient describes the action of intensive psychotherapy. *Psychiatric Quarterly, 30,* 211–248.

Hazan, C., & Shaver, P. (1987). Romantic love conceptualized as an attachment process. *Journal of Personality and Social Psychology, 52,* 511–524.

Hoch, A. (1910). Constitutional factors in the dementia praecox group. *Review of Neurology and Psychiatry, 8,* 463–475.

Hoffman, M. L. (1987). The contribution of empathy to justice and moral judgement. In N. Eisenberg & J. Strayer (Eds.), *Empathy and its development.* New York: Cambridge University Press.

Horney, K. (1945). *Our inner conflicts.* New York: Norton.

Hyler, S., Skodol, A. E., Kellman, H. D., Oldham, J. M., & Rosnick, L. (1990). Validity of the Personality Diagnostic Questionnaire—Revised. Comparison with two structured interviews. *American Journal of Psychiatry, 147,* 1043–1048.

Jacobson, E. (1964). *The self and the object world.* New York: International Universities Press.

Jung, C. J. (1971). Psychological types. In H. Read, M. Fordham, & G. Adler (Eds.), *The collected works* (Vol. 6). London: Routledge and Kegan Paul. (Original work published 1921)

Kantor, M. (1993). *Distancing: A guide to avoidance and avoidant personality disorder.* Westport, CN: Praeger.

Kendell, R. E. (1975). *The role of diagnosis in psychiatry.* Oxford: Blackwell Scientific Publications.

Kendler, K. S., Masterson, C. C., Ungaro, R., & Davis, K. L. (1984). A family history study of schizophrenic related personality disorders. *American Journal of Psychiatry, 141,* 424–427.

Kohut, H. (1971). *The analysis of the self: A systematic approach to the psychoanalytic treatment of narcissistic personality disorders.* New York: International Universities Press.

Kuipers, L., Leff, J., & Lam, D. (1992). *Family work for schizophrenia: A practical guide.* London: Gaskell.

Laing, R. D. (1965). *The divided self.* Harmondsworth, Middlesex: Penguin.

Lasch, C. (1984). *The minimal self.* London: Picador.

Lilly, J. C. (1956). Mental effects of reduction of ordinary levels of physical stimuli on intact, healthy persons. *Psychiatric research reports, no. 5,* 1–9. Washington, DC: American Psychiatric Association.

Livesley, W. J., West, M., & Tanney, A. (1985). Historical comment on DSM-III schizoid and avoidant personality disorders. *American Journal of Psychiatry, 142,* 1344–1347.

Macdiarmid, D. (1989). Self-cathexis and other-cathexis: Vicissitudes in the history of an observation. *British Journal of Psychiatry, 154,* 844–852.

Mahler, M. (1961). On sadness and grief in infancy and childhood. *Psychoanalytic study of the child, 18,* 307–324.

Main, M., & Goldwyn, R. (1990). Adult attachment rating and classification systems. In M. Main (Ed.), *A typology of human attachment organisation assessed in discourse, drawings and interview.* New York: Cambridge University Press.

Main, M., Kaplan, N., & Cassidy, J. (1986). Security in infancy, childhood and adulthood: A move to the level of representation. In I. Bretherton & E. Waters (Eds.), *Growing points and attachment theory and research. Monograph of the Society for Research in Child Development, 50,* Nos. 1–2.

Mazur, A. (1977). Interpersonal spacing on public benches in "contact" vs. "non-contact" cultures. *Journal of Social Psychology, 101,* 53–58.

McBride, G., King, M. G., & James, J. W. (1965). Social proximity: Effects on galvanic skin response in humans. *Journal of Psychology, 61,* 153–157.

McCord, J. (1982). *The psychopath and milieu therapy: A longitudinal study.* New York: Academic Press.

McCranie, E. J. (1971). Depression, anxiety, and hostility. *Psychiatric Quarterly, 45,* 117–133.

Milgram, S. (1974). *Obedience to authority.* New York: Harper & Row.

Millon, T. (1969). *Modern psychopathology: A biosocial approach to maladaptive learning and functioning.* Philadelphia, PA: Saunders.

Millon, T. (1981). *Disorders of personality, DSM III, Axis II.* New York: Wiley.

Millon, T. (1982). *Millon Clinical Multiaxial Inventory Manual.* Minneapolis, MN: National Computer Systems.

Millon, T. (1990). *Toward a new personology: An evolutionary model.* New York: Wiley.

Moore, R. I. (1985). Preface. In E. Peters (Ed.), *Torture.* New York: Blackwell.

Murray, H. (1938). *Explorations in personality.* New York: Oxford University Press.

Offord, D. R. (1982). Family backgrounds of male and female delinquents. In J. Gunn & D. P. Farrington (Eds.), *Abnormal offenders, delinquency and the criminal justice system.* Chichester: Wiley.

Ornitz, E. M. (1983). The functional neuroanatomy of infantile autism. *International Journal of Neuroscience, 19,* 85–124.

Parkes, C. M. (1973). Factors determining the persistence of phantom pain in the amputee. *Journal of Psychosomatic Research, 17,* 97–108.

Plutchik, R., Conte, H. R., & Karasu, T. B. (1994, June–July). The circumplex structure of personality disorders: An empirical study. Paper presented to the annual international meeting of the Society for Psychotherapy Research, York, England.

Presley, A. S., & Walton, H. J. (1973). Dimensions of abnormal personality. *British Journal of Psychiatry, 122,* 269–276.

Rado, S. (1956). Schizotypal organization: Preliminary report on a clinical study of schizophrenia. In S. Rado & G. E. Daniels (Eds.), *Changing concepts of psychoanalytic medicine.* New York: Grune & Stratton.

Rust, J. (1987). The Rust Inventory of Schizoid Cognitions (RISC): A psychometric measure of psychoticism in the normal population. *British Journal of Clinical Psychology, 26,* 151–152.

Sainsbury, P. (1955). *Suicide in London: An ecological study.* Maudsley Monographs No. 1. London: Chapman & Hall.

Seyfarth, R., & Cheney, D. (1992). Inside the mind of a monkey. *New Scientist, 133*(1802), 25–29.

Shaver, P. R., & Hazan, C. (1993). Adult romantic attachment: Theory and Evidence. In D. Perlman & W. H. Jones (Eds.), *Advances in Personal Relationships* (Vol. 4). London: Jessica Kingsley.

Sifneos, P. E. (1973). The presence of 'alexithymic' characteristics in psychosomatic patients. *Psychotherapy and Psychosomatics, 22,* 255–262.

Silverton, L. (1988). Crime and the schizophrenia spectrum—A diathesis-stress model. *Acta Psychiatrica Scandinavica, 78,* 72–81.

Slocum, J. (1948). *Sailing alone around the world.* London: Rupert Hart-Davis.

Smith, L., & Martinsen, H. (1977). The behavior of young children in a strange situation. *Scandinavian Journal of Psychology, 18,* 43–52.

Sroufe, L. A., & Waters, E. (1977). Heart rate as a convergent measure in clinical and developmental research. *Merrill-Palmer Quarterly, 23,* 3–25.

Stengel, E. (1941). On the aetiology of fugue states. *Journal of Mental Science, 87,* 572–599.

Stone, M. H. (1993). Long term outcome in personality disorders. In P. Tyrer & G. Stein (Eds.), *Personality Disorders Reviewed.* London: Gaskell.

Storr, A. (1983). A psychotherapist looks at depression. *British Journal of Psychiatry, 143,* 431–435.

Suedfeld, P. (1991). Groups in isolation and confinement: Environments and experiences. In A. H. Harrison, Y. A. Clearwater, & C. P. McKay (Eds.), *From Antarctica to outer space: Life in isolation and confinement.* New York: Springer Verlag.

Suedfeld, P., & Kristeller, J. L. (1982). Stimulus reduction as a technique in health psychology. *Health Psychology, 1,* 337–357.

Suttie, I. D. (1935). *The origins of love and hate.* London: Kegan Paul.

Tantam, D. (1988a). Lifelong eccentricity and social isolation I: Psychiatric, social and forensic aspects. *British Journal of Psychiatry, 153,* 777–782.

Tantam, D. (1988b). Lifelong eccentricity and social isolation II: Aspberger's syndrome or schizoid personality disorder? *British Journal of Psychiatry, 153,* 783–791.

Tsuang, M. T. (1982). *Schizophrenia: The facts.* London: Oxford University Press.

Waters, W., Matas, L., & Sroufe, L. A. (1975). Infants reactions to an approaching stranger: Description, validation and functional significance of wariness. *Child Development, 46,* 348–356.

West, M. A. (1987). Traditional and psychological perspectives on meditation. In M. A. West (Ed.), *The Psychology of Meditation*. Oxford: Clarindon Press.

Whitely, J. S. (1994). In pursuit of the elusive category. *British Journal of Psychiatry Review of Books, 7,* 14–17.

Williams, L. M., & Irwin, H. J. (1991). A study of paranormal belief, magical ideation as an index of schizotypy and cognitive style. *Personality and Individual Differences, 12,* 1339–1348.

Winnicott, D. W. (1953). Transitional objects and transitional phenomena. *International Journal of Psychoanalysis, 34,* 89–97.

Winnicott, D. W. (1956). On transference. *International Journal of Psychoanalysis, 37,* 382–395.

Wolff, S., & Cull, A. (1986). "Schizoid" personality and antisocial conduct: A retrospective case-note study. *Psychological Medicine, 16,* 677–687.

World Health Organization. (1992). *The ICD-10 classification of mental and behavioral disorders.* Geneva: Author.

Zeitlin, S. B., McNally, R. J., & Cassiday, K. L. (1993). Alexithymia in victims of sexual assault: An effect of repeated traumatization. *American Journal of Psychiatry, 150,* 661–663.

CHAPTER 8

Peculiarity

HOWARD BERENBAUM

As the chapters in this volume attest, the personality disorders encompass a wide array of personality characteristics. Several researchers have attempted to delineate the personality traits and dimensions that compose the personality disorders (Clark, 1990; Harkness, 1992; Livesley, Jackson, & Schroeder, 1992). Each of these researchers has identified one or more dimensions, factors, or clusters that include various manifestations of what I have chosen to call "peculiarity." For example, Harkness (1992) described 39 groupings of personality disorder diagnostic criteria, one of which was named "Has Very Odd or Unusual Beliefs and Experiences That Most People Would Consider Unusual, Strange, Fantastic, or Superstitious." Livesley et al. (1992) described 15 personality disorder factors, one of which was named "Cognitive Dysfunction" and included traits of depersonalization or derealization and schizotypal cognition. Clark (1990) described 15 personality disorder dimensions, one of which was named "Eccentric Thought" and included traits of recurrent illusions, depersonalization or derealization, magical thinking, ideas of reference, and clairvoyance. The peculiar phenomena described in these factors and dimensions could be divided into three categories:

1. Peculiar perceptions, as exemplified by recurrent illusions.
2. Peculiar thoughts and beliefs, as exemplified by magical thinking and clairvoyance.
3. Dissociative features such as depersonalization and derealization.

The goal of this chapter is to review what we know about the different aspects of peculiarity and their relationships to personality disorders. I will begin by describing the nature of these phenomena and will provide

---

I wish to thank Louise Fitzgerald and Gregory Miller for their helpful comments on an earlier draft of this chapter.

a brief description of how they can be measured. I will then discuss several of the most prominent theories concerning the development of peculiarity. Next, I will describe the manner in which the different aspects of peculiarity are associated with personality disorder categories and with other personality characteristics. Finally, I will summarize what we know about peculiarity and its relevance to the personality disorders and will provide recommendations for future research. I will argue that genetic factors and exposure to trauma constitute two significant pathways that can lead to peculiarity, and will discuss the relationships between these two pathways and personality disorders and schizophrenia.

THE NATURE OF PECULIARITY

One of the most important definitional issues concerning peculiar beliefs, perceptions, and dissociative experiences is whether they are dichotomous or continuous phenomena. For example, is it the case that one does or does not have peculiar beliefs, or is there a continuum of peculiar beliefs ranging from those that are not at all peculiar to those that are extremely peculiar? One reason this issue has received so much attention is that peculiar phenomena have been so strongly linked to categorically defined psychiatric disorders, notably psychotic and dissociative disorders. Peculiar beliefs have traditionally been studied in the form of delusions, and peculiar perceptions have traditionally been studied in the form of hallucinations. As pointed out by Strauss (1969), "the tendency to accept perceptual and ideational phenomena as dichotomous may stem from the high proportion of studies of schizophrenics and other psychotics" (p. 584). As is the case with peculiar perceptions and beliefs, most of the work examining dissociation has historically focused on dissociative disorders such as hysteria and multiple personality disorder. Several researchers have pointed out that hallucinations and delusions can be conceptualized and measured as continua (e.g., Chapman & Chapman, 1980; Strauss, 1969). Similarly, although psychopathologists may sometimes distinguish between "normal" dissociative experiences and "pathological" dissociative disorders (e.g., Nemiah, 1985), dissociation is "generally conceptualized as lying along a continuum from the minor dissociations of everyday life to major forms of psychopathology such as multiple personality disorder" (Bernstein & Putnam, 1986, p. 728). It should be pointed out, however, that psychopathologists are not unanimous in considering peculiar phenomena in continuous terms. For example, with respect to dissociation, Frankel (1990) stated, "The assumption of a continuum is open to question" (p. 827). Viewing the different facets of peculiarity as lying along continua is particularly important for understanding the personality disorders. Whereas individuals with psychotic and dissociative disorders exhibit peculiarity in its most extreme forms, individuals with personality disorders are likely to exhibit less severe forms of peculiarity that would not necessarily be considered hallucinations, delusions, or dissociation by those who would define these phenomena categorically.

To describe peculiar beliefs, it is helpful to examine them in their most extreme form, namely delusional beliefs. According to Oltmanns (1988), "Delusions are typically considered to be idiosyncratic beliefs, utterly lacking in social validation" (pp. 3–4). Oltmanns then went on to present the following list of seven defining characteristics of delusions, pointing out that none of these characteristics is necessary or sufficient to define delusions:

> (1) The balance of evidence for and against the belief is such that other people consider it completely incredible; (2) the belief is not shared by others; (3) the belief is held with firm conviction; (4) the person is preoccupied with (emotionally committed to) the belief; (5) the belief involves personal reference, rather than unconventional religious, scientific, or political conviction; (6) the belief is a source of subjective distress or interferes with the person's occupational or social functioning; and (7) the person does not report subjective efforts to resist the belief. (p. 5)

Beliefs vary in the degree to which they match each of these seven characteristics; the greater the degree to which each of these characteristics is matched, the more peculiar the belief can be considered. For example, the belief that UFOs probably exist might be considered somewhat peculiar, but not as peculiar as the belief that one's thoughts are definitely broadcast out loud.

Just as the nature of peculiar beliefs is clarified by examining delusions, the nature of peculiar perceptions can be illuminated by examining them in their most extreme form, hallucinations. Slade and Bentall (1988) defined hallucinations as "any percept-like experience which (a) occurs in the absence of an appropriate stimulus, (b) has the full force or impact of the corresponding actual (real) perception, and (c) is not amenable to direct and voluntary control by the experiencer" (p. 23). Heilbrun (1993) pointed out that an additional characteristic of hallucinations that was not included in the definition provided by Slade and Bentall is that the (mis)perception be persistent rather than transient. Many perceptions can be considered to meet at least some of the previously described defining characteristics of hallucinations (e.g., impact, persistence), at least to some degree. For example, hearing your name said aloud when at a party, when in fact your name was not said aloud, would meet at least some of those characteristics. The various characteristics might be met to lesser or greater degrees. For example, hearing your name said aloud at a party where others are speaking might be considered to meet the "absence of an appropriate stimulus" criterion less than would hearing your name said aloud when you are alone. In a similar vein, hearing your name said aloud one time at a party may be considered less "persistent" than hearing your name said aloud repeatedly throughout a party, which would be less "persistent" than hearing your name said aloud on a regular basis over the course of several weeks. Although all three cases of misperceiving one's name being said aloud might be considered instances of peculiar perceptions, they differ in severity. Peculiar perceptions can occur in all sensory modalities, though peculiar auditory and visual perceptions are most common. In the auditory modality, some psychopathologists have distinguished between peculiar perceptions perceived as emanating from outside one's head and peculiar perceptions perceived as emanating from inside one's head (e.g., Junginger & Frame, 1985). Historically, only those (mis)perceptions perceived as emanating from outside one's body were considered to be true hallucinations, whereas (mis)perceptions perceived as emanating from inside one's body were considered to be pseudohallucinations (e.g., Sedman, 1966).

The third aspect of peculiarity, dissociation, includes certain core aspects agreed on by almost all psychopathologists. According to Spiegel and Cardena (1991), "Dissociation can be thought of as a structured separation of mental processes (e.g., thoughts, emotions, conation, memory, and identity) that are ordinarily integrated" (p. 367). According to Frankel (1990), "At the heart of the idea of dissociation is a disconnectedness or lack of integration of knowledge, identity, memory, and control" (p. 828). Despite general agreement about the core of dissociation, many issues concerning the definition and conceptualization of the phenomenon remain controversial. As Frankel (1990) stated, "In reviewing the history of the use of the term dissociation, it is apparent that clarity is conspicuous by its absence. It is as if the core of the phenomenon is fairly readily recognizable and can be agreed on. However, as soon as one moves away to consider the other shades of experience, matters become less clear" (p. 827). Disagreement concerning the nature of dissociation may be a reflection of its complexity as well as the fact that it has received very little attention for most of this century (Hilgard, 1986). However, as pointed out by Erdelyi (1994), "Dissociationism has been around, persists, is ingrained in cognitive psychology, and will continue to be around because it is a fundamental reality of psychology" (p. 3), and Spiegel and Cardena (1991) describe the relatively recent resurgence of interest in dissociation. For example, two edited volumes devoted to the topic of dissociation have appeared in the past several years (Singer, 1990; Spiegel, 1994).

The various facets of dissociation were divided by Steinberg, Rounsaville, and Cicchetti (1990) into the following five types of features:

> (1) Amnesia represents a specific and substantial block of time that cannot be accounted for by memory; (2) depersonalization refers to detachment from oneself—a sense of "going through the motions" or of looking at oneself as an outsider; (3) derealization refers to the sense that one's surroundings are unreal; (4) identity confusion refers to subjective feelings of confusion, uncertainty, or puzzlement centered on patients' knowledge of their own identity; and (5) identity alteration focuses on behavioral manifestations of identity confusion, such as exhibiting a special knowledge or skill without knowing how this skill was acquired. (p. 77)

MEASUREMENT

A variety of instruments have been developed for measuring different aspects of peculiarity, the easiest of which to use are probably self-report questionnaires. In addition to self-report questionnaires, information concerning peculiarity can be obtained with several different interview measures. The instruments that assess peculiarity vary in their degree of specificity. For example, some instruments measure specific aspects of peculiarity (e.g., peculiar perceptions), whereas other instruments provide more global measurement of peculiarity. In addition, several instruments measure peculiarity as well as other characteristics of personality and psychopathology. Most of the instruments designed to measure peculiarity were developed by researchers who were primarily interested in studying schizophrenia or dissociative disorders; it has been uncommon for personality disorder researchers to develop such instruments.

Self-Report Questionnaires

Perhaps the most specialized and widely used instruments, at least for the purpose of conducting research on peculiarity among individuals who are not severely disturbed, are the Wisconsin psychosis proneness scales developed by the Chapmans and their colleagues. The Perceptual Aberration Scale (PABS; Chapman, Chapman, & Raulin, 1978) is a 35-item true-false questionnaire that measures peculiar perceptual experiences, particularly strange perceptions of one's own body (e.g., "Occasionally it has seemed as if my body had taken on the appearance of another person's body"). The Magical Ideation Scale (MIS; Eckblad & Chapman,

1983) is a 30-item true-false questionnaire that measures beliefs considered invalid according to the norms of industrialized, Western culture (e.g., "Some people can make me aware of them just by thinking about me"). Both the PABS and MIS have excellent internal consistency and good test-retest reliability (Chapman, Chapman, & Miller, 1982).

Two additional questionnaires that each measure only a single aspect of peculiarity are the Launay-Slade Hallucination Scale (LSHS; Launay & Slade, 1981), which assesses only peculiar perceptions, and the Paranormal Belief Scale (PBS; Tobacyk & Milford, 1983), which taps only peculiar beliefs. The PBS includes subscales assessing Traditional Religious Belief, Psi, Witchcraft, Superstition, Spiritualism, Extraordinary Life Forms, and Precognition. Neither of these instruments has been widely used by psychopathology researchers. The Schizotypal Personality Questionnaire (Raine, 1991) includes a variety of subscales including subscales that measure ideas of reference, odd beliefs/magical thinking, and unusual perceptual experiences. Three questionnaires developed by psychopathologists for the purpose of measuring both peculiar perceptions and beliefs are the Schizotypal Personality Scale (STA; Claridge & Broks, 1984), the Rust Inventory of Schizotypal Cognitions (RISC; Rust, 1988), and the schizophrenism subscale of the schizotypy scale developed by Venables, Wilkins, Mitchell, Raine, and Bailes (1990).

The most frequently used questionnaire for assessing dissociation is the Dissociative Experiences Scale (DES; Bernstein & Putnam, 1986; Carlson & Putnam, 1993). The DES is a 28-item scale with items scored on a visual analog scale, though a modified response format has recently been developed (Carlson & Putnam, 1993). The DES is intended to measure "experiences of disturbances in identity, memory, awareness, and cognition and feelings of derealization or depersonalization or associated phenomena such as déjà vu and absorption" (Bernstein & Putnam, 1986, p. 729). It has been found to have excellent internal consistency and good test-retest reliability (Bernstein & Putnam, 1986; Carlson & Putnam, 1993), and its criterion validity has been demonstrated in several studies that found elevated DES scores among individuals with dissociative disorders (Bernstein & Putnam, 1986; Carlson & Putnam, 1993). Individual differences in dissociation can also be assessed via the Questionnaire of Experiences of Dissociation (QED; Riley, 1988) and the Perceptual Alteration Scale (PAS; Sanders, 1986), though neither of these instruments has received nearly as much attention as the DES.

Several self-report questionnaires that are intended to measure a variety of aspects of personality and psychopathology include scales that measure peculiarity. Two questionnaires that are particularly relevant to the personality disorders are the Schedule for Nonadaptive and Adaptive Personality (SNAP; Clark, 1993; Clark, McEwen, Collard, & Hickok,

1993) and the Dimensional Assessment of Personality Pathology—Basic Questionnaire (DAPP-BQ; Schroeder, Wormworth, & Livesley, 1992). The SNAP includes an "Eccentric Perceptions" (EP) scale, and the DAPP-BQ includes a "Cognitive Distortion" (CD) scale; both scales measure multiple aspects of peculiarity. Peculiarity can also be assessed using the Bizarre Mentation (BM) scale of the MMPI-2 (Graham, 1993), which also measures multiple aspects of peculiarity. The advantage of these measures is that they are part of larger instruments that assess a broad range of characteristics relevant to personality and psychopathology. Their disadvantage is that although they provide dimensional scores of peculiarity, they do not provide measures of specific aspects of peculiarity as do more specialized instruments such as the DES and the MIS. For example, whereas a very high score on the MIS indicates that the individual has markedly peculiar beliefs, and a very high score on the DES indicates that the individual has extensive dissociative experiences, a very high score on the EP, CD, or BM scales does not indicate which specific aspect of peculiarity is deviant.

Information concerning peculiarity can also be garnered from questionnaires developed for evaluating personality disorders, such as the Millon Clinical Multiaxial Inventory III (MCMI-III; Millon, 1994), and the Personality Diagnostic Questionnaire—Revised (PDQ-R; Hyler, Skodol, Kellman, Oldham, & Rosnick, 1990). A recent discussion of such instruments was presented by Zimmerman (1994). These inventories were designed to provide information concerning the personality disorders, and thus inquire about peculiarity. However, these inventories do not provide dimensional peculiarity scores.

The different aspects of peculiarity, as measured by self-report questionnaires, are modestly positively correlated. For example, Kendler and Hewitt (1992) found that correlations between scores on the PABS, MIS, STA, and LSHS ranged from .32 to .65, with an average of .47. Tobacyk and Wilkinson (1990) found that scores on the PBS were positively correlated ($r = .46$) with scores on the MIS. Thalbourne (1994) found that PBS scores were positively correlated with scores on both the MIS ($r = .54$) and the PABS ($r = .43$). Thus, paranormal beliefs, as measured by the PBS, are as strongly correlated with measures of peculiarity developed by psychopathologists as such measures are correlated with each other. The relationship between dissociation and other aspects of peculiarity has not been examined. However, paranormal beliefs have been found to be associated with hypnotic susceptibility (Nadon, Laurence, & Perry, 1987; Wagner & Ratzeburg, 1987); because of the positive correlation between hypnotic susceptibility and dissociation (Roche & McConkey, 1990), these findings suggest that dissociation may be positively correlated with other aspects of peculiarity such as paranormal beliefs.

Interview Measures

The Structured Clinical Interview for DSM-IV Dissociative Disorders (SCID-D; Steinberg, 1993, 1994; Steinberg, Rounsaville, & Cicchetti, 1990) provides severity ratings of different dissociative symptoms, and can also be used for diagnosing DSM-IV dissociative disorders. The Dissociative Disorders Interview Schedule (DDIS; Ross et al., 1989) can be used for making DSM-III-R diagnoses of dissociative disorders, as well as other disorders frequently associated with dissociative disorders, such as somatization disorder and borderline personality disorder. The DDIS also includes a series of questions concerning Schneiderian symptoms of schizophrenia and can be used to derive a variety of different symptom severity scores.

Several interview rating scales have been developed for the purpose of measuring schizophrenia spectrum features and disorders. Khouri, Haier, Rieder, and Rosenthal (1980) developed the Symptom Schedule for the Diagnosis of Borderline Schizophrenia, which provides ratings of eight different phenomena such as nonspecific auditory hallucinations, altered body image, and dissociative experiences (e.g., derealization). Baron and colleagues developed the Schedule for Schizotypal Personalities (Baron, Asnis, & Gruen, 1981), which provides intensity scores for 10 different scales such as magical thinking and depersonalization/derealization. Kendler and colleagues developed the Structured Interview for Schizotypy (Kendler, Lieberman, & Walsh, 1989), which provides severity scores for a variety of schizotypic signs and symptoms, including magical thinking, illusions, and derealization.

Information concerning peculiarity can also be garnered from structured interviews developed for evaluating personality disorders, such as the Structured Interview for DSM-III-R Personality—Revised (SIDP-R; Pfohl, Blum, Zimmerman, & Stangl, 1989), the Personality Disorders Examination (PDE; Loranger, 1988; Loranger, Susman, Oldham, & Russakoff, 1987), and the Structured Clinical Interview for DSM-III-R Personality Disorders (SCID-II; Spitzer, Williams, Gibbon, & First, 1990). A discussion of such interview protocols was presented by Zimmerman (1994). These structured interviews were designed for making personality disorder diagnoses and thus inquire about peculiarity. As with self-report questionnaires that revolve around personality disorder categories, such as the PDQ-R, these structured interviews do not provide dimensional peculiarity scores.

ETIOLOGY

Although a great deal of theorizing and research has been devoted to various aspects of peculiarity, psychopathologists have generally not developed separate models of the etiology of peculiarity within the personality disorders. As a result, most of the work described in this section of the chapter does not revolve around the personality disorders. Almost all the work devoted to understanding peculiarity falls into one of three categories, the best developed of which concerns attempts to understand schizophrenia, its constituent signs and symptoms, and its antecedents and correlates. A second research tradition has focused on dissociation, particularly dissociative disorders, whereas the third and by far the smallest area of theorizing and research has examined paranormal beliefs. Unfortunately, work in each of these three domains has, with relatively few exceptions (e.g., Kihlstrom & Hoyt, 1988), proceeded relatively independently of one another. Researchers tend to study either schizophrenia or dissociation or paranormal beliefs, and each tends to publish in different outlets. Despite this relative independence, there are some interesting similarities in the kinds of explanations that have been developed within these three domains.

In the sections that follow, I will briefly review some of the etiologic factors, such as the roles of genes and stress, that have been most prominent in theories of peculiarity. The factors reviewed in this chapter are not intended to be exhaustive. In addition, the factors are presented independently even though integrative models (e.g., models that integrate neurophysiological and cognitive factors) can, and in fact, have been developed. More comprehensive coverage of the etiology of different facets of peculiarity can be found elsewhere (e.g., Oltmanns & Maher, 1988; Singer, 1990; Slade & Bentall, 1988; Spiegel, 1994).

Genetic Influences

Most models of peculiarity, including peculiarity among the personality disordered, have been influenced by, or have been part of, models of schizophrenia. There is abundant evidence that schizophrenia is genetically influenced (e.g., Gottesman & Shields, 1972; Kendler & Diehl, 1993). There is also evidence of a familial link between schizophrenia and schizotypal personality disorder (e.g., Gunderson, Siever, & Spaulding, 1983; Siever et al., 1990). Although such research has focused on diagnostic categories rather than specific signs and symptoms, it nonetheless suggests that peculiarity, which is a central feature of schizophrenia (Berenbaum & Fujita, 1994), is genetically influenced.

Although, as discussed in a later section, dissociation has been most strongly associated with trauma, it has also been hypothesized to be associated with genetic factors. According to Kihlstrom, Glisky, and Angiulo (1994), "Janet (1889/1907) thought that dissociation occurred in response to stress, but he also believed that certain people were constitutionally predisposed to dissociative disorder" (p. 117). Unfortunately, research examining genetic influences on dissociation has yet to be conducted. Researchers who study paranormal beliefs have not discussed the possibility that they may be influenced by genetic factors.

Several studies, mostly conducted within the past several years, have examined the familiality of, and potential genetic influences on, peculiarity as measured by self-report instruments. The results of three family studies that used the Perceptual Aberration Scale have been inconsistent. Grove et al. (1991) found evidence of significant sibling resemblance. In contrast, Clementz, Grove, Katsanis, and Iacono (1991) did not find evidence of significant parent-offspring or offspring-offspring resemblance. Finally, Berenbaum and McGrew (1993) found evidence of mother-offspring resemblance but not of father-offspring or offspring-offspring resemblance.

The results of twin studies have been considerably more consistent than have those of the family studies; all the twin studies examining peculiarity have found evidence of familial resemblance. Miller and Chapman (1993) found that PABS and MIS scores were both genetically influenced, with heritabilities of approximately 40%. Using the STA, Claridge and Hewitt (1987) found evidence of both genetic and shared environment effects, with heritability estimated at approximately 50%. Claridge and Hewitt (1987) noted "a tendency towards greater social environmental influence on females" (p. 311). Employing a variety of (sometimes abbreviated) peculiarity scales, Kendler and Hewitt (1992) found evidence of genetic influences on LSHS scores, as well as on magical ideation scores as measured by subsets of items from the STA and the MIS; heritability estimates ranged from approximately 40% to 55%. In contrast, these researchers found that perceptual aberration, as measured by subsets of items from the STA and the PABS, was influenced by common environment factors rather than by genetic factors. Using the DAPP-BQ, Livesley, Jang, Jackson, and Vernon (1993) found that scores on the Cognitive Distortion scale were influenced by both additive genetic and common environment factors, with heritability estimated at approximately 40%.

Information concerning potential genetic influences on peculiarity can also be obtained from a twin study conducted by Rose (1988) in which he examined genetic and environmental influences on factor analytically derived MMPI scales. One of the MMPI scales he used was labeled as "psychoticism" and is "characterized substantively by bizarre thinking and paranoid ideation" (Costa, Zonderman, McCrae, & Williams, 1985, p. 929). Rose found evidence of both genetic and shared environmental effects, with heritability estimated at approximately 60% in the total sample. Rose found that gender significantly influenced the relative genetic and shared environmental effects. In contrast to the results reported by Claridge and Hewitt (1987), Rose reported that genetic effects were stronger among women, and shared environmental effects were stronger among men. Thus, the preponderance of evidence suggests that peculiarity is familially influenced, with both genetic and shared environmental factors playing a role in its development. The relative contributions of genetic and shared environmental factors may vary as a function of gender, though the existing data are contradictory.

Neurophysiological Factors

Very little research has been conducted examining the neurophysiological correlates of dissociation. For example, the first study to examine the relationship between neurotransmitters and dissociation was published quite recently (Demitrack et al., 1993). Demitrack et al. (1993) found that in a sample of eating-disordered individuals, dissociation was associated with cerebrospinal fluid levels of serotonin and dopamine metabolites as well as with beta-endorphin levels. Because hypnotizability and dissociation are correlated, research examining the neurophysiological correlates of hypnotizability have been used to generate hypotheses concerning the neurophysiological correlates of dissociation. In a review of the neurophysiological evidence, Spiegel and Vermutten (1994) concluded that the frontal and temporal lobes, and possibly the right hemisphere, are the locations most likely to play a role in hypnosis and, by inference, dissociation.

The vast majority of the theorizing and research regarding the role of neurophysiological factors in peculiarity has been generated within the context of models of schizophrenia. As a result, some models have not specified which facets of peculiarity are posited to be influenced by different neurophysiological factors, but rather discuss "psychotic symptoms" or "positive symptoms of schizophrenia." The different neurophysiological models of peculiarity have varied in the degree to which they focused on (a) neurotransmitters; (b) brain regions; and (c) neural circuits or networks. Although these three neurophysiological aspects are presented separately in the following sections, many models have incorporated two or even all three of them.

Neurotransmitters

Hypotheses and evidence concerning the relationship between peculiarity and neurotransmitters have been strongly influenced by the relative ability of different pharmacological treatments to reduce or eliminate the psychotic symptoms of schizophrenia. One of the most influential theories of schizophrenia, the dopamine hypothesis, holds that schizophrenia is a manifestation of excessive dopaminergic activity. Most of the evidence supporting this hypothesis is based on observations of the effects of dopamine agonists and antagonists. Typical antipsychotic medications, such as haloperidol, are dopamine antagonists. Further, the clinical potency of such drugs is correlated with their dopamine antagonistic properties (e.g., Creese, Burt, & Snyder, 1976). Dopamine agonists, such as amphetamines, tend to worsen the symptoms of schizophrenia (e.g., Lieberman et al., 1984). Amphetamines can also induce psychotic symptoms such as paranoia and hallucinations in nonpsychiatric individuals (e.g., Angrist & Gershon, 1970).

Despite evidence that is consistent with excessive dopaminergic activity contributing to psychosis, data have also accumulated that are inconsistent with the simple dopamine hypothesis (Davis, Kahn, Ko, & Davidson, 1991). Consequently, more complicated models of the relationship between neurotransmitter functioning and psychosis have been developed. For example, Davis et al. (1991) proposed that positive symptoms of schizophrenia result from reduced prefrontal dopamine activity leading to excessive dopamine activity in mesolimbic dopamine neurons. The potential roles of other neurotransmitters, most notably serotonin and norepinephrine, have also been receiving increasing attention (e.g., Meltzer, 1989). In particular, there is growing evidence that psychotic symptoms may be associated with disturbances in the relative activity levels of different neurotransmitters (e.g., Hsiao et al., 1993; Kahn et al., 1993). An additional reason serotonin has been posited to play a role in peculiarity is that LSD, which can induce delusions and hallucinations, is known to affect serotonergic receptors.

Brain Regions

Hypotheses and evidence concerning the relationship between peculiarity and different brain regions has been strongly influenced by advances in brain-imaging techniques such as computerized axial tomography, positron emission tomography, and magnetic resonance imaging. There is abundant evidence of neuropathology in schizophrenia (e.g., Buchsbaum, 1990; Gur & Pearlson, 1993). Brain areas that have repeatedly been shown to be disturbed in schizophrenia include the frontal lobes (e.g., Weinberger, Berman, & Zec, 1986), the left hemisphere (e.g., Gur et al., 1983), and the temporolimbic system (e.g., McCarley et al., 1993).

Of attempts to link a specific aspect of peculiarity with a specific brain region, the potential connection between auditory hallucinations and the left hemisphere has probably received the most attention. Flor-Henry (1986) concluded, "Clinical and phenomenological, neuroanatomical and neurophysiological evidence indicates that auditory hallucinations in schizophrenia are reflections of altered neural structures responsible for verbal-linguistic expression" (p. 523). A very specific neuroanatomic region that has been posited to play a role in auditory hallucinations is the left superior temporal gyrus. Evidence supporting this link is based on (a) Penfield and Perot's (1963) observation that complex auditory hallucinations were elicited by electrical stimulation in the vicinity of the left superior temporal gyrus; and (b) the finding by Barta, Pearlson, Powers, Richards, and Tune (1990) of a strong association between left superior temporal gyrus volume and the severity of hallucinations in a sample of schizophrenic patients.

Neural Circuits

With advances in neuroscience, psychopathologists are developing models of psychosis that focus on neural circuits or networks (e.g., Carpenter, Buchanan, Kirkpatrick, Tamminga, & Wood, 1993; Weinberger, Berman, Suddath, & Torrey, 1992). Such models can integrate information concerning neurotransmitters, brain regions, and the functional significance of the circuit or network. For example, Gray, Feldon, Rawlins, Hemsley, and Smith (1991) proposed a complex model of positive symptoms of schizophrenia that emphasized:

> . . . the projections from the septohippocampal system, via the subiculum and the amygdala to nucleus acumbens, and their interaction with the ascending dopaminergic projection to the acumbens. Psychologically, the model emphasizes a failure in acute schizophrenia to integrate stored memories of past regularities of perceptual input with ongoing motor programs in the control of current perception. (p. 1)

Stress and Trauma

There is a long history of trauma being associated with dissociative phenomena such as hysteria and multiple personality disorder (e.g., Janet, 1889/1907; Prince, 1906–1907). A great deal of empirical research, much of it conducted fairly recently, has demonstrated that a history of childhood trauma, such as physical and sexual abuse, is associated with elevated levels of dissociation in adulthood. Such findings have been obtained in a wide variety of samples, including psychiatric patients (e.g., Chu & Dill, 1990), medical patients (e.g., Walker, Katon, Neraas,

Jemelka, & Massoth, 1992), college students (e.g., Sandberg & Lynn, 1992), professional women (Elliott & Briere, 1992), and randomly selected community residents (Vanderlinden, Van Dyck, Vandereycken, & Vertommen, 1993). Research documenting an association between stress and dissociation is not limited to childhood abuse. Cardena and Spiegel (1993) reported that dissociation levels were elevated in a sample of graduate students after they were exposed to an earthquake.

Although stress and trauma have also been posited to play a role in the development of other facets of peculiarity, such as hallucinations and delusions, the empirical evidence does not support an association between childhood trauma and the development of schizophrenia. Using data from the Los Angeles Epidemiological Catchment Area (ECA) study, Stein, Golding, Siegel, Burnam, and Sorenson (1988) found that childhood sexual abuse was not associated with increased lifetime prevalence of schizophrenia, whereas it was linked to an increased prevalence of mood and anxiety disorders. Although a history of child abuse may not be associated with the development of schizophrenia, there is evidence that trauma and stress are associated with psychotic symptoms. Goff, Brotman, Kindlon, Waites, and Amico (1991a, 1991b) found that in a sample of chronically psychotic outpatients, a history of childhood abuse was associated with delusions of possession and hearing voices inside the head. There is also evidence linking a history of childhood trauma with Schneiderian symptoms of schizophrenia (Ross & Joshi, 1992a). Consistent with such findings, Cardena and Spiegel (1993) reported that stress elicited by exposure to an earthquake led to an increase in Schneiderian symptoms. In addition, stress has been found to be associated with psychotic relapse among schizophrenic individuals (Birley & Brown, 1970; Ventura, Nuechterlein, Lukoff, & Hardesty, 1989). Finally, evidence for a link between stress and psychotic symptoms comes from studies of individuals during and following extreme stress (Comer, Madow, & Dixon, 1967; Mueser & Butler, 1987; Siegel, 1984).

Given the evidence that both dissociative experiences and psychotic symptoms are associated with stress and trauma, it should come as no surprise that paranormal beliefs have also been found to be associated with trauma. In a random sample of community residents, Ross and Joshi (1992b) found that belief in the paranormal was associated with a history of childhood trauma. Similarly, Irwin (1992) found that paranormal beliefs were associated with a history of childhood trauma in a sample of university students. Although there are no published data concerning the relationship between trauma and scores on questionnaire measures of peculiarity other than those measuring dissociation and paranormal beliefs, the relationship between PABS scores and childhood experience have been investigated. Edell and Kaslow (1991) found that compared with college students who had average PABS scores, students with deviantly high PABS scores reported that during childhood their parents were more critical and less supportive.

Cognitive Factors

One of the most frequently studied factors in schizophrenia is attentional disturbances. Individuals with schizophrenia have been found to exhibit a wide variety of information-processing deficits (e.g., Braff, 1989; Morice, 1990; Nuechterlein et al., 1992; Oltmanns & Neale, 1975). Thus, it is not surprising that cognitive disturbances have been posited to play a role in the development of psychotic symptoms (Strauss, 1993). For example, Walker and Lewine (1988) proposed that auditory processing deficits are associated with positive symptoms of schizophrenia. Elaborate models of the development of delusions have been proposed by Hemsley and Frith. Hemsley (1987a) proposed that "heightened awareness of irrelevant stimuli" and the "intrusion of unexpected/unintended material from long-term memory" (p. 183) contribute to the development of delusions. Frith (1987; Frith & Done, 1988) proposed that positive symptoms are the result of a disturbance in the internal monitoring of actions or "willed intentions." Such a disturbance is posited to lead to different types of delusions depending on the type of self-generated act that was not properly monitored. For example, a self-generated action whose source is not monitored might be believed to have been elicited by an irrelevant external stimulus. Consequently, "irrelevant external stimuli are imbued with false, personal significance" (Frith & Done, 1988, p. 440). Such an interpretation is hypothesized to give rise to delusions of reference.

Hemsley and Frith have also developed interesting models of the etiology of hallucinations. Hemsley (1987b) proposed that a disturbance in pigeonholing (the mechanism that leads perceptions to be influenced by "expectancies") leads to unexpected internally generated experiences being misattributed to external sources, thereby resulting in hallucinations. Frith (1979) had originally proposed a "defective filter" model of hallucinations. More recently, Frith (1987; Frith & Done, 1988) proposed that auditory hallucinations are the result of individuals not recognizing their own thoughts as emanating from themselves, and as a result they mistakenly attribute them to external sources.

Heilbrun (1993) has proposed that hallucinations are influenced by deviant attentional strategies, with both attentional hypervigilance and disengagement contributing to hallucinations. Heilbrun's views are based on his attempt to account for the rather complex sets of results of several studies conducted by him and his colleagues (e.g., Heilbrun, 1980; Heilbrun, Diller, Fleming, & Slade, 1986). In one particularly interesting study, Heilbrun, Blum, and Haas (1983) found that hallucinators (though only those with process as opposed to reactive schizophrenia) performed poorly at a task in which they had to detect the spatial location of sounds. In a somewhat similar study, Blyler and Maher (1993) also found that only a subset of hallucinating schizophrenics were deviant on an attentional task. Blyler and Maher (1993) examined the likelihood of "noise" being misperceived as words. Schizophrenics whose voices seemed to come from inside their heads did not differ from controls. In contrast, schizophrenics whose voices seemed to come from outside their heads misperceived more noises as words than did controls. Thus, the classic distinction between "true" hallucinations and "pseudohallucinations" may be related to the potential role of attentional disturbances in their development. Research examining nonpsychiatric individuals has also found an association between attentional disturbances and peculiar perceptions and beliefs. For example, several studies employing the PABS and MIS have found that individuals with deviant scores on these instruments tend to exhibit information-processing disturbances (e.g., Balogh & Merritt, 1985; Fernandes & Miller, in press; Lenzenweger, Cornblatt, & Putnick, 1991; Simons, MacMillan, & Ireland, 1982).

Just as information processing has played a major role in theorizing and research on psychosis, cognitive processes have also been central to theorizing and research on dissociation (e.g., Hilgard, 1986). Unlike research on schizophrenia, however, investigators studying dissociation have not focused on deficits in individual facets of information processing. For example, researchers have typically not hypothesized that dissociation is influenced by a general reduction in processing capacity, as is the case in schizophrenia (e.g., Nuechterlein & Dawson, 1984). Instead, dissociation researchers have been more likely to attend to the interconnectedness (or lack thereof), communication among, and relative activations and automaticity of different cognitive "modules," "processes," "subsystems," and "control systems" (e.g., Erdelyi, 1994; Hilgard, 1986). For example, Kihlstrom (1980, 1987) has described dissociations between declarative and procedural memory, between the episodic and semantic forms of declarative memory, and between implicit and explicit memory.

Absorption, Fantasy Proneness, Suggestibility, and Imagery

Absorption is a factor that has been posited to play a role in influencing dissociation. As described by Tellegen and Atkinson (1974), absorption is "a disposition for having episodes of 'total' attention that fully engage one's representational (i.e., perceptual, enactive, imaginative, and ideational) resources" (p. 268). Lynn and Rhue (1988) have stated that "the constructs of fantasy proneness, imaginative involvement, and absorption are not truly discriminable" (p. 36). There is considerable evidence demonstrating that absorption and hypnotizability are associated (e.g., Tellegen & Atkinson, 1974). Hypnotizability and dissociation are also associated (Roche & McConkey, 1990), thus lending support to the hypothesis that absorption and dissociation are related. As expected, when absorption and dissociation were examined in the same individuals, they were found to be positively correlated (Frischolz et al., 1991; Norton, Ross, & Novotny, 1990). Thus, it seems safe to conclude that dissociation is associated with absorption and related constructs such as fantasy proneness. However, it is impossible to draw firm conclusions about causation from correlational data. As pointed out by Kihlstrom et al. (1994), "The hypothesis that absorption, fantasy proneness, and hypnotizability reflect a dissociative diathesis is an interesting one, but it is far from proven" (p. 121).

Imagery, fantasy proneness, and suggestibility have also been posited to play a role in the development of hallucinations and other peculiar perceptions (e.g., Bentall, 1990). Several studies have found that hallucinations are associated with suggestibility in samples of psychiatric patients (Alpert, 1985; Mintz & Alpert, 1972; Young, Bentall, Slade, & Dewey, 1987). In a sample of nonpsychiatric participants, Jakes and Hemsley (1986) found an association between suggestibility and scores on the LSHS. Wilson and Barber (1981) have described an association between suggestibility, fantasy proneness, and hallucinatorylike experiences. Finally, Clark (1993) reported that in a college student sample, eccentric perceptions as measured by the SNAP were highly correlated ($r = .65$) with absorption as measured by the Multidimensional Personality Questionnaire.

Fantasy proneness and the need for absorbing experiences have also been posited to play a role in the development of belief in the paranormal (Irwin, 1992), and there is evidence consistent with this hypothesis. Council and Huff (1990) reported a strong positive correlation between fantasy proneness and paranormal experiences and beliefs. Paranormal beliefs have also been found to be associated with hypnotic susceptibility (Nadon et al., 1987; Wagner & Ratzeburg, 1987) and absorption (Nadon & Kihlstrom, 1987).

Socialization and Culture

Because beliefs and perceptions do not develop in a vacuum, it should come as no surprise that peculiarity is influenced by socialization and culture. An indisputable source of cultural variation in peculiarity concerns the specific content of delusions. In his review of the literature, Westermeyer (1988) concluded that there are "marked differences in delusional content across cultures" (p. 218) but that "the form or structure of delusions remains remarkably constant" (p. 218). Evidence for cross-cultural differences in the content of delusions comes from research examining delusions in different locations around the world (e.g., Murphy, Wittkower, Fried, & Ellenberger, 1963) and from research examining delusions in the same location at different points in time (e.g., Klaf & Hamilton, 1961).

As reviewed by Al-Issa (1977), there are also cross-cultural differences in hallucinations. In particular, research examining hallucinations in different locations around the world (e.g., Murphy et al., 1963) and research examining hallucinations in the same location at different points in time (e.g., Lenz, 1964, cited in Al-Issa, 1977) reveal cross-cultural differences in the relative prevalence of auditory and visual hallucinations. Al-Issa proposed, "Attitudes toward hallucinations may affect both the frequency and the content of hallucinatory experience and emotional response to it" (p. 583).

Cross-cultural differences in peculiar perceptions and beliefs are not limited to delusions and hallucinations. Chmielewski, Fernandes, Yee, and Miller (in press) found that Caucasian, African-American, Asian-American, and Latino college students differed significantly in their PABS and MIS scores, with Caucasians having the lowest scores on both scales. Tobacyk and Pirtilla-Backman (1992) found that university students from the United States had significantly stronger beliefs in the paranormal than did university students from Finland.

A fascinating discussion of cross-cultural aspects of dissociation is provided by Kirmayer (1994). According to Kirmayer (1994):

> Culture shapes dissociation through arranging contexts in which imaginative absorption or automaticity is appropriate and can be practiced (Noll, 1985), and by providing ethnopsychological concepts of memory and self and modes of narrative reconstruction to describe dissociative experiences. . . . Dissociation involves a gap or disturbance in normal patterns of integration of memory, self, and perception. We recognize this disruption against standards we have for the continuity, univocality, and rationality of the self. This is expressed in a temporal narrative centered on rational motives for our actions and responses. This depiction of the self is, to some extent, culture bound. (pp. 107, 114)

THE RELATIONSHIP BETWEEN PECULIARITY AND PERSONALITY DISORDER CATEGORIES

Within the personality disorders, peculiarity is typically thought of as a characteristic of individuals with Cluster A personality disorders (schizotypal, schizoid, and paranoid personality disorders). Of course, to say that there is a relationship between peculiarity and the Cluster A personality disorders is somewhat circular because both schizotypal and paranoid personality disorders include features of peculiarity among their diagnostic criteria (American Psychiatric Association [APA], 1994). However, it is not the case that peculiarity is unique to these two personality disorder categories. In particular, dissociative characteristics have been found to be common among individuals with borderline personality disorder. Zanarini, Gunderson, and Frankenburg (1990) reported that depersonalization and derealization were each present in approximately one-third of the patients they studied who had been diagnosed with borderline personality disorder. Research using the DES has found that the dissociation scores of individuals with borderline personality disorder are relatively high (e.g., Russ, Shearin, Clarkin, Harrison, & Hull, 1993); in fact, not only are the dissociation scores of individuals with borderline personality disorder higher than scores that are typical of nonpsychiatric controls, they are also higher than the scores typically obtained by individuals with anxiety and mood disorders (Carlson & Putnam, 1993).

Dissociation is not the only facet of peculiarity that is found among individuals with personality disorders outside of Cluster A. In particular, psychotic and psychoticlike characteristics have been associated with borderline personality disorder. In fact, Gunderson (1984) stated that "transient psychotic experiences are one of the central characteristics that define borderline personality disorder" (p. 117). The empirical evidence indicates that psychotic experiences are a common feature of borderline personality disorder. For example, George and Soloff (1986) found that among patients with borderline personality disorder, 29% had auditory hallucinations, 40% had visual illusions, and 52% exhibited "muddled thinking." Zanarini et al. (1990) found that among patients with borderline personality disorder, 68% exhibited odd thinking (e.g., marked superstitiousness, magical thinking) and 24% reported recurrent illusions. The rates of such experiences and perceptions were lower among patients with other personality disorders, but were hardly nonexistent—23.6% exhibited odd thinking, and 7.3% reported recurrent illusions. Pope, Jonas, Hudson, Cohen, and Tohen (1985) reported that of 33 individuals with borderline personality disorder, eight exhibited narrowly defined psychosis, with one person considered to have organic psychosis and seven considered to have functional psychosis. Twelve additional individuals were considered to have unusual psychotic features in that the psychotic features met at least two of the following criteria: (a) under voluntary control; (b) unconventional and fantastic, "i.e., fanciful or atypical symptoms in the absence of more typical symptoms such as ideas of reference" (p. 1286); and (c) unconventional response of symptoms to the environment, "i.e., sudden appearance or disappearance of the symptoms in a manner that would not be typical of ordinary psychotic symptoms" (p. 1286). All seven of the individuals who exhibited functional psychosis did so only when in the midst of manic or depressive episodes, suggesting that typical psychotic symptoms may only be present among individuals with borderline personality disorder who have concomitant mood disorders. However, Miller, Abrams, Dulit, and Fyer (1993) found that 27% of patients with borderline personality disorder exhibited narrowly defined psychotic symptoms, and that psychotic symptoms in these individuals could not be accounted for by comorbid mood and substance abuse disorders.

Several studies have examined the relationship between scores on self-report peculiarity questionnaires and personality disorders measured dimensionally in samples of psychiatric patients. Lenzenweger and Loranger (1989) found that scores on the PABS were positively correlated with all 11 personality disorders and were significantly correlated with schizoid, schizotypal, borderline, avoidant, dependent, and obsessive-compulsive personality disorders. Bailey, West, Widiger, and Freiman (1993) also found significant associations between scores on the PABS and non-Cluster A personality disorders. These investigators found that PABS scores were significantly associated with borderline and antisocial personality disorders, as well as with schizotypal personality disorder. Clark (1993) found that scores on the SNAP's EP scale were significantly positively correlated with paranoid, schizotypal, and borderline personality disorders. Clark (1993) found that EP scores were also positively, but not significantly, correlated with the remaining personality disorders. In contrast, Bailey et al. (1993) did not find statistically significant associations between MIS scores and non-Cluster A personality disorders, though the correlations were all positive, ranging from .18 to .23. Thus, across all these studies, all the personality disorders were positively correlated with peculiarity, though the specific correlations that were statistically significant varied somewhat from study to study.

The preceding studies all involved individuals who were receiving psychiatric treatment and were, in general, rather disturbed. Thus, it is possible that the high rates of psychotic and psychoticlike features among such individuals might be a reflection of Berkson's bias (Berkson, 1946) or some other form of bias (Galbaud du Fort, Newman, & Bland, 1993) that leads to rates of comorbid disturbance being exaggerated among individuals who seek treatment. However, this does not appear to be the case. Rosenberger and Miller (1989) studied a group of college students who were not recruited at a treatment facility, unlike the participants in the previously described studies; in fact only 12% of the Rosenberger and

Miller sample had received treatment for psychological problems. Despite being only mildly disturbed, at least one-third of their participants with borderline personality disorder reported either ideas of reference or recurrent illusions, and 11% reported magical ideation. Lenzenweger and Korfine (1992) examined the relationship between scores on the PABS and personality disorders measured dimensionally in a sample of college students. They found that compared with individuals with nondeviant PABS scores, individuals with deviantly high PABS scores had significantly higher scores on scales measuring compulsive, passive-aggressive, narcissistic, antisocial, histrionic, borderline, schizotypal, and paranoid personality disorder dimensions.

The results of the research described in this section indicate that peculiarity is not unique to the Cluster A personality disorders. Further, the presence of peculiarity among individuals with non-Cluster A personality disorders is not limited to measures of dissociation. For example, individuals with personality disorders often exhibit peculiar beliefs and perceptions. The strength of the association between peculiarity and borderline personality disorder is bound to be stronger using DSM-IV criteria than using DSM-III or DSM-III-R because of the addition of "transient stress-related paranoid ideation or severe dissociative symptoms" as a diagnostic criterion for borderline personality disorder in DSM-IV. The finding that peculiarity is not limited to the Cluster A personality disorders is also consistent with the findings reported by Schopp and Trull (1993). These authors stated:

> The results of this study challenge the DSM-III-R personality disorder Cluster groupings. . . . The results of this study also suggest that some features thought to be associated with personality disorder Clusters may be associated with personality pathology in general rather than with a particular subset of personality disorders. (p. 230)

THE RELATIONSHIP BETWEEN PECULIARITY AND OTHER PERSONALITY CHARACTERISTICS

Numerous studies have examined the relationship between peculiarity and other personality characteristics. There is considerable evidence indicating that individuals with higher levels of peculiarity also tend to report higher levels of neuroticism and negative affectivity. Moderately strong positive correlations have been found between various measures of neuroticism and EP, STA, RISC, MIS, PABS, SLHS, and DES scores (Bentall, Claridge, & Slade, 1989; Claridge & Hewitt, 1987; Clark, 1993; Kendler & Hewitt, 1992; Rust, Moncada, & Lepage, 1988; Silva & Ward,

1993). Not surprisingly, then, various measures of peculiarity have been found to be positively correlated with measures of depression and anxiety (Clark, 1993; Lenzenweger & Loranger, 1989; Norton et al., 1990).

In contrast to the findings regarding neuroticism, the correlations between peculiarity and extraversion have tended to be quite small (Bentall et al., 1989; Claridge & Hewitt, 1987; Clark, 1993; Kendler & Hewitt, 1992; Rust et al., 1988; Silva & Ward, 1993). Although the correlations between peculiarity and measures of impulsivity, disinhibition, and sensation seeking have been consistently positive (Bentall et al., 1989; Chapman, Chapman, & Miller, 1982; Claridge & Hewitt, 1987; Clark, 1993; Kendler & Hewitt, 1992; Launay & Slade, 1981; Rust et al., 1988; Silva & Ward, 1993; Tobacyk & Milford, 1983), they have generally not been as strong as have the correlations between peculiarity and neuroticism.

SUMMARY AND CONCLUSIONS

Peculiar beliefs and perceptions, as well as dissociative phenomena, appear to vary in their degrees of severity. In its more severe forms, peculiarity is most strongly associated with psychotic and dissociative disorders. There is abundant evidence, however, that peculiarity, especially in less severe forms, is reasonably common among individuals with personality disorders. Further, peculiarity is not limited to the Cluster A personality disorders. In particular, elevated levels of peculiarity appear to be associated with borderline personality disorder. Thus, researchers who wish to understand the personality disorders are likely to benefit from studying peculiarity, even if their main area of interest is not psychosis or the schizophrenia spectrum. Because peculiarity is relatively common among individuals with personality disorders, it would be wise for clinicians who work with individuals typically considered to have personality disorders to routinely assess this personality characteristic.

With respect to etiology, the evidence reviewed in this chapter leads me to propose that at least two significant pathways can lead to peculiarity. First, there is considerable evidence that genetic factors predispose individuals to peculiarity and schizophrenia spectrum disorders; thus, one pathway that leads to peculiarity has its origin in one or more as yet undetermined genes. There is, however, also considerable evidence that exposure to trauma contributes to peculiarity. Although the form most strongly associated with trauma is dissociation, it appears that other forms of peculiarity, such as peculiar beliefs and perceptions, are also linked to trauma. Thus, I propose that a second major pathway leading to peculiarity has its origin in exposure to trauma.

Although it has been common to assume that peculiarity is associated with schizophrenia and genetic factors, several researchers have discussed why adverse environmental factors might contribute to peculiarity. For example, Lynn and Rhue (1988) wrote: "Imaginative abilities may serve a functional role in minimizing physical and psychic pain and in preserving a relatively positive view of the abusive environment" (p. 40). Similarly, Epstein and Meier (1989) wrote: "Possibly, when individuals in their formative years feel helpless with respect to understanding and coping with emotionally significant events, they develop superstitious and magical ways of thinking in an attempt to establish some degree of understanding and control" (p. 344). The hypothesis that abusive environments contribute to peculiarity is supported by the data indicating a link between peculiarity and trauma, as well as by the evidence that peculiarity is influenced by shared environment (Claridge & Hewitt, 1987; Kendler & Hewitt, 1992; Livesley et al., 1993; Rose, 1988). The data demonstrating that peculiarity is influenced by shared environment are noteworthy because shared environment is generally found to have little influence on personality characteristics (e.g., Bouchard, 1994; Bouchard & McGue, 1990; Plomin & Daniels, 1987; but cf. Rose & Kaprio, 1987).

It will be important for future research to determine whether different aspects or types of peculiarity are differentially associated with trauma as opposed to a genetic vulnerability to schizophrenia. In addition to dissociative phenomena, other types of peculiarity that may be more strongly associated with trauma than with such genetic vulnerability are Schneiderian psychotic symptoms and hearing voices coming from inside one's head, both of which have been found to be associated with trauma (Cardena & Spiegel, 1993; Goff et al., 1991a, 1991b; Ross & Joshi, 1992a). An additional reason to suspect that Schneiderian psychotic symptoms may be more strongly associated with a history of trauma than with a genetic vulnerability to schizophrenia is the finding that schizophrenia, when operationally defined by Schneiderian symptoms, does not appear to be heritable (McGuffin, Farmer, Gottesman, Murray, & Reveley, 1984).

Although a history of trauma appears to contribute to peculiarity, there are both empirical and theoretical reasons not to consider trauma a significant contributor to schizophrenia. The empirical reason is that previous research has not found a significant association between trauma history and schizophrenia (e.g., Stein et al., 1988). The theoretical reason is that if one defines schizophrenia on the basis of etiology (Berenbaum, in press), individuals whose peculiarity developed as a result of trauma (as opposed to being influenced by a genetic diathesis) would not be considered to have true schizophrenia according to most models of schizophrenia (e.g., Meehl, 1990).

My proposal that two major pathways contribute to peculiarity can help account for data that are otherwise difficult to explain. If one posits that peculiarity reflects only genetic vulnerability to schizophrenia, it is difficult to explain why (a) there is a moderately strong association between peculiarity and borderline personality disorder (e.g., Zanarini et al., 1990); and (b) borderline personality disorder does not appear to be familially linked with schizophrenia (e.g., Gunderson et al., 1983; Loranger, Oldham, & Tulis, 1982). This pair of findings can be explained if one posits that the peculiarity exhibited by individuals with borderline personality disorder is a consequence of their having grown up in abusive environments, which appears to be the case for many such individuals (e.g., Herman, Perry, & van der Kolk, 1989; Weaver & Clum, 1993). A second finding that cannot be adequately explained by positing that peculiarity reflects genetic vulnerability to schizophrenia is that individuals with deviantly high scores on the PABS and MIS are at increased risk of concurrent and future mood disorder (Chapman, Chapman, Kwapil, Eckblad, & Zinser, 1994; Chapman, Edell, & Chapman, 1980; Eckblad & Chapman, 1983; Fujioka & Chapman, 1984). Keeping in mind that abusive childhood environments have been found to be associated with mood disorder (e.g., Stein et al., 1988), the link between peculiarity and mood disturbance ceases to be perplexing if one posits that many individuals with deviant levels of peculiarity developed their peculiar beliefs and perceptions in response to abusive environments.

It is not uncommon for researchers who examine the correlates of peculiarity to assume that those correlates are also associated with vulnerability to schizophrenia. My proposal that peculiarity can be an outcome of either a genetic predisposition to schizophrenia or a history of trauma suggests that researchers should be extremely cautious before drawing such conclusions. For example, Levin and Raulin (1991) found that college students with deviantly high PABS scores had more frequent nightmares than did controls. Although such results might indicate that nightmares are associated with vulnerability to schizophrenia, it seems even more likely, at least to me, that the findings can be accounted for by a history of trauma contributing to both peculiarity and nightmares.

It should be noted that it is quite possible that the two pathways to peculiarity share much in common. In particular, it is possible that many of the immediate antecedents, as well as the concurrent correlates, are shared regardless of the more distal etiologic factors. For example, factors such as attentional disturbances, heightened suggestibility, and even certain neurophysiological patterns may be part of a "common final pathway" to peculiarity. Along similar lines, it is likely that cultural factors influence the specific manifestation of peculiarity regardless of its etiologic origins. I hope that future theorizing and research will succeed in developing and testing comprehensive developmental models that can explain individual differences in peculiarity and its association with other aspects of psychopathology.

REFERENCES

Al-Issa, I. (1977). Social and cultural aspects of hallucinations. *Psychological Bulletin, 84,* 570–587.

Alpert, M. (1985). The signs and symptoms of schizophrenia. *Comprehensive Psychiatry, 26,* 103–112.

American Psychiatric Association. (1994). *Diagnostic and statistical manual of mental disorders* (4th ed.). Washington, DC: Author.

Angrist, B., & Gershon, S. (1970). The phenomenology of experimentally induced amphetamine psychosis: Preliminary observations. *Biological Psychiatry, 2,* 95–107.

Bailey, B., West, K. Y., Widiger, T. A., & Freiman, K. (1993). The convergent and discriminant validity of the Chapman scales. *Journal of Personality Assessment, 6,* 121–135.

Balogh, D. W., & Merritt, R. D. (1985). Susceptibility to Type A backward pattern masking among hypothetically psychosis-prone college students. *Journal of Abnormal Psychology, 94,* 377–383.

Baron, M., Asnis, L., & Gruen, R. (1981). The Schedule for Schizotypal Personalities (SSP): A diagnostic interview for schizotypal features. *Psychiatry Research, 4,* 213–228.

Barta, P. E., Pearlson, G. D., Powers, R. E., Richards, S. S., & Tune, L. E. (1990). Auditory hallucinations and smaller superior temporal gyral volume in schizophrenia. *American Journal of Psychiatry, 147,* 1457–1462.

Bentall, R. P. (1990). The illusion of reality: A review and integration of psychological research on hallucinations. *Psychological Bulletin, 107,* 82–95.

Bentall, R. P., Claridge, G. S., & Slade, P. D. (1989). The multidimensional nature of schizotypal traits: A factor analytic study with normal subjects. *British Journal of Clinical Psychology, 28,* 363–375.

Berenbaum, H. (in press). Toward a definition of schizophrenia. In G. A. Miller (Ed.), *The behavioral high-risk paradigm in psychopathology.* New York: Springer-Verlag.

Berenbaum, H., & Fujita, F. (1994). Schizophrenia and personality: Exploring the boundaries and connections between vulnerability and outcome. *Journal of Abnormal Psychology, 103,* 148–158.

Berenbaum, H., & McGrew, J. (1993). Familial resemblance of schizotypic traits. *Psychological Medicine, 23,* 327–333.

Berkson, J. (1946). Limitations of the application of fourfold table analysis to hospital data. *Biometrics Bulletin, 2,* 47–53.

Bernstein, E. M., & Putnam, F. W. (1986). Development, reliability, and validity of a dissociation scale. *Journal of Nervous and Mental Disease, 174,* 727–735.

Birley, J., & Brown, G. W. (1970). Crisis and life changes preceding the onset or relapse of acute schizophrenia: Clinical aspects. *British Journal of Psychiatry, 16,* 327–333.

Blyler, C. R., & Maher, B. A. (1993, October). *External origins of auditory hallucinations in schizophrenia.* Paper presented at the annual meeting of the Society for Research in Psychopathology, Chicago, IL.

Bouchard, T. J., Jr. (1994). Genes, environment, and personality. *Science, 264,* 1700–1701.

Bouchard, T. J., Jr., & McGue, M. (1990). Genetic and rearing environmental influences on adult personality: An analysis of adopted twins reared apart. *Journal of Personality, 58,* 263–292.

Braff, D. L. (1989). Sensory input deficits and negative symptoms in schizophrenic patients. *American Journal of Psychiatry, 146,* 1006–1011.

Buchsbaum, M. S. (1990). The frontal lobes, basal ganglia, and temporal lobes as sites for schizophrenia. *Schizophrenia Bulletin, 16,* 379–389.

Cardena, E., & Spiegel, D. (1993). Dissociative reactions to the San Francisco bay area earthquake of 1989. *American Journal of Psychiatry, 150,* 474–478.

Carlson, E. B., & Putnam, F. W. (1993). An update on the Dissociative Experiences Scale. *Dissociation, 6,* 16–25.

Carpenter, W. T., Jr., Buchanan, R. W., Kirkpatrick, B., Tamminga, C., & Wood, F. (1993). Strong inference, theory testing, and the neuroanatomy of schizophrenia. *Archives of General Psychiatry, 50,* 825–831.

Chapman, L. J., & Chapman, J. P. (1980). Scales for rating psychotic and psychotic-like experiences as continua. *Schizophrenia Bulletin, 6,* 476–489.

Chapman, L. J., Chapman, J. P., Kwapil, T. R., Eckblad, M., & Zinser, M. C. (1994). Putatively psychosis prone subjects 10 years later. *Journal of Abnormal Psychology, 103,* 171–183.

Chapman, L. J., Chapman, J. P., & Miller, E. N. (1982). Reliabilities and intercorrelations of eight measures of proneness to psychosis. *Journal of Consulting and Clinical Psychology, 50,* 187–195.

Chapman, L. J., Chapman, J. P., & Raulin, M. L. (1978). Body-image aberration in schizophrenia. *Journal of Abnormal Psychology, 87,* 399–407.

Chapman, L. J., Edell, W. S., & Chapman, J. P. (1980). Physical anhedonia, perceptual aberration, and psychosis proneness. *Schizophrenia Bulletin, 6,* 639–653.

Chmielewski, P. M., Fernandes, L. O. L., Yee, C. M., & Miller, G. A. (in press). Ethnicity and gender in scales of psychosis-proneness and mood disorders. *Journal of Abnormal Psychology.*

Chu, J. A., & Dill, D. L. (1990). Dissociative symptoms in relation to child-hood physical and sexual abuse. *American Journal of Psychiatry, 147,* 887–892.

Claridge, G., & Broks, P. (1984). Schizotypy and hemisphere function: I. Theoretical considerations and the measurement of schizotypy. *Personality and Individual Differences, 5,* 633–648.

Claridge, G., & Hewitt, J. K. (1987). A biometrical study of schizotypy in a normal population. *Personality and Individual Differences, 8,* 303–312.

Clark, L. A. (1990). Toward a consensual set of symptom clusters for assessment of personality disorder. In J. N. Butcher & C. D. Spielberger (Eds.), *Advances in personality assessment* (Vol. 8, pp. 243–266). Hillsdale, NJ: Erlbaum.

Clark, L. A. (1993). *SNAP—Schedule for Nonadaptive and Adaptive Personality: Manual for administration, scoring, and interpretation.* Minneapolis: University of Minnesota Press.

Clark, L. A., McEwen, J. L., Collard, L. M., & Hickok, L. G. (1993). Symptoms and traits of personality disorder: Two new methods for their assessment. *Psychological Assessment, 5,* 81–91.

Clementz, B. A., Grove, W. M., Katsanis, J., & Iacono, W. G. (1991). Psychometric detection of schizotypy: Perceptual aberration and physical anhedonia in relatives of schizophrenics. *Journal of Abnormal Psychology, 100,* 607–612.

Comer, N. L., Madow, L., & Dixon, J. J. (1967). Observations of sensory deprivation in a life-threatening situation. *American Journal of Psychiatry, 124,* 164–169.

Costa, P. T., Jr., Zonderman, A. B., McCrae, R. R., & Williams, R. B., Jr. (1985). Content and comprehensiveness in the MMPI: An item factor analysis in a normal adult sample. *Journal of Personality and Social Psychology, 48,* 925–933.

Council, J. R., & Huff, K. D. (1990). Hypnosis, fantasy activity and reports of paranormal experiences in high, medium and low fantasizers. *British Journal of Experimental and Clinical Hypnosis, 7,* 9–15.

Creese, I., Burt, D. R., & Snyder, S. H. (1976). Dopamine receptor binding predicts clinical and pharmacological potencies of antischizophrenic drugs. *Science, 192,* 481–483.

Davis, K. L., Kahn, R. S., Ko, G., & Davidson, M. (1991). Dopamine in schizophrenia: A review and reconceptualization. *American Journal of Psychiatry, 148,* 1474–1486.

Demitrack, M. A., Putnam, F. W., Rubinow, D. R., Pigott, T. A., Altemus, M., Krahn, D. D., & Gold, P. W. (1993). Relation of dissociative phenomena to levels of cerebrospinal fluid monoamine metabolites and beta-endorphin in patients with eating disorders: A pilot study. *Psychiatry Research, 49,* 1–10.

Eckblad, M., & Chapman, L. J. (1983). Magical ideation as an indicator of schizotypy. *Journal of Consulting and Clinical Psychology, 51,* 215–225.

Edell, W. S., & Kaslow, N. J. (1991). Parental perception and psychosis proneness in college students. *American Journal of Family Therapy, 19,* 195–205.

Elliott, D. M., & Briere, J. (1992). Sexual abuse trauma among professional women: Validating the Trauma Symptom Checklist-40 (TSC-40). *Child Abuse and Neglect, 16,* 391–398.

Epstein, S., & Meier, P. (1989). Constructive thinking: A broad coping variable with specific components. *Journal of Personality and Social Psychology, 57,* 332–350.

Erdelyi, M. H. (1994). Dissociation, defense, and the unconscious. In D. Spiegel (Ed.), *Dissociation: Culture, mind, and body* (pp. 3–20). Washington, DC: American Psychiatric Press.

Fernandes, L. O. L., & Miller, G. A. (in press). Compromised performance and abnormal psychophysiology associated with the Wisconsin scales of psychosis proneness. In G. A. Miller (Ed.), *The behavioral high-risk paradigm in psychopathology.* New York: Springer-Verlag.

Flor-Henry, P. (1986). Auditory hallucinations, inner speech, and the dominant hemisphere. *Behavioral and Brain Sciences, 9,* 523–524.

Frankel, F. H. (1990). Hypnotizability and dissociation. *American Journal of Psychiatry, 147,* 823–829.

Frischolz, E. J., Braun, B. G., Sachs, R. G., Schwartz, D. R., Lewis, J., Schaeffer, D., Westergaard, C., & Pasquotto, J. (1991). Construct validity of the Dissociative Experiences Scale (DES): I. The relation between the DES and other self report measures of dissociation. *Dissociation, 4,* 185–188.

Frith, C. D. (1979). Consciousness, information processing and schizophrenia. *British Journal of Psychiatry, 134,* 225–235.

Frith, C. D. (1987). The positive and negative symptoms of schizophrenia reflect impairments in the perception and initiation of action. *Psychological Medicine, 17,* 631–648.

Frith, C. D., & Done, D. J. (1988). Towards a neuropsychology of schizophrenia. *British Journal of Psychiatry, 153,* 437–443.

Fujioka, T. A. T., & Chapman, L. J. (1984). Comparison of the 2-7-8 MMPI profile and the perceptual aberration-magical ideation scale in identifying hypothetically psychosis-prone college students. *Journal of Consulting and Clinical Psychology, 52,* 458–467.

Galbaud du Fort, G., Newman, S. C., & Bland, R. C. (1993). Psychiatric comorbidity and treatment seeking: Sources of selection bias in the study of clinical populations. *Journal of Nervous and Mental Disease, 181,* 467–474.

George, A., & Soloff, P. H. (1986). Schizotypal symptoms in patients with borderline personality disorders. *American Journal of Psychiatry, 143,* 212–215.

Goff, D. C., Brotman, A. W., Kindlon, D., Waites, M., & Amico, E. (1991a). The delusion of possession in chronically psychotic patients. *Journal of Nervous and Mental Disease, 179,* 567–571.

Goff, D. C., Brotman, A. W., Kindlon, D., Waites, M., & Amico, E. (1991b). Self-reports of childhood abuse in chronically psychotic patients. *Psychiatry Research, 37,* 73–80.

Gottesman, I. I., & Shields, J. (1972). *Schizophrenia and genetics: A twin study vantage point.* San Diego, CA: Academic Press.

Graham, J. R. (1993). *MMPI-2: Assessing personality and psychopathology* (2nd ed.). New York: Oxford University Press.

Gray, J. A., Feldon, J., Rawlins, J. N. P., Hemsley, D. R., & Smith, A. D. (1991). The neuropsychology of schizophrenia. *Behavioral and Brain Sciences, 14,* 1–84.

Grove, W. M., Lebow, B. S., Clementz, B. A., Cerri, A., Medus, C., & Iacono, W. G. (1991). Familial prevalence and coaggregation of schizotypy indicators: A multitrait family study. *Journal of Abnormal Psychology, 100,* 115–121.

Gunderson, J. G. (1984). *Borderline personality disorder.* Washington, DC: American Psychiatric Press.

Gunderson, J. G., Siever, L. J., & Spaulding, E. (1983). The search for a schizotype: Crossing the border again. *Archives of General Psychiatry, 40,* 15–22.

Gur, R. E., & Pearlson, G. D. (1993). Neuroimaging in schizophrenia research. *Schizophrenia Bulletin, 19,* 337–353.

Gur, R. E., Skolnick, B. E., Gur, R. C., Caroff, S., Rieger, W., Obrist, W. D., Younkin, S., & Reivich, M. (1983). Brain function in psychiatric disorders: I. Regional cerebral blood flow in medicated schizophrenics. *Archives of General Psychiatry, 40,* 1250–1254.

Harkness, A. R. (1992). Fundamental topics in the personality disorders: Candidate trait dimensions from lower regions of the hierarchy. *Psychological Assessment, 4,* 251–259.

Heilbrun, A. B. (1980). Impaired recognition of self-expressed thought in patients with auditory hallucinations. *Journal of Abnormal Psychology, 89,* 728–736.

Heilbrun, A. B. (1993). Hallucinations. In C. G. Costello (Ed.), *Symptoms of schizophrenia* (pp. 56–91). New York: Wiley.

Heilbrun, A. B., Blum, N. A., & Haas, M. (1983). Cognitive vulnerability to hallucinations: Preferred imagery mode and spatial location of sounds. *British Journal of Psychiatry, 143,* 294–299.

Heilbrun, A. B., Diller, R., Fleming, R., & Slade, L. (1986). Strategies of disattention and auditory hallucinations in schizophrenics. *Journal of Nervous and Mental Disease, 174,* 265–273.

Hemsley, D. R. (1987a). An experimental psychological model for schizophrenia. In H. Hafner, W. F. Gattaz, & W. Janzarik (Eds.), *Search for the causes of schizophrenia* (pp. 179–188). Heidelberg: Springer-Verlag.

Hemsley, D. R. (1987b). Hallucinations: Unintended or unexpected? *Behavioral and Brain Sciences, 10,* 532–533.

Herman, J. L., Perry, J. C., & van der Kolk, B. A. (1989). Childhood trauma in borderline personality disorder. *American Journal of Psychiatry, 146,* 490–495.

Hilgard, E. R. (1986). *Divided consciousness: Multiple controls in human thought and action* (expanded ed.). New York: Wiley.

Hsiao, J. K., Colison, J., Bartko, J. J., Doran, A. R., Konicki, P. E., Potter, W. Z., & Pickar, D. (1993). Monoamine neurotransmitter interactions in drug-free and neuroleptic-treated schizophrenics. *Archives of General Psychiatry, 50,* 606–614.

Hyler, S. E., Skodol, A. E., Kellman, H. D., Oldham, J. M., & Rosnick, L. (1990). Validity of the Personality Diagnostic Questionnaire-Revised: Comparison with two structured interviews. *American Journal of Psychiatry, 147,* 1043–1048.

Irwin, H. J. (1992). Origins and functions of paranormal belief: The role of childhood trauma and interpersonal control. *Journal of the American Society for Psychical Research, 86,* 199–208.

Jakes, S., & Hemsley, D. R. (1986). Individual differences in reaction to brief exposure to unpatterned stimulation. *Personality and Individual Differences, 7,* 121–123.

Janet, P. (1907). *The major symptoms of hysteria: Fifteen lectures given in the medical school of Harvard University.* New York: Macmillan. (Original work published 1889)

Junginger, J., & Frame, C. L. (1985). Self-report of the frequency and phenomenology of verbal hallucinations. *Journal of Nervous and Mental Disease, 173,* 149–155.

Kahn, R. S., Davidson, M., Knott, P., Stern, R. G., Apter, S., & Davis, K. L. (1993). Effect of neuroleptic medication on cerebrospinal fluid monoamine metabolite concentrations in schizophrenia: Serotonin-dopamine interactions as a target for treatment. *Archives of General Psychiatry, 50,* 599–605.

Kendler, K. S., & Diehl, S. R. (1993). The genetics of schizophrenia: A current, genetic-epidemiologic perspective. *Schizophrenia Bulletin, 19,* 261–285.

Kendler, K. S., & Hewitt, J. (1992). The structure of self-report schizotypy in twins. *Journal of Personality Disorders, 6,* 1–17.

Kendler, K. S., Lieberman, J. A., & Walsh, D. (1989). The Structured Interview for Schizotypy (SIS): A preliminary report. *Schizophrenia Bulletin, 15,* 559–571.

Kihlstrom, J. F. (1980). Posthypnotic amnesia for recently learned material: Interactions with "episodic" and "semantic" memory. *Cognitive Psychology, 12,* 227–251.

Kihlstrom, J. F. (1987). The cognitive unconscious. *Science, 237,* 1445–1452.

Kihlstrom, J. F., Glisky, M. L., & Angiulo, M. J. (1994). Dissociative tendencies and dissociative disorders. *Journal of Abnormal Psychology, 103,* 117–124.

Kihlstrom, J. F., & Hoyt, I. P. (1988). Hypnosis and the psychology of delusions. In T. F. Oltmanns & B. A. Maher (Eds.), *Delusional beliefs* (pp. 66–109). New York: Wiley.

Kirmayer, L. J. (1994). Pacing the void: Social and cultural dimensions of dissociation. In D. Spiegel (Ed.), *Dissociation: Culture, mind, and body* (pp. 91–122). Washington, DC: American Psychiatric Press.

Klaf, F. S., & Hamilton, J. G. (1961). Schizophrenia: A hundred years ago and today. *Journal of Mental Science, 107,* 819–827.

Launay, G., & Slade, P. (1981). The measurement of hallucinatory predisposition in male and female prisoners. *Personality and Individual Differences, 2,* 221–234.

Lenzenweger, M. F., Cornblatt, B. A., & Putnick, M. (1991). Schizotypy and sustained attention. *Journal of Abnormal Psychology, 100,* 84–89.

Lenzenweger, M. F., & Korfine, L. (1992). Identifying schizophrenia-related personality disorder features in a nonclinical population using a psychometric approach. *Journal of Personality Disorders, 6,* 256–266.

Lenzenweger, M. F., & Loranger, A. W. (1989). Psychosis proneness and clinical psychopathology: Examination of the correlates of schizotypy. *Journal of Abnormal Psychology, 98,* 3–8.

Levin, R., & Raulin, M. L. (1991). Preliminary evidence for the proposed relationship between frequent nightmares and schizotypal symptomatology. *Journal of Personality Disorders, 5,* 8–14.

Lieberman, J. A., Kane, J. M., Gadaleta, D., Brenner, R., Lesser, M. S., & Kinon, B. (1984). Methylphenidate challenge as a predictor of relapse in schizophrenia. *American Journal of Psychiatry, 141,* 633–638.

Livesley, W. J., Jackson, D. N., & Schroeder, M. L. (1992). Factorial structure of traits delineating personality disorders in clinical and general population samples. *Journal of Abnormal Psychology, 101,* 432–440.

Livesley, W. J., Jang, K. L., Jackson, D. N., & Vernon, P. A. (1993). Genetic and environmental contributions to dimensions of personality disorder. *American Journal of Psychiatry, 150,* 1826–1831.

Loranger, A. W. (1988). *Personality Disorder Examination (PDE) manual.* Yonkers, NY: DV Communications.

Loranger, A. W., Oldham, J. M., & Tulis, E. H. (1982). Familial transmission of DSM-III borderline personality disorder. *Archives of General Psychiatry, 39,* 795–799.

Loranger, A. W., Susman, V. L., Oldham, J. M., & Russakoff, L. M. (1987). The Personality Disorders Examination (PDE): A preliminary report. *Journal of Personality Disorders, 1,* 1–13.

Lynn, S. J., & Rhue, J. W. (1988). Fantasy proneness: Hypnosis, developmental antecedents, and psychopathology. *American Psychologist, 43,* 35–44.

McCarley, R. W., Shenton, M. E., O'Donnell, B. F., Faux, S. F., Kikinis, R., Nestor, P. G., & Jolesz, F. A. (1993). Auditory P300 abnormalities and left posterior superior temporal gyrus volume reduction in schizophrenia. *Archives of General Psychiatry, 50,* 190–197.

McGuffin, P., Farmer, A. E., Gottesman, I. I., Murray, R. M., & Reveley, A. M. (1984). Twin concordance for operationally defined schizophrenia: Confirmation of familiality and heritability. *Archives of General Psychiatry, 41,* 541–545.

Meehl, P. E. (1990). Toward an integrated theory of schizotaxia, schizotypy, and schizophrenia. *Journal of Personality Disorders, 4,* 1–99.

Meltzer, H. Y. (1989). Clinical studies on the mechanism of action of clozapine: The dopamine-serotonin hypothesis of schizophrenia. *Psychopharmacology, 99*(Suppl.), 18–27.

Miller, F. T., Abrams, T., Dulit, R., & Fyer, M. (1993). Psychotic symptoms in patients with borderline personality disorder and concurrent Axis I disorder. *Hospital and Community Psychiatry, 44,* 59–61.

Miller, M. B., & Chapman, J. P. (1993, October). *A twin study of schizotypy in college-age males.* Paper presented at the annual meeting of the Society for Research in Psychopathology, Chicago, IL.

Millon, T. (1994). *Millon Clinical Multiaxial Inventory-III.* Minneapolis, MN: National Computer Systems.

Mintz, S., & Alpert, M. (1972). Imagery vividness, reality testing, and schizophrenic hallucinations. *Journal of Abnormal Psychology, 19,* 310–316.

Morice, R. D. (1990). Cognitive inflexibility and pre-frontal dysfunction in schizophrenia and mania. *British Journal of Psychiatry, 157,* 50–54.

Mueser, K. T., & Butler, R. W. (1987). Auditory hallucinations in combat-related chronic posttraumatic stress disorder. *American Journal of Psychiatry, 144,* 299–302.

Murphy, H. B. M., Wittkower, E. D., Fried, J., & Ellenberger, H. (1963). A cross-cultural survey of schizophrenic symptomatology. *International Journal of Social Psychiatry, 9,* 237–249.

Nadon, R., & Kihlstrom, J. F. (1987). Hypnosis, psi, and the psychology of anomalous experience. *Behavioral and Brain Sciences, 10,* 597–599.

Nadon, R., Laurence, J. R., & Perry, C. (1987). Multiple predictors of hypnotic susceptibility. *Journal of Personality and Social Psychology, 53,* 948–960.

Nemiah, J. C. (1985). Dissociative disorders (hysterical neurosis, dissociative type). In H. Kaplan & B. Sadock (Eds.), *Comprehensive textbook of psychiatry* (4th ed., pp. 942–957). Baltimore, MD: Williams & Wilkins.

Noll, R. (1985). Mental imagery cultivation as a cultural phenomenon: The role of visions in shamanism. *Current Anthropology, 26,* 443–461.

Norton, G. R., Ross, C. A., & Novotny, M. F. (1990). Factors that predict scores on the Dissociative Experiences Scale. *Journal of Clinical Psychology, 46,* 273–277.

Nuechterlein, K. H., & Dawson, M. E. (1984). Information processing and attentional functioning in the developmental course of schizophrenic disorders. *Schizophrenia Bulletin, 10,* 160–203.

Nuechterlein, K. H., Dawson, M. E., Gitlin, M., Ventura, J., Goldstein, M. J., Snyder, K. S., Yee, C. M., & Mintz, J. (1992). Developmental processes in schizophrenic disorders: Longitudinal studies of vulnerability and stress. *Schizophrenia Bulletin, 18,* 387–424.

Oltmanns, T. F. (1988). Approaches to the definition and study of delusions. In T. F. Oltmanns & B. A. Maher (Eds.), *Delusional beliefs* (pp. 3–11). New York: Wiley.

Oltmanns, T. F., & Maher, B. A. (1988). *Delusional beliefs.* New York: Wiley.

Oltmanns, T. F., & Neale, J. M. (1975). Schizophrenic performance when distractors are present: Attentional deficit or differential task difficulty. *Journal of Abnormal Psychology, 84,* 205–209.

Penfield, W., & Perot, P. (1963). The brain's record of auditory and visual experience. *Brain, 86,* 595–705.

Pfohl, B., Blum, N., Zimmerman, M., & Stangl, D. (1989). *Structured Interview for DSM-III-R Personality (SIDP-R).* Iowa City, IA: Department of Psychiatry, University of Iowa.

Plomin, R., & Daniels, D. (1987). Why are children in the same family so different from one another? *Behavioral and Brain Sciences, 10,* 1–60.

Pope, H. G., Jr., Jonas, J. M., Hudson, J. I., Cohen, B. M., & Tohen, M. (1985). An empirical study of psychosis in borderline personality disorder. *American Journal of Psychiatry, 142,* 1285–1290.

Prince, M. (1906–1907). Hysteria from the point of view of dissociated personality. *Journal of Abnormal Psychology, 1,* 170–187.

Raine, A. (1991). The SPQ: A scale for the assessment of schizotypal personality based on DSM-III-R criteria. *Schizophrenia Bulletin, 17,* 555–564.

Riley, K. C. (1988). Measurement of dissociation. *Journal of Nervous and Mental Disease, 176,* 449–450.

Roche, S., & McConkey, K. M. (1990). Absorption: Nature, assessment, and correlates. *Journal of Personality and Social Psychology, 59,* 91–101.

Rose, R. J. (1988). Genetic and environmental variance in content dimensions of the MMPI. *Journal of Personality and Social Psychology, 55,* 302–311.

Rose, R. J., & Kaprio, J. (1987). Shared experience and similarity of personality: Positive data from Finnish and American twins. *Behavioral and Brain Sciences, 10,* 35–36.

Rosenberger, P. H., & Miller, G. A. (1989). Comparing borderline definitions: DSM-III borderline and schizotypal personality disorders. *Journal of Abnormal Psychology, 98,* 161–169.

Ross, C. A., Heber, S., Norton, G. R., Anderson, D., Anderson, G., & Burchet, P. (1989). The Dissociative Disorders Interview Schedule: A structured interview. *Dissociation, 2,* 169–189.

Ross, C. A., & Joshi, S. (1992a). Schneiderian symptoms and childhood trauma in the general population. *Comprehensive Psychiatry, 33,* 269–273.

Ross, C. A., & Joshi, S. (1992b). Paranormal experiences in the general population. *Journal of Nervous and Mental Disease, 180,* 357–361.

Russ, M. J., Shearin, E. N., Clarkin, J. F., Harrison, K., & Hull, J. W. (1993). Subtypes of self-injurious patients with borderline personality disorder. *American Journal of Psychiatry, 150,* 1869–1871.

Rust, J. (1988). The Rust Inventory of Schizotypal Cognitions (RISC). *Schizophrenia Bulletin, 14,* 317–322.

Rust, J., Moncada, A., & Lepage, B. (1988). Personality dimensions through the schizophrenia borderline. *British Journal of Medical Psychology, 61,* 163–166.

Sandberg, D. A., & Lynn, S. J. (1992). Dissociative experiences, psychopathology and adjustment, and child and adolescent maltreatment in female college students. *Journal of Abnormal Psychology, 101,* 717–723.

Sanders, S. (1986). The Perceptual Alteration Scale: A scale measuring dissociation. *American Journal of Clinical Hypnosis, 29,* 95–102.

Schopp, L. H., & Trull, T. J. (1993). Validity of the DSM-III-R personality disorder clusters. *Journal of Psychopathology and Behavioral Assessment, 15,* 219–237.

Schroeder, M. L., Wormworth, J. A., & Livesley, W. J. (1992). Dimensions of personality disorder and their relationships to the big five dimensions of personality. *Psychological Assessment, 4,* 47–53.

Sedman, G. (1966). A comparative study of pseudohallucinations, imagery and true hallucinations. *British Journal of Psychiatry, 112,* 9–17.

Siegel, R. K. (1984). Hostage hallucinations: Visual imagery induced by isolation and life-threatening stress. *Journal of Nervous and Mental Disease, 171,* 264–272.

Siever, L. J., Silverman, J. M., Horvath, T. B., Klar, H., Coccaro, E., Keefe, R. S. E., Pinkham, L., Rinaldi, P., Mohs, R. C., & Davis, K. L. (1990). Increased morbid risk for schizophrenia-related disorders in relatives of schizotypal personality disordered patients. *Archives of General Psychiatry, 47,* 634–640.

Silva, P. de, & Ward, A. J. M. (1993). Personality correlates of dissociative experiences. *Personality and Individual Differences, 14,* 857–859.

Simons, R. F., MacMillan, F. W., III, & Ireland, F. B. (1982). Reaction-time crossover in preselected schizotypic subjects. *Journal of Abnormal Psychology, 91,* 414–419.

Singer, J. L. (1990). *Repression and dissociation: Implications for personality theory, psychopathology, and health.* Chicago, IL: University of Chicago Press.

Slade, P. D., & Bentall, R. P. (1988). *Sensory deception: A scientific analysis of hallucination.* Baltimore: Johns Hopkins University Press.

Spiegel, D. (1994). *Dissociation: Culture, mind, and body.* Washington, DC: American Psychiatric Press.

Spiegel, D., & Cardena, E. (1991). Disintegrated experience: The dissociative disorders revisited. *Journal of Abnormal Psychology, 100,* 366–378.

Spiegel, D., & Vermutten, E. (1994). Physiological correlates of hypnosis and dissociation. In D. Spiegel (Ed.), *Dissociation: Culture, mind, and body* (pp. 185–209). Washington, DC: American Psychiatric Press.

Spitzer, R. L., Williams, J. B. W., Gibbon, M., & First, M. (1990). *User's guide for the Structured Clinical Interview for DSM-III-R.* Washington, DC: American Psychiatric Press.

Stein, J. A., Golding, J. M., Siegel, J. M., Burnam, M. A., & Sorenson, S. B. (1988). Long-term psychological sequelae of child sexual abuse: The Los Angeles Epidemiologic Catchment Area study. In G. E. Wyatt & G. J. Powell (Eds.), *Lasting effects of child sexual abuse* (pp. 135–154). Newbury Park, CA: Sage Publications.

Steinberg, M. (1993). *Structured Clinical Interview for DSM-IV Dissociative Disorders (SCID-D).* Washington, DC: American Psychiatric Press.

Steinberg, M. (1994). Systematizing dissociation: Symptomatology and diagnostic assessment. In D. Spiegel (Ed.), *Dissociation: Culture, mind, and body* (pp. 59–88). Washington, DC: American Psychiatric Press.

Steinberg, M., Rounsaville, B., & Cicchetti, D. V. (1990). The Structured Clinical Interview for DSM-III-R Dissociative Disorders: Preliminary report on a new diagnostic instrument. *American Journal of Psychiatry, 147,* 76–82.

Strauss, J. S. (1969). Hallucinations and delusions as points on continua function. *Archives of General Psychiatry, 21,* 581–586.

Strauss, M. E. (1993). Relations of symptoms to cognitive deficits in schizophrenia. *Schizophrenia Bulletin, 19,* 215–231.

Tellegen, A., & Atkinson, G. (1974). Openness to absorbing and self-altering experiences ("absorption"), a trait related to hypnotic susceptibility. *Journal of Abnormal Psychology, 83,* 268–277.

Thalbourne, M. A. (1994). Belief in the paranormal and its relationship to schizophrenia-relevant measures: A confirmatory study. *British Journal of Clinical Psychology, 33,* 78–80.

Tobacyk, J. J., & Milford, G. (1983). Belief in paranormal phenomena: Assessment instrument development and implications for personality functioning. *Journal of Personality and Social Psychology, 44,* 1029–1037.

Tobacyk, J. J., & Pirtilla-Backman, A. M. (1992). Paranormal beliefs and their implications in university students from Finland and the United States. *Journal of Cross-Cultural Psychology, 23,* 59–71.

Tobacyk, J. J., & Wilkinson, L. V. (1990). Magical thinking and paranormal beliefs. *Journal of Social Behavior and Personality, 5,* 255–264.

Vanderlinden, J., Van Dyck, R., Vandereycken, W., & Vertommen, H. (1993). Dissociation and traumatic experiences in the general population of the Netherlands. *Hospital and Community Psychiatry, 44,* 786–788.

Venables, P. H., Wilkins, S., Mitchell, D. A., Raine, A., & Bailes, K. (1990). A scale for the measurement of schizotypy. *Personality and Individual Differences, 11,* 481–495.

Ventura, J., Nuechterlein, K. H., Lukoff, D., & Hardesty, J. P. (1989). A prospective study of stressful life events and schizophrenic relapse. *Journal of Abnormal Psychology, 98,* 407–411.

Wagner, M. W., & Ratzeburg, F. H. (1987). Hypnotic suggestibility and paranormal belief. *Psychological Reports, 60,* 1069–1070.

Walker, E. A., Katon, W. J., Neraas, K., Jemelka, R. P., & Massoth, D. (1992). Dissociation in women with chronic pelvic pain. *American Journal of Psychiatry, 149,* 534–537.

Walker, E., & Lewine, R. J. (1988). Negative symptom distinction in schizophrenia: Validity and etiological relevance. *Schizophrenia Research, 1,* 315–328.

Weaver, T. L., & Clum, G. A. (1993). Early family environments and traumatic experiences associated with border-line personality disorder. *Journal of Consulting and Clinical Psychology, 61,* 1068–1075.

Weinberger, D. R., Berman, K. F., Suddath, R., & Torrey, E. F. (1992). Evidence of dysfunction of a prefrontal-limbic network in schizophrenia: A magnetic resonance imaging and regional cerebral blood flow study of discordant monozygotic twins. *American Journal of Psychiatry, 149,* 890–897.

Weinberger, D. R., Berman, K. F., & Zec, R. F. (1986). Physiologic dysfunction of dorsolateral prefrontal cortex in schizophrenia: I. Regional cerebral blood flow evidence. *Archives of General Psychiatry, 43,* 114–124.

Westermeyer, J. (1988). Some cross-cultural aspects of delusions. In T. F. Oltmanns & B. A. Maher (Eds.), *Delusional beliefs* (pp. 212–229). New York: Wiley.

Wilson, S. C., & Barber, T. X. (1981). Vivid fantasy and hallucinatory abilities in the life histories of excellent hypnotic subjects ("somnambules"): Preliminary report with female subjects. In E. Klinger (Ed.), *Imagery: Vol. 2. Concepts, results, and applications* (pp. 133–149). New York: Plenum.

Young, H. F., Bentall, R. P., Slade, P. D., & Dewey, M. (1987). The role of brief instructions and suggestibility in the elicitation of auditory and visual hallucinations in normal and psychiatric subjects. *Journal of Nervous and Mental Disease, 175,* 41–48.

Zanarini, M. C., Gunderson, J. G., & Frankenburg, F. R. (1990). Cognitive features of borderline personality disorder. *American Journal of Psychiatry, 147,* 57–63.

Zimmerman, M. (1994). Diagnosing personality disorders: A review of issues and research methods. *Archives of General Psychiatry, 51,* 225–245.

CHAPTER 9

Paranoia

ALLAN FENIGSTEIN

Paranoia refers to a disordered mode of thought that is dominated by an intense, irrational, but persistent mistrust or suspicion of people, and a corresponding tendency to interpret the actions of others as deliberately threatening or demeaning. Because of the general expectation that others are against them or are somehow trying to exploit them, paranoid persons tend to be guarded, secretive, and ever vigilant, constantly looking for signs of disloyalty or malevolence in their associates. These expectations are easily confirmed: The hypersensitivity of paranoids turns minor slights into major insults, and even innocuous events are misinterpreted as harmful or vindictive. As a result, a pernicious cycle is set in motion whereby expectations of treachery and hostility often have the effect of eliciting such reactions from others, thus confirming and justifying the paranoid's initial suspicion and hostility.

Can these disordered thought processes and subsequent behaviors be described or understood in terms of personality characteristics? Although paranoia has traditionally been treated as a diagnostic category— as a mental problem from which someone either suffers or not—there may be sufficient reason to offer an alternative conceptualization that views paranoia as the outcome of a complex interplay of personality structures and processes. Like other aspects of personality, paranoia generally appears as a pervasive and consistent pattern of thought, feeling, and overt behavior, and there is a core element of that pattern that can be identified across a broad range of individuals, from the extremely dysfunctional to the apparently normal. This chapter, through a variety of different approaches, attempts to identify those basic traits or tendencies that give rise to paranoid phenomenon, in all of their varying manifestations.

In discussing paranoia as a personality disorder, several cautions need to be introduced. Although the term *paranoid personality disorder* is an accepted psychiatric diagnosis (American Psychiatric Association [APA], 1994), the term has become so much a part of ordinary vernacular, as in "you're being paranoid," that its clinical meaning can easily become obscured. To compound this potential confusion, paranoid features are explicitly identified in two other psychiatric disturbances, *delusional (paranoid) disorder* and *paranoid schizophrenia.* Moreover, the criteria for distinction among these disorders is problematic (e.g., Bernstein, Useda, & Siever, 1993; Munro, 1982; Turkat, 1985), and the utility of the distinction, in terms of etiology or treatment implications, has not been clearly established. For this reason, some researchers have found it useful to consider the different paranoid disorders as related syndromes, essentially characterized by a pervasive distrust and suspicion of others, existing along a continuum that varies in terms of the frequency and severity of paranoid thoughts, the degree to which reality is allowed to influence perceptions and interpretations, and the extent to which functioning is impaired (e.g., Bernstein et al., 1993; Sarason & Sarason, 1993). This continuum extends from paranoid personality disorder, which is nondelusional, but where suspicion, mistrust, and its sequelae occur so regularly that work and family life are often disrupted; to delusional (paranoid) disorder, involving a chronic, dysfunctional delusional system, although apart from the delusion, reality testing is reasonably appropriate and behavior is not obviously disturbed; and finally, to paranoid schizophrenia, a severe, incapacitating psychosis, involving a serious loss of contact with reality in which all thought is affected by the paranoid delusion.

The notion of a clearly defined disordered paranoid personality is further clouded by recent evidence suggesting that the concept of paranoia may need to be extended in a nonclinical direction, to include the thought processes that characterize ordinary persons (Fenigstein & Vanable, 1992; Sarason & Sarason, 1993; Thompson-Pope & Turkat, 1988). Consistent with the notion that personality disorders are often defined by otherwise common personality traits that are exhibited in a highly inflexible and maladaptive fashion (see DSM-IV, APA, 1994; Pervin, 1993), these studies suggest that almost everyone experiences paranoid thoughts or feelings on occasion; and that even within the general population, relatively stable *paranoid personalities*—involving characteristics such as suspiciousness, self-centeredness, scapegoating tendencies, and a generally hostile attitude—are readily identifiable and may serve as a useful analog of clinical paranoid disorders (e.g., Turkat, Keane, & Thompson-Pope, 1990). It should be noted, however, that there is currently insufficient evidence to determine whether these personality tendencies are continuous with more severe forms of paranoia.

A DIAGNOSTIC APPROACH

Because of the specific interest in developing a conception of paranoia as an integrated set of *personality* characteristics, that is, as a long-standing and pervasive pattern of thought, affect, and behavior, a detailed examination of the Paranoid Personality Disorder, despite its significant overlap with a variety of other paranoid manifestations, dysfunctional as well as normal, may provide a useful starting point for the present analysis of paranoia.

There is a surprising amount of disagreement as to what constitutes Paranoid Personality Disorder. The diagnostic system of the American Psychiatric Association, as represented by the *Diagnostic and Statistical Manual of Mental Disorders* (DSM), has changed the relevant diagnostic criteria in important ways over the years, and there is some controversy as to whether these changes derive from factors other than scientific evidence (e.g., Turkat et al., 1990). The DSM-III (APA, 1980) identified three major criteria for the disorder, along with a list of indications by which these criteria are manifested: pervasive, unwarranted *suspiciousness and mistrust* (e.g., expecting trickery or harm, guardedness); *hypersensitivity* (e.g., easily slighted, exaggerates difficulties); and *restricted affectivity* (e.g., appears cold, pride in rationality). The more recent versions, DSM-III-R (APA, 1987) and DSM-IV (APA, 1994), essentially identify only one criterion: a pervasive distrust and suspiciousness of others such that their motives are interpreted as malevolent, accompanied by a list of indications from which an individual need only present with a subset in recognition of the heterogeneity of the disorder. The single "suspiciousness" criterion, to some extent, subsumes the earlier element of "hypersensitivity" (although relegating it to a lesser status). However, the criterion of "restricted affectivity" has been effectively eliminated (although it continues to be discussed as an "associated feature"), largely on the basis of just two studies that found it to have poor diagnostic validity (Bernstein et al., 1993; Livesley, 1986), even though other elements of the DSM-IV (APA, 1994) "suspicion" criterion that were preserved also had questionable diagnostic efficiency (Bernstein et al., 1993).

There are also significant discrepancies between the DSM-IV (APA, 1994) criteria and the items used in the latest revision of the World Health Organization's *International Classification of Diseases* (ICD-10, 1992) for identifying Paranoid Personality Disorder. Both systems do agree on some characteristics: suspiciousness and a tendency to construe others' actions as hostile; bears grudges and is unforgiving of insults; and proneness to pathological jealousy. However, the following ICD criteria are unrepresented in the latest DSM: excessive sensitiveness to setbacks and rebuffs; a combative sense of personal rights out of keeping with the actual situation; a tendency toward excessive self-importance, manifested in a persistent self-referential attitude; and preoccupation with unsubstantiated conspiratorial explanations of events. At present, empirical data that might help resolve these inconsistencies do not exist. In light of these issues, the following description is best regarded as an amalgamation of a number of elements identified as critical by the varying diagnostic systems.

FEATURES OF THE PARANOID PERSONALITY

This examination, at least initially, will be largely descriptive, because little is known, although much has been theorized, about the origins or development of the paranoid personality disorder. Efforts to develop valid conceptualizations of the disorder have been hampered by a lack of empirical research, in part due to the difficulty of assembling samples of such persons (Turkat & Banks, 1987). Many of those with paranoid personality disorder function well enough to avoid coming to the attention of professionals, and their suspiciousness and intellectual arrogance usually prevent them from volunteering for treatment or participating in research. Whatever difficulties they have are usually attributed to others' problems, not their own; as Pretzer (1990) has noted, few paranoids enter therapy saying, "Doc, my problem is that I'm paranoid." In addition, paranoids often present symptoms, such as social difficulties and anger, that appear unrelated to the usual diagnostic criteria, thus leading to misdiagnosis. Although the prevalence of the disorder has been estimated at around 2% to 5% in the general population (APA, 1994), a more realistic picture of its actual occurrence is suggested by the many exploited inventors, morbidly jealous spouses, persecuted workers, fanatical reformers, and self-styled prophets who are often able to maintain themselves in the community without their paranoid condition being formally recognized.

Anyone starting out in a new situation or relationship may be cautious and somewhat guarded until confident that his or her fears are unwarranted. Those with paranoid personality disorder cannot abandon these concerns. Although not of sufficient severity to be considered delusional, theirs is a rigid, maladaptive, and pervasive pattern of thinking, feeling, and behavior, usually beginning by early adulthood, that is built on distrust, vigilance, and hostility. The conviction that others "have it in for them" represents their most basic and unrelenting belief; they feel constantly mistreated, and are especially adept at annoying and provoking others. Seeing the world as a threatening place, these individuals are preoccupied with hidden motives and the fear that someone may deceive or exploit them. They are inordinately quick to take offense, slow to forgive, and ready to counterattack at the first hint of criticism, real or imagined, even in their personal relationships.

Disordered paranoid personalities see references to themselves in everything that happens. If people are seen talking, the paranoid knows they are talking about him or her. If someone else gets a promotion, the other's advancement is seen as a deliberate attempt to humiliate the paranoid and downgrade his or her achievements. Even offers of help and concern are taken as implied criticisms of weakness or as subtle attempts at exploitation. The constant suspicions and accusations eventually strain interpersonal relations to the point where these individuals are in constant conflict with spouses, friends, and legal authorities. A particularly malignant form of this thinking is seen in paranoid jealousy, in which paranoids summon up any sign—even an apparent wrong number on the phone or a short delay in returning home—as evidence that a spouse is being unfaithful. When the jealousy becomes irrationally pathological, and these paranoids become convinced beyond all reason that their spouse is cheating, they may become violently dangerous (Fenigstein & Schleifer, 1993).

Given their hypersensitivity, information processing becomes highly selective. Any speck of evidence that seems to confirm the paranoid's suspicions is blown out of proportion, and any indication to the contrary is ignored or misinterpreted. Trivial incidents become accumulated, and unconnected "facts" are fit together to create false, but unshakable beliefs regarding mistreatment. Of course, given the ambiguity of social cues and signals, and the exceptional cunning of the paranoid's "enemies," virtually anything—a look, a sound, a feeling, for that matter, even the absence of anything, a particularly shrewd maneuver—is seen as confirmation of their suspicions.

Convinced that others are undermining their efforts or ruining their achievements, paranoid personalities tend to see themselves as blameless, instead finding fault for their own mistakes and failures in others, even to the point of ascribing evil motives to them. Many paranoids tend to be inveterate "injustice-detectors," inclined to take retributive actions of one sort or another, and constantly embroiled in litigation or letter-writing campaigns, in an attempt to redress imagined injustices. Those with disordered paranoid personalities also tend to overvalue their abilities, and have an inflated sense of their rationality and objectivity, making it extraordinarily difficult for them either to question their own beliefs or to accept or even appreciate another's point of view. Unable or unwilling to recognize the possibility of genuine dissent, simple disagreement by others becomes a sign of genuine disloyalty. The resulting obstinacy, defensiveness, and self-righteousness exasperates and infuriates others, and elicits responses that exacerbate the conflict and confirm the original paranoid expectations.

In addition to being argumentative and uncompromising, paranoids appear cold and aloof, and emotionally cut off from others. Intimacy is avoided and self-disclosure is difficult, partly because they fear betrayal, partly in an attempt to maintain total control over their affairs, and partly because of profound deficits in their capacity for joy, warmth, and nurturance. The resulting social isolation, by limiting the opportunity to check social reality and learn from others, only reinforces their egocentric perspective.

Compared with some other paranoid pathologies, those with disordered personalities tend not to progressively worsen, but rather reach a certain level of severity and stay there. They show considerably less disorganization of personality, and they do not develop the kind of systematic and well-defined delusions found in delusional disorders. General cognitive functioning, apart from the unwarranted distrust, remains essentially intact. However, the proverbial kernel of truth is often greater in the suspicions of disordered paranoid personalities than in those with delusional disorders; their accusations have more plausibility and their paranoid attitudes are more diffuse. Because of the complexity and pervasiveness of the paranoid personality disorder, work and family life are often impoverished, although some do manage to function adequately in society, often by carving out a social niche in which a moralistic and punitive style is acceptable or at least tolerated.

ASSESSING PARANOIA

By far, the most widely used objective test in clinical practice and research is the Minnesota Multiphasic Personality Inventory (MMPI), originally developed by Hathaway and McKinley in 1943, and subject to several revisions since then, although much of the form and content has remained the same. Items in the inventory (see below for samples) were empirically chosen on the basis of their ability to discriminate between the responses of patients with confirmed psychiatric diagnoses and those of normal controls. Although this assessment device was developed independently of any objectively established diagnostic criteria for paranoid personality disorder, high scores on the Paranoia (Pa) scale of the MMPI are interpreted as indicating suspiciousness, sensitivity, delusions of persecution, ideas of reference, rigidity, and externalizing defenses, corresponding reasonably well with both DSM and ICD criteria.

The Millon Clinical Multiaxial Inventory (MCMI, Millon, 1983) is another objective test for the assessment of clinical personality disorders, developed largely in accordance with the DSM-III (APA, 1980) classification system to which Millon was a significant contributor. This self-report, true-false inventory provides scores on 11 different personality patterns, including those corresponding to the paranoid personality disorder. An attempt to validate the 36-item Paranoia (P) subscale (Kreiner, Simonsen, & Mogenson, 1990) found that although some items, such as "I know I'm a superior person, so I don't care what people think," and "I have always 'tested' people to find out how much they can be trusted," were more likely to be endorsed by paranoids than nonclinical controls, other items, such as "I find it hard to sympathize with people who are always unsure about things," were significantly more likely to be identified as self-descriptive by the controls, compared with the paranoid patients. When these anomalous items were eliminated, the remaining 28 items showed good homogeneity and discriminant validity.

Given the difficulty of doing research on individuals diagnosed with paranoid personality disorder, Turkat and his colleagues (Thompson-Pope & Turkat, 1988; Turkat & Banks, 1987; Turkat et al., 1990), attempted to identify college subjects who could serve as an experimental analog of clinical paranoia. Unable to find a DSM-III-based assessment instrument in the existing literature, they used a battery of tests that they regarded as representative of the DSM-III (APA, 1980) criteria, including the Paranoid Ideation subscale of the Symptom Checklist-90 Revised (SCL 90R; Derogatis, 1978), the Fear of Negative Evaluation Scale (Watson & Friend, 1969), and the Superego Scale (Lazare, Klerman, & Armor, 1970), reflecting the DSM-specified characteristics of suspiciousness, hypersensitivity to interpersonal threat, and restricted affect, respectively. Subjects who scored highly on a weighted combination of these measures reported having more paranoid thoughts and experiences than controls, but similar amounts as a clinically diagnosed group of paranoid personalities, were more resistant to participation in research and more suspicious of being tricked by the experimenter, were more likely to interpret ambiguous situations as involving hostile intent, and were more likely to react to prosocial or accidental events with anger, suggesting that the behavioral tendencies of relatively normal "paranoid personalities" may be continuous with some of the characteristics of paranoid disorders.

Fenigstein and Vanable (1992) construed paranoid thought as an expression of a relatively normal and pervasive *egocentric* bias (e.g., Greenwald, 1980), in which events are seen as more relevant to the self than is actually the case. To investigate this phenomenon, a new measure of paranoia was developed explicitly for use with a nonclinical population, derived from several MMPI-based, paranoia-related scales reported in

Dahlstrom, Welsh, and Dahlstrom (1975). Because MMPI-related scales were all initially intended for a clinical paranoid population, items for the present scale were chosen on the basis of established paranoid criteria (Magaro, 1980; Millon, 1981) that were also judged as being potentially applicable to normal subjects: suspicion or mistrust of others' motives; belief that others are trying to influence one's behavior or control one's thinking; belief that people are against one; belief that people talk about, refer to, or watch one; and feelings of ill will, resentment, or bitterness. Some MMPI items that were part of the previously cited paranoia scales were not selected either because of their obscurity (e.g., "Everything tastes the same") or because they were so obviously psychotic (e.g., "I commonly hear voices without knowing where they come from") as to be inappropriate for the assessment of any moderate but presumably normal paranoid tendencies in college students. After numerous psychometric refinements, a final 20-item Paranoia Scale emerged (see Table 9.1).

The scale was shown to have a substantial degree of internal consistency, demonstrating a coefficient alpha of .84 ($N = 581$), and good reliability, with a test-retest correlation of .70 ($N = 107$) over a 6-month period, suggesting the existence of relatively stable personality tendencies toward paranoia in a normal population. Consistent with clinical descriptions of paranoia, validation studies found that this measure of paranoia was negatively related to interpersonal trust, and positively related to the inward expression of anger (resentment, boiling inside), a belief that powerful others were controlling events, and a corresponding need to assert personal control. Additional behavioral evidence for the construct validity of the scale found the scale to be associated with paranoid tendencies toward the personalistic interpretation of interpersonal events, that is, perceiving oneself as a target of others' behavior and feelings of being watched (Fenigstein & Vanable, 1992).

Normative data indicated a surprising willingness on the part of presumably normal college students to endorse paranoid characteristics as self-descriptive. Averaging across all the items in the scale, almost two-thirds of all subjects described a paranoid scale item as being at least slightly applicable to the self, and one-third of them endorsed the item as at least somewhat applicable to the self. These results tend to confirm what is reflected by the frequent use of the term *paranoia* in our language, and what is easily recognized in ordinary interactions: that on various occasions, many of us think that we are being talked about, or feel as if everything is going against us, often resulting in suspicion and mistrust of others, as if they were taking advantage of us or were somehow to blame for our difficulties. As suggested earlier, the point at which these thoughts and feelings spill over into the domain of psychopathology is a matter of some controversy.

TABLE 9.1   Paranoia Scale

Items on the Paranoia Scale

1. Someone has it in for me.
2. I sometimes feel as if I'm being followed.
3. I believe that I have often been punished without cause.
4. Some people have tried to steal my ideas and take credit for them.
5. My parents and family find more fault with me than they should.
6. No one really cares much what happens to you.
7. I am sure I get a raw deal from life.
8. Most people will use somewhat unfair means to gain profit or an advantage, rather than lose it.
9. I often wonder what hidden reason another person may have for doing something nice for you.
10. It is safer to trust no one.
11. I have often felt that strangers were looking at me critically.
12. Most people make friends because friends are likely to be useful to them.
13. Someone has been trying to influence my mind.
14. I am sure I have been talked about behind my back.
15. Most people inwardly dislike putting themselves out to help other people.
16. I tend to be on my guard with people who are somewhat more friendly than I expected.
17. People have said insulting and unkind things about me.
18. People often disappoint me.
19. I am bothered by people outside, in cars, in stores, etc. watching me.
20. I have often found people jealous of my good ideas just because they had not thought of them first.

From "Paranoia and Self-Consciousness" by A. Fenigstein and P. A. Vanable, 1992, *Journal of Personality and Social Psychology, 62,* p. 131. Copyright 1992 by the American Psychological Association. Reprinted with permission of the author.

One of the more interesting findings to emerge from repeated analyses of the Paranoia Scale (Fenigstein & Vanable, 1992) was that item responses seemed to be best explained by a single, general factor, which accounted for about 25% of the total variance. Despite the fact that apparently different criteria were used in selecting items for the scale (e.g., suspicion, ideas of reference, and hostility), the factor analytic evidence suggested that these characteristics all relate to a single, underlying attribute, although the nature of that unifying attribute is subject to dispute. Some theorists have identified *suspicion and mistrust* as the fundamental elements in paranoia (e.g., Kraepelin, 1921; Shapiro, 1965); others have focused on *hostility* as the essential aspect (e.g., Cameron, 1963; Gunderson, 1988); and Fenigstein (1995a) has identified *self-referential ideation* as the primary, organizing feature of paranoid behavior.

A DIMENSIONAL ANALYSIS OF PARANOIA

Although the DSM has traditionally used a categorical perspective, treating any given diagnosis, such as paranoid personality disorder, as a qualitatively distinct clinical syndrome, several problems exist concerning the validity, reliability, and internal consistency of that diagnosis (e.g., Frances & Widiger, 1986; Morey, 1988a, 1988b). For example, relatively few paranoid personalities are free of other personality disorder diagnoses (Bernstein et al., 1993). There is also some suggestion of a relationship between the delusional and the personality disorders involving paranoia (e.g., Kendler, Masterson, & Davis, 1985). Establishing the truth or falsity of an apparently paranoid belief, and separating these beliefs from the irrational beliefs occasionally held by normal individuals, is also problematic (e.g., Johnson, 1988; Oltmanns, 1988). Thus, it is difficult to argue that the paranoid personality disorder is a discrete and reliably identifiable entity with clear separations from either normality or other mental disorders. Instead, some researchers have concluded that the paranoid personality disorder is best considered a heterogeneous diagnostic category, even in regard to the defining features of the category (e.g., Bernstein et al., 1993).

As a partial response to these issues, the DSM-IV (APA, 1994) explicitly acknowledges an alternative to the categorical approach. The alternative, dimensional perspective suggests that a personality disorder may represent maladaptive variants of personality traits that merge imperceptibly into other disorders and into normality. Diagnostic classification is based on quantification of attributes rather than assignment to categories. The critical task then becomes one of identifying the most fundamental dimensions or characteristics that underlie the domain of normal and pathological personality functioning. Although the relationship between the dimensional and the categorical models remains under active investigation, exploring these dimensions and their interrelationships may lead to the development of a more empirically based, informative, and reliable understanding of the various syndromes and their etiology.

One attempt at developing such trait dimensions for the paranoid personality disorder took a construct validity approach (Livesley & Schroeder, 1990) in which the disorder was defined in terms of prototypical features or behavioral exemplars, initially derived from the diagnostic literature, and subsequently confirmed by clinicians' ratings. The 11 dimensions associated with the paranoid personality disorder, in decreasing order of clinically rated prototypicality, were *vindictiveness* (an unrelenting need to "get back" at one's enemies), *suspiciousness* (including misinterpreting the intentions and actions of others, and a sense of the world as hostile and threatening), *hypervigilance* for any sign of threat, *hypersensitivity* to real or imagined negative evaluation, *reluctance to confide in others, avoidance of blame or responsibility,* even when justified, along with *attributing problems to the external world, a fixed, rigid cognitive style, easily angered, resentful of authority,* and *fear of humiliation.*

These dimensional features of paranoid personality disorder were found to exhibit satisfactory levels of internal consistency in both a clinical sample, as well as in the general population. Factor analyses also yielded similar two-factor solutions for both groups. The first factor, involving vindictiveness, suspiciousness, hypervigilance, and blame avoidance, corresponds to the core features of the DSM-IV (APA, 1994) criteria for this diagnosis. In contrast to the DSM, however, clinical judges placed greater emphasis on the second factor that emerged, involving such interpersonal features as hypersensitivity, fear of social hurt, and resentment of powerful others, as well as the rigid, cognitive style of paranoids. The similarity in factor structure across the two samples suggests that the major difference between the clinical and normal samples may be quantitative, as represented by the degree to which similar personality features are present, and thus may be taken as support for a dimensional classification of paranoid personality characteristics.

CAUSES OF PARANOIA

Another means of attempting to identify the major personality characteristics that make up paranoid behavior is through an examination of the causal mechanisms that have been theorized as explanations for paranoia.

Biological Bases

Genetic Contribution

Although there is relatively little research on the role of heredity in causing paranoia, family studies suggest that features of the paranoid personality disorder occur disproportionately more often among biological relatives of those who have either delusional (paranoid) disorders or paranoid schizophrenia, suggesting that these syndromes, and the paranoid features that characterize each of them, may have some genetic basis, although the findings, particularly with respect to schizophrenia, have been inconsistent (e.g., Kendler & Gruenberg, 1982; Kendler, Masterson, & Davis, 1985).

Biochemistry

No identifiable biochemical substrate or demonstrable neuropathology relates specifically to paranoid thought or delusions; there is no brain system whose dysfunction specifically produces the psychological characteristics associated with paranoia. However, paranoid symptoms are sometimes a by-product of physical illness, organic brain disease, or drug intoxication (Manschreck & Petri, 1978). Among organic illnesses, hypothyroidism, multiple sclerosis, Huntington's disease, and epileptic disorders, as well as Alzheimer's disease and other forms of dementia are commonly associated with paranoid features. In some people, alcohol stimulates a paranoid reaction even in small doses, and paranoia is a common feature of alcohol hallucinosis and alcohol withdrawal delirium. Chronic abuse of drugs, such as amphetamines, cocaine, marijuana, PCP, LSD, or other stimulants or psychedelic compounds may result in some of the symptoms of paranoid personality disorder. These drugs may also exacerbate symptoms in persons already suffering from a paranoid disorder. Although the abuse of drugs may lead to paranoid symptoms, thus suggesting a possible biochemical pathway, it needs to be reiterated that no such pathway has been identified; whatever drug effects have been found may be psychologically, and not biochemically, mediated.

Psychological Bases

In the absence of a clear organic basis or effective drug treatment for paranoia, most researchers have sought to identify the psychological mechanisms that explain how paranoid ideas become fixed in the mind.

Psychodynamic Approaches

Repressed Homosexuality

Of all psychological theories, Freud's (1915/1956) is perhaps the best known, although it is increasingly being challenged. He believed that paranoia was a form of repressed homosexual love. According to Freud, paranoia arises, at least in men, when a child's homosexual feelings for his father are preserved but driven into the unconscious, from which they reemerge during an adult emotional crisis, converted into suspicions and delusions by the defense mechanism of projection—the attribution of one's own unacknowledged wishes and impulses to another person. Before reaching consciousness, the impulses undergo a transformation that disguises their homosexual origin; for example, a man suffering from paranoid jealousy, unable to acknowledge that he himself loves another man, projects that feeling onto his wife and becomes convinced that it is his wife who loves the man.

Although it may be possible to find paranoid aspects in the personality of a homosexual, there are other explanations for the relationship, the most parsimonious being that homosexuals have a great deal to fear in contemporary society (e.g., Colby, 1977); that is, if a homosexual was not paranoid to begin with, society offers many opportunities to learn to be so. Perhaps most problematic for the psychoanalytic view is that many paranoids are *aware* of their homosexual interests.

Although Freud's theory of unconscious homosexuality has been largely discredited, projection is still recognized as a basic mechanism used by paranoids to defend against their unacceptable feelings and impulses (Millon, 1981; Shapiro, 1965). For example, paranoids will explain their sense of helplessness by pointing to the control exerted by others; or they will transform self-critical ideas into the belief that others are criticizing them. Viewing others as hostile serves a number of functions for paranoids: not only does it justify their feelings of being threatened, it may actually elicit the other's anger, in the process confirming their suspicions, and leaving them feeling weakly vulnerable, but morally righteous. As Shapiro (1965) has argued, by projecting onto others that which is actually true, but cannot be acknowledged in the self, the paranoid reduces guilt, defends against inner conflicts, sustains an unrealistic self-image, and experiences less distress than would result from a more realistic view.

Developmental and Interpersonal Approaches

Failure, Inferiority, and Low Self-Esteem

Related to the traditional dynamic view, with its emphasis on defensiveness, is Colby's (1977, 1981) cognitive-behavioral model. Based on a computer simulation of paranoid responses that are sufficiently realistic so as to be indistinguishable from the responses of a paranoid client, as judged by experienced interviewers, the model argues that paranoia is actually a set of strategies constructed to defend against feelings of shame and embarrassment. Paranoid individuals are assumed to be especially vulnerable to intolerably high levels of humiliation and shame, largely due to a strong, inner belief that they are somehow inadequate or unworthy, especially in situations where they may be the object of ridicule, or are falsely accused. Rather than accept the blame and consequent shame themselves, paranoids blame someone else and assert that they were the ones being victimized. Presumably, the anger or anxiety resulting from attributing problems to persecution by malevolent others is less aversive than the humiliation experienced when holding oneself responsible for the events.

An underlying assumption of this perspective is that the lives of paranoids are replete with failures in critical life situations, often stemming from their rigidity and social ineptitude, and compounded by their inability to understand how they have alienated others. The continual exposure to rejection and ridicule helps account for their fear of negative evaluation (Livesley & Schroeder, 1990), hypersensitivity to criticism, and social isolation (Turkat & Maisto, 1985), and also explains the overwhelming sense of inadequacy that Colby (1981) views as the basis for their cognitive strategy.

Faulty Development

The role of personal failures is echoed in other approaches that view paranoid thinking as stemming from the development of immature and distorted personality patterns, part of which may be traced to early family dynamics. Paranoids, even as children, are often described as having been aloof, suspicious, secretive, stubborn, and resentful of punishment. Rarely is there a history of normal play with other children, or good socialization with warm, affectionate relationships (Swanson, Bohnert, & Smith, 1970). Their family background is often characterized by parental dominance, mistreatment, and a lack of consistent love, resulting in a basic lack of trust (e.g., Cameron, 1974; Turkat, 1985).

Based on his clinical observations, Turkat (1985) emphasized the child's early interactions with parents as a major source of low self-esteem. Growing up amid completely unreasonable parental expectations and a need to conform to those expectations, paranoid persons may dread being watched and judged, presumably because that reminds them of their parents, who were distant, demanding, and capricious. Overly critical parental demands, in turn, interfered with the child's acceptance by peers, resulting in ostracism and humiliation. These social failures further undermined self-esteem and led to deeper social isolation and mistrust. Turkat (1985) hypothesized that these children subsequently spent a lot of time ruminating about isolation and mistreatment by peers, and eventually concludes, as Colby (1981) had suggested in his analysis, that the reason for their persecution was that they were special and that others were jealous. Although the resulting paranoid view of others perpetuated their isolation, the self-serving nature of the explanation effectively reduced distress over that isolation.

The Paranoid "Illumination" and the
Paranoid Pseudo-Community

Other theorists have focused, not on early family history, but on the later emergence of a fixed, unyielding paranoid belief system. Given paranoids' rigidity, self-importance, and suspiciousness, they are likely to become a target of actual discrimination and mistreatment (Lemert, 1962); and ever alert to such occurrences, they are likely to find abundant "proof," both real and imagined, of persecution. The cycle of misunderstanding is then perpetuated by the paranoids' subsequent responses. Their belief that others are plotting against them results in hostile, defensive behavior which, in turn, elicits the others' anger and irritability. The paranoids' inability to consider the others' perspective—that they may be operating out of defensiveness against the paranoids' antagonism and belligerence—only exacerbates conflicts.

As failures and seeming betrayals mount, the paranoid, to avoid self-devaluation, searches for "logical" explanations and becomes more vigilant in scrutinizing the environment, looking for hidden meanings, and asking leading questions. Eventually, a meaningful picture, in the form of the "paranoid illumination," crystallizes and everything begins to make sense: The paranoid has been singled out for some obscure reason, and others are working against him or her. Failure is not because of any personal inadequacy, but rather because of some conspiracy or plot directed at him or her. With this as a fundamental defensive premise, the individual proceeds to distort and falsify the facts to fit the premise, and gradually develops a logical, fixed delusional system, referred to as the "pseudo-community" (Cameron, 1963), in which the paranoid organizes surrounding people (real and imaginary) into a structured group whose sole purpose is centered on his or her victimization. As each additional experience is misconstrued and interpreted in light of this new understanding, more and more events, persons, and experiences become effectively incorporated into the delusional system. This pathological "paranoid construction," for all its distortion of reality and loss of critical judgment, provides a sense of identity and importance not otherwise available (Meissner, 1978). Because these beliefs meaningfully integrate all the vague, disturbing, amorphous, and unrelated "facts" of his or her existence, the paranoid is unwilling to accept any other explanation and is impervious to reason or logic; any questioning of the belief only reinforces the suspicion that the interrogator has sold out to the enemy.

Cognitive Approaches

Anomalous Perceptions

A theory by Maher (1974, 1988) offered the intriguing hypothesis that delusions are the result of a cognitive attempt to account for aberrant or anomalous sensory experiences. For example, research has shown that persons with visual or hearing loss—because of either heightened suspiciousness or an attempt to deny the loss—may conclude that others are conspiring to conceal things from them (e.g., Zimbardo, Andersen, & Kabat, 1981). The experience of many elderly people, who are a high-risk group for paranoia (e.g., Christenson & Blazer, 1984), provides a particularly good example of this phenomenon. These individuals, because of physical disability or social isolation, often feel especially vulnerable. These realistic feelings may then be converted to paranoia by an unacknowledged loss of hearing. That is, an awareness of themselves as potential victims of greedy relatives or petty criminals, together with an increased sense that others are whispering, may contribute to a growing suspicion that others are whispering about them, or perhaps planning to exploit them. When the others angrily deny the accusation, that only strengthens their belief that they are being plotted against and intensifies the cycle of hostility and mistrust.

The occurrence of paranoia in those with degenerative brain disorders, such as Alzheimer's disease, may be explained through a similar process. These diseases commonly involve a disruption of memory that victims may be unable or unwilling to recognize. As a result, failures of memory become anomalous experiences that need to be explained. For example, not being able to locate one's keys is transformed into the belief that someone else has stolen or misplaced them. This suspicion is then likely to be supported by actual perceptions, such as seeing one's child speaking to the doctor, to produce the conviction that others are conspiring to confuse the patient in order to put the person away.

The general hypothesis that anomalous experience may be the basis for paranoia assumes that logical processes lead to illogical conclusions. That is, the cognitive process by which delusional beliefs are formed are assumed to be very similar to those operating in the formation of normal beliefs: In effect, delusions are not the result of disturbed thought, but arise because of abnormal sensory or perceptual experiences. Anomalous experiences demand an explanation, and in the course of developing hypotheses and testing them through observations, the delusional insight is confirmed through selective evidence. This explanation offers relief in the form of removing uncertainty, and the relief in turn works against abandonment of the explanation.

Stress and the Need for Control

Maher's analysis, extended to other forms of strange or unusual experiences, may account for the often observed association between paranoia and stress. An acute episode of paranoid thinking sometimes manifests itself after sudden, stressful social or situational changes, such as emigration, economic deprivation, prison, induction into military service, or even leaving a family home (Bernstein et al., 1993). Although these conditions are multifaceted, they are all, in a sense, anomalous experiences associated with extreme social isolation, unfamiliarity with the appropriate rules of behavior, a sense of vulnerability to exploitation, and a general loss of control over life. In some ways, paranoid thought, by providing an explanation, albeit an illogical one for these feelings, may serve to impose meaning, comfort, and control in an otherwise confusing or hostile environment (e.g., Heider, 1958).

The paranoid belief that others are responsible for his or her own misfortunes or distress, although threatening and irrational, may still be preferable to taking personal responsibility for his or her difficulties. In addition to deflecting blame away from the self, the blaming of others may also render apparently random occurrences more understandable. For example, the paranoid invention of conspiratorial plots in modern society may be seen as an attempt to provide order and a sense of control to what in reality are unconnected and uncontrollable events. Similarly, ethnographers have identified entire cultures which may be described as paranoid: confronted with natural disasters, they refuse to believe that accidents happen randomly; it is far more psychologically satisfying to attribute misfortune to human malice and find an enemy to blame. In this regard, it is possible that the paranoid thinking which often develops as a result of acute drug intoxication, or aging (and its concomitant sensory loss and social isolation), or degenerative brain disorders, may also be mediated by the confusion and vulnerability inherent in these conditions, and the consequent need of the sufferer to impose some form of order and meaning on the situation.

Biases in Information Processing

Some of the approaches discussed thus far have emphasized that, apart from the paranoid construction itself, the cognitive functioning of paranoids is essentially intact. In fact, given their delusional system, paranoid reactions are not unlike the biased tendencies of many individuals with strong belief systems, who are likely to exaggerate, distort, or selectively focus on events that are consistent with their beliefs. Once paranoids suspect that others are working against them, they start carefully noting the slightest signs pointing in the direction of their suspicions, and ignore all evidence to the contrary (Swanson et al., 1970). With this frame of reference, it is quite easy, especially in a highly competitive, somewhat ruthless world, for any event, no matter how innocuous, to be selectively incorporated into the delusion. This, in turn, leads to a vicious cycle: suspicion, distrust, and criticism of others drives people away, keeps paranoids in continual friction with others, and generates new incidents for distortion and magnification.

A Self-Focus Theory of Paranoid Thought

Although these information-processing biases help to explain how paranoid beliefs are maintained once they are established, they do not address the question of the origin of paranoid beliefs. Some insight into that issue may be gained through an analysis of paranoid thought. The essence of paranoia is a malfunctioning of the capacity to assign meanings and understand causes for events (e.g., Magaro, 1980). Ordinarily, these cognitive processes operate in a reasonably logical and objective fashion. In paranoia, such objective assessments are overwhelmed by judgments and interpretations that bear little relation to reality, but instead are perverted in a distinctly self-referential fashion. Even when there is no basis for making any connection to the self, paranoids tend to perceive others' behavior as if it was relevant to the self so that, for example, the laughter or conversation of others in the distance is assumed to be self-directed and malicious, or the appearance of a stranger on the street is taken to mean that one is being watched or plotted against. It is this interpretational bias on which the fundamental suspicion and mistrust of paranoids may be predicated. This conceptualization is by no means intended to reduce the complexity of paranoid thought to simple errors of self-referent processing, but the persistent misperception of oneself as the target of others' malevolent thoughts and actions, commonly referred to as an idea or delusion of reference, is the hallmark characteristic of almost all forms of paranoid thought (e.g., Cameron, 1943; Greenwald, 1980; Magaro, 1980; Maher, 1988; Oltmanns, 1988). Why do paranoids consistently go beyond the information given and feel singled out or targeted by others for unkind treatment?

Paranoia and Self-Focus

Part of the explanation for the aberrant social processing of paranoids is hinted of by the characterization of the disorder as a self-focused style of functioning. Paranoia has long been described in terms involving excessive self-consciousness or self-focus (e.g., Kraepelin, 1915; Millon & Everly, 1985; Shapiro, 1965). That characterization partly derives from the paranoid's phenomenological preoccupation with self and isolation from others, but it also reflects certain elements of paranoid thought and behavior that relate to the process of self-focus. Kraepelin (1915) first recognized that heightened self-consciousness is an inherent part of paranoid personalities, and others followed. Cameron (1943), for example, described the paranoid woman whose preoccupation with how she looked created a readiness to detect ridicule or criticism from others; in effect, her own self-consciousness led her to incorrectly impute self-referent thoughts to others. Shapiro (1965), too, noted that the simple awareness of attention from another is capable of precipitating paranoid feelings of exposure and vulnerability. Similarly, Laing (1969) argued that the self-conscious awareness of oneself as an object of awareness to others leads to a heightened paranoid sense of being seen and of being the object of other people's interest. Only recently, however, has the hypothesized relationship between self-focused attention and paranoia been subjected to systematic experimental examination (Fenigstein, 1984; Fenigstein, 1995a; Fenigstein & Vanable, 1992).

This research basically examined the notion that to see oneself as an object of attention to others, leaves a person susceptible to the paranoid idea of being targeted by others' thoughts and behaviors. Previous research has shown that attention to the self facilitates the ease of access to information related to the self (e.g., Carver & Scheier, 1978; Fenigstein & Levine, 1984; Hull & Levy, 1979; Hull, Van Treuren, Ashford, Propsom, & Andrus, 1988), making the self more salient or "available" (Tversky & Kahneman, 1973), and more likely to be interjected into the interpretation of others' behavior. It was hypothesized that as a result, insignificant and irrelevant events would become transformed into ones that appear to have personal relevance for the self (e.g., Fenigstein, 1984; Wicklund & Hormuth, 1981). That is, self-focus may be important, not so much because it directs *perception* to particular behaviors or events (e.g., Hull & Levy, 1979; Hull et al., 1988), but rather because it affects the tendency to *misconstrue* those behaviors as if they were relevant to the self. If paranoids, as suggested, are prone toward self-focused attention, that may explain their tendency to overconceptualize events in terms of the self, and read self-referent content into neutral or innocuous stimuli.

Theory and research on self-focused attention have suggested an important distinction between awareness of the internal aspects of the self, such as private thoughts and feelings, and awareness of the self as a social object (e.g., Carver & Scheier, 1981; Fenigstein, 1987; Fenigstein, Scheier, & Buss, 1975). When attention is directed toward the external, public aspects of the self that are potentially observable by others, the implications for paranoia may be even more obvious. Awareness of one's own observability to others can easily induce a feeling of visibility or conspicuousness, resulting in the (not altogether illogical) paranoid assumption that others are very much aware of your presence and thus are likely to be acting with you in mind (e.g., Fenigstein, 1979). It is not unreasonable at that point to make self-referent interpretations of others' behavior, and perceive oneself as a target of others' intended malevolence.

Self-Attention and Ideas of Reference

The first set of studies to be discussed examined the idea that when a person is aware of being an object of attention to others, he or she is more likely to infer that others are also attending to the person. In one study (Fenigstein, 1984, Experiment 3), subjects were presented with a series of hypothetical social situations involving the self and another, and were asked to make a judgment as to whether the behavior of the other was in some way targeted toward them (see Table 9.2). Subjects dispositionally

TABLE 9.2 Self-as-Target Questionnaire

Situations

1. You are giving a public lecture and before you finish, some people get up and leave. How likely is it that:
   (a) the people left because the lecture was boring*
   (b) the people left because of an important prior commitment

2. You are walking down the hallway when an acquaintance walks right by without saying hello to you. How likely is it that:
   (a) the other person was preoccupied and didn't notice you
   (b) the other person wanted to avoid a conversation with you*

3. While you are working, your boss unexpectedly stops by. How likely is it that:
   (a) this was simply a convenient time for the boss to drop in
   (b) the boss was there to check up on you*

4. Two of your friends are talking at some distance from you. They notice you, and shortly afterward, they begin to laugh. How likely is it that:
   (a) they were laughing at you*
   (b) they were laughing at a joke one of them told

5. About halfway through an exam period, two people turn in their papers. How likely is it that:
   (a) they finished early because they knew the material better than you*
   (b) they gave up early

6. Shortly after you begin a new job, the person who had been working with you changes shifts. How likely is it that:
   (a) the other person had to change schedules because of conflicting obligations
   (b) the other person didn't want to work with you*

7. While working in a personnel office where you've had access to personal records, your supervisor informs you that those records are now off-limits. How likely is it that:
   (a) you are suspected of misusing personal information*
   (b) this reflects a general change in policy

8. Your date asks to go home early. How likely is it that:
   (a) your date is not feeling very well
   (b) your date does not want to spend any more time with you*

Note: * Indicates the self-relevant option. From "Self-Consciousness and the Overperception of Self as a Target," by A. Fenigstein, 1984, *Journal of Personality and Social Psychology, 47*, p. 866. Copyright 1984 by the American Psychological Association. Reprinted with permission.

high in public self-consciousness (who tended to focus on the publicly observable aspects of themselves) compared with those low on that dimension, were significantly more likely to construe interpersonal situations in personalistic terms and perceive the self as a target.

In a related study (Fenigstein, 1984, Experiment 2), subjects, participating in groups of 10, were told that the experimenter had designated, presumably on a random basis, one member of the group to participate in a demonstration, and were then asked to estimate the probability that either they or the person seated next to them had been targeted as the chosen one. Public self-consciousness again strengthened subjects' beliefs that they, rather than the other person, had been singled out by the experimenter.

Another investigation (Fenigstein, 1993) attempted to test the effects of self-consciousness on self-referential inferences in a more naturalistic setting. Medical students often suffer from a syndrome in which, after hearing or reading about some disease or illness, they begin to imagine themselves suffering from the described symptoms. A similar phenomenon has on occasion been observed in students of abnormal psychology. This effect, to some extent, may be explained by students' interpreting the information within a self-referential framework, as a result of which the symptoms take on more personal meaning than they should. If self-attention heightens the tendency to perceive events personally, then self-conscious persons should be more prone to this syndrome. That is, if persons are presented with information about a disorder at the same time that they are attending to themselves, they should be more likely to process the information in relation to the self. Research confirmed this hypothesis. After listening to a lecture on depression that discussed only some of the relevant symptoms, students high in public self-consciousness were significantly more likely than low self-conscious students to self-report symptoms of depression, but only those symptoms that had been discussed in the lecture.

These studies all suggest that as a result of their own preoccupation with themselves as social objects, persons high in public self-consciousness have difficulty avoiding the inference that others are acting with them in mind or that events in some way relate to them. Because such self-referential inferences are one of the defining characteristics of paranoid thought, this research suggests a clear relationship between self-consciousness and paranoid ideation. This relationship was confirmed by studies that consistently found moderately strong correlations of about .40 between measures of public self-consciousness and responses to the Paranoia Scale, which measures suspicion, ideas of reference, and feelings of victimization (Fenigstein & Vanable, 1992).

Self-Attention and Feeling Observed

A set of studies by Fenigstein and Vanable (1992) examined the relationship between self-attention and a classical manifestation of paranoia, the feeling of being watched. The underlying assumption in this research was that publicly self-conscious persons, because of their preoccupation with how they are seen by others, would be likely to assume, even in the absence of any direct evidence, that they are actually the object of observation by others. In one study (Fenigstein & Vanable, 1992,

Study 2), subjects sat in a room containing a two-way mirror for a 5-minute period, either simply waiting prior to the start of the "real" experiment, or working on an anagram task. Although the mirror obviously suggested the possibility of being observed, it was hypothesized that public self-consciousness would increase the extent to which subjects accepted that possibility. As predicted, public self-consciousness was significantly associated with subjects' beliefs, measured as part of a mood manipulation check, that they were being watched while they were in the room.

In an attempt to extend these findings beyond the laboratory, feelings of being watched were investigated among students eating in a large dining hall (Fenigstein, Schneider, & Bothe, 1994). The earlier findings were confirmed: Despite reporting that they themselves did not watch others as they went for their food or ate at their tables, subjects were likely to assume that others were watching them, and the perceived difference between self-as-observer and self-as-observed was clearly exacerbated by public self-consciousness.

In the studies reported thus far, a correlational design was used in which self-attention, measured in terms of dispositional public self-consciousness, was related to paranoid phenomena. In no case did private self-consciousness relate to paranoid symptoms. The last study in this series (Fenigstein & Vanable, 1992, Study 3) used an experimental design in which self-focus was experimentally manipulated, so as to increase the plausibility and generalizability of a self-attentional interpretation. Self-directed attention was induced in the context of a story-construction task, by providing subjects with a list of words, some of which were first-person pronouns, which had to be incorporated into a written story. Control subjects were given a list that differed only in having third-person pronouns replace the first-person ones. Manipulation checks confirmed that self-focus was significantly stronger in the experimental group. Stories were written while subjects were in a room with a two-way mirror and, as in the previous study, the dependent variable of interest was subjects' beliefs that they were being observed. As expected, subjects who wrote about themselves, compared with the group who wrote about others, were much more likely to report feelings of being observed while constructing the story. Once again, directing one's own attention toward the self heightened the sense that one was an object of attention to others.

To the extent that both ideas of reference and feelings of being watched are prominent features of paranoia, these studies together offer convergent evidence for the notion that paranoid ideation is related to self-directed attention. In addition, the last study in the series, by using an experimental manipulation, rather than a dispositional measure, of self-attention, shed some light on the question of causal relationships by demonstrating that the paranoid experience of observability was heightened as a function of attention directed toward the self. Given the similarity in paradigms across all the studies presented, it may be reasonable to infer that analogous causal mechanisms were operating in each case. That is, these studies suggest that self-attention can produce a variety of effects that are remarkably similar to those observed in paranoia.

Self-Attentional Mediating Mechanisms

Personalism and Paranoia

Although the studies discussed thus far have focused primarily on paranoid ideas of reference (the objectively unwarranted feeling that one is the object of other people's interest, thoughts, and behavior), these findings may be related to a number of other critical aspects of paranoid thought. In particular, to interpret events as if they were intentionally directed toward the self is to engage in personalistic thinking (Heider, 1958; Jones & Davis, 1965). Personalism is associated with more extreme internal attributions for others' behavior, especially when that behavior has negative implications for the self, presumably because such occurrences are more hedonically important than positive ones, and so are more demanding of an explanation. That is, when the actions of others hurt someone, even when the occurrence is unintentional, personalism would lead the victim to interpret the others' behavior in terms of their personal intent or dispositions.

The concept of personalistic attributions may offer some critical insights into many of the interpersonal dynamics of paranoia. For example, paranoids rarely accept the idea that bad things just happen (e.g., Millon, 1981; Shapiro, 1965); rather, they are inclined to believe that it is someone else's doing. That is, they are likely to perceive the event in self-referential terms and make a personalistic interpretation (e.g., Fenigstein & Vanable, 1992). For the paranoid, the negative event itself is evidence for others' malevolent intentions toward them. Given the attribution of intent, minor slights become major insults, and the bearing of grudges or difficulty in emotional control becomes somewhat more understandable. Eventually, the accumulation of such occurrences constitutes evidence for a view of the world as a hostile and threatening place. Once the assumption of ubiquitous danger is accepted, other manifestations of paranoia become comprehensible: suspicion and guardedness; selective attention and memory for signs of trickery or exploitation; misinterpretation of apparently harmless events as malevolent; readiness to take offense and counterattack; and blaming others for all of one's difficulties. As a result, hostilities become intensified, suspicions are confirmed, and enemies are found everywhere. In addition, as suggested previously, the perception of intent serves a number of ego-related concerns, in particular, by shifting blame away from the self, and by providing a sense of control. Thus, self-consciousness, through the mediating mechanism of personalistic inferences, may relate to a variety of paranoid behaviors (e.g., Fenigstein, 1979).

Egocentrism and Paranoia

Another mechanism through which self-focus may relate to paranoia is by interfering with the ability to take another's perspective; in effect, self-focused thought, by locking persons into their own perspective, may diminish their capacity for considering other viewpoints. One of the critical elements of paranoid thinking is the utter inability to understand the motivations and perspectives of others (e.g., Millon, 1981) or to examine the broader context of behavior (e.g., Shapiro, 1965). Not only are paranoids more likely to take another's behavior personally, they are less likely to correct that misinterpretation by altering their point of view. Regarding their own behavior as so obviously benign or as an appropriate response to threat or conflict, they assume that their good intentions are also obvious to others and fail to appreciate that to the other, they may appear menacing. Rather than consider the way in which their behavior provokes hostility, they become completely consumed by the idea that they are the innocent victim of the other's unwarranted hostility.

Although social withdrawal and isolation may account, in part, for this deficit in perspective taking, research suggests that self-focused attention may also play a role in the self-centeredness of paranoids (Fenigstein & Abrams, 1993). In a series of studies involving a variety of attitudes and behaviors, as well as causal inferences, Fenigstein and Abrams had subjects answer questions, both from their own perspective, and from the perspective of hypothetical others in the same situation. It was found that attention focused toward the public aspects of self consistently increased the assumption that others thought and acted in the same way as the self. That is, when making inferences about the general preferences or attitudes of others, or when making judgments about another's causal perspective, subjects who were self-focused used their own position as a basis for generating inferences about the position of others. Thus, to the extent that self-focus heightens the salience of one's own perspective, it may be suggested that the narrowness and rigidity of paranoid thought—their failure to examine events critically or in a broader context, their extreme selectivity in processing information, and their unwillingness to consider alternative perspectives—may, in part, result from their self-focused style of thought.

A PARANOID SELF-SCHEMA

The research and theory presented thus far has focused on paranoia as a system of thought in which perceptions and interpretations of events, as a function of self-focused thought, are overly biased in the direction of self-concerns and self-perspectives. A question that arises at this point is why the paranoid is prone to such a high degree of self-attention; what, in effect, draws attention inward? To some extent, that may derive from the way in which paranoids conceive of and think about themselves, that is, the nature of their self-schemas.

The remarkably rigid and biased nature of paranoid thought, dominated by fixed expectations and the repetitive search only for confirmation of them (e.g., Shapiro, 1965) is consistent with the idea of schematic processing (e.g., Fiske & Taylor, 1991; Nisbett & Ross, 1980). Given the self-referent nature of paranoid thought (Fenigstein & Vanable, 1992; Greenwald, 1980; Shapiro, 1965), it was hypothesized that paranoids might operate on the basis of an extremely salient and attention-grabbing paranoid self-schema, organized around basic issues of threat and vulnerability (Fenigstein, 1995b). Without specifying the origins of the paranoid's schematic beliefs, which may be acquired through faulty learning or developmental conditions, it may be argued that when the schema is activated, paranoids attempt to select out, exaggerate, or misinterpret information so that it is consistent with the schema, even if that means distorting information to achieve congruence.

The concept of a paranoid schema, to a large extent, derives from recent cognitive information-processing approaches to the study of psychopathology (e.g., Beck & Freeman, 1990), which emphasize the role of fixed and faulty schemas, or informational structures, in the organization of thoughts, perceptions, and emotions. This approach has been largely concerned with pathology related to negative *affect,* such as depression or anxiety (e.g., Beck, 1967, 1976). Paranoia, however, is characterized predominantly by disordered *thought,* not affect, and thus may be even more amenable to a cognitive analysis. A schematic perspective, in particular, seems especially applicable to paranoia in that the distinguishing characteristic of paranoid thought is not just its dysfunctional character, but its remarkable *rigidity* (Shapiro, 1965); paranoid suspicions are so chronic and compelling as to admit no exceptions. As suggested by the concept of schematic processing, the paranoid examines information with extraordinary prejudice, dismissing whatever is irrelevant or inconsistent, and seizing any clue that is confirmatory. That schemas are woven into the person's usual cognitive processes (e.g., Fiske & Taylor, 1991) also helps to explain the paranoid's characteristic failure to recognize that any of their beliefs are faulty.

An examination of the cognitive and interpersonal components of paranoia (e.g., Millon, 1981; Pretzer, 1990; Shapiro, 1965) suggests a pattern of behavior involving feelings of almost constant threat from malevolent and deceptive others, a sense of personal vulnerability, and a consequent need for vigilance and self-protection. The unrelenting and self-threatening nature of these concerns (as expressed by the sense that "they're all out to get me") argues for a highly accessible self-schema that is capable, not only of readily drawing attention, but of also facilitating the personalistic interpretation of events. The resulting pattern of arbitrary conclusions provides particularly clear examples of what is meant by schema-driven cognitive biases (e.g., Beck et al., 1990).

The existence of a paranoid self-schema was examined with the use of the orienting task procedure (Craik & Tulving, 1975; Rogers, Kuiper, & Kirker, 1977). Subjects, who were pretested on the Paranoia scale (Fenigstein & Vanable, 1992), were asked to make judgments on a series of trait adjectives that were either neutral, depressive, or paranoid in content (see Table 9.3). Judgments were of three types: semantic, asking about the meaning of the word, other-referent, asking how well the word applies to others, and self-referent, asking how well the word

TABLE 9.3   Content Ratings of Selected
Paranoid Trait Terms

Paranoid Terms	Descriptive of Paranoia
Angry	3.03
Betrayed	4.19
Cautious	4.44
Cold	3.31
Criticized	4.25
Envious	4.03
Exploited	4.06
Guarded	4.19
Hostile	3.63
Inflexible	3.15
Jealous	3.69
Mistrustful	3.81
Persecuted	4.69
Secretive	4.09
Suspicious	4.59
Threatened	4.75
Vigilant	3.47
Vulnerable	4.56

Rated on a scale of 1 to 5, with higher numbers indicating greater descriptiveness.

describes the self. Consistent with the notion of a well-articulated paranoid self-schema, it was found that only those subjects who scored high
in Paranoia demonstrated a "self-reference effect" (e.g., Rogers,
Kuiper, & Kirker, 1977): They showed higher incidental recall for paranoid compared with depressive or neutral words, but only when those
words had been processed with reference to the self. Additional findings
pointed to the intrusiveness of this schema by showing that paranoid
subjects were especially likely to project their own characteristics and
perceive others as paranoid. Findings also indicated that the characteristics of the paranoid self-schema were distinguishable from those associated with depression.

These data regarding a paranoid self-schema are informative, not only
because they suggest an effective conduit for paranoid biases in the perception, interpretation, and recall of information, but also because they
suggest an interesting reciprocal relationship between self-focused
thought and the paranoid self-schema. By fostering personalistic inferences, so that events are perceived as being directed toward the self, self-
attention may transform trivial, unintentional, or benign events into
deliberate insults or attacks, facilitating the sense of being surrounded
by malevolent others, and feeding the sense of self as vulnerable and
threatened. The highly salient nature of these self-related fears and concerns, on the one hand, suggests a particularly high level of self-focus.
Self-attention, in turn, may heighten the perception of intended harm,
and so on. The vicious cycle that emerges from these dynamics may be
responsible for the extraordinary rigidity and intransigence of paranoid
thought.

The highly interpersonal nature of the paranoid's concerns—as a target
of other's malevolence—may also help resolve the apparent paradox between the publicly self-conscious nature of the paranoid and the paranoid's
tendency toward externalizing blame. Although research has consistently
demonstrated that self-directed attention increases causal attributions to
the self (e.g., Buss & Scheier, 1976; Duval & Wicklund, 1973), the highly
self-conscious paranoid individual tends to blame others for negative outcomes. What needs to be emphasized, however, is that attributions are not
simply a function of self-attention, but rather are determined by the nature of the self to which attention is directed (Fenigstein & Levine, 1984).
The paranoid self is explicitly defined in terms of threat from others, control by others, and a sense of personal vulnerability to those external
forces. To focus on those attributes is to directly confront the extent to
which others are responsible for negative events. That is, more than simply an ego-protective strategy (e.g., Greenwald, 1980; Snyder, Stephan, &
Rosenfield, 1976), the paranoid's blaming others for problems may be an
accurate reflection of a distorted worldview.

IMPLICATIONS OF A SCHEMATIC ANALYSIS

The notion of a well-integrated self-schema is central to the present conceptualization of paranoid thought. Despite the apparently diverse manifestations of paranoia (e.g., ideas of reference, feelings of threat, and a sense of suspicion and ill will), it may be argued that these characteristics are all related to a relatively coherent set of self-perceptions that both imply others' malevolence toward the self, and describe a personal sense of vulnerability related to that perceived threat.

The fundamental paranoid tendency toward personalistic interpretations of social information seems especially compatible with the notion of a highly intrusive self-schema, which may account both for the self-focus of paranoids, as well as their tendency to transform insignificant events into ones that appear to have personal relevance to the self. Moreover, when that self-structure explicitly involves elements of threat from others, self-referent perceptions of the self as a target may become especially intransigent. To perceive themselves as the intentional target of others' malevolence leads paranoids to expect deception and harm in interpersonal situations, and to conclude that only by being constantly vigilant for signs of trickery and malevolence can they protect themselves. Taking almost everything personally also helps to explain some of the more emotional elements of paranoia, such as their boiling anger, vindictiveness, and unwillingness to forgive.

More generally, it may be suggested that the highly rigid and inflexible style of thinking often associated with paranoia (e.g., Fenigstein, 1994; Shapiro, 1965) parallels a number of important elements of schematic processing. For example, paranoia involves a tendency to exaggerate, distort, or selectively focus on the hostile or threatening aspects of others—suggesting a form of perceptual bias that is clearly associated with schema-based cognition. This vigilance, of course, may have the unintended consequence of revealing malicious intent even when the actual intentions are benign.

Schematic thinking also tends to be self-confirming and self-fulfilling, which is an especially insidious aspect of paranoid behavior. Paranoids typically engage in an intense search for confirmation of their expectancies, and their suspicions often ensure that even discrepant information will provide evidence for their beliefs regarding the malevolence or deceptiveness of others. In addition, the paranoid's own schematically appropriate behavior—guarded, accusatory, protective—may provoke others to act precisely as anticipated. These tendencies may also help account for the intransigence, egocentricity, and all-encompassing character of the paranoid explanatory system. That is, paranoid thinking may be the prototypical example of many of the schematically driven biases or errors in information processing that characterize much of ordinary human thought (e.g., Fiske & Taylor, 1991; Nisbett & Ross, 1980).

TREATMENT OF PARANOIA

Treatment of paranoia is extraordinarily difficult for a number of reasons. First, little is known about the causes that presumably are to be treated. Second, it is difficult for paranoids to recognize a problem when they are locked into their own perspective and are reluctant to accept another's viewpoint. Finally, it is nearly impossible for therapists to penetrate the barrier of suspiciousness. For all these reasons, paranoids are unlikely and unwilling to enter therapy; and once in therapy, their wariness often leads them to sabotage treatment, or to break it off prematurely. Paranoids also generally refuse to take responsibility for their treatment, because the only problems they see are those created by the people intent on harming them. In addition, the disclosure of personal information or other aspects of therapy may represent a loss of control, especially to male paranoids.

Mistrust obviously serves to undermine the therapeutic relationship. Any expression of friendliness or concern by the therapist is likely to arouse suspicion or be taken as confirmation that others are trying to humiliate them. Any questions or suggestions are seen as criticisms or attacks. Even if therapy improves other aspects of the paranoids' functioning, their delusional system is so strenuously defended, and so easily confirmed by "clues" detected in the therapeutic situation, that it often remains intact, yielding a highly unfavorable prognosis for complete recovery.

Behavioral theory assumes that paranoids have learned to be hypersensitive to the judgments of others, and as a result, they behave in ways that invite just the sort of reaction they anticipate and fear. As others begin to avoid them, they become socially isolated and develop increasingly elaborate suspicions that maintain the isolation. With behavior therapy, clinicians try to break the cycle by first teaching the patient to be less sensitive to criticism through the use of relaxation and anxiety management, and then improving social skills by training the patient to act in ways that will not invite attack or avoidance. The patient can also be given help with recognition and avoidance of situations that produce or increase delusions. Paranoid thinking can in some cases be altered by aversive conditioning or the removal of factors that reinforce maladaptive behavior.

Because of the paranoid patients' guardedness and insistence on their own correctness, another effective therapeutic approach focuses on trust building rather than direct confrontation of the delusional beliefs. Perhaps the most powerful strategy is to establish rapport by forming a therapeutic alliance in which the therapist recognizes whatever kernel of truth exists in a paranoid system, and acknowledges the delusional beliefs as powerful, convincing, and understandable. The therapist may then try to identify the ways in which these beliefs may interfere with the patient's goals or create frustration for others as well as for the patient. The patient's paranoid reactions have usually driven others away or incited them to counterattack, heightening the cycle of suspicion and hostility. The therapist can sometimes bring about change by providing a different, empathic response that serves as a model of nonparanoid behavior. The task is then to help the paranoid become more competent at discriminating real threats from perceived ones, perhaps through some form of cognitive restructuring, and the final step is the development of more adaptive responses to real or even ambiguous threats.

REFERENCES

American Psychiatric Association. (1980). *Diagnostic and statistical manual of mental disorders* (3rd ed.). Washington, DC: Author.

American Psychiatric Association. (1987). *Diagnostic and statistical manual of mental disorders* (3rd ed., rev.). Washington, DC: Author.

American Psychiatric Association. (1994). *Diagnostic and statistical manual of mental disorders* (4th ed.). Washington, DC: Author.

Beck, A. T. (1967). *Depression: Clinical, experimental, and theoretical aspects.* New York: Harper & Row.

Beck, A. T. (1976). *Cognitive therapy and emotional disorders.* New York: International Universities Press.

Beck, A. T., & Freeman, A. M. (1990). *Cognitive therapy of personality disorders.* New York: Guilford.

Bernstein, D. P., Useda, D., & Siever, L. J. (1993). Paranoid personality disorder: Review of the literature and recommendations for DSM-IV. *Journal of Personality Disorders, 7,* 53–62.

Buss, D. M., & Scheier, M. F. (1976). Self-awareness, self-consciousness, and self-attribution. *Journal of Research in Personality, 10,* 463–468.

Cameron, N. (1943). The development of paranoic thinking. *Psychological Review, 50,* 219–233.

Cameron, N. (1963). *Personality development and psychopathology: A dynamic approach.* Boston: Houghton-Mifflin.

Cameron, N. (1974). Paranoid conditions and paranoia. In S. Arieti & E. Brody (Eds.), *American handbook of psychiatry* (Vol. 3, pp. 676–693). New York: Basic Books.

Carver, C. S., & Scheier, M. F. (1978). Self-focusing effects of dispositional self-consciousness, mirror presence, and audience presence. *Journal of Personality and Social Psychology, 36,* 324–332.

Carver, C. S., & Scheier, M. F. (1981). *Attention and self-regulation: A control theory approach to human behavior.* New York: Springer-Verlag.

Christenson, R., & Blazer, D. (1984). Epidemiology of persecutory ideation in an elderly population. *American Journal of Psychiatry, 141,* 1088–1091.

Colby, K. M. (1977). Appraisal of four psychological theories of paranoid phenomenon. *Journal of Abnormal Psychology, 86,* 34–59.

Colby, K. M. (1981). Modeling a paranoid mind. *Behavioral and Brain Sciences, 4,* 515–560.

Craik, F. I. M., & Tulving, E. (1975). Depth of processing and the retention of words in episodic memory. *Journal of Experimental Psychology: General, 104,* 268–294.

Dahlstrom, W. G., Welsh, G. S., & Dahlstrom, L. F. (1975). *An MMPI Handbook: Vol. 2. Research applications.* Minneapolis, MN: University of Minnesota.

Derogatis, L. D. (1978). *Symptom Checklist—90 Revised.* Copyright: Author.

Duval, S., & Wicklund, R. A. (1973). Effects of objective self-awareness on attributions of causality. *Journal of Experimental Social Psychology, 9,* 17–31.

Fenigstein, A. (1979). Self-consciousness, self-attention, and social interaction. *Journal of Personality and Social Psychology, 37,* 75–86.

Fenigstein, A. (1984). Self-consciousness and the overperception of self as a target. *Journal of Personality and Social Psychology, 47,* 860–870.

Fenigstein, A. (1987). On the nature of public and private self-consciousness. *Journal of Personality, 55,* 543–554.

Fenigstein, A. (1993). *Self-attention and the abnormal psychology student's syndrome.* Unpublished manuscript.

Fenigstein, A. (1994). Paranoia. In V. S. Ramachandran (Ed.), *Encyclopedia of human behavior.* San Diego, CA: Academic Press.

Fenigstein, A. (1995a). Paranoia and self-focused attention. In A. Oosterwegel & R. A. Wicklund (Eds.), *The self in European and North American culture.* Amsterdam: Kluwer Academic Publishers.

Fenigstein, A. (1995b). *Paranoid thought and schematic processing.* Proceedings of the American Psychological Society, New York.

Fenigstein, A., & Abrams, D. (1993). Self-attention and the egocentric assumption of shared perspectives. *Journal of Experimental Social Psychology, 29,* 287–303.

Fenigstein, A., & Levine, M. (1984). Self-attention, concept activation, and the causal self. *Journal of Experimental Social Psychology, 20,* 231–245.

Fenigstein, A., Scheier, M. F., & Buss, A. H. (1975). Public and private self-consciousness: Assessment and theory. *Journal of Clinical and Consulting Psychology, 43,* 522–527.

Fenigstein, A., & Schleifer, D. (1993). *Paranoia, self-consciousness, and domestic violence.* Unpublished manuscript.

Fenigstein, A., Schneider, M., & Bothe, S. (1994). *Observed and observer: The effects of self-consciousness.* Unpublished manuscript.

Fenigstein, A., & Vanable, P. A. (1992). Paranoia and self-consciousness. *Journal of Personality and Social Psychology, 62,* 129–138.

Fiske, S. T., & Taylor, S. E. (1991). *Social cognition* (2nd ed.). New York: McGraw-Hill.

Frances, A. J., & Widiger, T. (1986). The classification of personality disorders: An overview of problems and solutions. In R. E. Hales & A. J. Frances (Eds.), *Annual Review* (Vol. 5, pp. 240–257). Washington, DC: American Psychiatric Association.

Freud, S. (1956). A case of paranoia running counter to the psychoanalytical theory of the disease. In E. Jones (Ed.), *Collected papers* (Vol. 2). London: Hogarth. (Original work published 1915)

Greenwald, A. G. (1980). The totalitarian ego: Fabrication and revision of personal history. *American Psychologist, 35,* 603–618.

Gunderson, J. G. (1988). Personality disorders. In A. M. Nicholi (Ed.), *The new Harvard guide to psychiatry* (pp. 337–357). Cambridge, MA: Belknap Press.

Hathaway, S. R., & McKinley, J. C. (1943). *The Minnesota Multiphasic Personality Inventory.* Minneapolis: University of Minnesota Press.

Heider, F. (1958). *The psychology of interpersonal relations.* Hillsdale, NJ: Erlbaum.

Hull, J. G., & Levy, A. S. (1979). The organizational functions of self: An alternative to the Duval and Wicklund model of self-awareness. *Journal of Personality and Social Psychology, 37,* 756–768.

Hull, J. G., Van Treuren, R., Ashford, S., Propsom, P., & Andrus, B. W. (1988). Self-consciousness and the processing of self-relevant information. *Journal of Personality and Social Psychology, 54,* 452–465.

Johnson, M. K. (1988). Discriminating the origin of information. In T. F. Oltmanns & B. A. Maher (Eds.), *Delusional beliefs* (pp. 34–65). New York: Wiley.

Jones, E. E., & Davis, K. E. (1965). From acts to dispositions: The attribution process in person perception. In L. Berkowitz (Ed.), *Advances in experimental social psychology* (Vol. 2). New York: Academic Press.

Kendler, K. S. (1980). The nosologic validity of paranoia (simple delusional disorder). *Archives of General Psychiatry, 37,* 699–706.

Kendler, K. S., & Gruenberg, A. M. (1982). Genetic relationship between paranoid personality disorder and the "schizophrenic spectrum" disorders. *American Journal of Psychiatry, 139,* 1185–1186.

Kendler, K. S., Masterson, C. C., & Davis, K. L. (1985). Psychiatric illness in first degree relatives of patients with paranoid psychosis, schizophrenia, and medical controls. *British Journal of Psychiatry, 147,* 524–531.

Kraepelin, E. (1915). *Psychiatrie: Ein lehrbuch* [Psychiatry: A textbook] (7th ed.). Leipzig, Germany: Barth.

Kraepelin, E. (1921). *Manic-depressive insanity and paranoia.* Edinburgh: Livingstone.

Kreiner, S., Simonsen, E., & Mogensen, J. (1990). Validation of a personality inventory scale: The MCMI P-scale (paranoia). *Journal of Personality Disorders, 4,* 303–311.

Laing, R. D. (1969). *The divided self.* London: Penguin Press.

Lazare, A., Klerman, G. L., & Armor, D. J. (1970). Oral, obsessive, and hysterical personality patterns. *Journal of Psychiatric Research, 7,* 275–290.

Lemert, E. M. (1962). Paranoia and the dynamics of exclusion. *Sociometry, 25,* 2–25.

Livesley, W. J. (1986). Trait and behavioral prototypes of personality disorder. *American Journal of Psychiatry, 143,* 728–732.

Livesley, W. J., & Schroeder, M. L. (1990). Dimensions of personality disorder: The DSM-III-R Cluster A diagnoses. *Journal of Nervous and Mental Disease, 178,* 627–635.

Magaro, P. A. (1980). *Cognition in schizophrenia and paranoia: The interpretation of cognitive processes.* Hillsdale, NJ: Erlbaum.

Maher, B. A. (1974). Delusional thinking and perceptual disorder. *Journal of Individual Psychology, 30,* 98–113.

Maher, B. A. (1988). Anomalous experience and delusional thinking: The logic of explanations. In T. F. Oltmanns & B. A. Maher (Eds.), *Delusional beliefs* (pp. 15–33). New York: Wiley.

Manschreck, T., & Petri, M. (1978). The paranoid syndrome. *Lancet, 2,* 251–253.

Meissner, W. W. (1978). *The paranoid process.* Northvale, NJ: Jason Aronson.

Millon, T. H. (1981). *Disorders of personality.* New York: Wiley.

Millon, T. H. (1983). *Millon Clinical Multiaxial Inventory (MCMI) manual* (3rd ed.). Minneapolis, MN: National Computer Systems.

Millon, T. H., & Everly, G. (1985). *Personality and its disorders.* New York: Wiley.

Morey, L. C. (1988a). Personality disorders in DSM-III and DSM-III-R: Convergence, coverage, and internal consistency. *American Journal of Psychiatry, 145,* 573–577.

Morey, L. C. (1988b). The categorical representation of personality disorder: A cluster analysis of DSM-III-R personality features. *Journal of Abnormal Psychology, 97,* 314–321.

Munro, A. (1982). Paranoia revisited. *British Journal of Psychiatry, 141,* 344–349.

Nisbett, R. E., & Ross, L. (1980). *Human inference: Strategies and shortcomings of social judgement.* Englewood Cliffs, NJ: Prentice-Hall.

Oltmanns, T. F. (1988). Approaches to the definitions and study of delusions. In T. F. Oltmanns & B. A. Maher (Eds.), *Delusional beliefs* (pp. 3–12). New York: Wiley.

Pervin, L. A. (1993). *Personality: Theory and research* (6th ed.). New York: Wiley.

Pretzer, J. (1990). Paranoid personality disorder. In A. T. Beck, A. Freeman, & Associates. *Cognitive therapy of personality disorders* (pp. 97–119). New York: Guilford.

Rogers, T. B., Kuiper, N. A., & Kirker, W. S. (1977). Self-reference and the encoding of personal information. *Journal of Personality and Social Psychology, 35,* 677–688.

Sarason, I. G., & Sarason, B. R. (1993). *Abnormal psychology: The problem of maladaptive behavior* (7th ed.). Englewood Cliffs, NJ: Prentice-Hall.

Shapiro, D. (1965). *Neurotic styles.* New York: Basic Books.

Snyder, M. L., Stephan, W. G., & Rosenfield, D. (1976). Egotism and attribution. *Journal of Personality and Social Psychology, 33,* 435–441.

Swanson, D. W., Bohnert, P. J., & Smith, J. A. (1970). *The paranoid.* Boston: Little, Brown.

Thompson-Pope, S. K., & Turkat, I. D. (1988). Reactions to ambiguous stimuli among paranoid personalities. *Journal of Psychopathology and Behavioral Assessment, 10,* 21–32.

Turkat, I. D. (1985). Formulation of paranoid personality disorder. In I. D. Turkat (Ed.), *Behavioral case formulation* (pp. 161–198). New York: Plenum.

Turkat, I. D., & Banks, D. S. (1987). Paranoid personality and its disorder. *Journal of Psychopathology and Behavioral Assessment, 9,* 295–304.

Turkat, I. D., Keane, S. P., & Thompson-Pope, S. K. (1990). Social processing errors among paranoid personalities. *Journal of Psychopathology and Behavioral Assessment, 12,* 263–269.

Turkat, I. D., & Maisto, S. A. (1985). Application of the experimental method to the formulation and modification of personality disorders. In D. H. Barlow (Ed.), *Clinical handbook of psychological disorders* (pp. 503–507). New York: Guilford.

Tversky, A., & Kahneman, D. (1973). Availability: A heuristic for judging frequency and probability. *Cognitive Psychology, 5,* 207–232.

Watson, D., & Friend, R. (1969). Measurement of social evaluation anxiety. *Journal of Consulting and Clinical Psychology, 43,* 384–395.

Wicklund, R. A., & Hormuth, S. E. (1981). On the functions of the self: A reply to Hull & Levy. *Journal of Personality and Social Psychology, 40,* 1029–1037.

World Health Organization. (1992). *International statistical classification of diseases and related health problems* (10th ed.). New York: Author.

Zimbardo, P. G., Andersen, S. E., & Kabat, L. G. (1981). Induced hearing deficit generates experimental paranoia. *Science, 212,* 1529–1531.

CHAPTER 10

Obsessiveness

BRUCE PFOHL

Any student of human behavior who is preoccupied with compiling a comprehensive list of personality traits must eventually include obsessiveness—a trait to which such students often feel a natural affinity. This chapter will consider the terms "obsessiveness" and "compulsiveness" as referring to the same basic personality trait. In psychology and psychiatry, the term compulsion is usually applied to behaviors and the term obsession to mental events. At the level of personality, both terms represent aspects of the same domain of character. For example, the individual who is obsessed with organization and order is likely to feel compelled to make lists and publish rules.

Official diagnostic manuals have not yet obtained consensus about the best terminology for this personality feature. The *Diagnostic and Statistical Manual of Mental Disorders* of the American Psychiatric Association has displayed an ironic level of indecisiveness (often a clue to underlying obsessiveness) by switching back and forth between the terms "compulsive personality disorder" and "obsessive-compulsive personality disorder" with each of the first four editions of the manual. At least two other terms in the literature are used to describe obsessiveness. Freudians often use the term "anal" character type, reflecting the psychosexual stage they consider crucial to the development of this trait and the *International Classification of Diseases* (ICD-10) uses the term, "anakastic" personality.

Early descriptions of obsessiveness by personality theorists tended to view the concept not as a single trait component among a constellation of personality dimensions but rather as a broad personality type that enveloped virtually all aspects of interpersonal functioning. In 1921, Abraham expanded on the Freudian concept of the anal type with a rich description of character traits that have been concisely summarized in a review by Oldham and Frosch (1988):

Abraham emphasized the compulsive person's pleasure in indexing, classifying, and compiling lists, his tendency to arrange things symmetrically and to divide things with minute exactness, and his ambivalence toward order or cleanliness betrayed by fastidiousness on the surface but disarray or lack of cleanliness underneath. He also noted the compulsive person's pleasure in possession, often resulting in an inability to throw away worn out or worthless objects. The compulsive's penchant to postpone every action is combined with an often unproductive perseverance and preoccupation with preserving correct social appearances. Yet, in close personal relationships, the compulsive refuses to accommodate himself to others, expects compliance, has an exaggerated criticism of others, and insists on controlling interactions with others. Finally, Abraham noted the generally morose or surly attitude of the compulsive, reflecting a state of constant tension. (p. 245)

MEASUREMENT OF OBESSIONALITY

Concise descriptions are useful, but empirical research requires a reliable system of measurement. Lazare, Klerman, and Armor (1966, 1970) were the first to systematically measure obsessionality using a self-report measure that was validated by factor analysis. The Lazare-Klerman Trait Scale (LKTS) consists of 200 true-false items. Three dimensions are measured, the oral (dependent), obsessive, and hysterical personality constructs. The components that make up the obsessive dimension are listed in Table 10.1. A comparison of the DSM-IV (American Psychiatric Association [APA], 1994) criteria for Obsessive-Compulsive Personality Disorder (OCPD) in Table 10.1 with the LKTS content areas reveals more similarity than differences.

Most self-report personality measures have avoided the use of traditional personality "types" as their starting point and have instead attempted to let traits and factor structures define the scales. An obsessive-compulsive factor has generally emerged from these analyses, but it tends to be a more narrowly defined component that can vary independently from many other dimensions of personality. For example, the Neuroticism, Extroversion, Openness to Excellence Personality Inventory (NEO-PI; Costa & McCrae, 1985) includes a Conscientiousness Factor with the following facets: competence, order, dutifulness, achievement striving, self-discipline, and deliberation. The Schedule for Normal and Abnormal Personality (SNAP; Clark, 1992), covers many of the same components with the following trait scales: Propriety, Workaholism, (low) impulsivity, and (low) disinhibition.

The Minnesota Multiphasic Personality Inventory (MMPI; Hathaway, 1989) includes an Obsessive-Compulsive scale (CPS) that McCann

TABLE 10.1   Scales and Criteria Sets for Measuring Obsessive-Compulsive Personality Traits

LKTS Obsessionality Dimension	MCMI-II Scale 7 and Subfactors[b]
Orderliness	Restraint
Strong Superego	Interpersonal Ambivalence
Perseverance	(low) Sensation Seeking
Obstinacy	Irritable/Intolerant
Rigidity	
Parsimony	**SNAP Selected Trait Scales**
Emotional Constriction	**Encompassing Compulsiveness**
(Rejection of others)[a]	Propriety
(Self-Doubt)[a]	Workaholism
	(low) Impulsivity
MMPI Compulsive Scale and Subfactors[b]	(low) Disinhibition
Obsessive Preoccupation	
Indecisiveness/Worry	**DSM-IV**
	Preoccupation with Details/Rules
NEO-PI Conscientiousness Factor	Perfectionism
Competence	Devotion to Work
Order	Overconscientiousness
Dutifulness	"Pack Rat"
Achievement Striving	Reluctant to Delegate
Self-Discipline	Miserly
Deliberation	Rigidity and Stubbornness

[a] Items in parentheses were not consistently supported by factor analyses.
[b] Component factors were suggested by analyses of a clinical sample by McCann (1992).

(1992) found may have at least two subfactors—Obsessive Preoccupation and Indecisiveness/Worry. Finally Scale 7 of the Millon Clinical Multiaxial Inventory (MCMI-II; Millon, 1987) captures many of the same concepts that, according to McCann, may include four subfactors—restraint, interpersonal ambivalence, (low) sensation seeking, and irritable/intolerant.

In addition to trait measures of the compulsiveness dimension, some of these same instruments and some structured interviews purport to assess the presence or absence of the DSM-IV category of Obsessive-Compulsive Personality Disorder (OCPD). The full text of the DSM-IV defines the threshold for each of the eight criteria in such a way that distress or impairment must be present. This contrasts with most of the preceding trait scales in which abnormality is defined in terms of deviation from the mean. For example, an individual who scores two standard deviations above the mean on the NEO-PI Conscientiousness Factor does not necessarily have distress or impairment.

Research would be considerably simplified if the various approaches to measuring obsessiveness-compulsive personality traits all agreed with each other. At best, there is moderate correlation between measures. For example, Soldz (1993) and colleagues found that Scale 7 on MCMI-II shows a moderate positive correlation with the Conscientiousness Factor on the NEO-PI and a slightly weaker negative correlation with the Extroversion Factor of the NEO-PI. In contrast, the same investigators report that when the OCPD is measured using the Personality Disorder Examination (PDE; Loranger, 1994), a clinical semistructured interview, there is a moderate *negative* correlation with the NEO-PI Conscientiousness Factor. Soldz and colleagues suggest that instruments such as the PDE (which are based directly on DSM OCPD criteria) identify individuals with levels of obsessive personality traits that cause impairment and that this impairment leads to a reduction in some of the behaviors measured by the NEO-PI as Conscientiousness.

This explanation is supported by two other studies. Schroeder, Wormworth, and Livesley (1992) found a strong correlation between the Compulsivity scale of the Dimensional Assessment of Personality Pathology—Basic Questionnaire (DAPP-BQ) and the Conscientiousness scale of the NEO-PI in a general population sample. In contrast, Trull (1992) found a negative correlation between the same NEO-PI scale and OCPD as measured by the Structured Interview for DSM-III Personality Disorder (SIDP), a semistructured clinical interview, in a sample of psychiatric outpatients. Pitman and Jenike (1989) report a lack of correspondence between obsessionality as measured on the LKTS scale and a clinician-rated diagnosis of OCPD in a series of obsessive-compulsive disorder patients and healthy controls.

The overall score on the MMPI Compulsive scale (CPS) shows little or no correlation with the MCMI Obsessive-Compulsive Scale (Scale 7). McCann (1992) compared these two instruments in a diagnostically mixed group of psychiatric inpatients and found that the CPS could be broken down into four identifiable factors and that Scale 7 included at least two factors (see descriptors in Table 10.1). The Irritable/Intolerant factor on Scale 7 was significantly correlated with the Indecisive/Worry factor on the CPS, but the latter was even more strongly correlated with the Interpersonal Ambivalence factor on Scale 7.

The alternative personality trait measures of obsessiveness cannot be considered interchangeable. However, even among instruments that were designed to directly assess DSM Obsessive-Compulsive Personality Disorder, the agreement is poor (Reich, 1987).

THE NATURE AND CAUSE OF OBSESSIVENESS

Earlier in this century, psychoanalysts proposed that obsessive-compulsive personality traits resulted from conflicts between parent and child during the anal stage of psychosexual development when toilet training becomes a major issue. Pollak (1979) reviews more than a dozen studies that attempt to systematically assess obsessiveness as a function of childhood experience with toilet training without establishing any clear connection. More recent studies also fail to find a relationship between parental child-rearing practices and obsessiveness in offspring. Benjaminsen, Jorgensen, Kragh-Hansen, and Pedersen (1984) used a fairly comprehensive self-report measure of memories of parental rearing practices among 200 healthy volunteers and found no correlation between this measure and the obsessive scale on the LKTS.

Some of the most interesting findings for personality research come from genetic research employing the twin study method. Higher concordance rates for personality traits among monozygotic versus dizygotic twins represent a powerful argument for a genetic effect, particularly when monozygotic twins raised apart show a similar high concordance rate. Bergman and colleagues (1993) studied several hundred pairs of twins identified by the Swedish Twin Registry. They reported that genetic influences accounted for 29% of the variance on the NEO-PI's Conscientiousness factor. Tellegen and colleagues (1988) found heritabilities in the 40% range for measures of control and achievement using the Multidimensional Personality Questionnaire (MPQ) to study twins from the Minnesota Twin Registry.

Not all genetic studies of obsessiveness have been positive. Torgersen (1980) applied the twin method to a set of twins from a mixed community/clinical sample in Sweden and failed to find a significant genetic effect on the obsessive scale of LKTS. Loehlin, Horn, and Willerman (1981) used an adoption methodology and failed to find a significant genetic association for the conscientiousness factor of the California Psychological Inventory (CPI).

Loehlin (1992) completed a meta-analysis of six adoption studies and found that the variance was generally explained by genetic effects and nonshared environment. He notes that few studies suggest that shared environment accounts for a significant amount of personality variance. In other words, the environment that two individuals growing up in the same household share in common appears to account for little in determining obsessive-compulsiveness personality traits (or most other personality traits). This suggests that the environmental effects that do influence personality traits are highly specific to an individual. It is important to fully consider the implications of this finding. It seems astounding that living in the same house, sharing the same family rituals, experiencing the same parental role models, walking down the same neighborhood streets, and going to the same schools has virtually no measurable effect for most personality traits. Although no two individuals share exactly the same environment, the absence of a shared environment effect suggests that the environmental factors that do influence personality disorder must be extremely capricious. Yet it hardly seems tenable that individual experiences such as getting lost in a department store at age 6 or receiving a teddy bear instead of a doll for a birthday present has a powerful effect on personality while all the elements that families share have no measurable effect. Smith (1993) has suggested that much of the nongenetic variance in personality may be explained by ". . . the brain itself, as an inherently indeterminate dynamic system." If this is true, our ability to understand the influence of environment on personality may be no more precise than our ability to predict which tree in a forest will be struck by lightning.

Cloninger (1987) has suggested that a number of key personality traits may be directly influenced by the activity of specific neurotransmitters. He has developed a personality questionnaire, the Tridimensional Personality Questionnaire (TPQ) to measure these personality traits. Although he does not propose an obsessive-compulsive factor as such, he does propose a trait called, "Harm Avoidance" that he believes is related to serotonin activity in the brain. Low serotonin activity has been related to Obsessive-Compulsive Disorder (Zohar, Insel, Zohar-Kadouch, Hill, & Murphy, 1988) and high serotonin activity to impulsiveness (Brown et al., 1982), which can be viewed as the antithesis of the rigidity and overcontrol that defines OCPD. Studies examining the association between measures of serotonin activity and personality have yielded mixed results (Pfohl, Black, Noyes, Kelley, & Blum, 1990).

A final clue to the possible origins of obsessiveness comes from studies of the effects of brain lesions on personality. Cummings (1993) provides a recent review of the literature and concludes that connections between the frontal lobes and thalamus play a critical role in inhibiting impulsivity. Patients with frontal lobe injuries exhibit problems with flexibility in responding to environmental demands, and surgical lesions of the midline frontal tracts appear to reduce symptoms of obsessive-compulsive disorder.

These limited findings can hardly be considered a complete explanation of the obsessive-compulsive personality dimension, but the available fragments suggest that this personality dimension may someday be shown to be controlled by the activity of specific neurotransmitter systems operating in localized brain regions which develop under the influence of still to be delineated genetic and environmental influences.

ASSOCIATED TRAITS AND PSYCHOPATHOLOGY

Obsessiveness would appear to be unlikely to occur in the presence of certain other personality types such as histrionic or borderline personality disorder, especially when defined broadly as a personality type. For example, the DSM-IV criteria for OCPD would appear to be the antithesis of borderline personality disorder, which is defined with such words as impulsiveness, unstable relationships, affective instability; or histrionic personality disorder, which is described with such words as exaggerated expression of emotion, shallow, impressionistic, and lacking in detail. In contrast, paranoid personality might be expected to overlap somewhat with a broad definition of obsessiveness because DSM-III-R uses such words as bears grudges, questions loyalty and trustworthiness of others, and, is reluctant to confide in others.

Table 10.2 presents the rates of comorbid DSM personality diagnoses reported in several different studies of involving clinical populations. It shows that even personality types which appear antithetical to obsessive-compulsive personality may be comorbid. This finding may relate to the fact that the presence of almost any psychiatric disorder can be demonstrated to increase the relative risk for almost any other psychiatric disorder (Kessler et al., 1994). The lack of specificity in comorbidity rates may reflect the existence of one or more dimensions of psychopathology that cross the traditional categories of psychiatric disorder.

Nestadt and colleagues (1994), examined this issue in a large general population sample collected as part of the Baltimore component of the Epidemiologic Catchment Area (ECA) study. Psychiatrists rated 93 DSM-III-R personality characteristics for each subject. These data were then subjected to dichotomous factor analysis to reduce the influence of more severely disordered individuals who might otherwise skew the distribution. Most of the variance was accounted for by five factors that generally crossed the boundaries of the various DSM-III-R personality disorders. However, the investigators found that obsessive-compulsive personality disorder was less multifactorial than most other personality disorders in that nearly all the criterion traits for this disorder loaded on a single factor labeled "scrupulousness."

Several other studies, some using clinical samples, also report that OCPD is more unifactorial than other DSM personality disorders (Hyler & Lyons, 1988; Kass, Skodol, Charles, Spitzer, & Williams, 1985). It is possible that the previously noted overlap with other personality disorders occurs because the other disorders are relatively more heterogeneous and contain a number of different factors of which obsessiveness is only one factor and not because obsessive-compulsive personality disorder is multifactorial. This possibility is not necessarily incompatible with the previously mentioned studies, which show, for example, that OCPD loads on several of the NEO-PI factors; it is possible that a rotation of the NEO-PI factors could yield a single factor that would correlate strongly with OCPD.

TABLE 10.2 Percentage of Obsessive-Compulsive PD Patients with Selected Comorbid PD Diagnoses

Authors	Criteria	OCPD Cases	Sample Size	Paranoid (%)	Histrionic (%)	Borderline (%)	Narcissistic (%)	Avoidant (%)
Pfohl et al. (1986)	DSM-III	7	131	0	43	29	14	29
Zanarini et al. (1988)	DSM-III	17	253	17	39	72	28	50
Morey (1988)	DSM-III-R	23	291	22	13	9	30	56
Skodol et al. (1988)	DSM-III-R	21	97	33	24	86	48	62
Pfohl & Blum (1991)	DSM-III-R	31	112	52	36	26	16	52
Pfohl & Blum (1991)	Modified*	19	112	68	37	16	26	47

Note: From "Obsessive-Compulsive Personality Disorder: A Review of Available Data and Recommendations for DSM-IV," by B. Pfohl and N. Blum, 1991, *Journal of Personality Disorders, 5*, p. 371. Copyright 1991 by Guilford Press. Reprinted by permission.

* The modified criteria are identical to DSM-III-R criteria except Criterion 5 was deleted from the compulsive PD criteria and five of the remaining eight criteria were required for diagnosis.

It is also worth considering whether obsessiveness is a relevant risk factor for psychiatric syndromes other than personality disorder. Despite the similarity in names, several reviews of the literature have concluded there is at best a weak association between obsessive-compulsive disorder and various measures of obsessive-compulsive personality (Pfohl & Blum, 1991; Pollak, 1979). Studies do not support that obsessive-compulsive disorder is simply a more extreme form of obsessive personality. On the other hand, the presence of OCPD traits appears to predict an increased risk for anxiety disorders, especially generalized anxiety disorder and social phobia (Nestadt, Romanoski, Samuels, Folstein, & McHugh, 1992).

A number of investigators have reported obsessionality as a risk factor for clinical depression (Lichtermann, Minges, & Heun, 1992). A recent review notes that the relationship appears to be inconsistent and perhaps dependent on the exact scales used to measure obsessionality (Pfohl & Blum, 1991). Trull (1992) reported on a population-based sample of 468 young adults who were assessed for a variety of clinical syndromes and followed longitudinally. The Conscientiousness scale on the NEO-PI was negatively associated with various types of substance abuse as well as being a negatively associated risk for major depression.

DIRECTIONS FOR FUTURE RESEARCH

As with any personality dimension, the value of the obsessive-compulsive personality construct rests on its internal consistency, longitudinal stability, and predictive validity. At the present time, researchers face a difficult choice of alternative instruments for defining and measuring this construct because the various measures are far from interchangeable. The best approach may be to select at least two instruments. This will increase the number of data sets that can be directly compared with each other and will allow for the comparison of the performance of different instruments against measures of predictive validity.

More research should be directed toward understanding why measures that at least superficially appear to measure the same construct can be uncorrelated or even negatively correlated. Some of the discrepancy can be explained by the differences between pathological levels of obsessive-compulsive personality traits and the ranges of these traits seen in a general population. The Schedule for Nonadaptive and Adaptive Personality (SNAP) may prove a useful tool for exploring the effects of severity pathology on measurement because the SNAP includes items measuring the DSM criteria for personality disorders as well as items measuring nonpathological levels of personality traits.

There may be another reason for poor agreement among different measures of compulsivity. For any data set, there are multiple factor rotations (different ways of defining factors), all of which account for the same proportion of total variance. Even when two different personality instruments each have factors labeled compulsivity, the compulsivity on one instrument might correlate with several different factors on the second instrument and vice versa. In this case, empirical research may offer little help in determining which rotation is "right."

Solutions that cannot be determined mathematically may need to be addressed bureaucratically. The real value of the DSM system is not that all the diagnoses are valid, but that the various criteria sets represent a common language and a common starting point for research that will inevitably lead to iterative changes in the diagnostic criteria. It may be very helpful to the field of personality disorder research for psychiatrists and psychologists to define a common set of "official" personality dimensions that could serve as a common language. Alternative approaches and factor structures would still be studied, but the performance of alternative approaches would all be measured against the official benchmark. The PD definitions in DSM-IV are not adequate for this purpose because the criteria are defined around pathological levels of impairment and because the personality categories do not represent a coherent factor structure.

Eventually, genetics, neurobiology, and even psychopharmacology may help define the most appropriate personality dimensions. The most productive strategy for genetic research may be to simultaneously study genetic associations for Axis I and Axis II disorders because a number of the disorders seem to be related to genetic factors that cross both axes. Investigations of inheritance patterns for different personality traits may provide a useful guide for refining concepts and definitions. This will be especially true if a single major gene can be associated to a given personality trait. In contrast, if it turns out that all major personality traits are highly polygenetic, inheritance patterns may be equally compatible with a variety of factor solutions.

Even if personality traits are polygenetic, a specific factor structure may be favored by biological factors such as neurotransmitter activity. Finally, studies suggesting that psychoactive medications may have a role in the treatment of certain personality pathology (Soloff, 1990) have important implications for how personality traits are defined. As Kramer (1993) has pointed out, developments in psychopharmacology have greatly influenced the way psychiatric syndromes have been defined over the past 30 years. It is quite possible that psychopharmacology may have a role to play in how we conceptualize personality in the future.

REFERENCES

American Psychiatric Association. (1994). *Diagnostic and statistical manual of mental disorders* (4th ed.). Washington, DC: Author.

Benjaminsen, S., Jorgensen, J., Kragh-Hansen, L., & Pedersen, L. L. (1984). Memories of parental rearing practices and personality features. *Acta Psychiatrica Scandinavia, 69,* 426–434.

Bergman, C. S., Chipuer, H. M., Plomin, R., Pedersen, N. L., McClearn, G. E., Nesselroade, J. R., Costa, P. T., Jr., & McCrae, R. R. (1993). Genetic and environmental effects on openness to experience, agreeableness, and conscientiousness: An adoption/twin study. *Journal of Personality, 61,* 159–178.

Brown, G. L., Ebert, M. H., Goyer, P. F., Jimerson, D. C., Klein, W. J., Bunney, W. E., & Goodwin, F. K. (1982). Aggression, suicide, and serotonin. Relationships to CSF amine metabolites. *American Journal of Psychiatry, 139,* 741–746.

Clark, L. A. (1992). *Manual for the Schedule for Normal and Abnormal Personality.* Minneapolis: University of Minnesota Press.

Cloninger, C. R. (1987). A systematic method for clinical description and classification of personality variants: A proposal. *Archives of General Psychiatry, 44,* 573–588.

Costa, P. T., Jr., & McCrae, R. R. (1985). *The NEO Personality Inventory manual.* Odessa, FL: Psychological Assessment Resources.

Costa, P. T., Jr., & McCrae, R. R. (1992). The five-factor model of personality and its relevance to personality disorders. *Journal of Personality Disorder, 6,* 343–359.

Hathaway, S. R. (1989). MMPI-2: *Minnesota Multiphasic Personality Inventory-2: Manual for administration and scoring.* Minneapolis: University of Minnesota Press.

Hyler, S. E., & Lyons, M. (1988). Factor analysis of the DSM-III personality disorder clusters: A replication. *Comprehensive Psychiatry, 29,* 304–308.

Kass, F., Skodol, A. E., Charles, E., Spitzer, R. L., & Williams, J. B. (1985). Scaled ratings of DSM-III personality disorders. *American Journal of Psychiatry, 142,* 627–630.

Kessler, R. C., McGonagle, K. A., Zhao, S., Nelson, C. B., Hughes, M., Eshleman, S., Wittchen, H. U., & Kendler, K. S. (1994). Lifetime and 12-month prevalence of DSM-III-R psychiatric disorders in the United States. Results from the National Comorbidity Survey. *Archives of General Psychiatry, 51,* 8–19.

Kramer, P. D. (1993). *Listening to prozac.* New York: Viking.

Lazare, A., Klerman, G., & Armor, D. J. (1966). Oral, obsessive and hysterical personality patterns. *Archives of General Psychiatry, 14,* 624–630.

Lazare, A., Klerman, G., & Armor, D. J. (1970). Oral, obsessive and hysterical personality patterns: Replication of factor analysis in an independent sample. *Journal of Psychiatric Research, 7,* 275–279.

Lichtermann, M. W., Minges, J., & Heun, R. (1992). Personality traits in subjects at risk for unipolar major depression: A family study perspective. *Journal of Affective Disorder, 24,* 153–163.

Loehlin, J. C. (1992). *Genes and environment in personality development.* Newbury Park, CA: Sage Publications.

Loehlin, J. C., Horn, J. M., & Willerman, L. (1981). Personality resemblance in adoptive families. *Behavior Genetics, 11,* 309–330.

Loranger, A. W. (1994). The International Personality Disorder Examination: The World Health Organization/Alcohol, Drug Abuse, and Mental Health Administration international pilot study of personality disorders. *Archives of General Psychiatry, 51,* 215–224.

McCann, J. T. (1992). A comparison of two measures for obsessive-compulsive personality disorder. *Journal of Personality Disorder, 6,* 18–23.

Millon, T. (1987). *Manual for the Millon Clinical Multiaxial Inventory-II (MCMI-II).* Minneapolis, MN: National Computer Systems.

Nestadt, G., Eaton, W. W., Romanoski, A. J., Garrison, R., Folstein, M. F., & McHugh, P. R. (1994). Assessment of DSM-III personality structure in a general-population survey. *Comprehensive Psychiatry, 35,* 54–63.

Nestadt, G., Romanoski, A. J., Samuels, J. F., Folstein, M. F., & McHugh, P. R. (1992). The relationship between personality and DSM-III Axis I disorders in the general population. *American Journal of Psychiatry, 149,* 1228–1233.

Pfohl, B., Black, D., Noyes, R., Kelley, M., & Blum, N. (1990). A test of the Tridimensional Personality Theory: Association with diagnosis and platelet imipramine binding in obsessive-compulsive disorder. *Biologic Psychiatry, 28,* 41–46.

Pfohl, B., & Blum, N. (1991). Obsessive-compulsive personality disorder: A review of available data and recommendations for DSM-IV. *Journal of Personality Disorder, 5,* 363–375.

Pfohl, B., Coryell, W., Zimmerman, M., & Stangl, D. (1986). DSM-III personality disorders: Diagnostic overlap and internal consistency of individual DSM-III criteria. *Comprehensive Psychiatry, 27,* 21–34.

Pitman, R. K., & Jenike, M. A. (1989). Normal and disordered compulsivity: Evidence against a continuum. *Journal of Clinical Psychiatry, 50,* 450–452.

Pollak, J. M. (1979). Obsessive-compulsive personality: A review. *Psychological Bulletin, 86,* 225–241.

Pollak, J. M. (1987). Relationship of obsessive-compulsive personality to obsessive-compulsive disorder: A review of the literature. *Journal of Psychology, 121,* 137–148.

Reich, J., Noyes, R., & Troughton, E. (1987). Comparison of instruments to measure DSM-III Axis II. In T. Millon (Ed.), *Proceedings of the Millon Clinical Multiaxial Inventory Conference 1986* (pp. 223–235). Minneapolis, MN: National Computer Systems.

Schroeder, M. L., Wormworth, J. A., & Livesley, W. J. (1992). Dimensions of personality and their relationships to the big five dimensions of personality. *Psychological Assessment, 4,* 47–53.

Soldz, S. (1993). Diagnostic agreement between the Personality Disorder Examination and the MCMI-II. *Journal of Personality Assessment, 60,* 486–499.

Soloff, P. H. (1990). What's new in personality disorders? An update on pharmacologic treatment. *Journal of Personality Disorders, 4,* 223–243.

Soloff, P. H., Anselm, G., Nathan, S., Schulz, P., Ulrich, R. F., & Perel, J. M. (1986). Progress in pharmacotherapy of borderline disorders. *Archives of General Psychiatry, 43,* 691–697.

Tellegen, A., Lykken, D. T., Bouchard, T. J., Wilcox, K. J., Segal, N. L., & Rich, S. (1988). Personality similarity in twins reared apart and together. *Journal of Personality and Social Psychology, 54,* 1031–1039.

Torgersen, S. (1980). The oral, obsessive and hysterical personality syndromes: A study of hereditary and environmental factors by means of the twin method. *Archives of General Psychiatry, 37,* 1272–1277.

Trull, T. J. (1992). DSM-III-R personality disorders and the five-factor model of personality: An empirical comparison. *Journal of Abnormal Psychology, 101,* 553–560.

Trull, T. J., & Sher, T. (1994). Relationship between the five-factor model of personality and Axis I disorders in a nonclinical sample. *Journal of Abnormal Psychology, 103,* 350–360.

Zohar, J., Insel, T. R., Zohar-Kadouch, R. C., Hill, J. L., & Murphy, D. L. (1988). Serotonergic responsivity in obsessive-compulsive disorder. *Archives of General Psychiatry, 45,* 167–172.

CHAPTER 11

Sensation Seeking

MARVIN ZUCKERMAN

COMPONENTS OF THE SENSATION SEEKING TRAIT

There is general agreement that personality disorders represent extreme and maladaptive extremes of normal dimensions of personality (Livesley, Schroeder, Jackson, & Jang, 1994). In this chapter, I will present the thesis that a component of certain personality disorders is a trait I call "Impulsive Unsocialized Sensation Seeking" (ImpUSS, Zuckerman, 1989, 1993a, 1993b, 1994a, 1994b). This trait is one of a basic set of five traits defined by factor analyses of scales regarded as markers for basic dimensions of personality or temperament (Zuckerman, Kuhlman, & Camac, 1988; Zuckerman, Kuhlman, Thornquist, & Kiers, 1991), many of which have been used in studies of the psychobiology of personality (Zuckerman, 1991). The three components of this supertrait are impulsivity, socialization, and sensation seeking. The close link between impulsivity and sensation seeking had been noted for some years (Zuckerman, 1979; Zuckerman, 1993a) and recent factor analyses of items adapted from the scales used in the earlier study (Zuckerman, 1991) revealed a replicable supertrait incorporating both impulsivity and sensation seeking items (ImpSS; Zuckerman, Kuhlman, Joireman, Teta, & Kraft, 1993). Because Barratt and Stanford have discussed the trait of impulsivity in Chapter 4 in this volume, I will focus primarily on the unsocialized sensation seeking component in this chapter.

ImpUSS is highly related to the dimension called "Psychoticism" (P) by H. J. Eysenck and S. B. G. Eysenck (1976) and their P scale (Eysenck, Eysenck, & Barrett, 1985) proved to be one of the best markers for this dimension in factor analyses limited to three factors (Zuckerman et al., 1993). However, the P dimension also includes aggression scales that comprise a third factor in our "alternative" five-factor model (Zuckerman et al., 1993). The ImpSS scale is also strongly (negatively) related to the Conscientious scale, and our Aggression-Hostility scale is strongly (negatively) related to the Agreeableness factor of the "big five" (Costa & McCrae, 1992).

THE SENSATION SEEKING SCALE (SSS)

The ImpSS scale is relatively new and most of the previous research has been done with older forms of the SSS. The concept of sensation seeking has been most recently defined as "The seeking of novel, intense, and complex forms of sensation and experience and the willingness to take risks for the sake of such experience" (Zuckerman, 1994a). Forms IV and V of the SSS incorporated four subscales derived from factor analyses of items. The four subscales may be described in terms of their items as follows:

Thrill and Adventure Seeking (TAS) items express the desire to engage in risky sports or activities providing unusual sensations or out of the ordinary range of experiences such as mountain climbing, parachuting, or scuba diving.

Experience Seeking (ES) items express the desire to expand one's experience through the mind and the senses, through music, art, travel, and an unconventional, nonconforming life style.

Disinhibition (Dis) items refer to the seeking of sensation through social occasions such as parties, social drinking, and attitudes reflecting cynicism and desire for a variety of sexual partners.

Boredom Susceptibility (BS) items reflect a strong aversion to sameness, lack of change, or predictability in activities and friends and a general restlessness when there is no novelty or change.

Form IV of the SSS used a *General Scale* derived from previous factor analyses of a more limited set of items in earlier forms, whereas the SSS-V uses a *Total Score,* which is simply the sum of the four subscales.

SENSATION SEEKING IN PERSONALITY DISORDERS

Personality Disorders in the DSM-IV

Impulsive sensation seeking and a lack of socialization are traits that have long been associated with certain personality disorders. Three of the four personality disorders in Cluster B of the *Diagnostic and Statistical Manual of Mental Disorders* (DSM-IV; American Psychiatric Association [APA], 1994) incorporate ImpUSS traits in their description. In *antisocial personalities,* "decisions are made on the spur of the moment, without foresight, and without consideration for the consequences to self or others," and these personalities have ". . . a reckless disregard for the safety of themselves or others" (APA, 1994, p. 646) as manifested in speeding and reckless driving, driving when drunk, reckless sexual behavior, and substance abuse. They are also characterized as having a "history of many sexual partners" and an "inability to tolerate boredom" (p. 647). Persons who engage in all these exemplars of antisocial behavior have been found to be high sensation seekers as defined by scores on the SSS (Zuckerman, 1994a). Impulsive sensation seeking is also a central part of earlier descriptions of the psychopathic personality by Cleckley (1976) and Quay (1965). Two of the items in Hare's (1991) Psychopathy Checklist-Revised are "need for stimulation/proneness to boredom" and "impulsivity."

In DSM-IV, the *borderline personality* is characterized by "impulsivity in at least two areas that are potentially self-damaging" (APA, 1994, p. 651) such as gambling, spending money irresponsibly, binge eating, substance abuse, engaging in unsafe sex, and driving recklessly. Unlike the antisocial personality, however, the borderline personality is also characterized by highly reactive depressive moods and a neurotic fear of rejection. The *histrionic personality* is described as sexually provocative or seductive and someone who "craves novelty, stimulation, and excitement and has a tendency to become bored with their usual routine" (APA, 1994, p. 656). Most of the research on sensation seeking has been done on delinquency, conduct disorder, antisocial personality disorder, and criminality. There is one study of sensation seeking in the borderline personality and none of histrionic personality.

Substance abuse (both alcoholism and drug abuse) is a clinical disorder with a high degree of comorbidity with antisocial personality disorder (Wolf et al., 1988). Disinhibition and experience seeking are prominent motives for substance abuse and therefore the sensation seeking personality would be expected to be found with high frequency in substance abusers compared with abstainers and normal users of substances.

Each type of disorder usually involves a high level of more than one personality trait (Widiger & Costa, 1994). In this sense they may be regarded as "types" rather than "trait" extremes. Traits like sensation seeking are not necessarily pathological even in the extreme ranges. It is only when combined with extremes on other traits that they become involved in disorders. Most high sensation seekers are not antisocial, for instance, but most antisocial personalities are high sensation seekers. It is the combination of sensation seeking, impulsivity, *and* lack of socialization that underlies the antisocial personality disorder. The form of expression taken by a trait is also of crucial importance in determining whether it will be maladaptive. A potentially neurotic personality may be compensated by the use of predominantly mature defenses (Vaillant, 1994). In one environment, a high sensation seeker may find adequate expressions in risky sports or disinhibited but not antisocial behavior; but in another environment, drugs and criminality may be the primary expression for the trait.

Conduct Disorder and Antisocial Personality Disorder

To be diagnosed as an adult personality disorder, one must be at least 18 years of age and have a history of conduct disorder before the age of 15 (APA, 1994). Thus the antisocial personality disorder is defined as a long-standing disorder in order to exclude the kinds of delinquency that appear in many children in preadolescence and adolescence but disappear with the attainment of adult maturity. Conduct disorders in children are defined by truancy, running away from home, starting fights, using weapons, rape, sadistic behavior toward people or animals, vandalism, fire setting, lying, and stealing.

Russo et al. (1991) developed a children's version of the SSS containing a total score and only two subscales resembling the adult TAS and BS scales. Children from a child guidance clinic were divided into three groups: conduct disorder (CD), attention deficit with hyperactivity (ADHD), and anxiety disorder (ANX). The CD group had the highest scores, but when the subjects who had both CD and ANX disorders were compared with controls, they were not higher than nonclinic controls. The distinction between CD with and without anxiety resembles a distinction made between primary and secondary psychopaths: the primary psychopath is said to have little anxiety or depression whereas the secondary psychopath has considerable anxiety in addition to impulsivity. The secondary psychopath is regarded as a neurotic who uses acting-out as a method of defense.

Russo et al. (1993) revised the children's SSS; the new scale includes three subscales: TAS, Social Disinhibition, and Drug and Alcohol Attitudes. A new CD group scored higher than the non-CD clinic cases on all three scales, but did not differ significantly from normal children on any of the scales. The difference between this result in the two studies may be due to the absence of a BS scale in the second version of the children's SSS. The non-CD cases were lower than normals on all three scales.

Whereas highly anxious children might be expected to be low on sensation seeking, theory and observation would predict that hyperactive children would be high, rather than low on this trait. Hyperactives need a lot of variety in stimulation to keep them from becoming restless and inattentive. Stimulant drugs tend to normalize their behavior suggesting that their lack of attention and hyperactivity stem from an underaroused nervous system and a consequent need for novel and intense stimulation to raise their arousal levels. But Salkind (1981) reported similar findings to those of Russo using another children's SSS. One study, however, found that hyperactive children scored higher than normals on an SSS form more like the adult SSS in form and content (Shaw & Brown, 1990).

Primary and secondary psychopaths were compared in studies by Blackburn (1978, 1987) and Emmons and Webb (1974). Blackburn (1978) and Emmons and Webb classified prison inmates into three groups: primary psychopaths, secondary psychopaths, and nonpsychopaths. Both studies used psychometric criteria to make the distinction between primary and secondary types, but different criteria were used in the two studies. Both used the MMPI Psychopathic Deviate (*Pd*) scale to distinguish psychopaths from nonpsychopaths, but Blackburn used a sociability scale whereas Emmons and Webb used an anxiety scale to make the distinction between primary and secondary psychopaths. In both studies, the SSS IV Dis scale best discriminated between the three groups, although other SS subscales also significantly differentiated them. The primary psychopath had the highest scores, the nonpsychopathic prisoners had the lowest scores, and the secondary psychopath had intermediate scores on the SSS. A similar finding of a difference between psychopathic and nonpsychopathic prisoners was reported by Deforest and Johnson (1981) for the SSS Total Score.

Blackburn (1987) later developed scales to classify prisoners and found evidence for two factors, Belligerence (*B*) and Withdrawal (*W*). Primary psychopaths were defined as those who scored high on *B* and low on *W*, whereas secondary psychopaths were described as those who scored high on both *B* and *W*. A control group consisted of prisoners who scored low on both scales. Primary psychopaths were higher than secondary psychopaths on the Total and Dis scales of the SSS-V, but neither of these groups differed significantly from the controls who tended to score slightly higher than the secondary psychopaths on the SSS.

Many of the items constituting the *B* factor were drawn from scales for hostility and aggression as well as impulsivity and psychopathic deviancy scales. Berman and Paisey (1984) found that juvenile offenders who were sentenced for crimes of violence had higher scores on the General SSS (Form IV), as well as Dis, ES, TAS, and BS subscales, than offenders convicted for simple property crimes. Farley and Farley (1972) compared incarcerated female delinquents who scored high or low on the SSS and found that the highs made more escape attempts, were punished for disobeying the warders, and engaged in more fighting than the low sensation seekers. Farley (personal communication, 1973) said that similar results were found for incarcerated male delinquents. Shoham, Askenasy, Rahav,

Chard, and Addi (1989) classified adult prisoners as violent and nonviolent and found that violent prisoners had higher scores on the SSS General Scale (no other scales were used). Although the violent prisoners were younger, they had spent a longer time in jail during their careers, a sign of psychopathy. Breivik (personal communications, 1991, 1993) found that Norwegian prisoners convicted for robbery, murder, or other violent or drug-related crimes had higher SSS scores than those convicted for sexual or economic crimes and their scores were at the level of a group of adventurous noncriminal sportsmen.

Although juvenile and adult offenders do not seem to differ as a group from their peers, sensation seeking separates the more violent and psychopathic offenders from the ordinary, nonviolent felons. However, much delinquent behavior goes on in adolescents that does not result in imprisonment for the offenders. A number of studies have shown that self-reported delinquency and crime in anonymously administered questionnaires correlates with sensation seeking (Horvath & Zuckerman, 1993; Perez & Torrubia, 1985; Simo & Perez, 1991; Wallbank, 1985; Wasson, 1981). Newcomb and McGee (1991) and White, LaBouvie, and Bates (1985) found that sensation seeking not only related concurrently to delinquent behavior but also predicted later delinquency in young adolescents.

Diagnosis of antisocial personalities from self-report psychometric instruments alone is a dubious procedure given their famous ability to lie when it suits their purposes. Hare and Cox (1978) devised a Psychopathy Check List (PCL) to be used by raters after an extensive review of the case history and an intensive interview with the subject. Subjects are rated on 22 characteristics that combine behavioral characteristics and personality trait definitions from Cleckley (1976). A factor analysis of the PCL found two replicable factors: Factor 1 includes personality characteristics such as egocentricity, insincerity, lack of strong emotions and empathy with others; Factor 2 describes criteria based on objective records of antisocial behavior rather than the kind of inferential data in Factor 1 (Harpur, Hare, & Hakstian, 1989). Not surprisingly, Factor 2 shows the higher correlations with diagnosis of antisocial personality, behavior in prison, and parole violations.

Sensation seeking and socialization scales correlated significantly with Factor 2 (SSSTotal $r = .39$; Soc $r = -.44$) and the Total PCL, but not at all with Factor 1 ratings (Harpur et al., 1989). The Eysenck Personality Questionnaire (EPQ) P scale also correlated with Factor 2 ratings ($r = .22$). An impulsivity scale did not correlate with either factor. The MMPI Pd and Ma (hypomania) scales also correlated significantly with Factor 2 but not with Factor 1. However, Thornquist and Zuckerman (in press) found that only ImpSS and Agg-Host scales from the Zuckerman-Kuhlman Personality Questionnaire (ZKPQ) correlated with PCL Total and only ImpSS and the EPQ *P* score correlated with Factor 1 ratings, but in this study none of the personality measures correlated with Factor 2 ratings! Even the significant correlations were low for the total group of prisoners, but when the group was divided into ethnic groups, the significant correlations were found only in the whites; none of the correlations were significant in the black subgroup, and only two approached significance in the Hispanic group. ImpSS was related to rated psychopathy (Total PCL) in both studies, but the PCL factor responsible for the correlation was different in the two studies; the Thornquist and Zuckerman study found that the relationship was limited to a white population of prisoners and was not found in blacks or Hispanics. Perhaps the concept of an antisocial personality has certain cultural limitations, or else the concept of sensation seeking as assessed by the SSS has cultural limitations. African-Americans generally score lower than white Americans on all the subscales of the SSS except Disinhibition (Zuckerman, 1979), but this is not true of the ImpSS scale of the ZKPQ which has less culture-bound content.

Substance Abuse

Substance abuse is one of the typical expressions of the antisocial personality. Most persons start abusing alcohol and drugs because these substances provide either direct pleasure and euphoria through central nervous system effects, or indirect pleasure through social disinhibition and enhancement of sexual pleasure (Zuckerman, 1983, 1987a, 1987b). However, once dependency is added to abuse, the drugs are primarily used just to feel normal and to avoid withdrawal discomforts. Sensation seeking is a major personality factor in the individual's experimental use, and abuse stages. High sensation seekers are more prone to drink heavily and more willing to try a variety of drugs beginning with marijuana and sometimes progressing to hard drugs including stimulants, opiates, and narcotics. Sensation seeking is related to the variety, frequency, and dosage of drugs used but not to any particular drug of abuse.

A Theoretical Aside

The findings that use of both central nervous system (CNS) stimulants, such as amphetamine, and CNS depressants, such as opiates, attracted high sensation seekers posed a problem for the earlier theory of sensation seeking (Zuckerman, 1969) based on an optimal level of reticulocortical arousal. However, recent psychopharmacological investigations have found that amphetamine and cocaine stimulants and opiate depressants have their rewarding effects at the two ends of the medial forebrain bundle (stimulants at the nucleus accumbens and opiates at the ventral tegmental area), both acting to release the neurotransmitter dopamine. Amphetamine injected into the nucleus accumbens and opiates injected into the ventral tegmental area both facilitate feeding and perhaps other kinds of reward such as sex (Wise, 1994). These kinds of findings led to a change to the idea of dopaminergic pathways mediating reward and an optimal level of catecholamine system arousal, rather than the optimal level of cortical arousal, as the basis for the trait of sensation seeking (Zuckerman, 1979, 1984). The intense sensations and experiences sought by the sensation seeker may be due more to their capacity to stimulate these primary reward areas of the brain than to activate the reticulocortical arousal system. However, drugs and intense experiences also release norepinephrine, which mediates another cortical arousal system so that cortical arousal may be a secondary effect of excitation of limbic areas. But it is the reward euphoria, not the cortical arousal, that is the point of sensation seeking. If it were just a matter of cortical arousal, this could be achieved by running around the block several times or drinking several cups of coffee with no need to parachute jump or take cocaine.

Classifications of Substance Abusers

As with criminality, sensation seeking is a factor dividing the more antisocial and chronic substance abuser from other abusers. Malatesta, Sutker, and Treiber (1981) contrasted two groups of alcoholics in terms of their history of involuntary admissions to a detoxification facility. The group with the more chronic history of public drunkenness, as assessed by number of admissions to the facility, scored significantly higher on all the SS scales. Both groups were equivalent in terms of age, education, and years of drinking, but the higher sensation seeking group more often violated social norms by displaying their drunkenness in public and running afoul of the police in the course of their binge. Cloninger (1987) described two subgroups of alcoholics: Type I with a relatively late onset often precipitated by environmental stressors and Type II with an early onset, a high genetic loading, and alcohol-related social complications such as job loss, criminal behavior, arrests, drunken driving, and the use of illegal drugs as well as alcohol. Type II alcoholics scored higher than Type I alcoholics and nonalcoholic controls on sensation seeking scales (von Knorring, Bohman, von Knorring, & Oreland, 1985) and on an ImpUSS factor (sensation seeking + impulsiveness − socialization; von Knorring, von Knorring, Smigan, Lindberg, & Edholm, 1987).

Ball, Carroll, Babor, and Rounsaville (1995) devised a similar classification for cocaine abusers. In comparison with Type A abusers, Type B abusers had higher rates of premorbid risk factors such as a family history of substance abuse and childhood behavior symptoms, an earlier onset and more years of cocaine abuse with higher dosages and more frequent use, criminality, aggression and a violent history, and antisocial personality. Type Bs also scored significantly higher than Type As on all of the sensation seeking subscales.

Ball, Carroll, and Rounsaville (1994) found that sensation seeking correlated not only with extent of cocaine use, but also with lifetime use of amphetamines, opiates, hallucinogens, sedatives, and solvents, thus confirming conclusions from earlier research that general sensation seeking is related to extent and variety of drug abuse but not specifically to any particular drug of abuse (Zuckerman, 1983, 1987a). Among their drug-abusing population Ball et al. also found that the General SSS was higher in those who received childhood diagnoses of attention deficit/hyperactivity and conduct disorders, and concurrent adult diagnoses of antisocial personality, alcohol abuse/dependence, and "depressive" disorders. Ball et al. (1995) extended these findings using the ImpSS scale from the ZKPQ in a group of cocaine abusers seeking treatment and found that ImpSS correlated significantly with addiction severity indexes for alcoholism and general drug abuse as well as age of onset, last cocaine use, family history of substance abuse, history of violence, and suicide attempts.

Pathological Gambling Disorder

Although pathological gambling does not involve a substance, it shares many behavioral characteristics with substance abuse disorders. Gambling, like alcohol, for most people is simply a recreational form of sensation seeking, but for a few, it is a highly addictive and uncontrollable impulse that causes severe social and legal consequences. Actually, cross-addictions of gambling to alcohol and drugs are common (Lesieur, Blume, & Zoppa, 1986) perhaps indicating common personality factors such as antisocial and sensation-seeking traits. Custer and Milt (1985) describe the compulsive gambler as someone who needs change, stimulation, and excitement; loves risk, challenge, and adventure; and is easily bored. The description is a perfect fit to sensation seeking.

Actual studies of sensation seeking in pathological gamblers have yielded inconsistent results. Studies of gamblers seeking treatment or in treatment have either showed lower than normative scores or scores not different from those of controls (Allcock & Grace, 1988; Blaszczynski, McConaghy, & Frankova, 1990; Blaszczynski, Wilson, & McConaghy, 1986). However, studies of heavy gamblers who were not seeking treatment, or self-defined as pathological or compulsive gamblers, found them to be higher on sensation seeking or risk taking than low-stake or social gamblers, nongamblers, or exclusively lottery players (Kuley & Jacobs,

1988; Kusyszyn & Rutter, 1985). Furthermore, within groups of gamblers, sensation seeking is correlated with the particular patterns associated with pathological gambling, such as "chasing" after losing and arousal during betting (Anderson & Brown, 1984; Dickerson, Hinchy, & Fabre, 1987).

Personality Disorders Other than Antisocial Personality Disorder

Sensation seeking has not been widely studied in personality disorders other than antisocial personality. However, one study compared male patients diagnosed as borderline personality with a group of "non-Cluster B" personality disorders (avoidant, obsessive-compulsive, schizoid, schizotypal) and normal controls (Reist, Haier, DeMet, & Chicz-DeMet, 1990). The borderline personality disorder patients were significantly higher than both the non-Cluster B personality disorders and the controls on the Total and all the SS subscales except Thrill and Adventure Seeking. The other types of personality disorders did not differ from the controls on any of the SSS scales. In contrast, both borderlines and other personality disorders were higher than controls on scales for anxiety and depression, but the two personality disorder groups were not different on these measures. These findings substantiate the clinical impression that borderlines share the impulsive sensation seeking trait with antisocial personalities, and the dysphoric emotional traits with other personality disorders.

Cyclothymia and Depressive Personality

Although cyclothymia and depressive personalities are not classified as personality disorders, they represent long-standing personality manifestations in contrast to the episodic and more severe expressions seen in bipolar and unipolar clinical disorders. Sensation seeking is high in persons with bipolar disorders regardless of whether they are in a normal phase (Zuckerman & Neeb, 1979), or a depressed or manic phase (Cronin & Zuckerman, 1992) of the disorder. Similarly, major depressive disorders scored low on the SSS during and after recovery from a depressive episode (Carton, Jouvent, Bungener, & Widlöcher, 1992). Apparently, the bipolar and unipolar patients are characterized by sensation seeking aspects of cyclothymia (high SS) and depressive personality (low SS) as part of a personality disorder that accompanies and may also precede the development of the clinical disorder. Even the offspring of bipolars, who have not yet developed the clinical disorder, have high sensation seeking scores (Nurnberger et al., 1988).

BIOLOGICAL CONNECTIONS BETWEEN SENSATION SEEKING AND PERSONALITY DISORDERS

Heredity

Studies of identical and fraternal twins reared together (Fulker, Eysenck, & Zuckerman, 1980), and twins separated after birth and reared apart in different families (Lykken, personal communication, 1992) have shown a high degree of heritability for the trait of sensation seeking (about 60%) and a lack of influence of shared environment. The environmental influences affecting sensation seeking, as for most other broad personality traits, are largely those that are specific to different family members (e.g., specific friends, spouses, lovers). Most of the personality disorders described in this chapter have also been found to have substantial heritability in twin and adoption and familial incidence studies. However, the role of the genotype for personality traits in the clinical traits is not clear and requires special kinds of model testing described by Carey and DiLalla (1994). The finding of high sensation seeking scores in offspring of bipolar patients (Nurnberger et al., 1988), for instance, implies that the sensation seeking genotype is involved in the genotype for bipolar disorder, but is not the direct mediator for the disorder. One strategy is to look for biological traits that are genetic markers for both the disorder and the personality trait.

Monoamine Oxidase (MAO)

Monoamine oxidase assayed from blood platelets constitutes the kind of genetic marker that bridges the genotype-phenotype chasm. Platelet MAO in humans is normally distributed and highly reliable and stable over short time intervals. The level of MAO does show an increase in brain, platelets, and plasma with age but the changes are slow. At all ages, females have higher levels of MAO than males. There are two types of MAO in the human brain, A and B. Platelets contain only the B type, which in the brain seems to be more closely linked with the deamination or catabolic breakdown of the neurotransmitter dopamine than the other monoamines, norepinephrine and serotonin (Murphy, Aulach, Garrick, & Sunderland, 1987). However, platelet MAO activity may be determined by the same set of genes regulating levels of central serotonin turnover, and MAO in the brain is most highly concentrated in serotonergic-rich areas (Oreland, Wilberg, & Fowler, 1981). Thus far, no direct correlations between platelet and MAO in selected brain areas have been found, but indirect assessments suggest that there is a connection, if only limited to certain brain areas (Bench et al., 1991).

Platelet MAO in humans yields nearly total heritabilty in twin studies, comparable to what is found for human height measurements. Studies of the genetic mechanism for MAO suggest only one or two gene loci with two to five alleles to describe the population distribution (Cloninger, von Knorring, & Oreland, 1985; Rice, McGuffin, & Shaskan, 1982). The level of MAO has been found to vary inversely with several personality traits including sensation seeking, impulsivity, and sociability, but the most consistent correlations have been found with sensation seeking (Zuckerman, 1994a); high sensation seekers have low MAO levels. The correlations are low and usually produced by subjects in the lowest decile of the MAO distribution. In 9 of 13 groups, however, the correlations were significant, and in 11 of 13 groups the correlations were negative in sign. What makes these correlations interesting is not their strength (the median correlation is only $-.24$) but consistent findings linking MAO to behavioral and psychopathological phenomena also linked to sensation seeking (Zuckerman, Buchsbaum, & Murphy, 1980).

Coursey, Buchsbaum, and Murphy (1979) selected males with very low MAO levels in the general population and found that they reported more convictions for criminal offenses and used more alcohol, tobacco, and illegal drugs than those with high MAO levels. Shekim et al. (1986) found that MAO was low in 6- to 12-year-old boys with attention disorder, and negatively related to measures of impulsivity and attentiveness. The level of MAO is low in diagnosed antisocial (Lidberg, Modin, Oreland, Tuck, & Gillner, 1985) and borderline (Reist et al., 1990) personality disorders than in normal controls. It is also low in alcoholics (Major & Murphy, 1978), particularly Type II alcoholics (von Knorring et al., 1985), and drug abusers (Sher, Bylund, Walitzer, Hartmann, & Ray-Prenger, 1994), including heavy users of marijuana, barbiturates, amphetamines, hallucinogens, and cocaine. In the latter study, as in studies of personality and behavior and MAO, it was the lowest 10% of the MAO distribution that produced the significant relationships with drug use. Other studies have also found low MAO levels related to substance abuse (Hallman, von Knorring, von Knorring, & Oreland, 1990; Pandey, Fawcett, Gibbons, Clark, & Davis, 1988; Stillman, Wyatt, Murphy, & Rausher, 1978; von Knorring, Oreland, & von Knorring, 1987).

The genetic link between MAO and substance abuse was demonstrated in a study by Purchall, Coursey, and Buchsbaum (1980) where a substantial correlation was found between MAO in children and alcoholism in parents. Among the parents of low MAO children, 19% were diagnosed as alcoholic and 14% as antisocial personalities; but among the parents of high MAO children only 3% of the parents were diagnosed in alcoholic or antisocial categories.

The study by Sher et al. (1994) found both MAO and sensation seeking were related to extent of drug use. Sensation seeking was the stronger correlate so that authors attempted to see if sensation seeking mediated the weaker relationship between MAO and drug use. They found that controlling for the effect of sensation seeking through multiple regression produced little change in the MAO-drug use relationship. Both MAO and sensation seeking were making relatively independent contributions to the prediction of drug use.

Low MAO is found in a spectrum of disorders characterized by disinhibition. It may be hypothesized that the low MAO represents either a dysregulation of dopamine in certain areas of the brain or a weak serotonergic system, or both. A sensation seeking trait in the high normal range may be related to a weaker version of psychopathy or mania, or one without the factors that produce low socialization.

Testosterone

Testosterone in normal males is positively related to sensation seeking, particularly the disinhibitory form (Daitzman & Zuckerman, 1980). Low disinhibiters have normal testosterone levels for their age and highly disinhibited males have higher than normal levels. Testosterone is also related to sociability, dominance, self-acceptance, and heterosexual experience. High testosterone males tend to score *low* on socialization and self-control (scales that constitute the negative pole of the $P-$ImpUSS factor). In women, testosterone is also related to sociability and sexiness and to lack of inhibition, impulsivity, and lack of conformity to the culturally prescribed "female role" (Baucom, Beach, & Callahan, 1985).

Unprovoked aggression is one of the manifestations of antisocial personality. Psychopathic criminals are more dangerous than other criminals because they may kill or injure others for "kicks" (arousal) alone. The relationship between physical aggression and testosterone is clearer in other species than in humans. In males of many other species, the hormone is related to dominance and aggression. Although testosterone in humans is related to dominance, there is little correlation between self-report scales of aggressiveness and testosterone in humans, an exception being the study by Schalling (1987) in which scales for verbal and general aggression and a liking of physical sports were related to testosterone. However, among male delinquents (Mattson, Schalling, Olweus, Low, & Svensson, 1980) and adult prisoners of both sexes (Dabbs, Carr, Frady, & Riad, 1995; Dabbs, Ruback, Frady, Hopper, & Sgoritas, 1988; Kreuz & Rose, 1972; Rada, Laws, & Kellner, 1976), those with histories of particularly violent and unprovoked crimes had higher testosterone levels than other criminals. Ehrenkranz, Bliss, and Sheard (1974) found that high testosterone was associated with either social dominance or aggression in male prisoners while in prison. Perhaps the more dominant prisoners delegate others to carry out their aggressive tasks. Dabbs et al. (1995) reported that high testosterone prisoners were more likely to violate prison rules. In other species, the most dominant (alpha) male rarely has to fight because he is seldom challenged by other males. Challenges to dominance in humans usually do not take the form of physical aggression. Chronic aggression is often associated with criminality, and testosterone distinguishes these types of criminals from others.

Testosterone is associated with normal dominance and sociability, but is also associated with lack of socialization and self-control in normal males, and lack of inhibition and impulsivity in normal females. However, in prisoners of both sexes, high testosterone is associated with a history of aggression and violence. As discussed previously, chronic violence in offenders is associated with more antisocial and sensation seeking tendencies, distinguishing the primary psychopath from the secondary type and other nonpsychopathic criminals.

A study of the effects of self-administration of anabolic-androgenic steroids by male athletes revealed that the steroids produced mania, hypomania, and major depressions in a significant number of them (Pope & Katz, 1994). There was a direct relationship between dosage of steroids and likelihood of manic and depressive episodes. Irrational and violent aggressive behavior often accompanied manic or hypomanic episodes. Although there was a slightly greater incidence of antisocial personality disorder and substance abuse among the users of steroids, most were not taking other drugs at the time they were using the steroids. The results suggest that steroid use can trigger disinhibitory disorders and aggressive behavior that is not normally characteristic of the persons using these steroids.

Augmenting/Reducing of the Cortical Evoked Potential: A Marker for Disinhibition

The cortical evoked response (EP) to a stimulus of a particular intensity is a complex wave form that shows a high degree of similarity in identical twins (Buchsbaum, 1974), but not in fraternal twins or other siblings. When stimulation is done across a range of stimulus intensities, the resulting relationship between stimulus intensity and amplitude of the EP is called "augmenting/reducing" (Buchsbaum & Silverman, 1968). A marked increase of EP amplitude with increases in stimulus intensity defines the augmenting end of the continuum whereas little change in EP amplitude with increasing stimulus intensity or a decrease of EP magnitude at the highest intensities is an index of reducing. Although phrased in terms of a dichotomy, the distribution of slope measures is continuous and normally distributed. Reducing represents a protective cortical function, whereas extreme augmenting may represent a failure of cortical inhibition or a marker for a "strong nervous system" in the Pavlovian sense of resistance to transmarginal inhibition for the effects of strong stimulation.

Beginning with a study by Zuckerman, Murtaugh, and Siegel (1974) of the visual evoked potential, many other studies (summarized in Zuckerman, 1990) have shown that the disinhibition subscale of the SSS is related to augmenting of the EP in both visual and auditory modalities. Figure 11.1 shows the mean visual EP amplitudes at 5 levels of stimulus intensity for high and low disinhibiters in the study by Zuckerman et al. (1974), and Figure 11.2 shows the relationship between auditory EPs and stimulus intensity in the study by Zuckerman, Simons, and Como (1988). For both visual and auditory modalities, the high disinhibiters tended to show an augmenting pattern, whereas the low disinhibiters showed a reducing

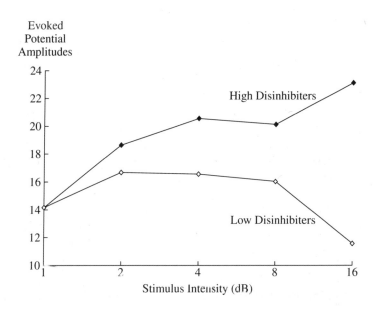

Figure 11.1 Mean visual evoked potential (EP) amplitudes of high and low scorers on the Disinhibition subscale of the Sensation Seeking Scale as a function of stimulus intensity. From "Sensation Seeking and Cortical Augmenting-Reducing," by M. Zuckerman et al., 1974, *Psychophysiology, 11,* p. 539. Copyright 1974 by the Society for Psychophysiological Research. Reprinted with the permission of Cambridge University Press.

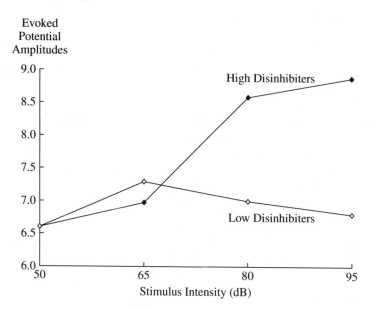

Figure 11.2   Mean auditory evoked potential (EP) amplitudes of high and low scorers on the Disinhibition subscale of the Sensation Seeking Scale as a function of stimulus intensity for the short interstimulus interval condition (2 seconds). From "Sensation Seeking and Stimulus Intensity as Modulators of Cortical, Cardiovascular, and Electrodermal Response: A Cross-Modality Study," by M. Zuckerman, R. F. Simons, and P. G. Como, 1988, *Personality and Individual Differences, 9,* p. 368. Copyright 1988 by Pergamon Press. Reprinted by permission.

pattern. Barratt, Pritchard, Faulk, and Brandt (1987) reported that impulsivity is also related to augmenting of the visual EP.

Augmenting of EP in contrast to reducing is found in alcoholics (Coger, Dymond, Serafetinides, Lowenstein, & Pearson, 1976; von Knorring, 1976), delinquents (Silverman, Buchsbaum, & Stierlin, 1973), and bipolar mood disorders, even when they are not in the manic state (Buchsbaum, Landau, Murphy, & Goodwin, 1973). These findings provide another biological link between ImpUSS and disinhibitory disorders.

Animal Models for Augmenting/Reducing Types

Animal models for psychopathology are important for a biological approach because they allow experimental tests of the involvement of the brain in various disorders (Hannin & Usdin, 1977). Investigators extended the EP augmenting/reducing paradigm to cats and found that cats showing the augmenting pattern tend to be exploratory, active, and aggressive whereas reducer cats tend to be emotional, tense, and inhibited

(Hall, Rappaport, Hopkins, Griffin, & Silverman, 1970; Lukas & Siegel, 1977; Saxton, Siegel, & Lukas, 1987). Although the augmenter cats performed well on a fixed interval schedule, they showed a disadvantage on a schedule requiring the maintenance of a low rate of response (requiring a capacity to inhibit response in order to avoid loss of reward) (Saxton et al., 1987). In contrast, the reducer cats were good at this task because they could inhibit responses when necessary.

The augmenting/reducing index at the optimal time bands of the EP has substantial heritability in humans (Buchsbaum, 1974). Siegel, Sisson, and Driscoll (1993) investigated the genetically influenced correlates of augmenting/reducing in rats by contrasting two strains: the Roman High Avoidance (RHA) and the Roman Low Avoidance rats (RLA). The high avoidance rats were bred on the basis of their capacity to learn an active avoidance response, whereas the low avoidance rats were bred from those who tended to freeze rather than run and therefore took long to learn the avoidance response. A strain of inbred rats is nearly equivalent to a colony of cloned twins with very little genetic variation left after many generations of inbreeding. When they are bred for one behavioral trait, other traits are usually also bred because of their similarity in the distinctive biological bases.

The two strains of rats were clearly differentiated in EP augmenting/reducing. Nearly all the RHA rats were augmenters, and nearly all the RLA rats were reducers or weaker augmenters. There was very little overlap between the two strains in the augmenting measure. Table 11.1 shows some of the other behavioral and biological characteristics differentiating the two strains. The RHA augmenting rats showed more

TABLE 11.1   Characteristics of Roman Low Avoidance (RLA) and Roman High Avoidance (RHA) Rats

	RLA (Reducers)	RHA (Augmenters)
Active Avoidance	Less (freezing)	More
Open-Field		
Activity	Less	More
Defecation	More	Less
Shock-Induced Aggression	Less aggressive	More aggressive
Alcohol Drinking	Less	More
Barbiturates	Little tolerance	High tolerance
Maternal Behavior	More	Less time in nest with young
Hypothalamic Self-Stimulation	More sensitive	Less sensitive low intensities
	More escapes	Fewer escapes high intensities
Stress Effects:		
Prefrontal cortex	No change DA	Increased DA (DOPAC)
Hypothalamus	Increased 5–HT	Less change 5–HT (serotonin)
	Increased CRF	Less change CRF
Pituitary	Increased ACTH	Less change ACTH

exploratory activity in a novel situation (the open field) and less emotional-fearful response to this situation (defecation) than the RLAs. The RHAs were more aggressive when shocked. The RHAs showed more tolerance for barbiturates and a greater attraction to alcohol. The RHA females showed less maternal behavior (time in the nest). In many ways, the RHA rats have characteristics of the human antisocial personality, and the RLA rats resemble the avoidant personality.

Biological reactivity differences between the two strains give some clues as to the source of the behavioral differences. The RHAs were less sensitive to low intensities of hypothalamic brain self-stimulation (intrinsic reward) but were more responsive to high intensities of stimulation than the RLAs, who tended to flee from such intense "pleasure" stimulation. Their responses to stress differentiated the two strains. The RLAs showed a marked serotonergic (5-HT) response in the hypothalamus and a strong response along the hypothalamic-pituitary pathway with increased corticotropin-releasing factor (CRF) and adrenocorticotropic hormone (ACTH) release. The RHAs showed little of this classical stress response but curiously had increased dopamine release from the prefrontal cortex.

Dopamine is involved in reward-directed activity, and its release in the precentral cortex might facilitate the active avoidance response bred into this strain. The level of MAO is low in human high sensation seekers, and the Type B MAO measured from platelets is particularly important in regulation of dopamine in the brain. Low levels of MAO would mean that more dopamine is available in the neurons and this could make the system more reactive. Serotonin, which serves behavioral inhibition, may be more reactive in the low sensation seeking human as it is in the RLA-reducing rat.

Correlations have been found between EP augmenting/reducing and MAO and serotonin in humans. Consistent with the common correlates of augmenting, MAO, and serotonin in personality and psychopathology are the findings that augmenters tend to have low levels of both MAO (Buchsbaum et al., 1973) and CSF 5-HIAA (the serotonin metabolite) (von Knorring & Perris, 1981) relative to higher levels in reducers. Zimeldine, which inhibits the reuptake of serotonin thereby potentiating responsivity of serotonergic neurons, changes the augmenting pattern to a reducing one in humans (von Knorring & Johansson, 1980). This latter finding suggests a direct role for serotonin in the inhibition of cortical response at higher intensities of stimulation.

GENDER AND AGE

Sensation seeking is higher in men than in women; it increases with age, reaching a peak in late adolescence or the early 20s, and thereafter declines with increasing age (Zuckerman, 1979, 1994a). Antisocial personality, the disorder most closely associated with sensation seeking, is 3 to 7 times more frequent in men than in women and diminishes in intensity with age. In fact, some say that age is the only cure for psychopathy. Risk taking, crime, and automobile accidents due to reckless driving are also related to sensation seeking and are most frequent in young males during adolescence and early 20s.

The level of MAO is low in high sensation seekers, lower in men than in women, and it rises with age. Augmenting/reducing of the EP does not show consistent relationships to gender, but augmenting decreases and reducing increases with age. Testosterone is, of course, higher in men than in women, peaks in males during adolescence, and declines thereafter along with changes in sexual desire and frequency of sexual activity. Dopamine and other catecholamines decline with age. Could these parallels between sensation seeking, risk taking, psychopathologies, and their biological correlates in gender differences and age changes imply a causal effect? It must be admitted that the direction of causation is not always clear. Sexual stimulation and activity might stimulate testosterone as well as the other way around. The MAO influence, possibly through its regulation of dopamine, is more difficult to explain in terms of a behavioral effect because it is so stable over short time periods and strongly genetic in origin. Gonadal hormones, however, do lower MAO levels so that their variations might affect the brain enzyme.

Possibly the best way to conceptualize the role of biological factors in personality and psychopathology is as something between state and trait, or cause and effect. Feedback systems regulate most biochemical processes from neuronal to systems activities. Behavior could be regarded as part of these systems. In a feedback system, there is no single cause but a chain of events triggered by a shift in equilibrium. The environment is one source of disequilibrium and the brain is another. The enzymes such as MAO, which regulate the systems and are responsible for limits of variation, may be the key to understanding the relatively stable traits or broad-situation habits of reaction that we call "personality." Disorders may be due to deficits in regulators or imbalances between neurotransmitters such as dopamine and serotonin, which have antagonistic excitatory and inhibitory effects on approach behavior.

To use an automotive metaphor: Dopamine is the accelerator, controlling the speed of the drive toward reward, and serotonin is the brake, stopping or slowing the movement when signals of danger appear on the road. Of course, there is the frontal lobe at the wheel integrating the information from sensory areas, steering, and accelerating or braking. A psychopath has a sensitive accelerator, a responsive motor, and worn brakes, whereas a manic has a jammed accelerator and no brakes. In response to a yellow (caution) traffic signal, the impulsive brain accelerates and the inhibited brain slows. The disinhibited, impulsive, unsocialized brain goes through the red as well as the yellow traffic light. The problem with the metaphor is that there is little provision for the feedback mechanisms that regulate the brain's neurotransmitter systems (although one might say that the speedometer is broken or the brain has suffered a prefrontal lobotomy). Figure 11.3 shows part of the metaphor translated into behavioral mechanisms and the neurotransmitters, enzymes, and hormones governing them. Dopaminergic pathways underlie the approach mechanism, serotonin the inhibition mechanism, and norepinephrine the arousal mechanism. What must be noted is the interaction between all monoamine systems and their joint influence in traits like impulsive, unsocialized sensation seeking, characterized by strong approach, and weak inhibition and arousal mechanisms. This is probably an oversimplified model ignoring other neurotransmitters, receptors, enzymes, and hormones involved in personality and its disorders. But no one ever claimed that nature is simple, and the brain is the most complicated of all the organs. Evolution has built a structure something like a Victorian house to which successive generations have added new wings.

Mechanistic metaphors are distasteful to humanistic and cognitive psychologists, who prefer their own metaphors involving "selves" or

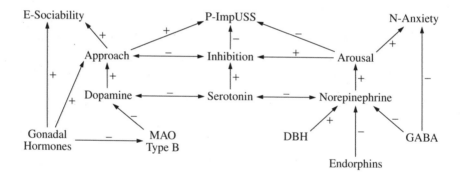

Figure 11.3   A psychopharmacological model for Impulsive Unsocialized Sensation Seeking (ImpUSS) and Neuroticism-Anxiety (N-Anxiety) with underlying behavioral and physiological mechanisms (Approach, Inhibition, and Arousal) and neurotransmitters, enzymes, and hormones involved. MAO = monoamine oxidase, DBH = dopamine-beta-hydroxylase, GABA = gamma-aminobutyric acid. Interaction between behavioral and biochemical factors indicated (+) for agonistic and (−) for antagonistic actions. Single-headed arrows indicate the hypothesized direction of influence; double-headed arrows indicate a two-way interaction between the factors. From *Behavioral Expressions and Biosocial Bases of Sensation Seeking,* by M. Zuckerman, 1994a, p.380, New York: Cambridge University Press. Copyright 1994 by Cambridge University Press. Reprinted by permission.

"schemas." But all scientific theory involves metaphor. The job of the life sciences is to determine which metaphor is best at describing, understanding, and predicting the complex phenomena of behavior. Perhaps each is suitable to its own level of analysis and "all shall win prizes." But then as Freud (1920/1958) predicted:

> Biology is truly a land of unlimited possibilities; we may expect it to give us the most surprising revelations, and we cannot guess what answers it will return in a few dozen years to the questions we have put to it. They may be of a kind which will blow away the whole of our artificial structure of [psychological] hypotheses. (p. 60)

REFERENCES

Allcock, C. C., & Grace, D. M. (1988). Pathological gamblers are neither impulsive nor sensation-seekers. *Australian and New Zealand Journal of Psychiatry, 22,* 307–311.

American Psychiatric Association. (1994). *Diagnostic and statistical manual of mental disorders* (4th ed.; DSM-IV). Washington, DC: Author.

Anderson, G., & Brown, R. I. (1984). Real and laboratory gambling, sensation-seeking and arousal. *British Journal of Psychology, 75,* 401–410.

Ball, S. A. (1995). The validity of an alternative five factor measure of personality in cocaine abusers. *Psychological Assessment, 7,* 148–154.

Ball, S. A., Carroll, K. M., Babor, T. F., & Rounsaville, B. J. (1995). Subtypes of cocaine abusers: Support for a Type A/Type B distinction. *Journal of Consulting and Clinical Psychology, 63,* 115–124.

Ball, S. A., Carroll, K. M., & Rounsaville, B. J. (1994). Sensation seeking, substance abuse, and psychopathology in treatment seeking and community cocaine users. *Journal of Consulting and Clinical Psychology, 62,* 1053–1057.

Barratt, E. S., Pritchard, W. S., Faulk, D. M., & Brandt, M. E. (1987). The relationship between impulsiveness subtraits, trait anxiety, and visual N100-augmenting-reducing: A topographic analysis. *Personality and Individual Differences, 8,* 43–51.

Baucom, D. H., Besch, P. K., & Callahan, S. (1985). Relation between testosterone concentration, sex role identity and personality among females. *Journal of Personality and Social Psychology, 48,* 1218–1226.

Bench, C. J., Price, G. W., Lammetsma, A. A., Cremer, J. C., Luthra, S. R., Turton, D., Dolan, R. J., Kettler, R., Dingemanse, J., DaPrada, M., Biziere, K., McClelland, G. R., Jamieson, V. L., Wood, N. D., & Frachowiak, R. S. (1991). Measurement of human cerebral monoamine oxidase type B (MAO-B) activity with positron emission tomography (PET): A dose ranging study with the reversible inhibitor Ro 19-6327. *European Journal of Clinical Pharmacology, 40,* 169–173.

Berman, T., & Paisey, T. (1984). Personality in assaultive and non-assaultive juvenile male offenders. *Psychological Reports, 54,* 527–530.

Blackburn, R. (1978). Electrodermal and cardiovascular correlates of psychopathy. In R. D. Hare & D. Schalling (Eds.), *Psychopathic behavior: Approaches to research.* New York: Wiley.

Blackburn, R. (1987). Two scales for the assessment of personality disorder in antisocial populations. *Personality and Individual Differences, 8,* 81–93.

Blaszczynski, A., McConaghy, N., & Frankova, A. (1990). Boredom proneness in an impulse control disorder. *Psychological Reports, 67,* 35–42.

Blaszczynski, A., Wilson, A. C., & McConaghy, N. (1986). Sensation seeking and pathological gambling. *British Journal of Addiction, 81,* 113–117.

Buchsbaum, M. S. (1974). Average evoked response and stimulus intensity in identical and fraternal twins. *Physiological Psychology, 2,* 365–370.

Buchsbaum, M. S., Landau, S., Murphy, D. L., & Goodwin, F. K. (1973). Average evoked response in bipolar and unipolar affective disorders: Relationship to sex, age of onset, and monoamine oxidase. *Biological Psychiatry, 7,* 199–212.

Buchsbaum, M. S., & Silverman, J. (1968). Stimulus intensity control and the cortical evoked response. *Psychosomatic Medicine, 30,* 12–22.

Carey, G., & DiLalla, D. L. (1994). Personality and psychopathology: Genetic perspectives. *Journal of Abnormal Psychology, 103,* 32–43.

Carton, S., Jouvent, R., Bungener, C., & Widlöcher, D. (1992). Sensation seeking and depressive mood. *Personality and Individual Differences, 13,* 843–849.

Cleckley, H. (1976). *The mask of sanity* (5th ed.). St. Louis, MO: Mosby.

Cloninger, C. R. (1987). Neurogenic adaptive mechanisms in alcoholism. *Science, 236,* 410–416.

Cloninger, C. R., von Knorring, L., & Oreland, L. (1985). Parametric distribution of platelet monoamine oxidase activity. *Psychiatry Research, 15,* 133–143.

Coger, R. W., Dymond, A. M., Serafetinides, E. A., Lowenstam, I., & Pearson, D. (1976). Alcoholism: Averaged visual evoked response amplitude-intensity slope and symmetry in withdrawal. *Biological Psychiatry, 11,* 435–443.

Costa, P. T., Jr., & McCrae, R. R. (1992). *NEO-PI-R: Revised Personality Inventory.* Odessa, FL: Psychological Assessment Resources.

Coursey, R. D., Buchsbaum, M. S., & Murphy, D. L. (1979). Platelet MAO activity and evoked potentials in the identification of subjects biologically at risk for psychiatric disorders. *British Journal of Psychiatry, 134,* 372–381.

Cronin, C., & Zuckerman, M. (1992). Sensation seeking and bipolar affective disorder. *Journal of Personality and Individual Differences, 13,* 385–387.

Custer, R., & Milt, H. (1985). *When luck runs out.* New York: Facts on File.

Dabbs, J. M., Jr., Carr, T. S., Frady, R. L., & Riad, J. K. (1995). Testosterone, crime, and misbehavior among 692 prison inmates. *Personality and Individual Differences, 18,* 627–633.

Dabbs, J. M., Jr., Ruback, R. B., Frady, R. L., Hopper, C. H., & Sgoritas, D. S. (1988). Saliva testosterone and criminal violence among women. *Personality and Individual Differences, 9,* 269–275.

Daitzman, R. J., & Zuckerman, M. (1980). Disinhibitory sensation seeking, personality, and gonadal hormones. *Personality and Individual Differences, 1,* 103–110.

Deforest, F. D., & Johnson, L. S. (1981). Modification of stimulation seeking behavior in psychopaths using hypnotic imagery conditioning. *American Journal of Clinical Hypnosis, 23,* 184–194.

Dickerson, M., Hinchy, J., & Fabre, J. (1987). Chasing, arousal and sensation seeking in off-course gamblers. *British Journal of Addiction, 82,* 673–680.

Ehrenkranz, J., Bliss, E., & Sheard, M. H. (1974). Plasma testosterone: Correlation with aggressive behavior and social dominance in man. *Psychosomatic Medicine, 36,* 469–475.

Emmons, T. D., & Webb, W. W. (1974). Subjective correlates of emotional responsivity and stimulation seeking in psychopaths, normals, and acting-out neurotics. *Journal of Consulting and Clinical Psychology, 42,* 620–625.

Eysenck, H. J., & Eysenck, S. B. G. (1976). *Psychoticism as a dimension of personality.* New York: Crane, Russak, & Company.

Eysenck, S. B. G., Eysenck, H. J., & Barrett, P. (1985). A revised version of the psychoticism scale. *Personality and Individual Differences, 6,* 21–29.

Farley, F. H., & Farley, S. V. (1972). Stimulus seeking motivation and delinquent behavior among institutionalized delinquent girls. *Journal of Consulting and Clinical Psychology, 39,* 140–147.

Freud, S. (1955). Beyond the pleasure principle. In J. Strachey (Ed.), *The standard edition of the complete psychological works of Sigmund Freud* (Vol. 21, pp. 175–196). London: Hogarth Press. (Original work published 1920)

Fulker, D. W., Eysenck, S. B. G., & Zuckerman, M. (1980). The genetics of sensation seeking. *Journal of Personality Research, 14,* 261–281.

Hall, R. A., Rappaport, M., Hopkins, H. K., Griffin, R. B., & Silverman, J. (1970). Evoked response and behavior in cats. *Science, 170,* 998–1000.

Hallman, J., von Knorring, A. L., von Knorring, L., & Oreland, L. (1990). Clinical characteristics of female alcoholics with low platelet monoamine oxidase activity. *Alcoholism: Clinical and Experimental Research, 14,* 227–231.

Hannin, I., & Usdin, E. (1977). *Animal models for psychiatry and neurology.* New York: Pergamon.

Hare, R. D. (1991). *The Hare psychopathy checklist-Revised.* Toronto: Multi-Health Systems.

Hare, R. D., & Cox, D. N. (1978). Clinical and empirical conceptions of psychopathy and the selection of subjects for research. In R. D. Hare & D. Schalling (Eds.), *Psychopathic behaviour: Approaches to research* (pp. 1–22). Chichester: Wiley.

Harpur, T. J., Hare, R. D., & Hakstian, R. (1989). Two-factor conceptualization of psychopathy: Construct validity and assessment implications. *Psychological Assessment, 1,* 6–17.

Horvath, P., & Zuckerman, M. (1993). Sensation seeking, risk appraisal, and risky behavior. *Personality and Individual Differences, 14,* 41–52.

Kreuz, L. E., & Rose, R. M. (1972). Assessment of aggressive behavior and plasma testosterone in a young criminal population. *Psychosomatic Medicine, 34,* 321–332.

Kuley, N. B., & Jacobs, D. F. (1988). The relationship between dissociative-like experiences and sensation seeking among social and problem gamblers. *Journal of Gambling Behavior, 4,* 197–207.

Kusyszyn, I., & Rutter, R. (1985). Personality characteristics of male heavy gamblers, light gamblers, nongamblers, and lottery players. *Journal of Gambling Behavior, 1,* 59–64.

Lesieur, H. R., Blume, S. B., & Zoppa, R. M. (1986). Alcoholism, drug abuse, and gambling. *Alcoholism: Clinical and Experimental Research, 10,* 33–38.

Lidberg, L., Modin, I., Oreland, L., Tuck, J. R., & Gillner, A. (1985). Platelet monoamine oxidase activity and psychopathy. *Psychiatry Research, 16,* 339–343.

Livesley, J., Schroeder, M. L., Jackson, D. N., & Jang, K. L. (1994). Categorical distinctions in the study of personality disorder: Implications for classification. *Journal of Abnormal Psychology, 103,* 6–17.

Lukas, J. H., & Siegel, J. (1977). Cortical mechanisms that augment or reduce evoked potentials in cats. *Science, 196,* 73–75.

Major, L. F., & Murphy, D. L. (1978). Platelet and plasma amine oxidase activity in alcoholic individuals. *British Journal of Psychiatry, 132,* 548–554.

Malatesta, V. J., Sutker, P. B., & Treiber, F. A. (1981). Sensation seeking and chronic public drunkeness. *Journal of Consulting and Clinical Psychology, 49,* 292–294.

Mattson, A., Schalling, D., Olweus, D., Low, H., & Svensson, J. (1980). Plasma testosterone, aggressive behavior, and personality dimensions in young male delinquents. *Journal of the American Academy of Child Psychiatry, 19,* 476–490.

Murphy, D. L., Aulach, C. H., Garrick, N. A., & Sunderland, T. (1987). Monoamine oxidase inhibitors as antidepressants: Implications for the mechanism action of antidepressants and the psychology of the affective disorders. In H. Y. Meltzer (Ed.), *Psychopharmacology: The third generation of progress* (pp. 545–552). New York: Raven.

Newcomb, M. D., & McGee, L. (1991). The influence of sensation seeking on general and specific problem behaviors from adolescence to young adulthood. *Journal of Personality and Social Psychology, 61,* 614–628.

Nurnberger, J. I., Jr., Hamovit, J., Hibbs, E. D., Pellegrini, D., Guroff, J. J., Maxwell, M. E., Smith, A., & Gershon, E. S. (1988). A high-risk study of primary affective disorder: Selection of subjects, initial assessment, and 1- to 2-year follow-up. In D. L. Dunner, E. S. Gershon, & J. E. Barrett (Eds.), *Relatives at risk for mental disorder.* New York: Raven.

Oreland, L., Wilberg, A., & Fowler, C. J. (1981). Monoamine oxidase activity as related to monoamine oxidase activity and monoaminergic function in the brain. In B. Angrist (Ed.), *Recent advances in neuropsychopharmacology,* Vol. 31. Oxford: Pergamon.

Pandey, G. N., Fawcett, J., Gibbons, R., Clark, D. C., & Davis, J. M. (1988). Platelet monoamine oxidase in alcoholism. *Biological Psychiatry, 24,* 15–24.

Perez, J., & Torrubia, R. (1985). Sensation seeking and antisocial behaviour in a student sample. *Personality and Individual Differences, 6,* 401–403.

Pope, H. G., & Katz, D. L. (1994). Psychiatric and medical effects of anabolic-androgen steroid use: A controlled study of 160 athletes. *Archives of General Psychiatry, 51,* 375–382.

Purchall, L. B., Coursey, R. D., Buchsbaum, M. S., & Murphy, D. L. (1980). Parents of high risk subjects defined by levels of monoamine oxidase activity. *Schizophrenia Bulletin, 6,* 338–346.

Quay, H. C. (1965). Psychopathic personality as pathological stimulation seeking. *American Journal of Psychiatry, 122,* 180–183.

Rada, R. T., Laws, D. R., & Kellner, R. (1976). Plasma testosterone levels in the rapist. *Psychosomatic Medicine, 38,* 257–258.

Reist, C., Haier, R. J., DeMet, E., & Chicz-DeMet, A. (1990). Platelet MAO activity in personality disorders and normal controls. *Psychiatry Research, 33,* 221–227.

Rice, J., McGuffin, P., & Shaskan, E. G. (1982). A commingling analysis of platelet monoamine oxidase activity. *Psychiatry Research, 7,* 325–335.

Russo, M. F., Lakey, B. B., Christ, M. A. G., Frick, P. J., McBurnett, K., Walker, J. L., Loeber, R., Stouthammer-Loeber, M., & Green, S. M. (1991). Preliminary development of a sensation seeking scale for children. *Personality and Individual Differences, 12,* 399–405.

Russo, M. F., Stokes, G. S., Lahey, B. B., Christ, M. A. G., McBurnett, K., Loeber, R., Stouthammer-Loeber, M., & Green, S. M. (1993). A sensation seeking scale for children: Further refinement and psychometric development. *Journal of Psychopathology and Behavioral Assessment, 15,* 69–86.

Salkind, N. J. (1981). Stimulation seeking and hyperactivity in young children. *Journal of Pediatric Psychology, 6,* 97–102.

Saxton, P. M., Siegel, J., & Lukas, J. H. (1987). Visual evoked potential augmenting/reducing slopes in cats-2. Correlations with behavior. *Personality and Individual Differences, 8,* 511–519.

Schalling, D. (1987). Personality correlates of plasma testosterone levels in young delinquents: An example of person-situation interaction? In S. Mednick, E. Moffitt, & S. A. Stack (Eds.), *The causes of crime: New biological approaches* (pp. 283–291). Cambridge, England: Cambridge University Press.

Shaw, G. A., & Brown, G. (1990). Laterality and creativity concomitants of attention problems. *Developmental Neuropsychology, 6,* 39–57.

Shekim, W. O., Bylund, D. B., Alexson, J., Glasner, R. D., Jones, S. B., Hodges, K., & Perdue, S. (1986). Platelet MAO and measures of attention disorder deficit and hyperactivity. *Psychiatry Research, 18,* 179–188.

Sher, K. J., Bylund, D. B., Walitzer, K. S., Hartmann, J., & Ray-Prenger, C. (1994). Platelet monoamine oxidase (MAO) activity: Personality, substance abuse, and the stress-response-dampening effect of alcohol. *Experimental and Clinical Psychopharmacology, 2,* 53–81.

Shoham, S. G., Askenasy, J. J., Rahav, G., Chard, F., & Addi, A. (1989). *Personality and Individual Differences, 10,* 137–145.

Siegel, J., Sisson, D. F., & Driscoll, P. (1993). Augmenting and reducing of visual evoked potentials in Roman High- and Low-Avoidance rats. *Physiology and Behavior, 54,* 707–711.

Silverman, J., Buchsbaum, M., & Stierlin, H. (1973). Sex differences in perceptual differentiation and stimulus intensity control. *Journal of Personality and Social Psychology, 25,* 309–318.

Simo, S., & Perez, J. (1991). Sensation seeking and antisocial behavior in a junior high school sample. *Personality and Individual Differences, 12,* 965–966.

Stillman, R. C., Wyatt, R. J., Murphy, D. L., & Rauscher, F. P. (1978). Low platelet monoamine oxidase activity and chronic marijuana use. *Life Sciences, 23,* 1577–1582.

Thornquist, M. H., & Zuckerman, M. (in press). Psychopathy, passive avoidance learning and basic dimensions of personality. *Personality and Individual Differences.*

Vaillant, G. E. (1994). Ego mechanisms of defense and personality psychopathology. *Journal of Abnormal Psychology, 103,* 44–50.

von Knorring, L. (1976). Visual averaged-evoked responses in patients suffering from alcoholism. *Neuropsychobiology, 2,* 233–238.

von Knorring, A. L., Bohman, M., von Knorring, L., & Oreland, L. (1985). Platelet MAO activity as a biological marker in subgroups of alcoholism. *Acta Psychiatrica Scandinavia, 72,* 51–58.

von Knorring, L., & Johansson, F. (1980). Changes in the augmenter-reducer tendency and in pain measures as a result of treatment with a serotonin reuptake inhibitor: Zimeldine. *Neuropsychobiology, 6,* 313–318.

von Knorring, L., Oreland, L., & von Knorring, A. (1987). Personality traits and platelet MAO activity in alcohol and drug abusing teenage boys. *Acta Psychiatrica Scandinavia, 75,* 307–314.

von Knorring, L., & Perris, C. (1981). Biochemistry of the augmenting-reducing response in visual evoked potentials. *Neuropsychobiology, 7,* 1–8.

von Knorring, L., von Knorring, A., Smigan, L., Lindberg, U., & Edholm, M. (1987). Personality traits in subtypes of alcoholics. *Journal of Studies on Alcohol, 48,* 523–527.

Wallbank, J. (1985). Antisocial and prosocial behavior among contemporary Robin Hoods. *Personality and Individual Differences, 6,* 11–19.

Wasson, A. S. (1981). Susceptibility to boredom and deviant behavior at school. *Psychological Reports, 48,* 901–902.

White, H. R., LaBouvie, E. W., & Bates, M. E. (1985). The relationship between sensation seeking and delinquency: A longitudinal analysis. *Journal of Research in Crime and Delinquency, 22,* 197–211.

Widiger, T. A., & Costa, P. T., Jr. (1994). Personality and personality disorders. *Journal of Abnormal Psychology, 103,* 92–102.

Wolf, A. W., Schubert, D. S. P., Patterson, M. B., Grande, T. P., Brocco, K. J., & Pendleton, L. (1988). Associations among major psychiatric disorders. *Journal of Consulting and Clinical Psychology, 56,* 292–294.

Zuckerman, M. (1969). Theoretical formulations. In J. P. Zubek (Ed.), *Sensory deprivation: Fifteen years of research.* New York: Appleton-Century Crofts.

Zuckerman, M. (1979). *Sensation seeking: Beyond the optimal level of arousal.* Hillsdale, NJ: Erlbaum.

Zuckerman, M. (1983). Sensation seeking: The initial motive for drug abuse. In E. Gottheil, K. A. Druley, T. E. Skoloda, & H. M. Waxman (Eds.), *Etiological aspects of alcohol and drug abuse* (pp. 202–220). Springfield, IL: Thomas.

Zuckerman, M. (1984). Sensation seeking: A comparative approach to a human trait. *Behavioral and Brain Sciences, 7,* 413–471.

Zuckerman, M. (1987a). Biological connection between sensation seeking and drug abuse. In J. Engel & L. Oreland (Eds.), *Brain reward systems and abuse* (pp. 165–176). New York: Raven.

Zuckerman, M. (1987b). Is sensation seeking a predisposing trait for alcoholism? In E. Gottheil, K. A. Druley, S. Pashkey, & S. P. Weinstein (Eds.), *Stress and Addiction* (pp. 283–301). New York: Bruner/Mazel.

Zuckerman, M. (1989). Personality in the third dimension: A psychobiological approach. *Personality and Individual Differences, 10,* 391–418.

Zuckerman, M. (1990). The psychophysiology of sensation seeking. *Journal of Personality, 58,* 313–345.

Zuckerman, M. (1991). *Psychobiology of personality.* Cambridge, England: Cambridge University Press.

Zuckerman, M. (1993a). Sensation seeking and impulsivity: A marriage of traits made in biology? In W. G. McCown, J. L. Johnson, & M. B. Shure (Eds.), *The impulsive client: Theory, research, and treatment* (pp. 71–91). Washington, DC: American Psychological Association.

Zuckerman, M. (1993b). Personality from top (traits) to bottom (genetics) with stops at each level between. In J. Hettema & I. J. Deary (Eds.), *Foundations of personality* (pp. 73–100). Dordrecht, Netherlands: Kluwer Academic Publishers.

Zuckerman, M. (1994a). *Behavioral expressions and biosocial bases of sensation seeking*. New York: Cambridge University Press.

Zuckerman, M. (1994b). Impulsive unsocialized sensation seeking: The biological foundations of a basic dimension of personality. In J. E. Bates & T. D. Wachs (Eds.), *Temperament: Individual differences at the interface of biology and behavior* (pp. 219–255). Washington, DC: American Psychological Association.

Zuckerman, M., Buchsbaum, M. S., & Murphy, D. L. (1980). Sensation seeking and its biological correlates. *Psychological Bulletin, 88,* 187–214.

Zuckerman, M., Kuhlman, D. M., & Camac, C. (1988). What lies beyond E and N? Factor analyses of scales believed to measure basic dimensions of personality. *Journal of Personality and Social Psychology, 54,* 96–107.

Zuckerman, M., Kuhlman, D. M., Joireman, J., Teta, P., & Kraft, M. (1993). A comparison of three structural models for personality: The big three, the big five, and the alternative five. *Journal of Personality and Social Psychology, 65,* 757–768.

Zuckerman, M., Kuhlman, D. M., Thornquist, M., & Kiers, H. (1991). Five (or three) robust questionnaire scale factors of personality without culture. *Personality and Individual Differences, 12,* 929–941.

Zuckerman, M., Murtaugh, T. T., & Siegel, J. (1974). Sensation seeking and cortical augmenting-reducing. *Psychophysiology, 11,* 535–542.

Zuckerman, M., & Neeb, M. (1979). Sensation seeking and psychopathology. *Psychiatry Research, 1,* 255–264.

Zuckerman, M., Simons, R. F., & Como, P. G. (1988). Sensation seeking and stimulus intensity as modulators of cortical, cardiovascular, and electrodermal response: A cross-modality study. *Personality and Individual Differences, 9,* 361–372.

Author Index

Subject Index